"**Art, like morality,** consists of drawing the line somewhere." G.K. CHESTERTON

American Illustration 12

The 12th annual of American
editorial, book, advertising, posters/maps,
graphics, unpublished work and video.

Edited by Edward Booth-Clibborn
Designed by Frankfurt Balkind Partners

editor)
Edward Booth-Clibborn

publisher)
Kenneth Fadner

designers)
Kent Hunter and Ruth Diener,
Frankfurt Balkind Partners

cover and divider illustrations)
Johan Vipper,
Frankfurt Balkind Partners

production manager)
Tina Moskin,
Frankfurt Balkind Partners

production coordinators)
Mark Heflin and Jay Heflin

printed by)
Dai Nippon, Hong Kong

special thanks to)
Parsons School of Design for providing the space and equipment for the American Illustration 12 competition.

If you are a practicing illustrator, artist, or student, and would like to **submit work** to the next annual competition, write to)

American Illustration
5 East 16th Street, 11th floor
New York, NY 10003
212.647.0874

distributor to the USA Trade)
Rizzoli International Publications
300 Park Avenue South
New York, NY 10010-3599

distributor to United Kingdom and World Direct Mail)
Internos Books
12 Percy Street
London W1P 9FB U.K.

book trade for the rest of the world)
Hearst Books International
1350 Avenue of the Americas
New York, NY 10019

Contents

Introduction

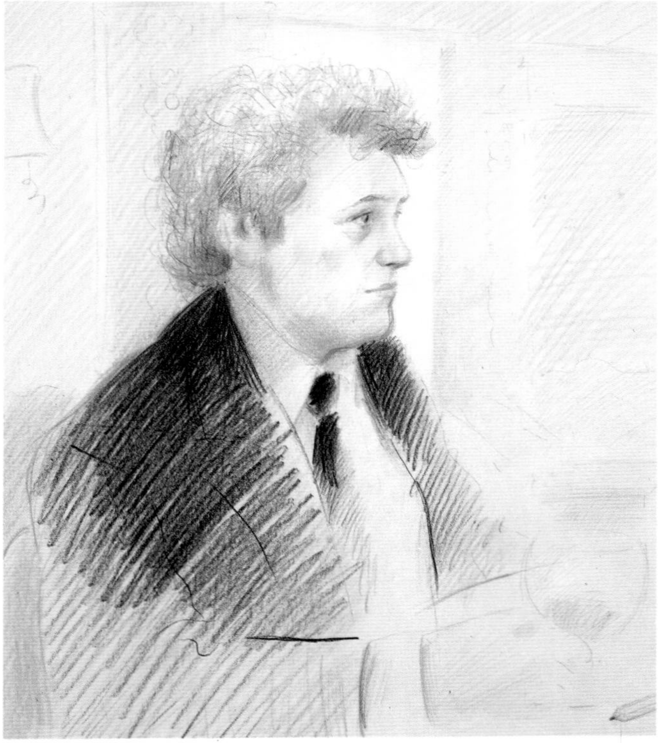

portrait by **Adrian George**

The judging for this edition of "American Illustration" took place in March of 1993 with a jury of seven people, all of whom I would like to thank for their time, enthusiasm, wit and wisdom. ¤ **With** the publication of this twelfth annual we have reached a point where a definite style of American illustration has emerged. This is especially true of the work from the younger people whose submissions we have accepted over the last few years; people who have since become very successful as American illustrators. ¤ **But** there is a disturbing trend behind this success. ¤ **Put** simply, too many people are copying other people's work. ¤ **This** year, for example, the jury rejected quite a number of items produced by people who, to put it bluntly, can only be described as rip-off artists. ¤ **Tragically**, the artists who suffer most are the people like Edward Sorel, Guy Billout, Bob Blechman and Brad Holland whose highly original work is so often plagiarized. ¤ **Who** is to blame for this? ¤ **I fear** that it begins in art schools, where students are pressured into producing portfolios designed to get them work, rather than to show off the individual talents. ¤ **It** is also a sad reflection of the visual communications business in general, where people are increasingly prepared to pay less for a copyist than they would for the original thinker. ¤ **It** seems to me that there is only one way to stamp this out, and that is that copyists' work should not be recognized. ¤ **Our** jury has done their part, particularly by dismissing every copyist's submission and including the exceptionally imaginative work for the windows of Bloomingdales by Jessie Hartland and Josh Gosfield's fine work for Barneys' windows. I believe it takes real talent to be able to see the broad applications open to illustration and then have the vision to carry fresh ideas through to the end. ¤ **It** is work like this–and much else beside–which shows that, after twelve years, "American Illustration" is very much here to stay as the benchmark of excellence in a highly competitive world.

Edward Booth-Clibborn

Jessica Helfand

Jessica Helfand has been design director at the "Philadelphia Inquirer Sunday Magazine" since July, 1990. During this time, the magazine has won over 60 awards in graphic design and photography from the Society of Newspaper Designers and the American Institute of Graphic Arts, among others. ∞ Prior to this, she was a designer with Roger Black Studio in New York, where she worked on the redesigns of numerous American and European publications including "Mother Earth News," "McCalls" and "Grazia." ∞ She has lectured at the University of Pennsylvania, and has been guest critic at Yale University, Temple University's School of Journalism, University of the Arts and Tyler School of Art in Philadelphia. Helfand judged this year's Illustrator's Club of Washington show, and last year's competition sponsored by the Philadelphia chapter of the American Society of Magazine Photographers. Her work has appeared in numerous publications including the Print Regional Design Annual and the Communication Arts annuals in both photography and illustration. She holds a B.A. and a M.F.A. in graphic design from Yale University.

favorite deadly sin: lust

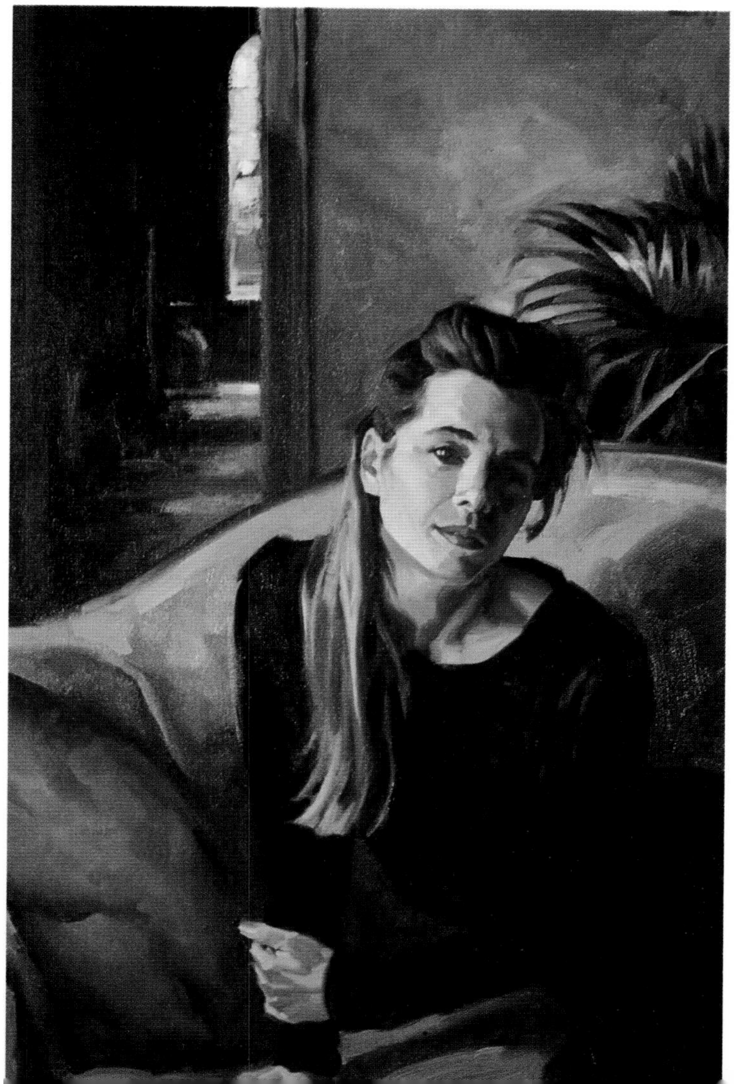

portrait by **Gregory Manchess**

Kandy Littrell

Kandy Littrell is senior art director for covers at "Newsweek." In addition to her past freelance work with Random House and Houghton Mifflin, she has held various posts at "The New York Times Magazine," "New England Monthly," and "Rolling Stone." ∞ As an illustrator, Kandy's work has appeared in such publications as "Ms. Magazine," "National Lampoon," "Psychology Today," and "Savvy." Throughout her career, her efforts have been awarded by The Art Directors Club of New York, Communication Arts, and SPD, to name a few.

favorite deadly sin: lust

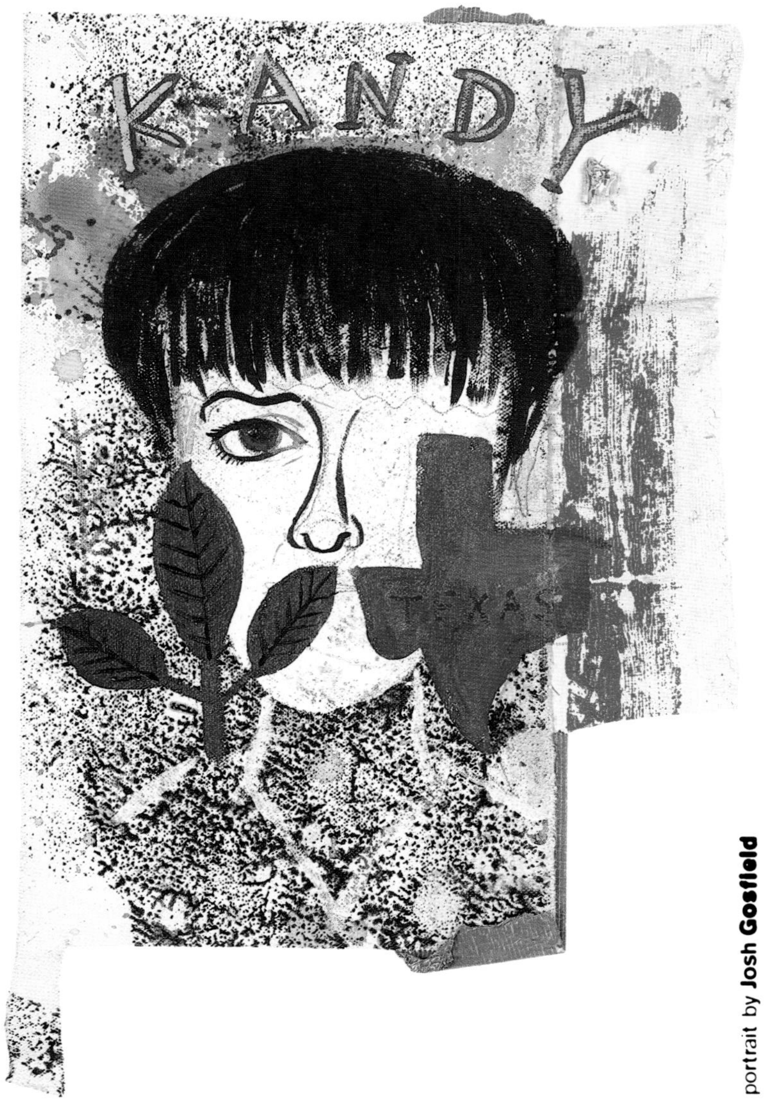

portrait by Josh Gosfield

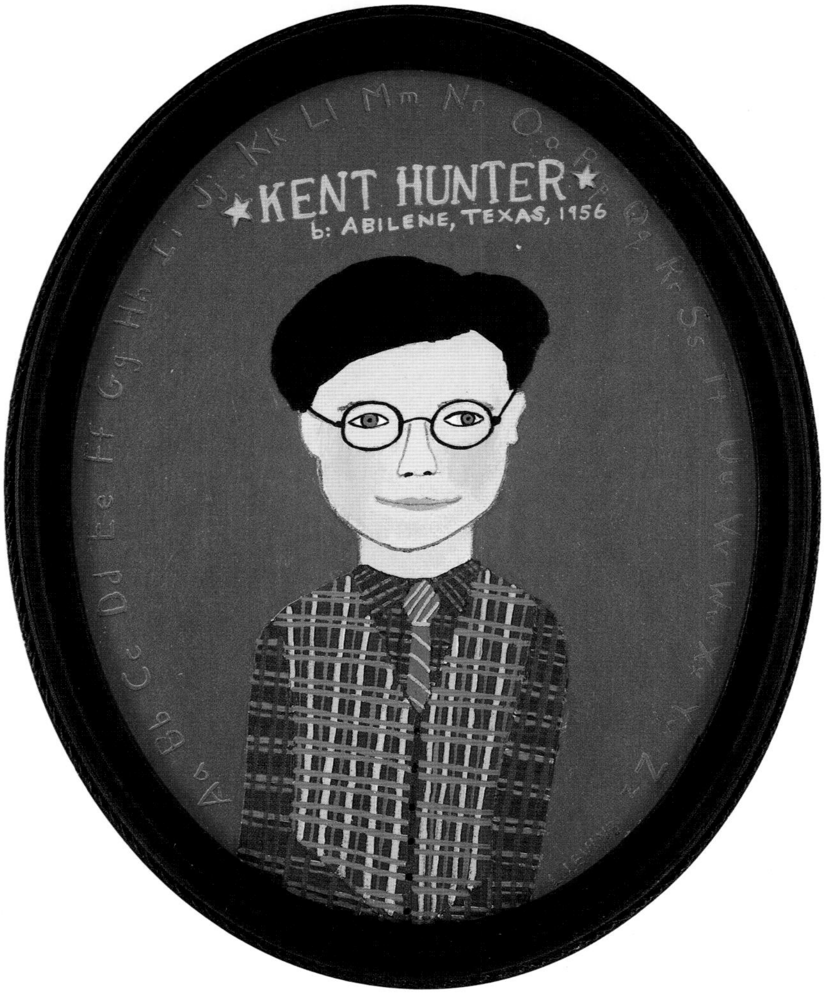

portrait by **Laura Levine**

favorite deadly sin: sloth

Kent Hunter is Executive Design Director and a principal of Frankfurt Balkind Partners, an integrated communications agency based in New York and Los Angeles and San Francisco. Known for its innovative approach to annual reports, the firm is increasingly working in video and multi-media, utilizing their expertise in **advertising and entertainment marketing. The firm's work for Time Warner, MTV, The Limited,** MCI, and others has won every major design award. ∞ Kent is a past vice-president of the New York chapter of the American Institute of Graphic Arts, has judged numerous design shows and gives lectures around the country. He passionately collects folk art.

Kent **Hunter**

Gail **Anders**on

Gail Anderson has worked at "Rolling Stone" with Fred Woodward since 1987, the past three years as deputy art director. She served as the assistant designer at "The Boston Globe Magazine" from 1985-87 and as a designer at **Vintage Books prior to that. Her work has received awards from the Society of Publication Designers, the Type Directors Club, AIGA, The Art Directors Club, and Communication Arts Magazine. She is co-author with Steven Heller of "Graphic Wit: The Art Of Humor In Design," and "The Savage Mirror: The Art of Contemporary Caricature." They are currently working together on "American Typography," a survey of modern type. A School of Visual Arts graduate, Gail now teaches design in SVA's Continuing Education program. Her work is represented in the permanent collection of** the Cooper-Hewitt Design Resource and she serves on the Executive Committee of AIGA's New York chapter.

favorite deadly sin: sloth

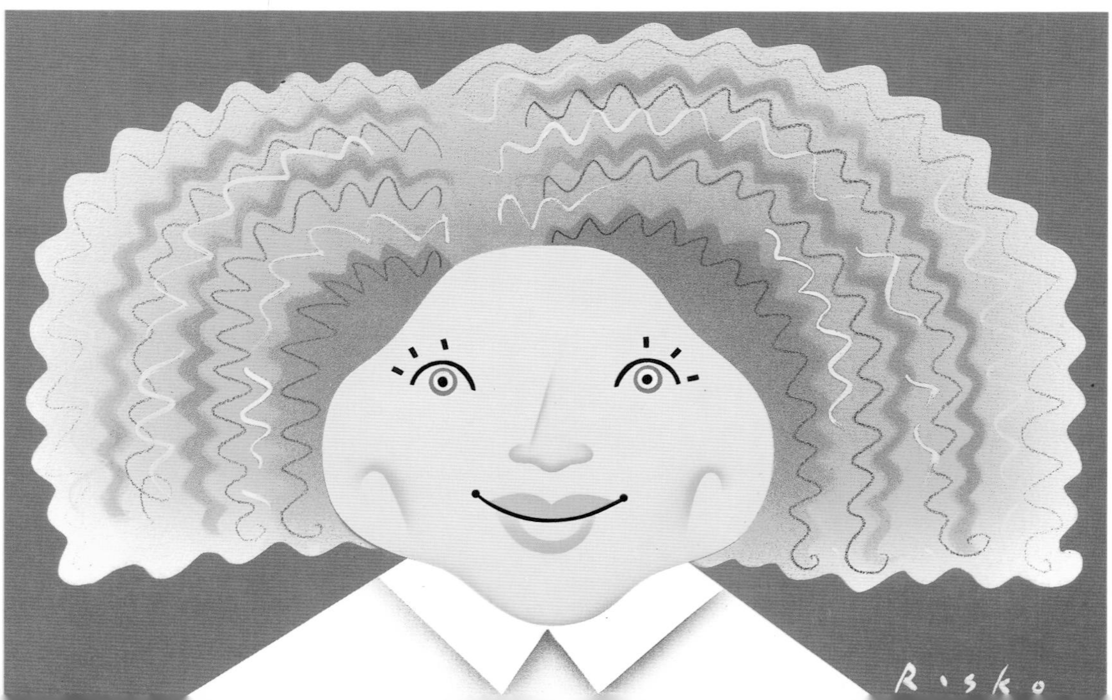

portrait by **Robert Risko**

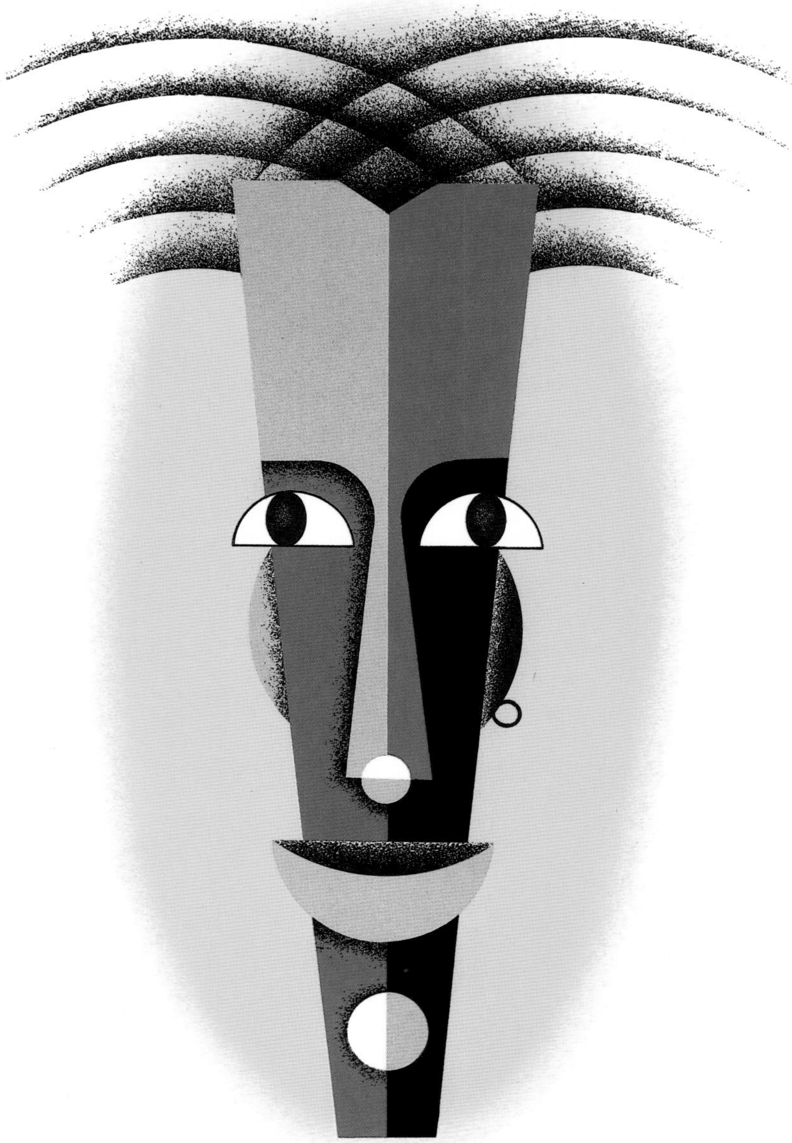

favorite deadly sin: sloth

portrait by **Terry Allen**

Richard Baker was born in Kingston, Jamaica where he learned to Rub-A-Dub Style all night long to the tunes of Big Youth. Faced with the career choices of working for the Royal Postal Service or selling kali weed, he **headed no'th to The Big Apple. ∞ After graduating from the School of Visual Arts, he moved to Boston to work as a designer and art director for The Boston Globe. He then went to work** for The Washington Post Magazine as its art director for three years. He is currently back in New York working as art director at Vibe Magazine. ∞ He sometimes still thinks about a career in sales and postal service.

Richard Baker

Mark Koudys

Mark Koudys is Canadian, and therefore an extremely nice and polite person. He grew up in an octagonal house just outside Niagara Falls, which may or may not account for the many facets to his work and character today, but must **certainly explains his fear and loathing of tourism and honeymoons. Currently he is a principal of Atlanta Art and Design in Toronto, which specializes in editorial design and corporate communications programs. His work has been recognized by The American Institute for Graphic Arts, Society of Publication Designers, Communication Arts, Graphis and the Toronto Art Directors Club. His surname comes from Dutch parents, it's pronounced "cowt-ice," and it means "cold-ice," which raises the question of** what other kind of ice they have in Holland...but perhaps it is not a question which need concern us any further here...

favorite deadly sin: lust

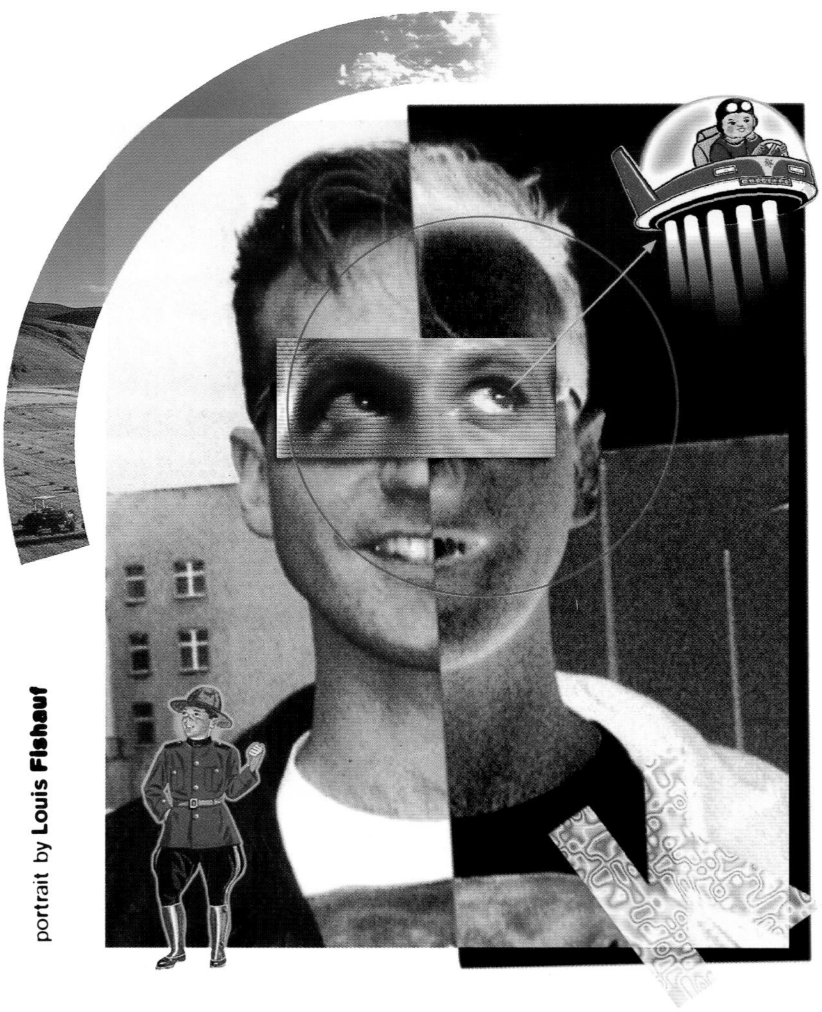

portrait by **Louis Fishauf**

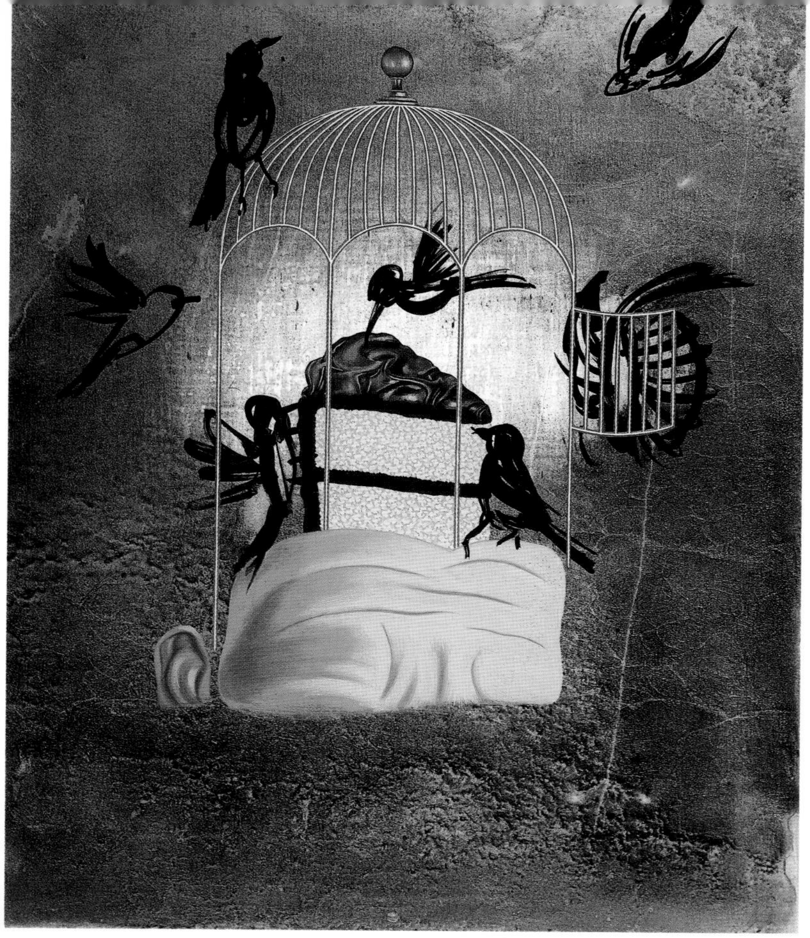

portrait by **Ruth Marten**

favorite deadly sin: anger

Mirko Ilić was born in Bosnia in 1956. He started to publish his work at the age of seventeen. His work ranged from **comics and illustrations to art direction for film, theater posters, album covers and book covers. In 1986** **he emigrated to the U.S. where he continued to work for a wide range of clients, primarily as** **an illustrator. He has art directed "Time International" and is currently art directing the Op-Ed page of "The** New York Times." Mirko has been awarded a gold medal by the Society of Illustrators and by the Society of Publication Designers.

Mi**rko Ilić**

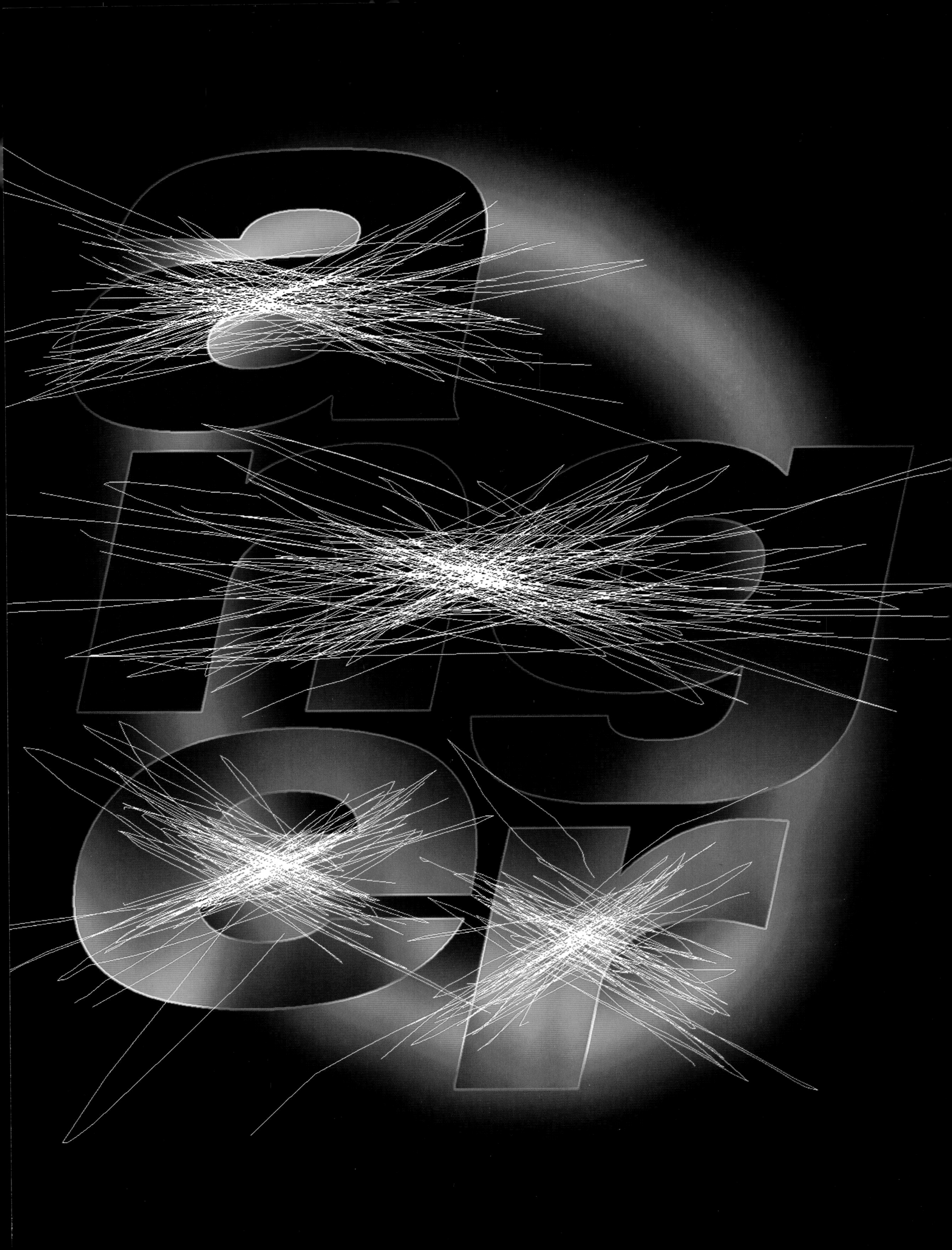

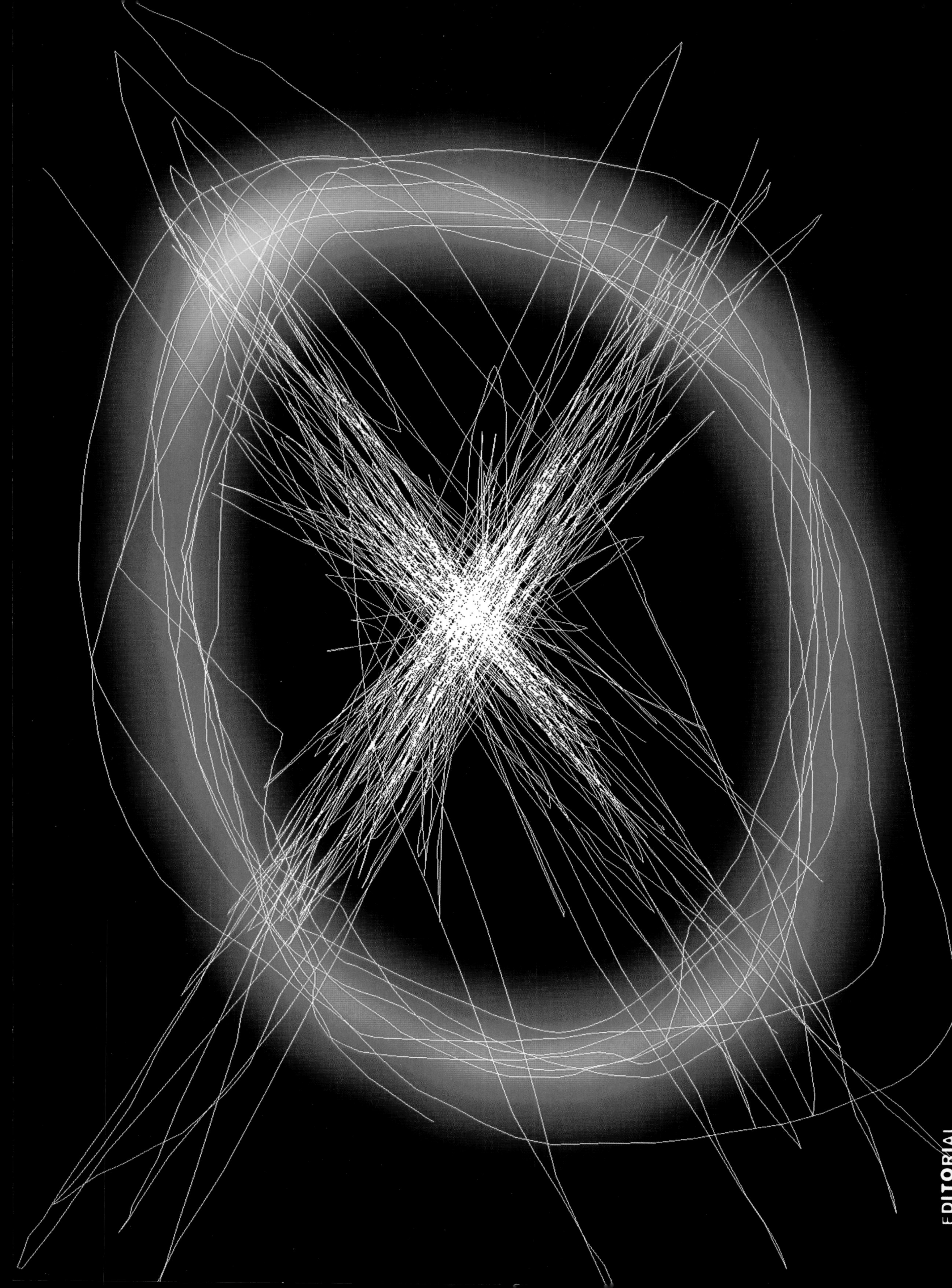

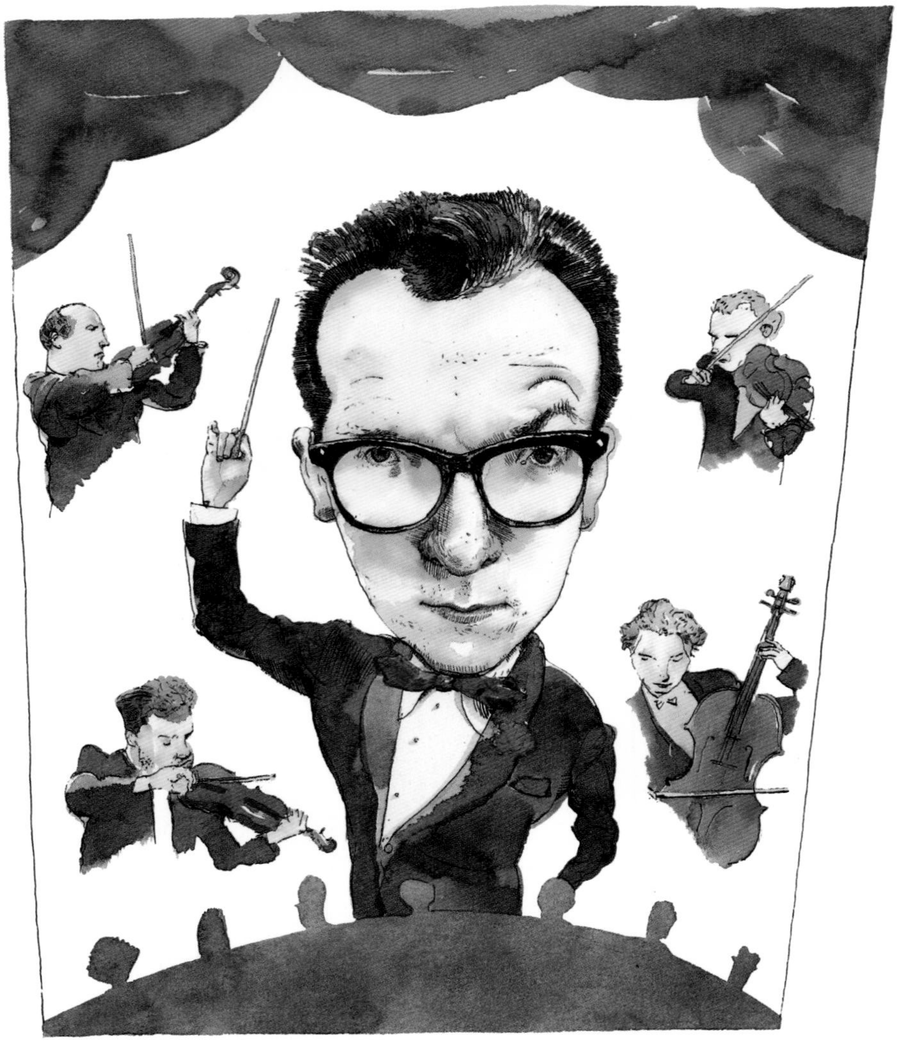

Barry Blitt

Art Directors) Chris Curry and Lee Lorenz **Editor)** Tina Brown **Publication)** The New Yorker **Date)** March 22, 1993
Publisher) Condé Nast Publications, Inc. **Medium)** Pen and ink, watercolor
Elvis Costello and the Brodsky Quartet as depicted for the feature "Goings on About Town."

17

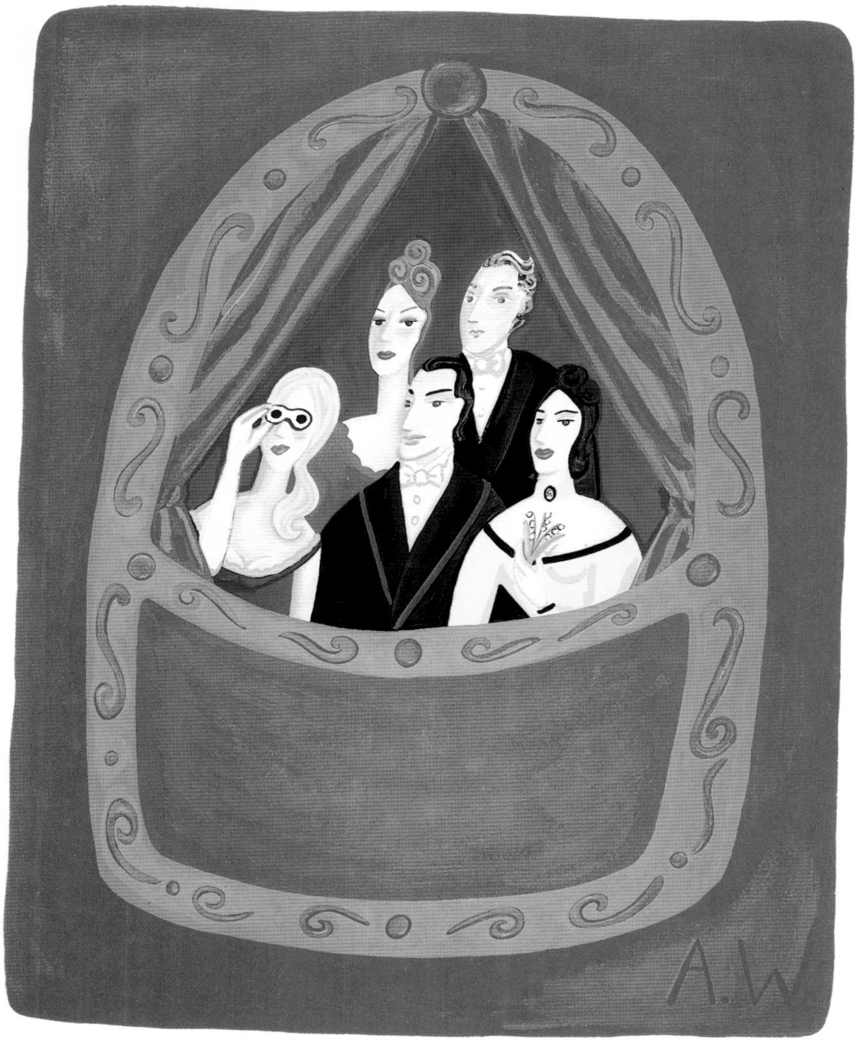

Alexandra Weems

Art Director) Chris Curry Editor) Tina Brown **Publication) The New Yorker** Publisher) Condé Nast Publications, Inc.
Medium) Gouache on BFK Rives One of two **Illustrations commissioned** for The New Yorker's "Night Life" section.

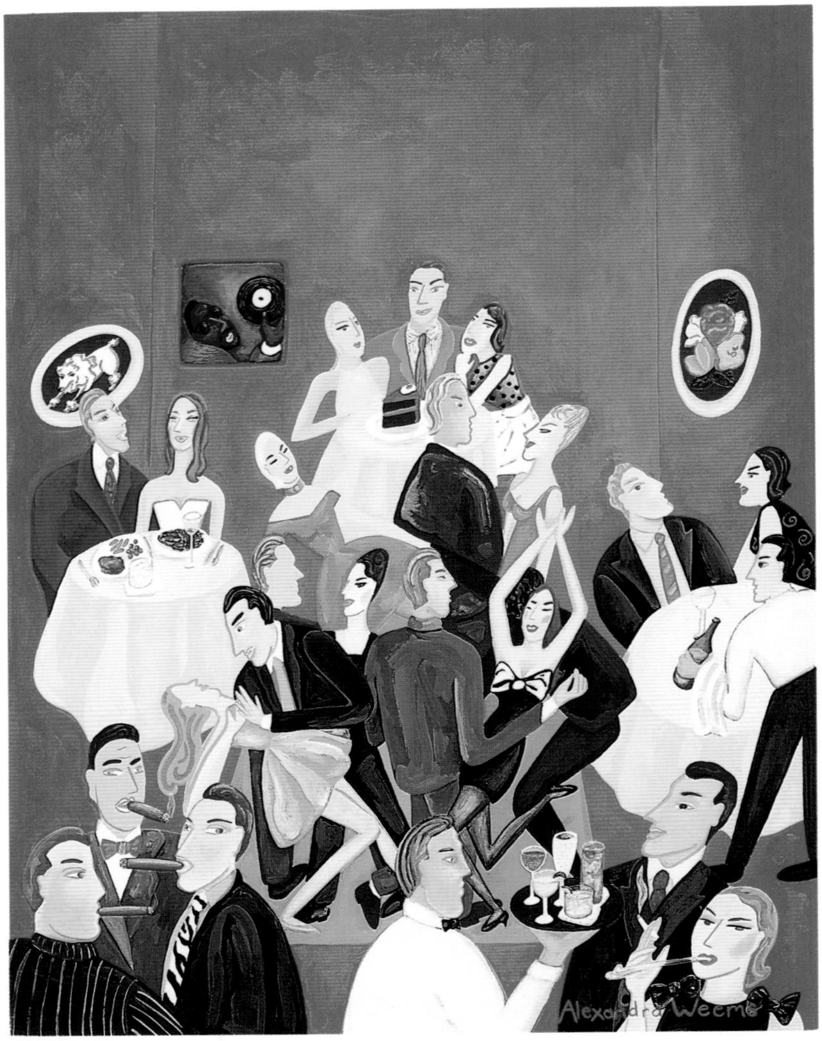

Alexandra Weems

Art Director) Chris Curry Editor) Tina Brown **Publication) The New Yorker** Publisher) Condé Nast Publications, Inc.
Medium) Gouache on BFK Rives The second of two **illustrations commissioned** for The New Yorker's "Night Life" section (above).

∞

Art Director) Pamela Berry Writer) Michael Kaplan **Publication) US Magazine** Date) August 1992 Publisher) Straight Arrow Publishers, Inc.
Medium) Gouache on paper Cable sex shows were the **subject of the article "You** Get What You Pay For" **feat**uring this illustration (right).

Maira Kalman

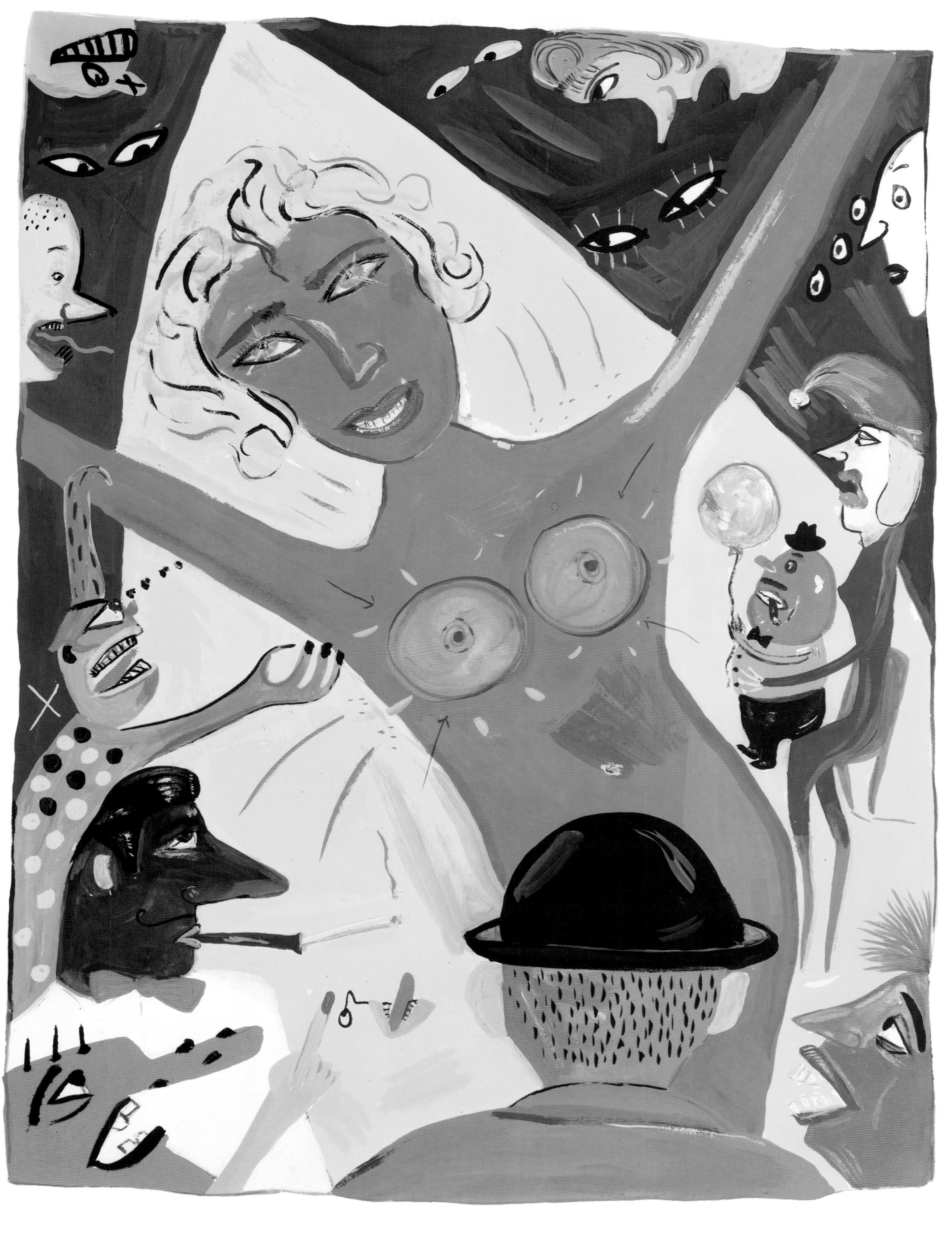

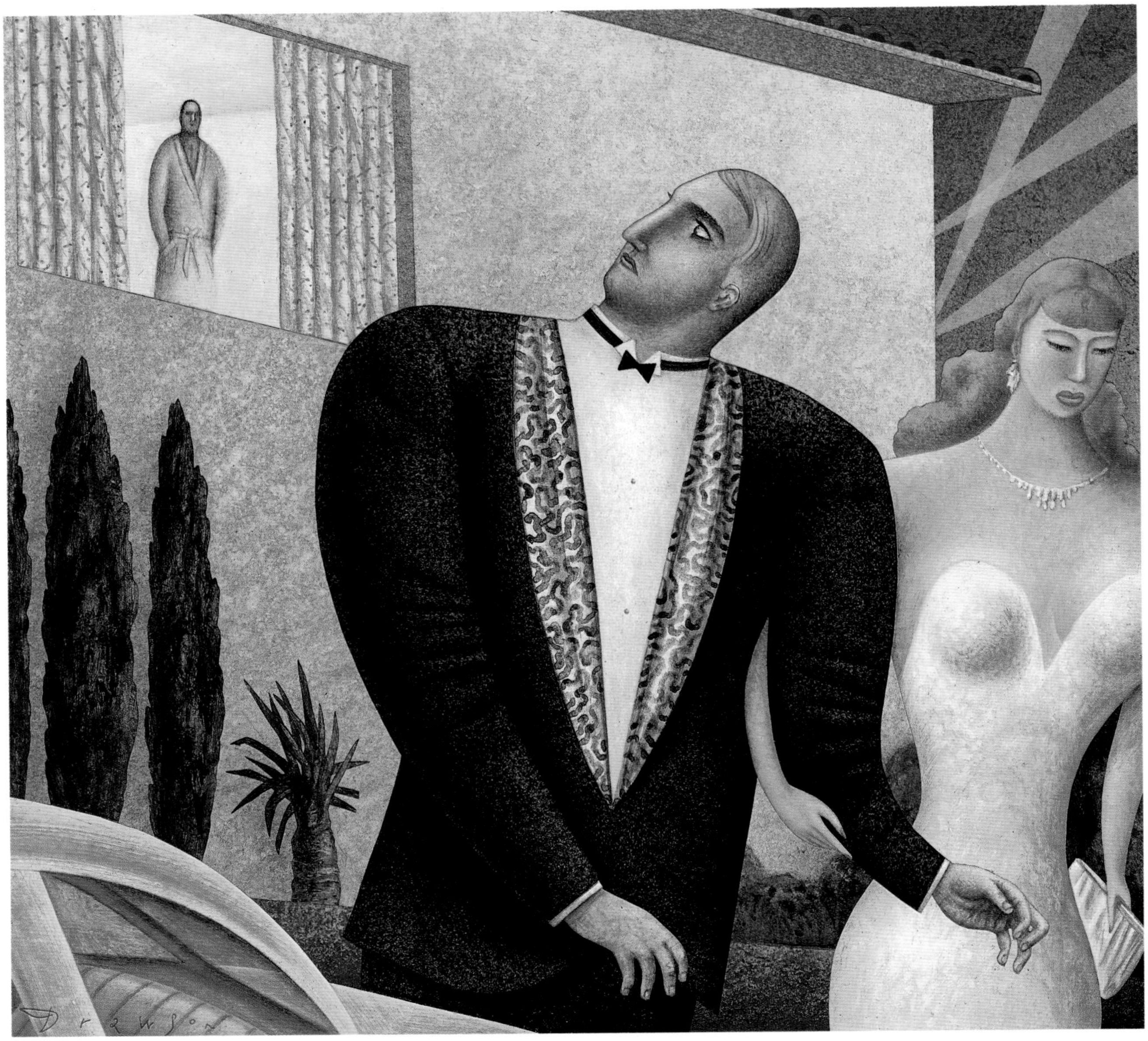

Blair Drawson

Art Director) Pamela Berry Publication) US Magazine Date) February 1992 Publisher) Straight Arrow Publishers, Inc.
Medium) Acrylic This image illustrated the article "What It's Like to be Gay in Hollywood."

Designer) Darrin Perry Editor) Chris Hunt Writer) Gary Smith Publication) Sports Illustrated Date) July 22, 1992. Publisher) The Time Inc. Magazine Company Medium) Pen and ink, dyes The unsophisticated American traveler is depicted here for the article "A Pain in Spain."

Maurice Vellekoop

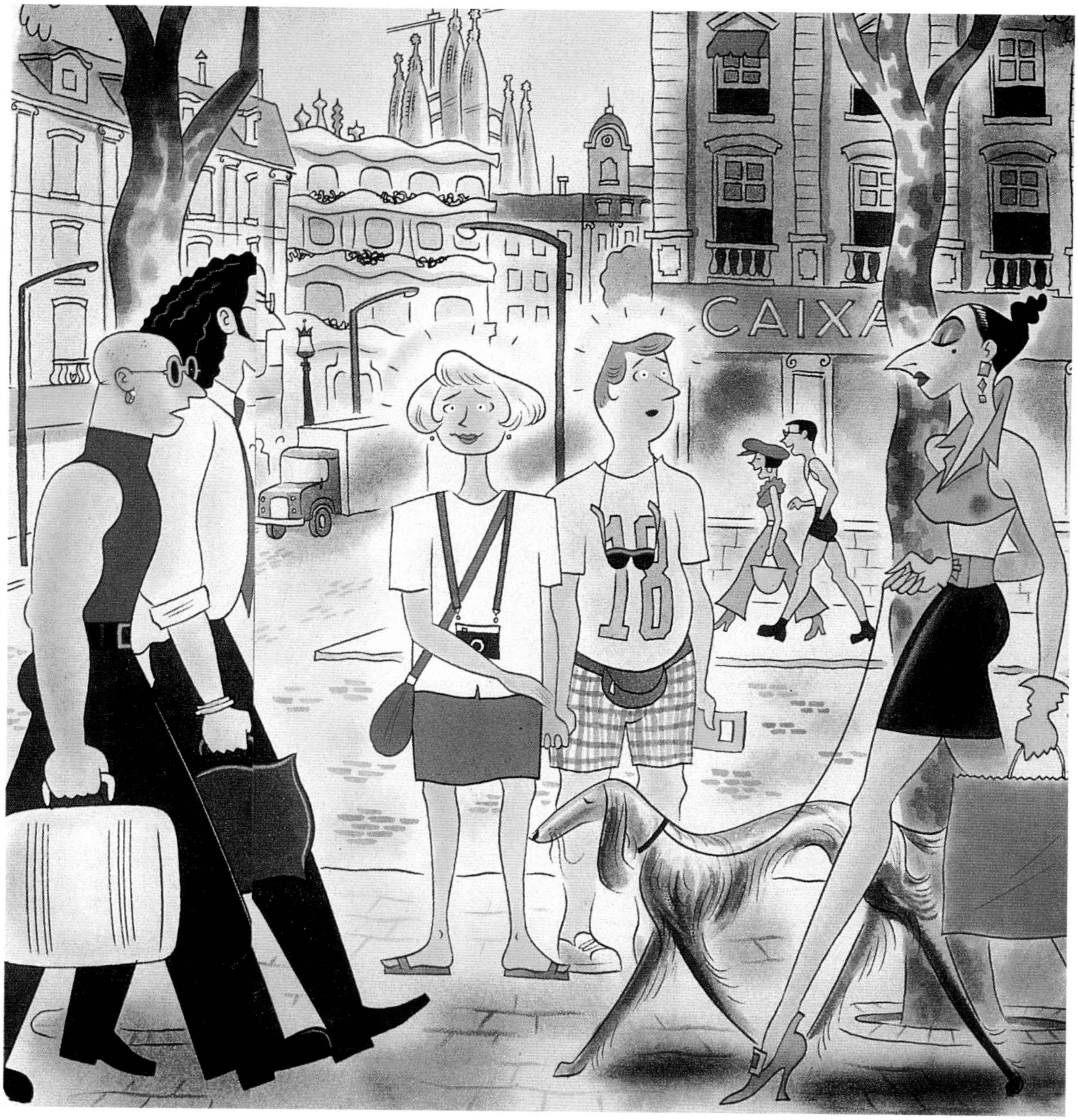

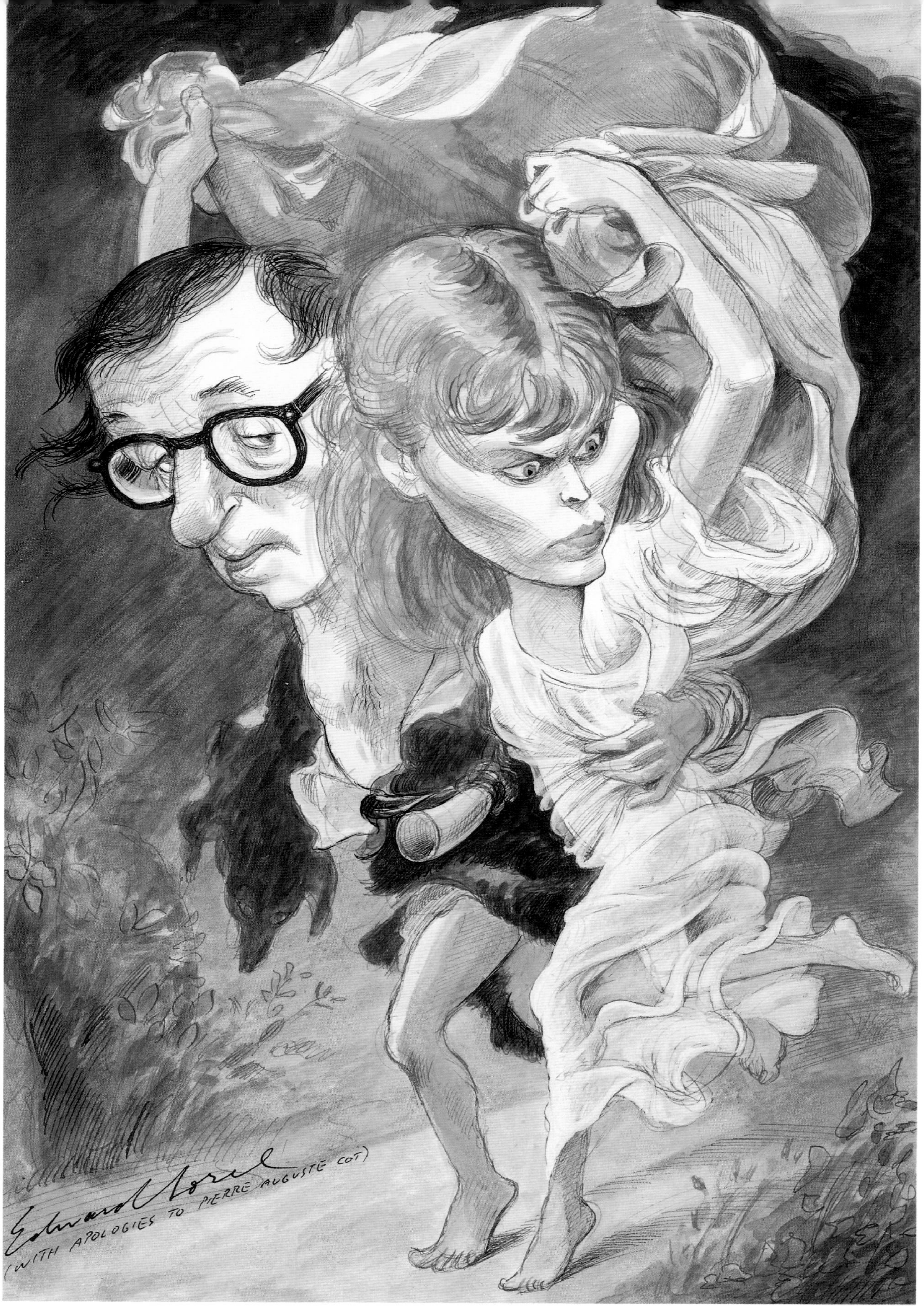

Edward Sorel

Art Director) Fred Woodward **Writer) Peter Travers** Publication) Rolling Stone
Date) October 1, 1992 Publisher) **Straight Arrow Publishers,** Inc. Medium) Pen and ink, watercolor
This parody of Pierre Cot's painting accompanied the review of Woody Allen's movie "Husbands and Wives."

Art Directors) Dwayne Flinchum and Suzette Ruys Editor) Bob Guccione Writer) Kit Reed
Publication) Omni Magazine Date) March 1993 Publisher) General Media Publication Group Medium) Oil on canvas
This illustration of a crazed woman being chased by dogs was created for the article "Like My Dress."

Sandra Hendler

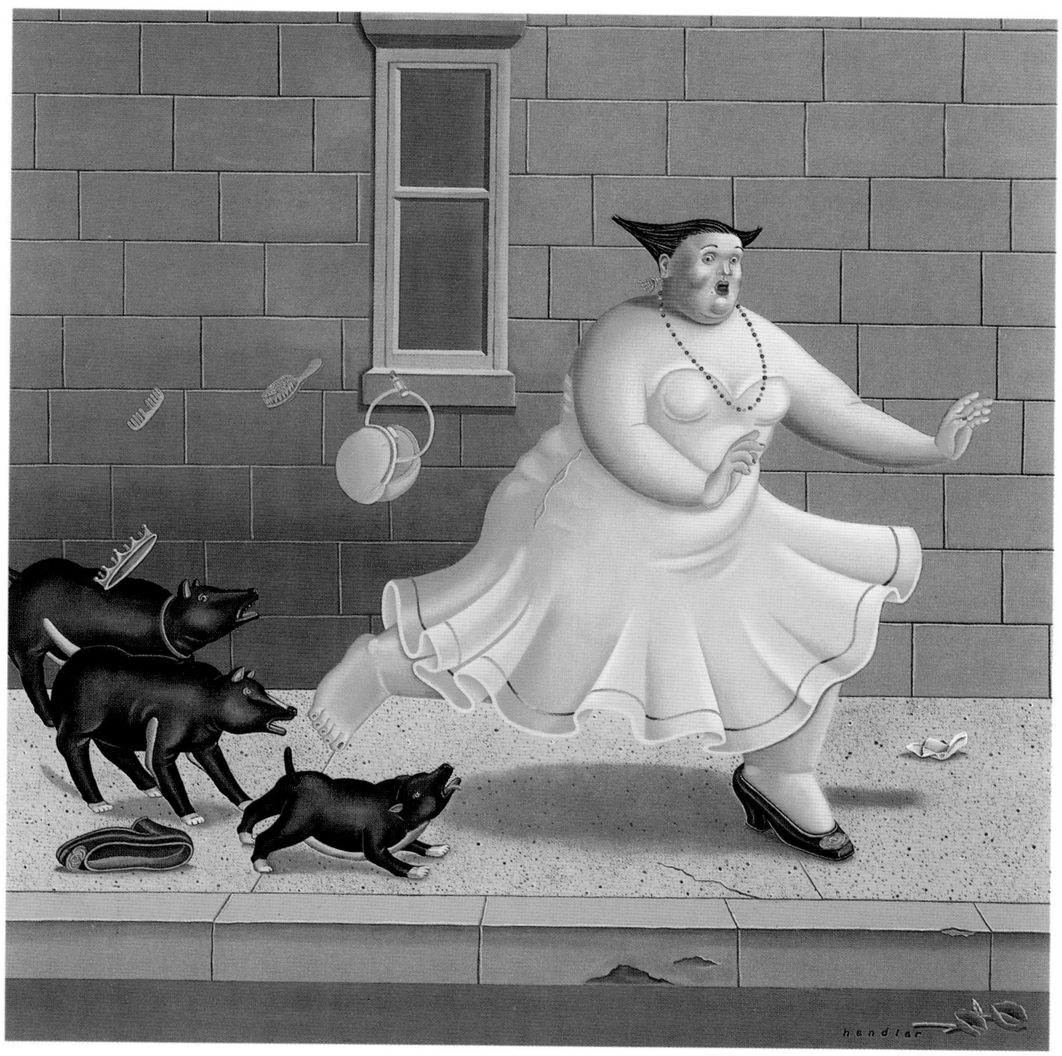

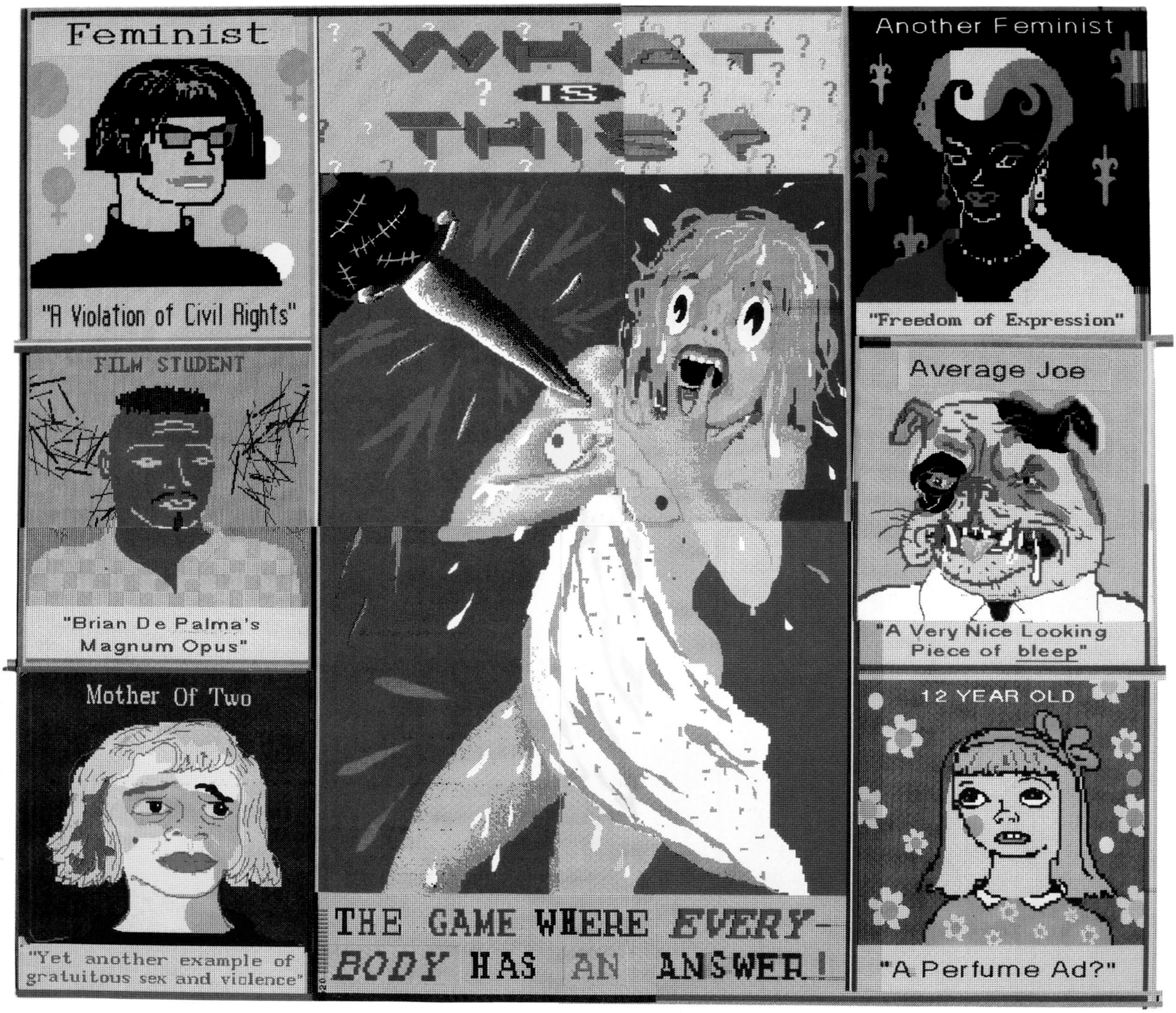

Georganne Deen

Art Director) Judy Garlan Editor) Jack Beatty Writer) Wendy Kaminer Publication) The Atlantic Monthly
Date) November 1992 Publisher) The Atlantic Monthly Company Medium) AMIGA Computer/Diablo Printer
A critique of feminists' participation in the anti-pornography movement inspired this image.

Art Directors) Rudolph C. Hoglund **and Jane Frey** **Editor) Jo**hanna McGeary **Writer) John** Kohan
Publication) Russia **Special Issue of Time Magazine Date) December 7, 1992** **Publisher) The Time Inc.** Magazine Company
Medium) **Paint and collage This collage accompanied the article "Can Russia Escape Its** Past?"

Janet Woolley

25

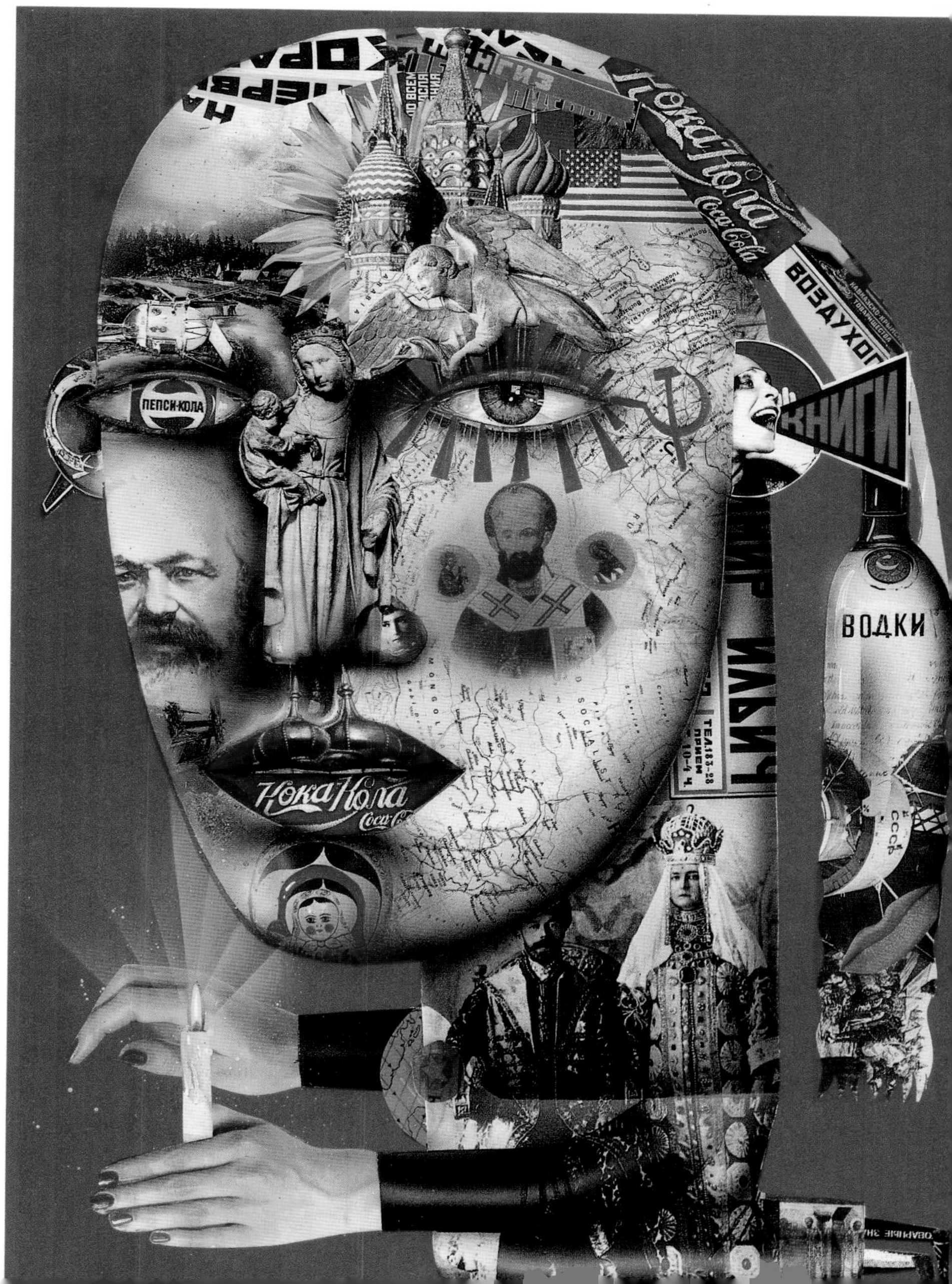

Art Director) Kerig Pope Designer) Tom Staebler Writer) Alex Haley Publication) Playboy Date) July 1992
Publisher) Playboy Enterprises, Inc. Medium) Acrylic This illustration accompanied the article "Malcolm X Remembered."

Brad Holland

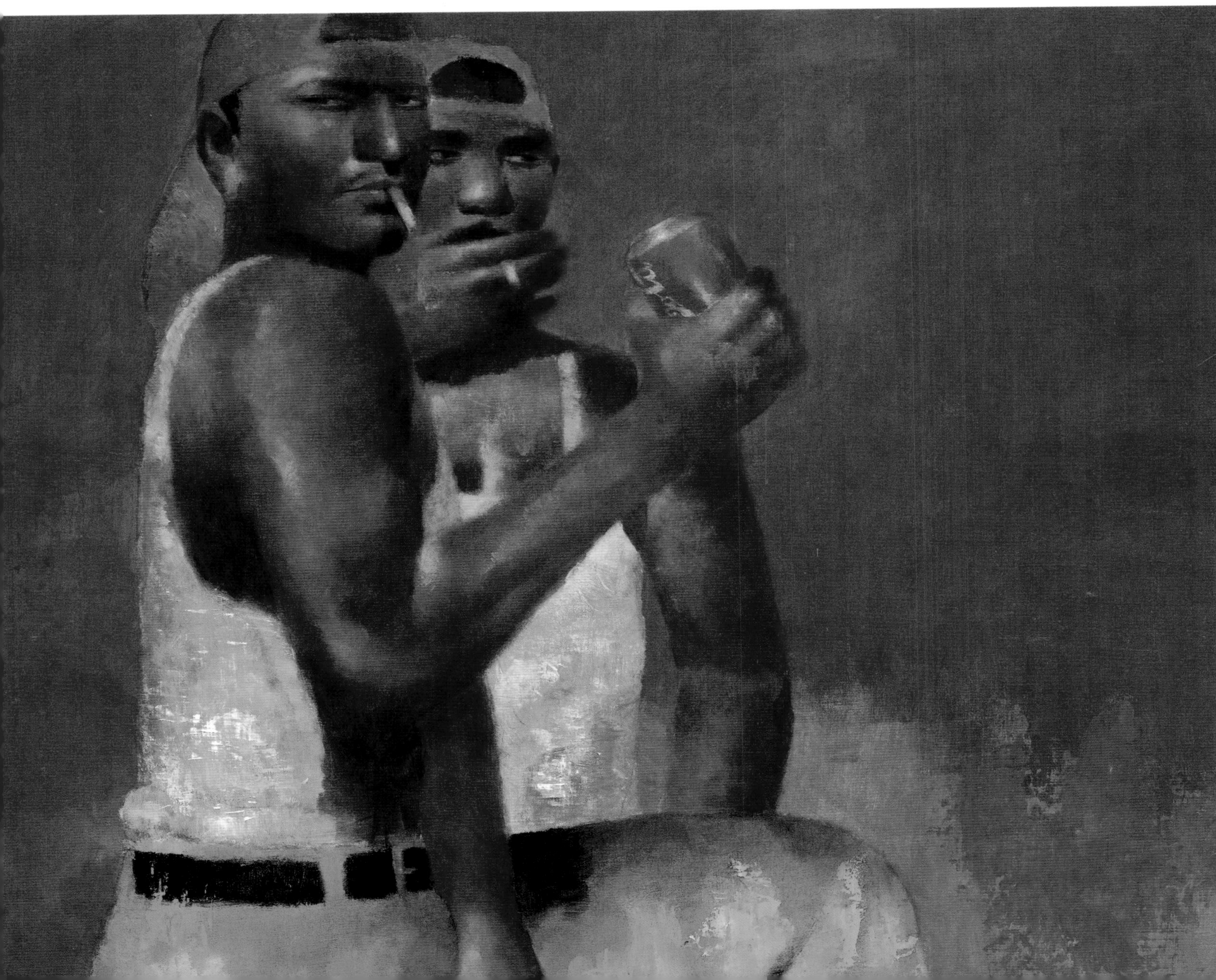

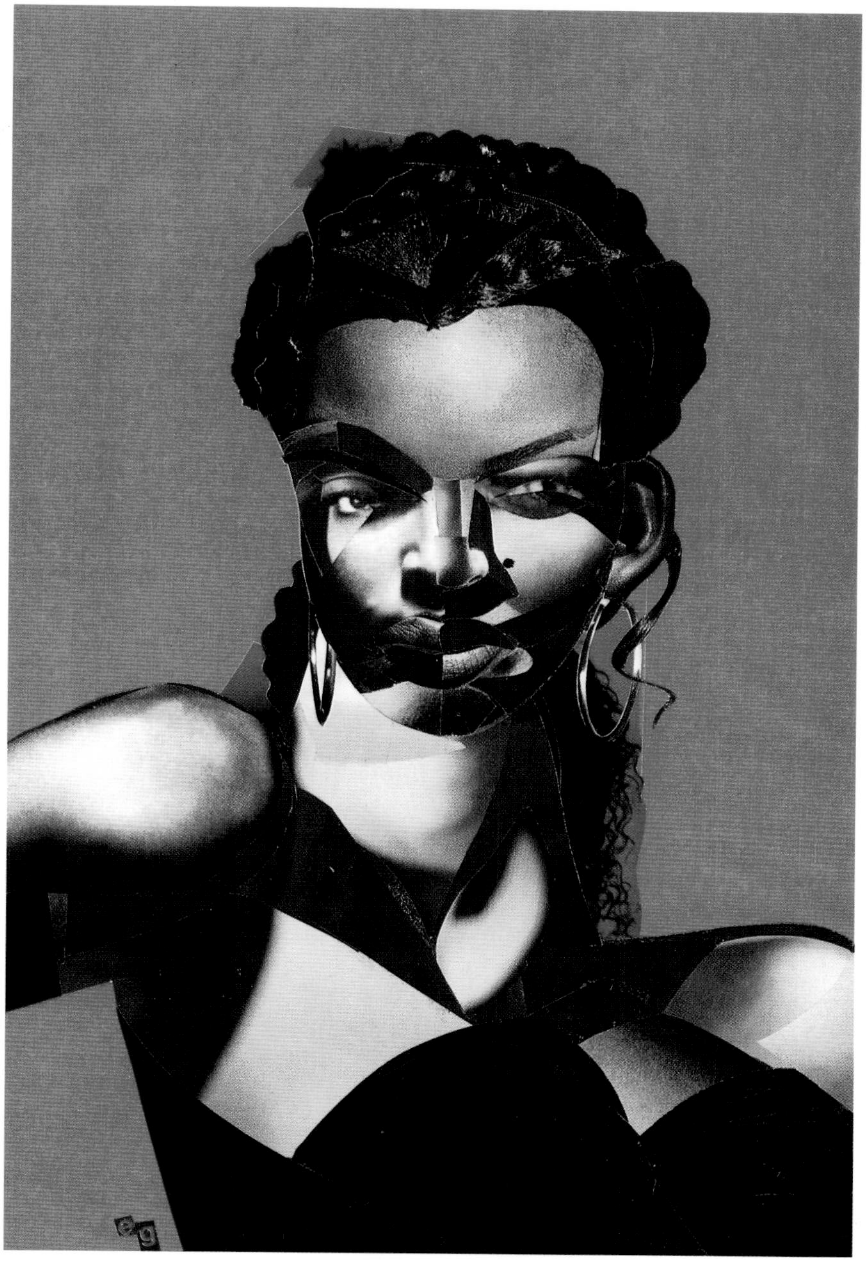

Edmund Guy

Art Director) Fred Woodward Writer) Mark Coleman **Publication) Rolling Stone** Date) November 26, 1992 Publisher) Straight Arrow Publishers, Inc. Medium) Collage The article "**Neneh's Hot 'Homebrew'**" featured this portrait of the singer Neneh Cherry.

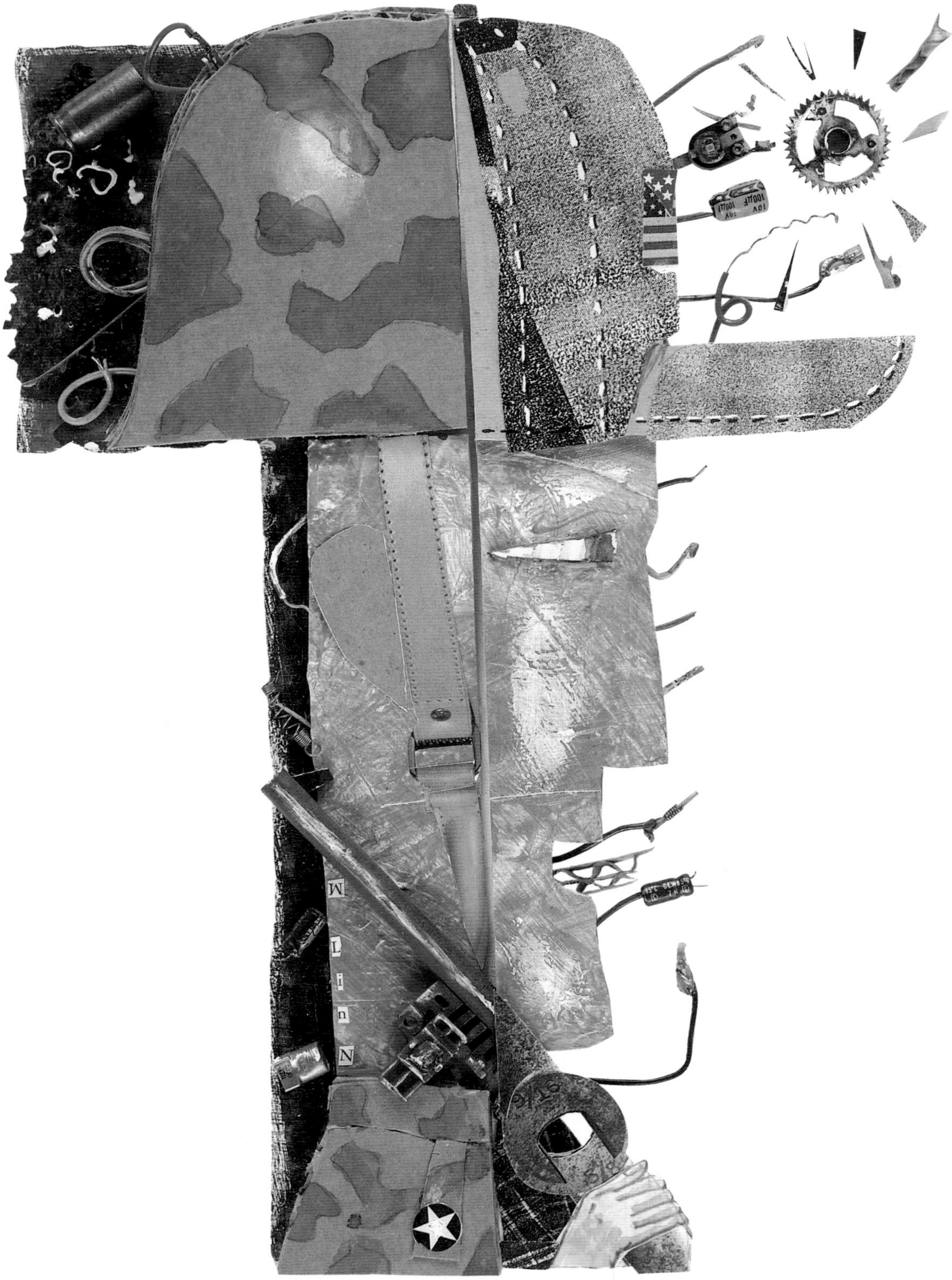

Warren Linn

Art Director) Mirko Ilić Editor) David Shipley Writer) Ann Markusen Publication) The New York Times Date) November 22, 1992 Publisher) New York Times Company Medium) Collage and acrylic This illustration accompanied the article "Turning Off the War Machine" for the New York Times Op-Ed page.

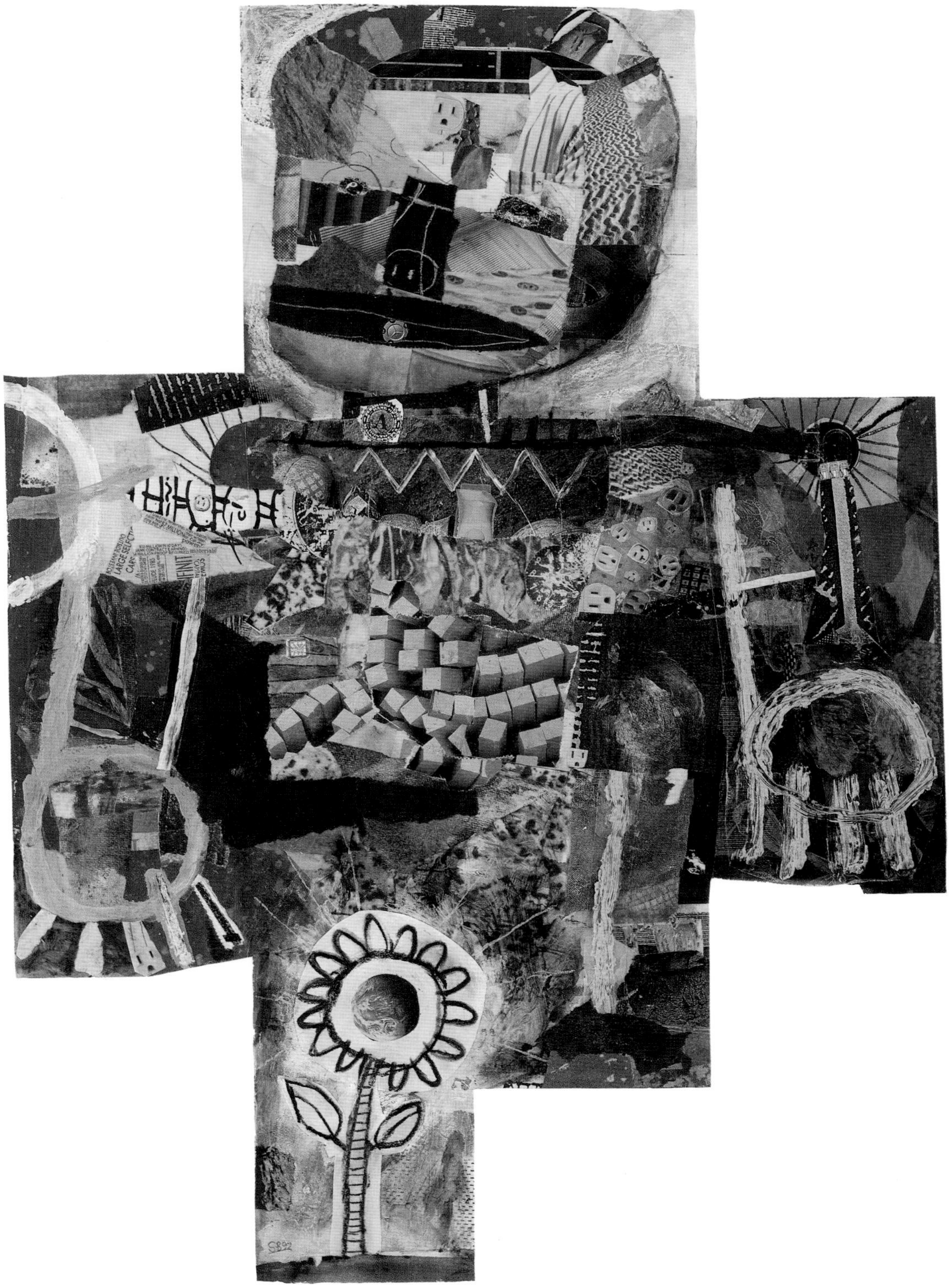

Stephen Byram

Art Director) Mirko Ilić Editor) David Shipley Writer) T. Rosack Publication) The New York Times Date) June 1992 Publisher) New York Times Company Medium) Mixed media This illustration accompanied an essay on environmental and commerce issues for the Times Op-Ed page.

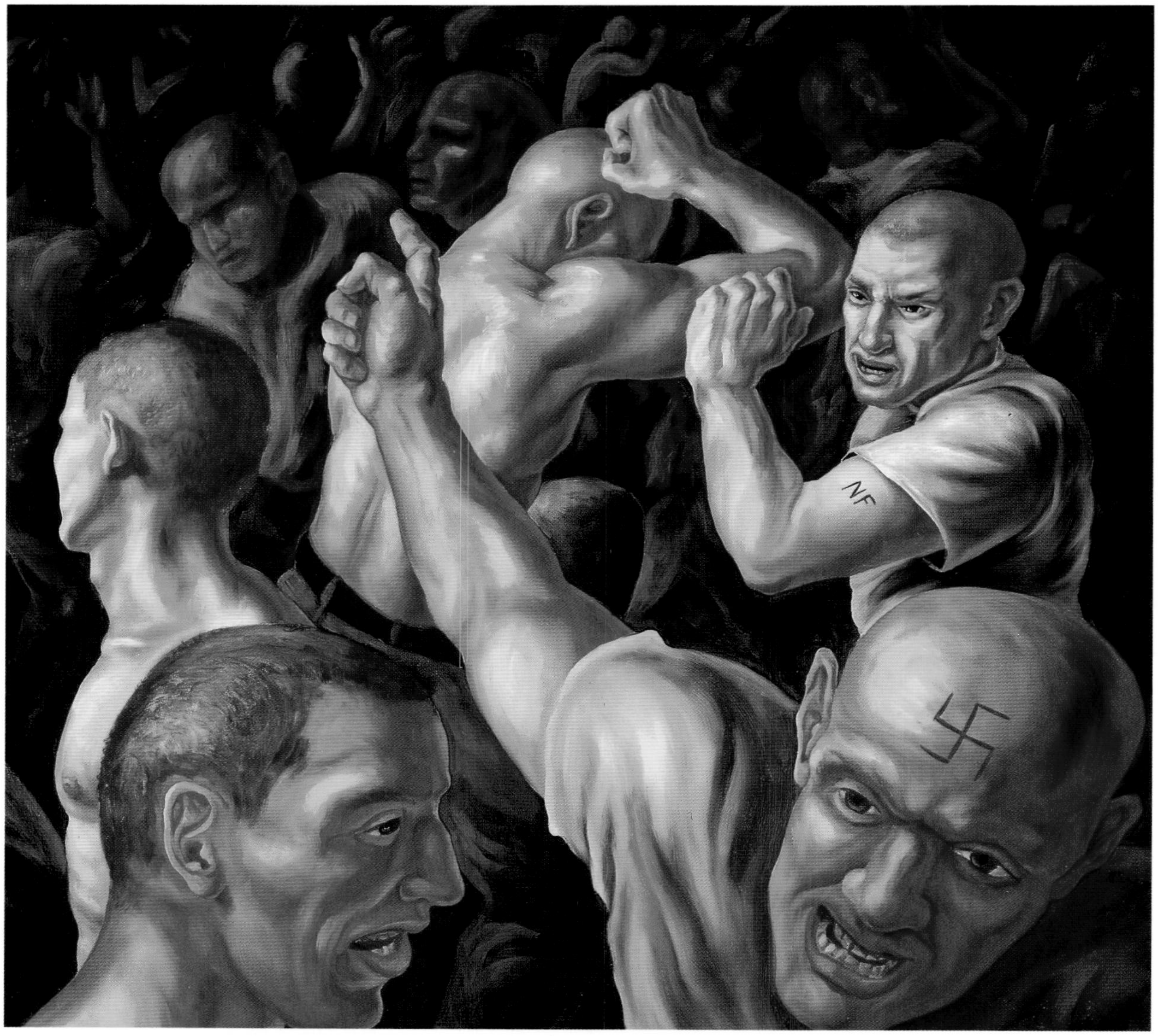

Owen Smith

Art Director) Janet Froelich Designer) Kandy Littrell Writer) Bill Buford Publication) The New York Times Magazine Date) April 26, 1992 Publisher) New York Times Company Medium) Oil on board This illustration depicts violent, chaotic dancing at an event organized by the National Front, a British Neo-Nazi group.

Art Director) Fred Woodward Publication) Rolling Stone Date) September 17, 1992
Publisher) Straight Arrow Publishers, Inc. Medium) Graphite and gouache Appearing on the Contents page, this illustration ran with the heading "The Bush Years, Supreme Cruelty."

Sue Coe

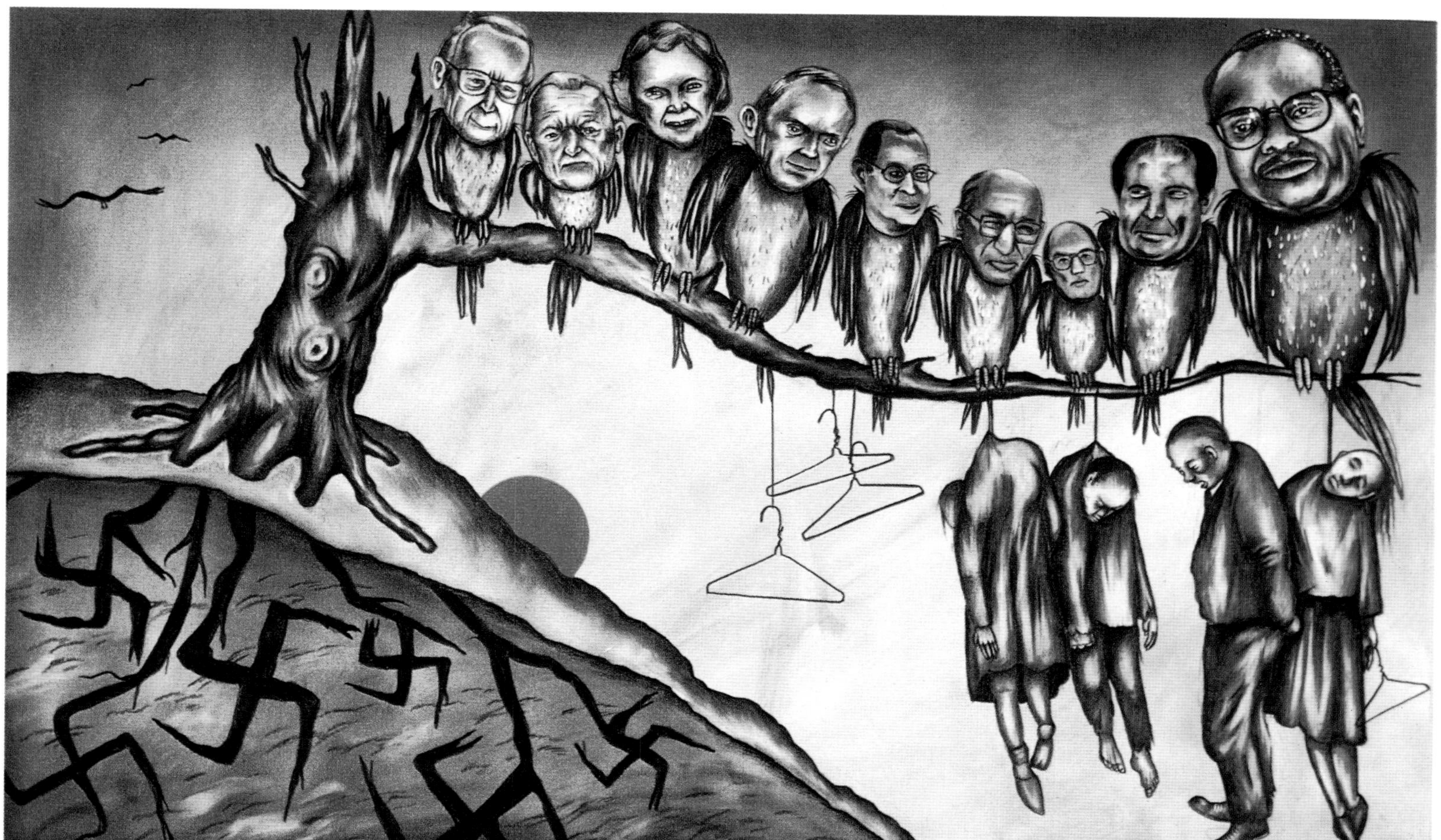

Art Director) Fred Woodward Publication) Rolling Stone Date) September 3, 1992
Publisher) Straight Arrow Publishers, Inc. Medium) Graphite and gouache "The Bush Years, The Environmental President" was the heading for this illustration, appearing on the Contents page.

Sue Coe

32

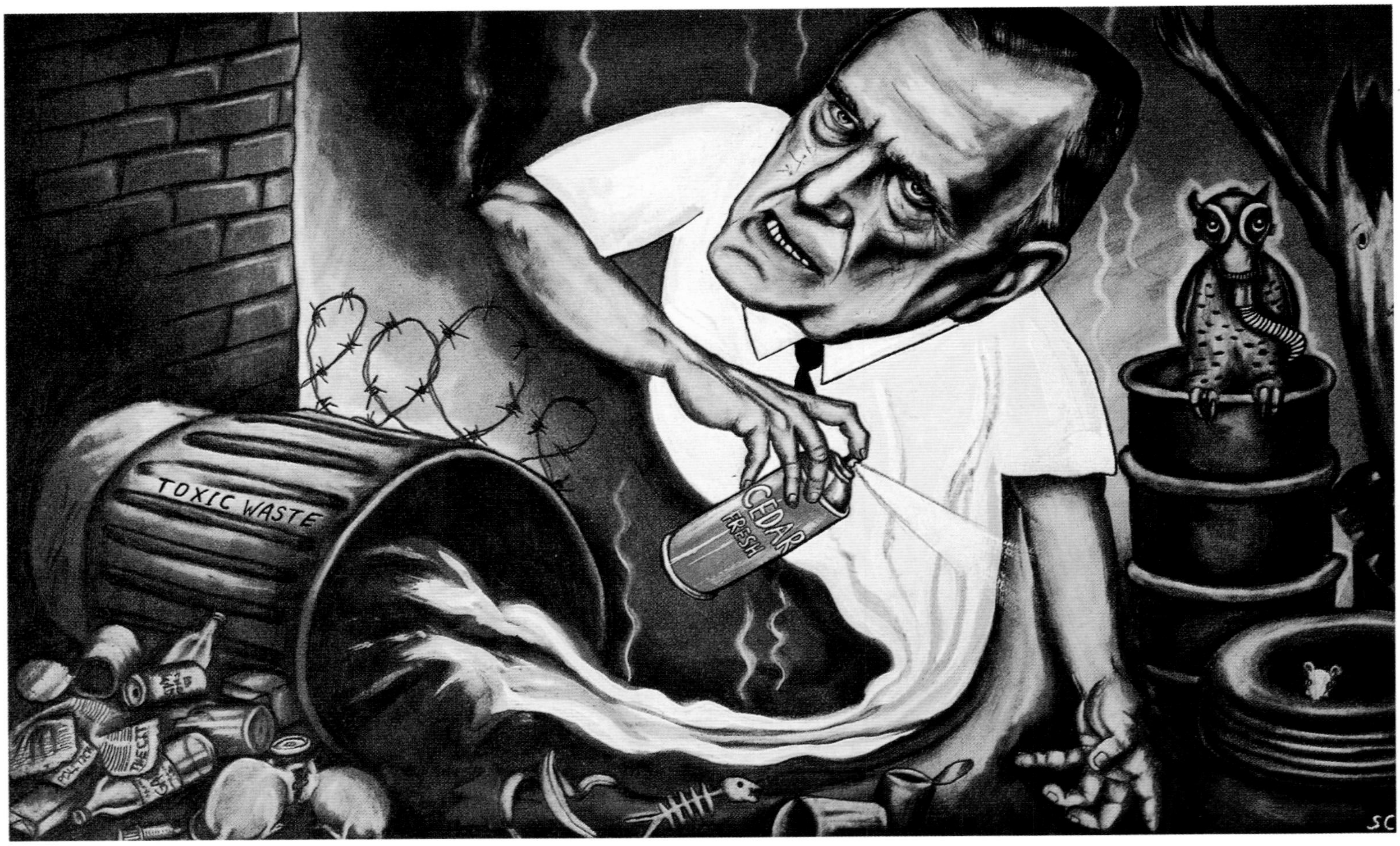

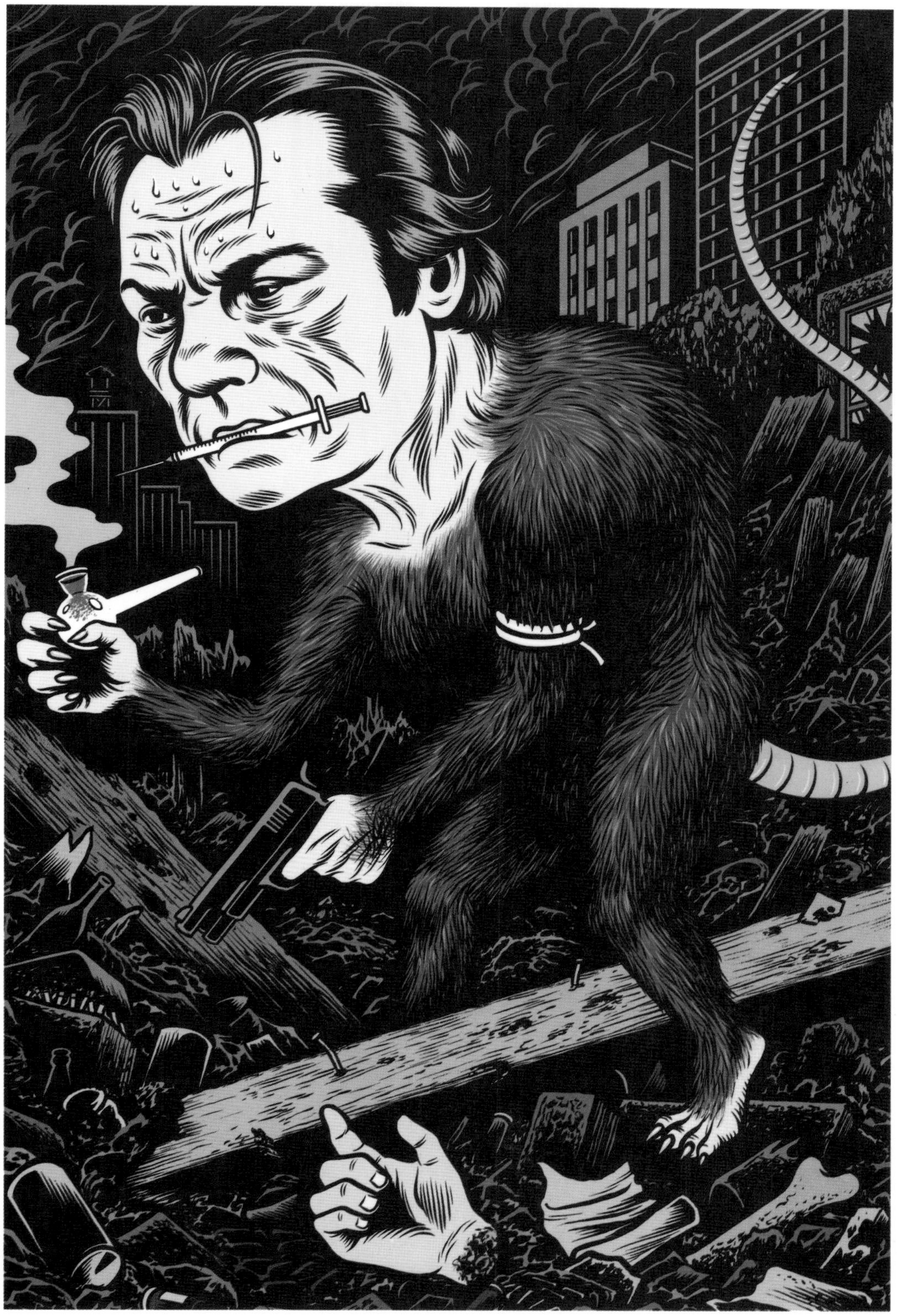

Charles Burns

Art Director) Fred Woodward Writer) Peter Travers Publication) Rolling Stone Date) November 26, 1992 Publisher) Straight Arrow Publishers, Inc. Medium) Mixed media A review of "The Bad Lieutenant" was accompanied by this depiction of its star, Harvey Keitel.

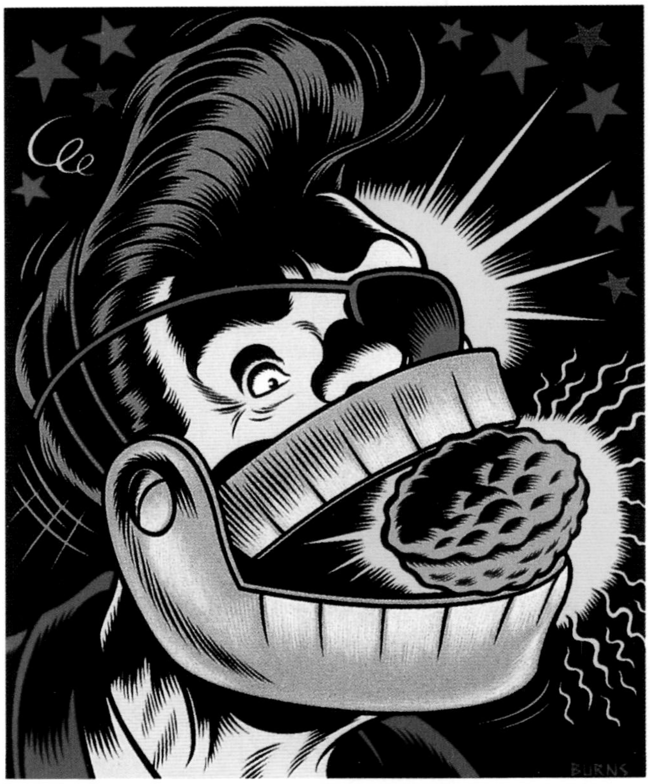

Charles Burns

Art Director) Chris Curry **Editor) Tina Brown** Publication) The New Yorker
Date) December 14, 1992 Publisher) **Condé Nast Publications, Inc.** Medium) Pantone paper and ink
This illustration was found in **the "Night Life" section** of The New Yorker (above).

∞

Art Director) Fred Woodward Publication) Rolling **Stone Date) October** 15, 1992 Publisher) Straight Arrow Publishers, Inc.
Medium) Mixed media The 25th an**niversary issue featured** this portrait of James Brown (right).

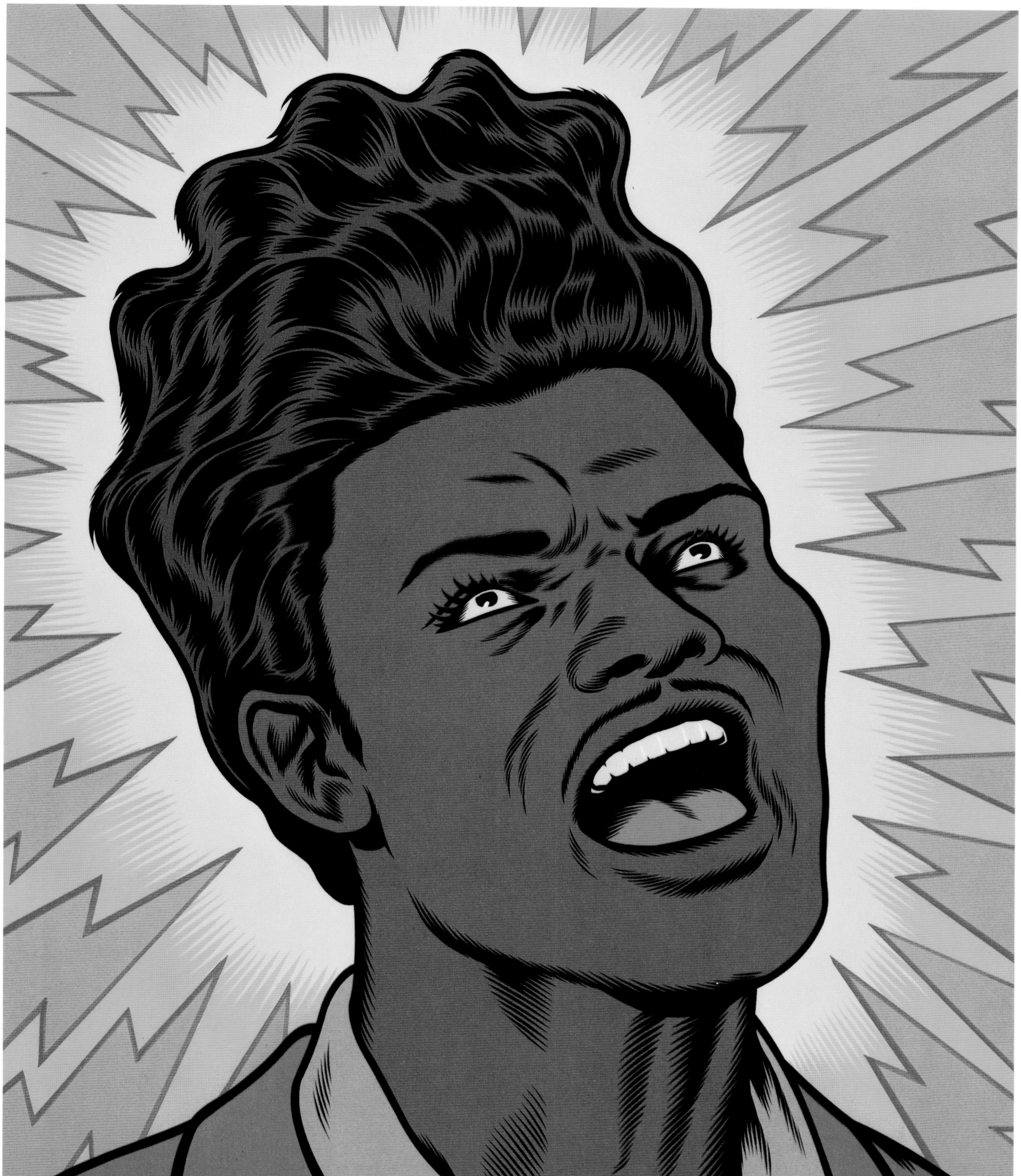

Art Director) Robert Priest Writer) Steve Friedman Publication) GQ Magazine Date) February 1993
Publisher) Condé Nast Publications, Inc. Medium) Mixed media The question,
"Can sex put undue strain on your heart?" was asked in the feature "Personal Best."

Charles Burns

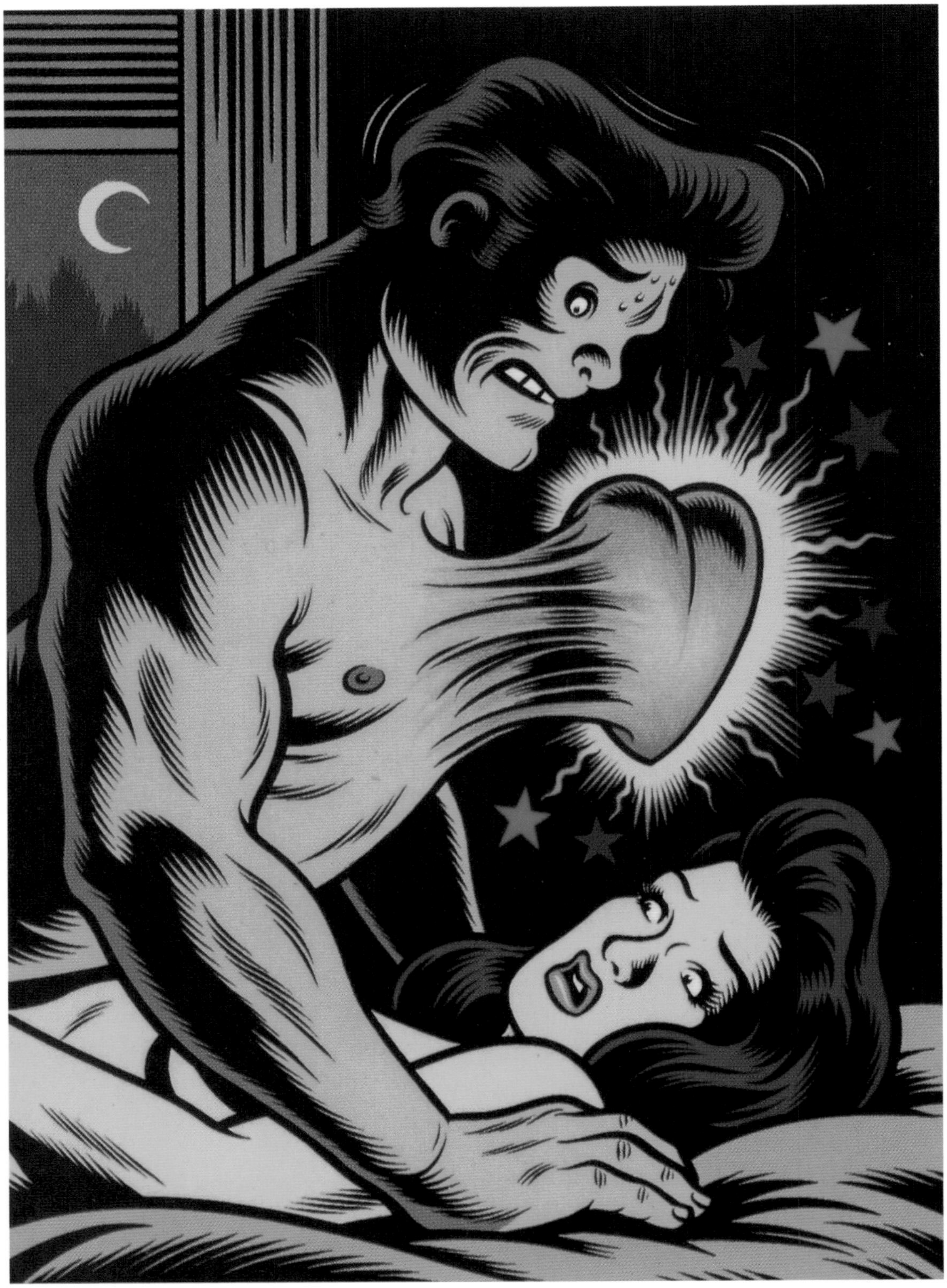

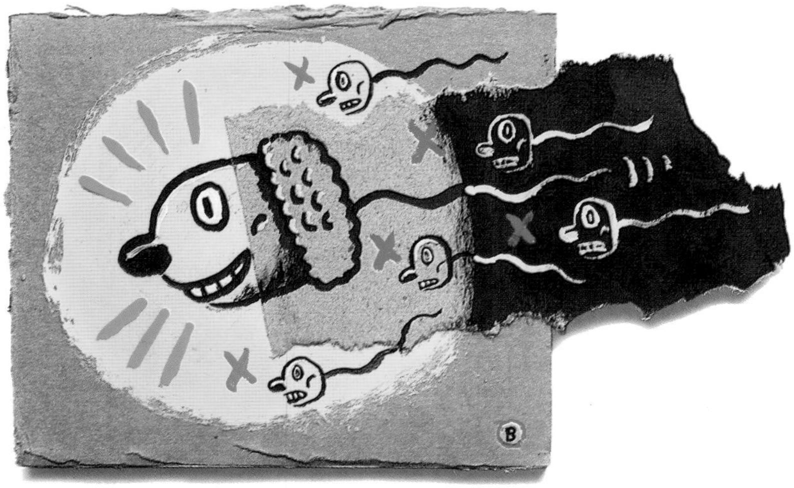

Gary Baseman

Art Director) Susan Gockel Dazzo Writer) Kathleen Clute Publication) American Health Magazine
Date) April 1992 Publisher) Reader's Digest Publications, Inc. Medium) Mixed media
The article "Mighty Sperm From Little Acorns" discusses the potency of sperm with acorn shaped heads.

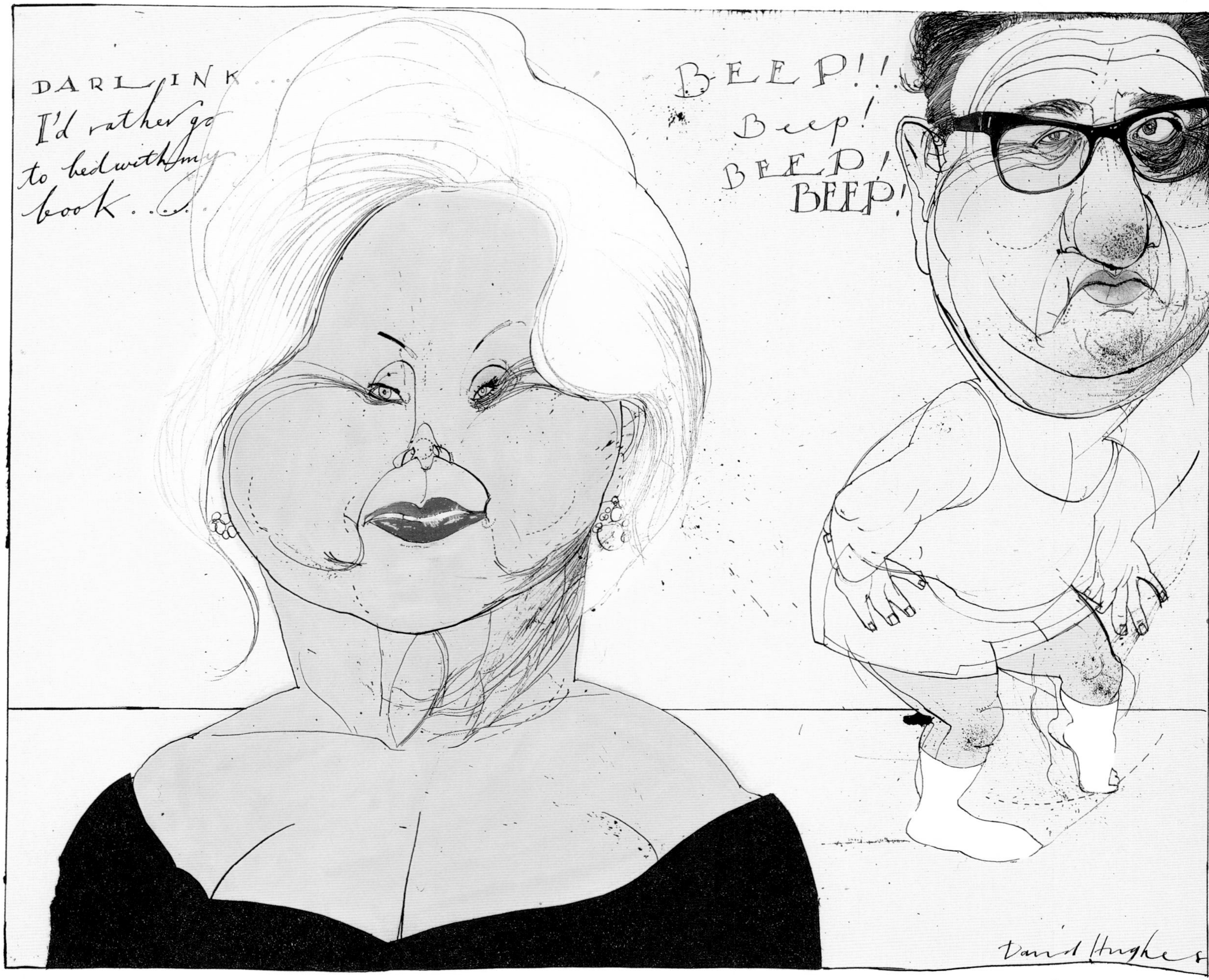

David Hughes

Art Director) Richard Baker Designer) Kelly Doe Editor) Bob Thompson Writer) Peter Carlson Publication) The Washington Post Magazine Date) July 26, 1992 Publisher) The Washington Post Company Medium) Gouache and ink
"When Henry Met Zsa Zsa," a humorous look at celebrity autobiographies, featured this illustration.

Art Director) Charles Churchward **Writer) Anthony Summers** Publication) Vanity Fair Date) March 1993 Publisher) Condé **Nast Publications, Inc.** **Medium)** Gouache This illustration ran with the article "Hidden Hoover," **which revealed one of** his more interesting pastimes.

Robert Risko

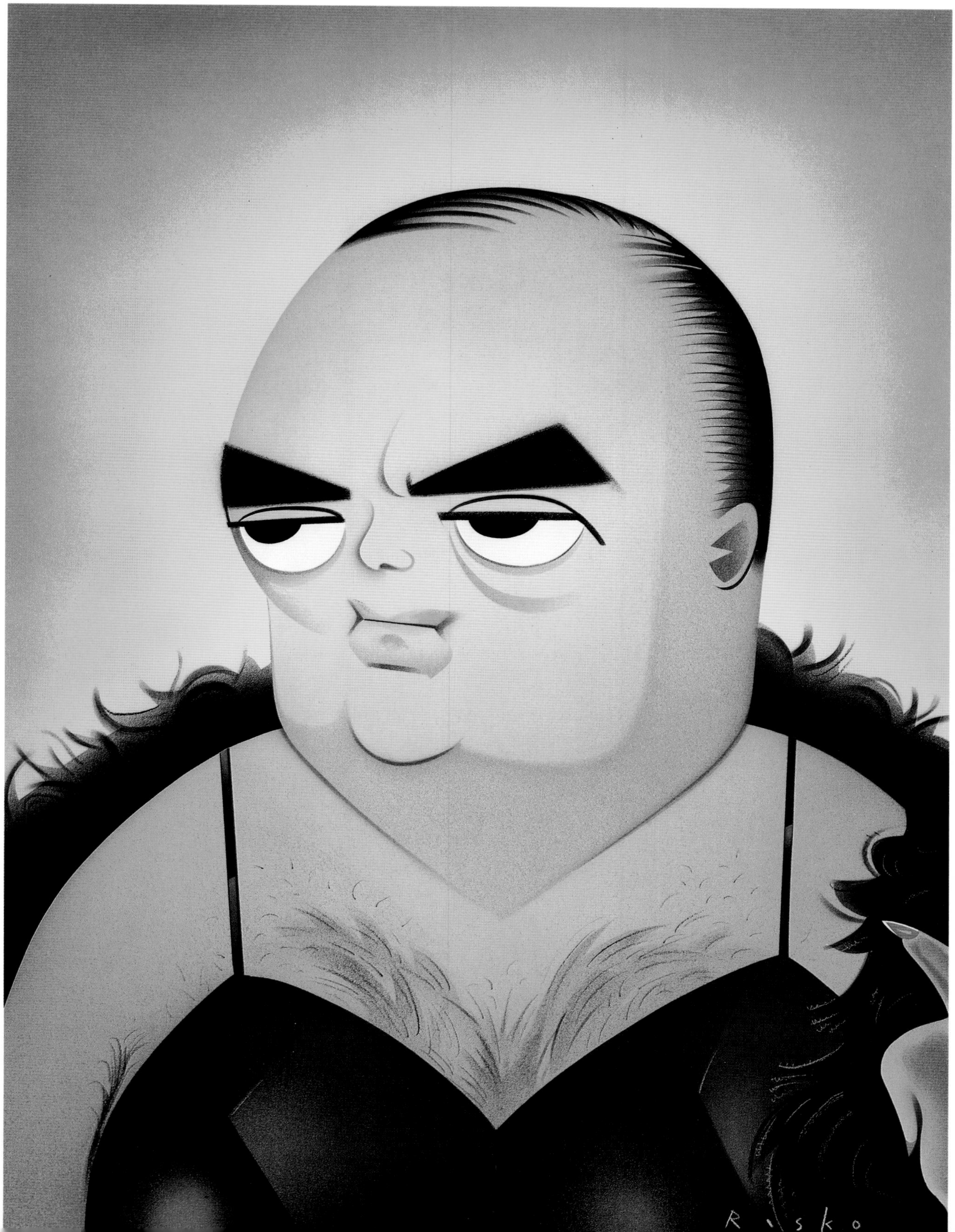

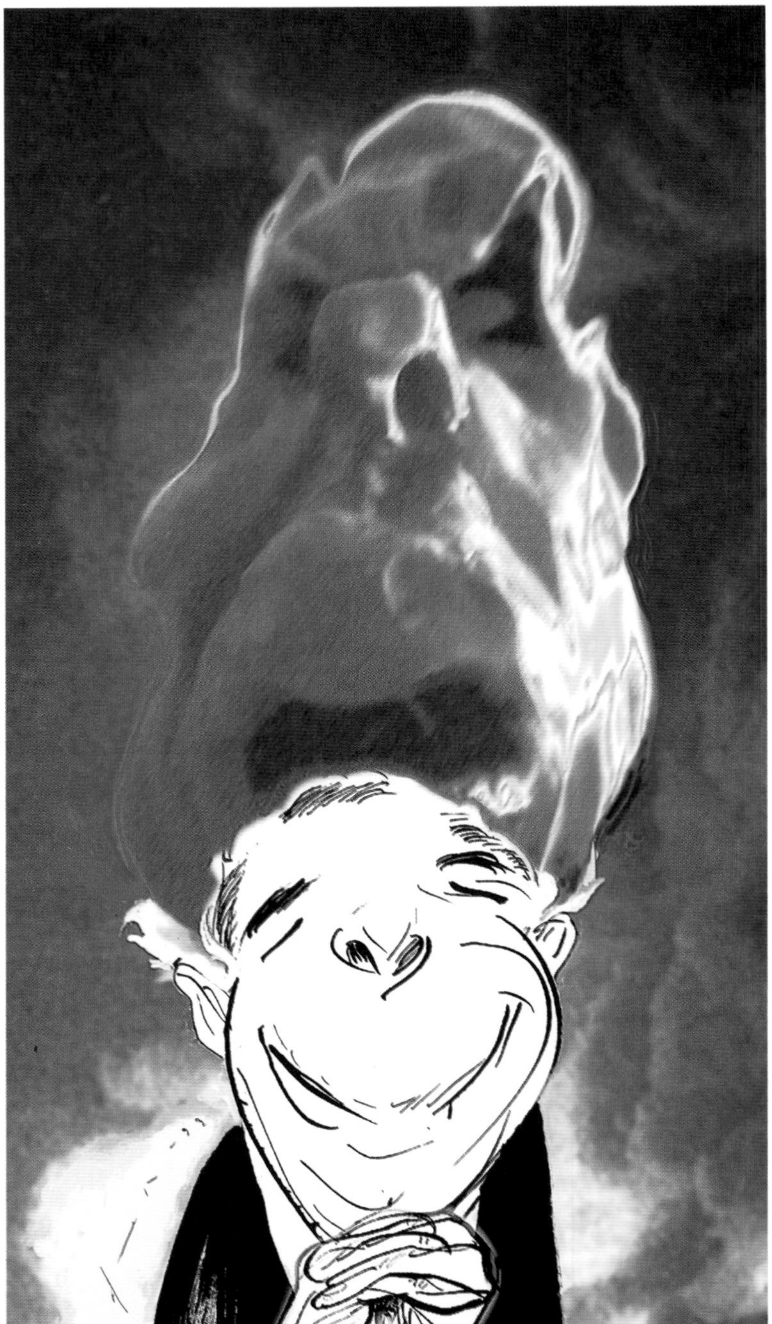

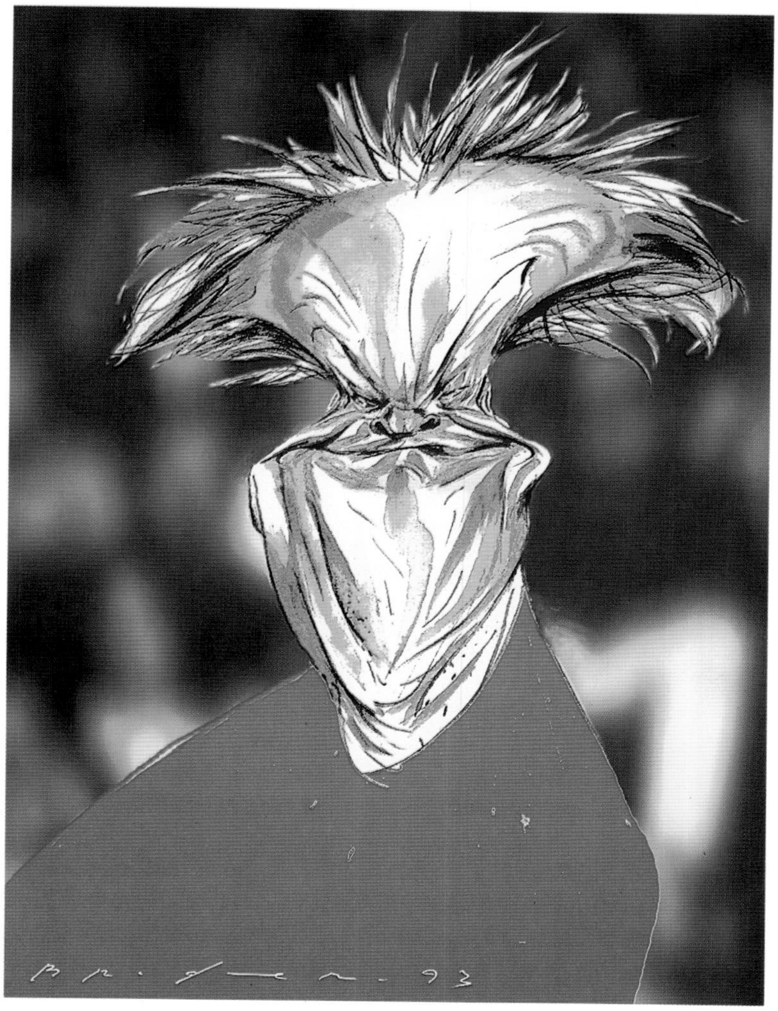

Steve Brodner

Art Director) Pamela Berry Publication) US Magazine Date) March 1993 Publisher) Straight Arrow Publishers, Inc.
Medium) Mixed media using computer The caricature of Jack Nicholson highlights the actor's features (above).

∞

Art Director) Adam Smith Publication) Mirabella Date) April 1993 Publisher) Murdoch Publications
Medium) Mixed media using computer This caricature of Sol Wachtler was created with the computer (left).

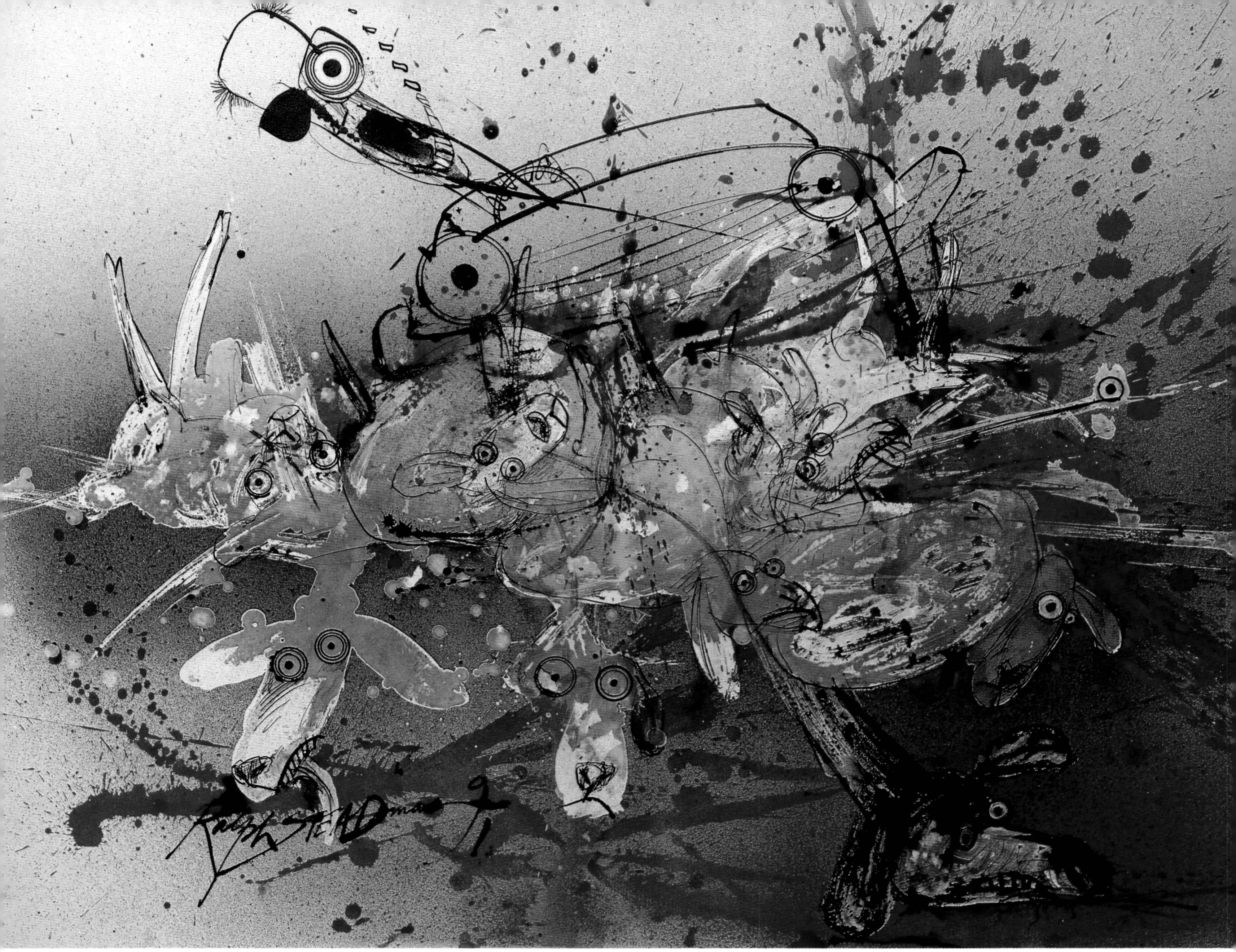

Ralph Steadman

Art Director) **Fred Woodward** Writer) **Hunter S. Thompson** Publication) **Rolling Stone** Date) **January** 23, 1992
Publisher) Straight Arrow **Publishers, Inc.** Medium) **Mixed media** **The article** "Fear and Loathing in ELKO" featured this image.

Art Director) Lisa Powers Editor) Kenneth Auchincloss Writers) Steven Strasser, Bill Powell, Peter McKillop, Frank Gibney Jr., George Wehrfritz Publication) Newsweek International Date) December 21, 1992 Publisher) The Washington Post Company Medium) Linoleum cut The quest for democracy in Asia is represented in this illustration for the article "People Power."

Frances Jetter

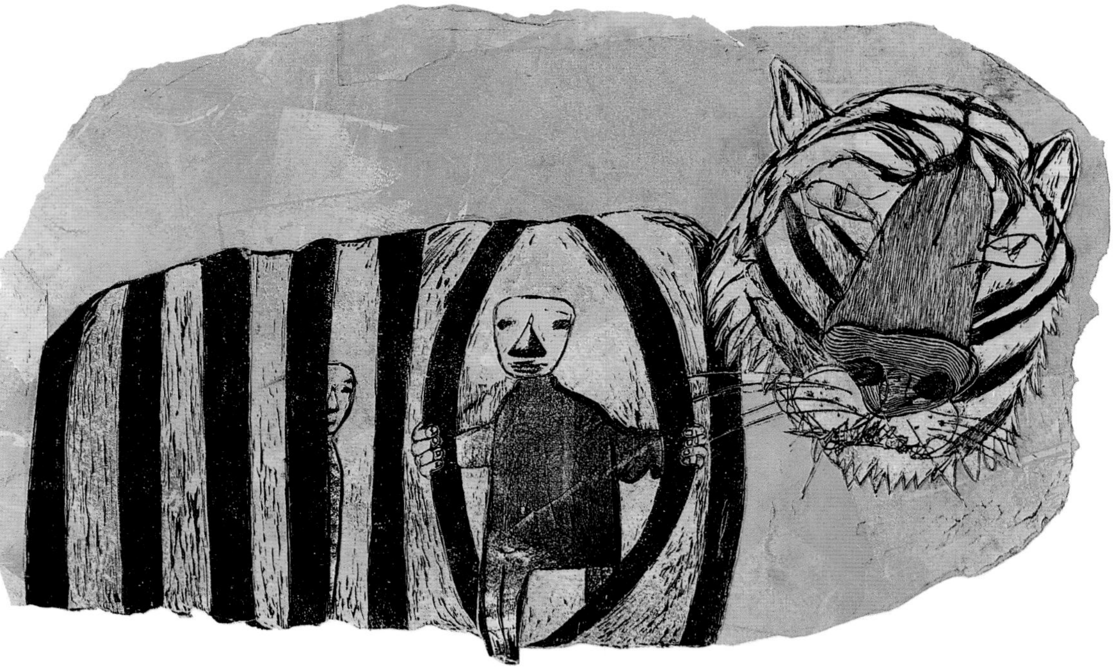

Art Director) Jane Palecek Editor) Eric Schrier Writer) David Sharp Publication) Health Date) April 1992
Publisher) Hippocrates Partners Medium) Acrylic The article "Send in the Crowds" was accompanied by this illustration.

Blair Drawson

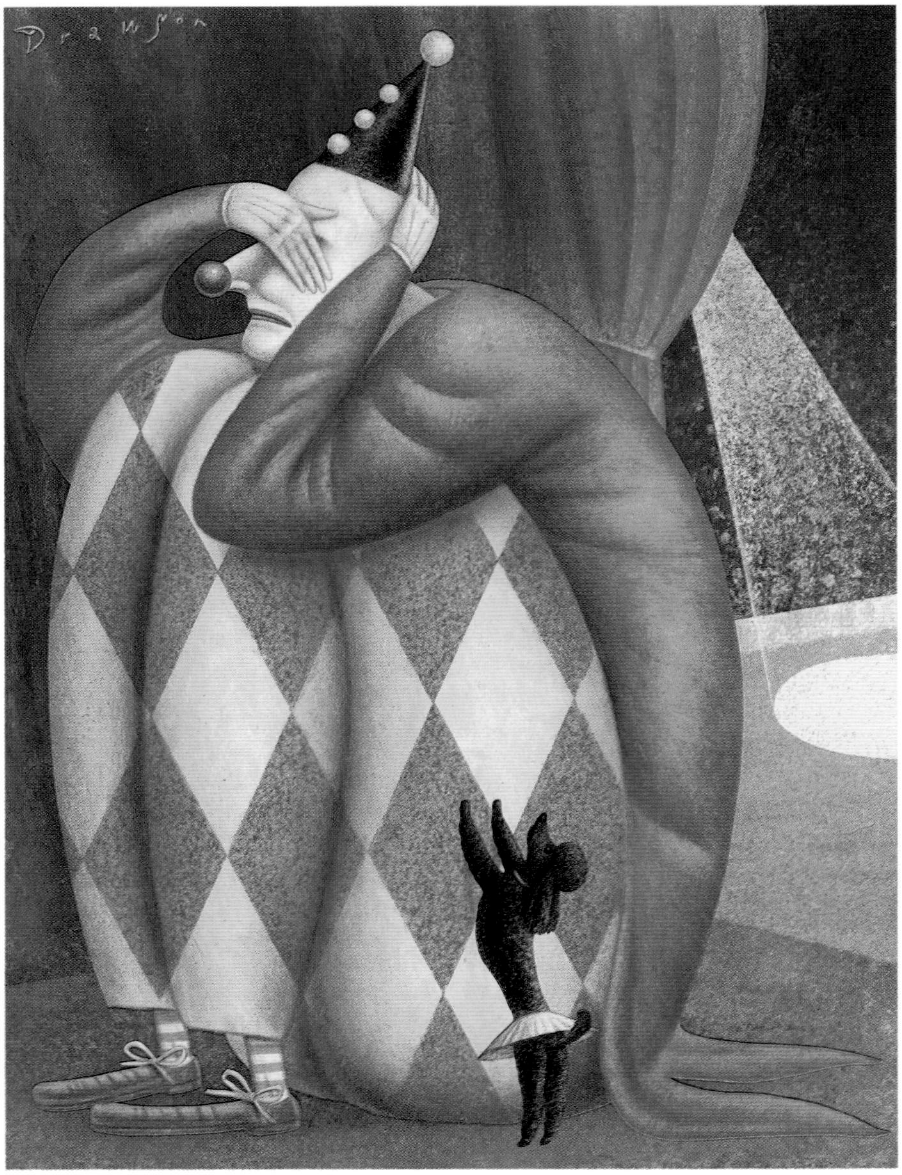

Art Director) Joan Ferrell Editor) Deborah Wilburn Writer) Paula M. Siegel Publication) Working Mother Magazine Date) January 1993
Publisher) Lang Communications Medium) Pastel The painful consequences of a child's shame are depicted in this image.

Wiktor Sadowski

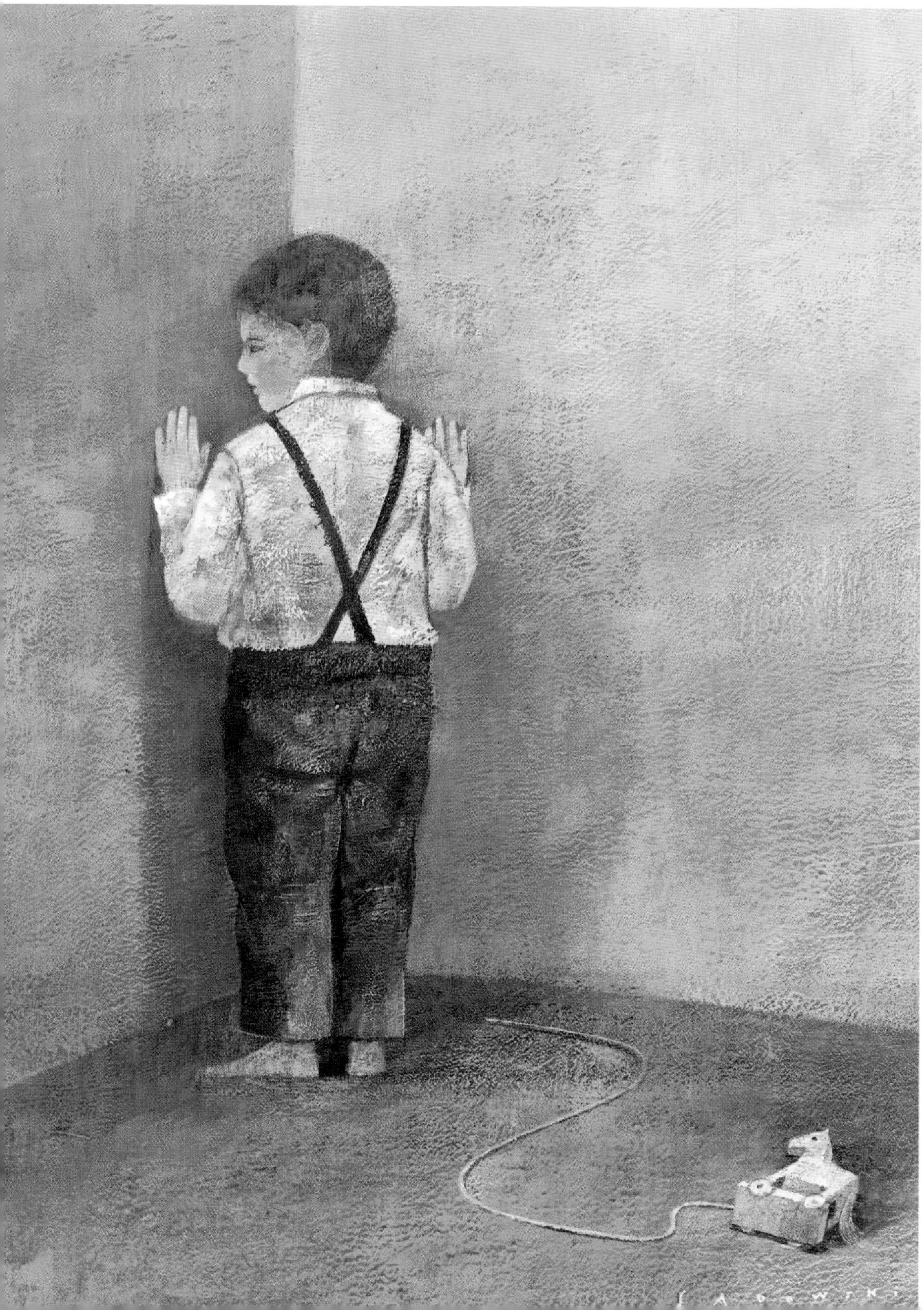

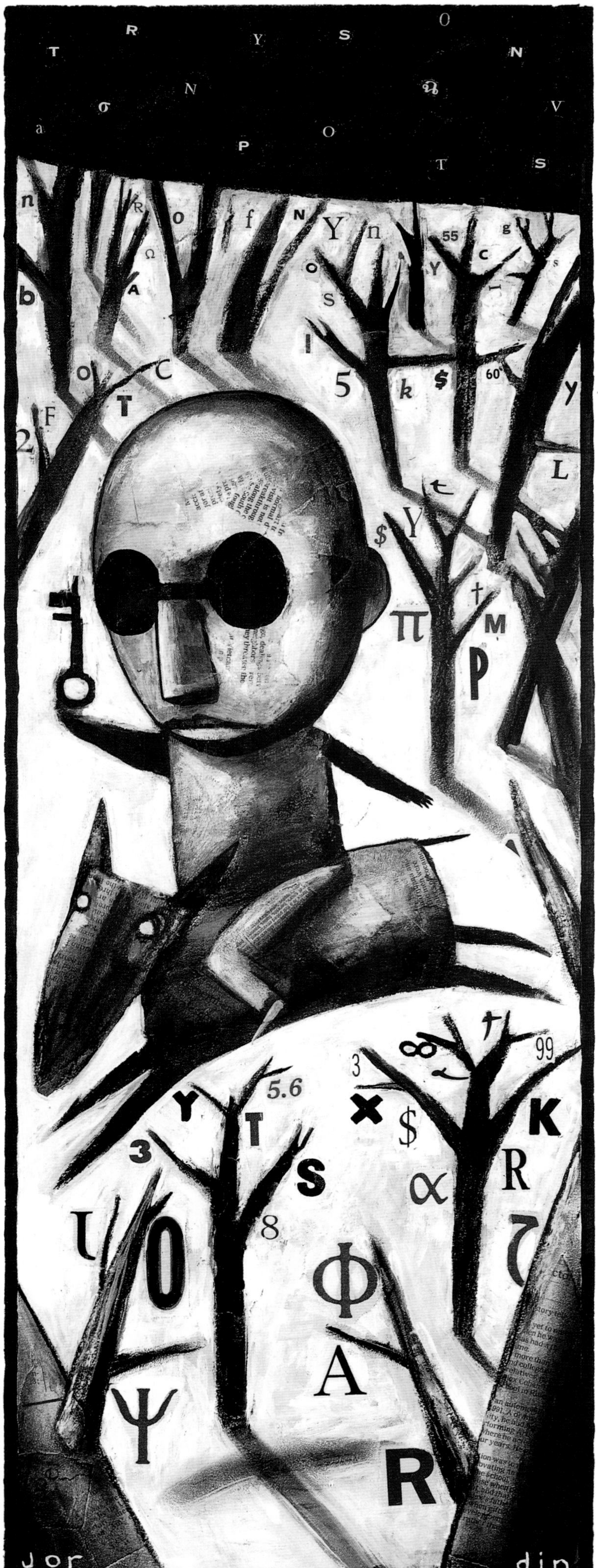
jor
din

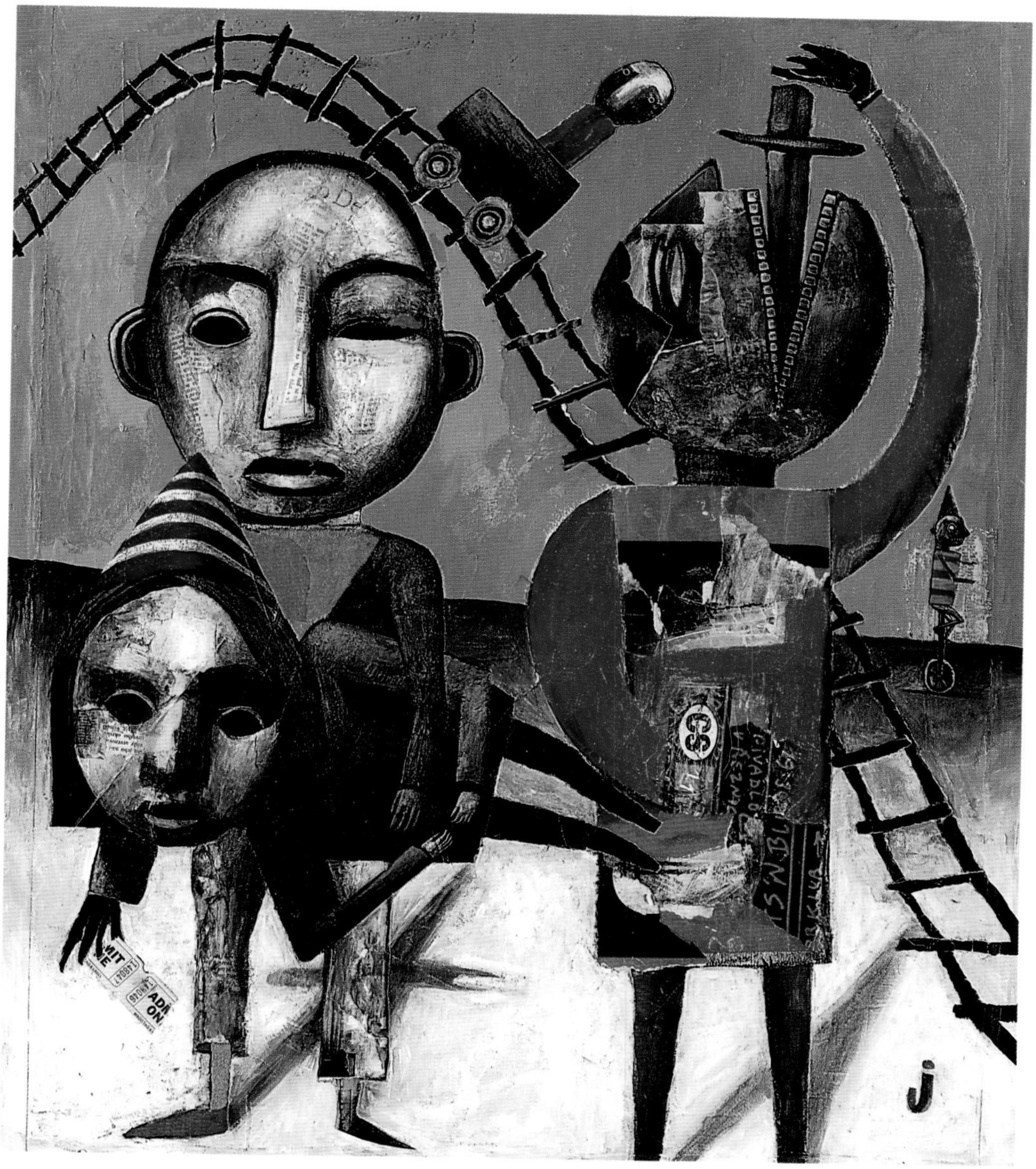

Jordin Isip

Art Director) David Carson Editor) Marvin Scott Jarrett Publication) Ray Gun Date) April 1993 Publisher) Ray Gun Publishing, Inc. Medium) Mixed media An interpretation of the song "Breadcrumb Trail" by the Slint band for the feature "Sound in Print" (above).

∞

Art Director) Kate Thompson Editor) M. Mark Writer) Erik Davis Publication) Voice Literary Supplement Date) March 1993 Publisher) VV Publishing Corporation Medium) Mixed media "A Computer, A Universe," an article which explored the possibilities of an online cosmological program, included this illustration (left).

Art Director) Laura N. Frank Editor) Earl W. Foell Writer) Zbigniew Brzezinski
Publication) World Monitor Magazine Date) March 1993 Publisher) The Christian Science Publishing Society
Medium) Mixed-media This illustration accompanied the article entitled "Power and Morality."

Jordin Isip

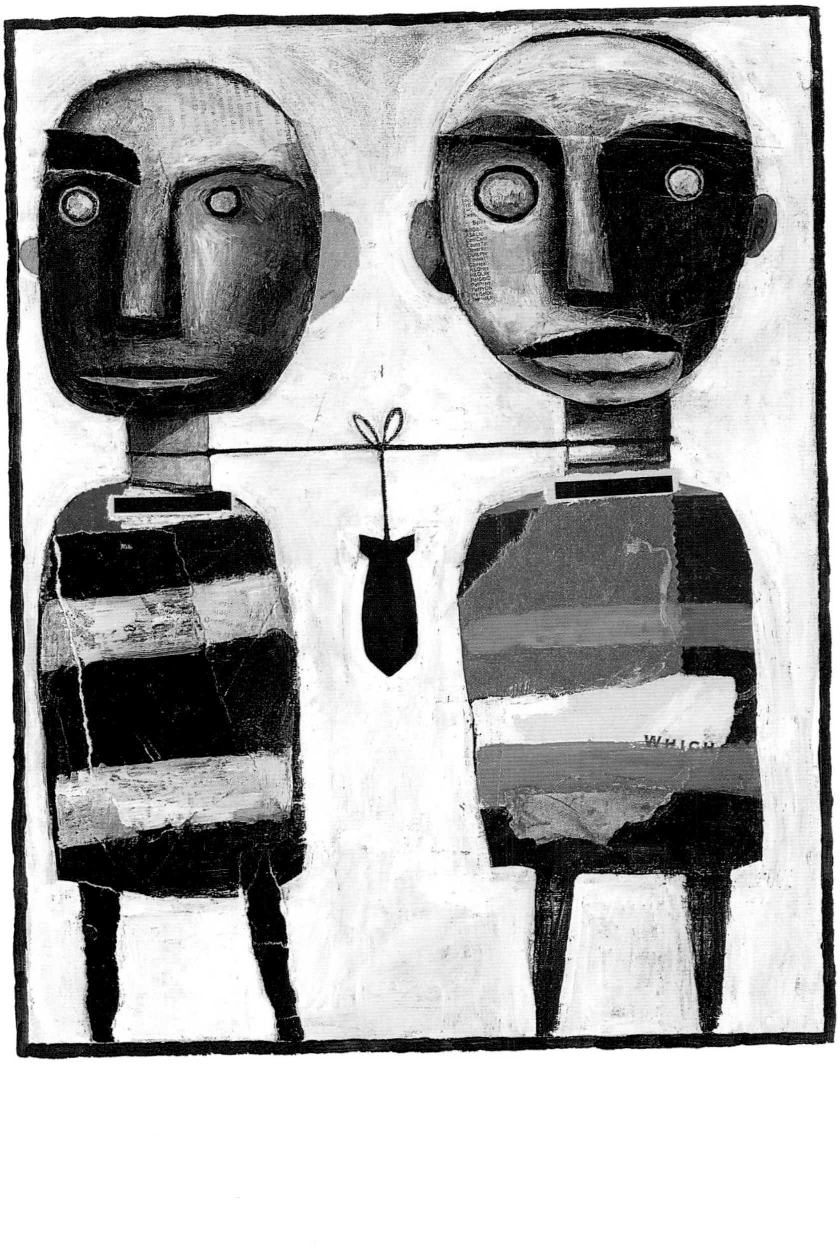

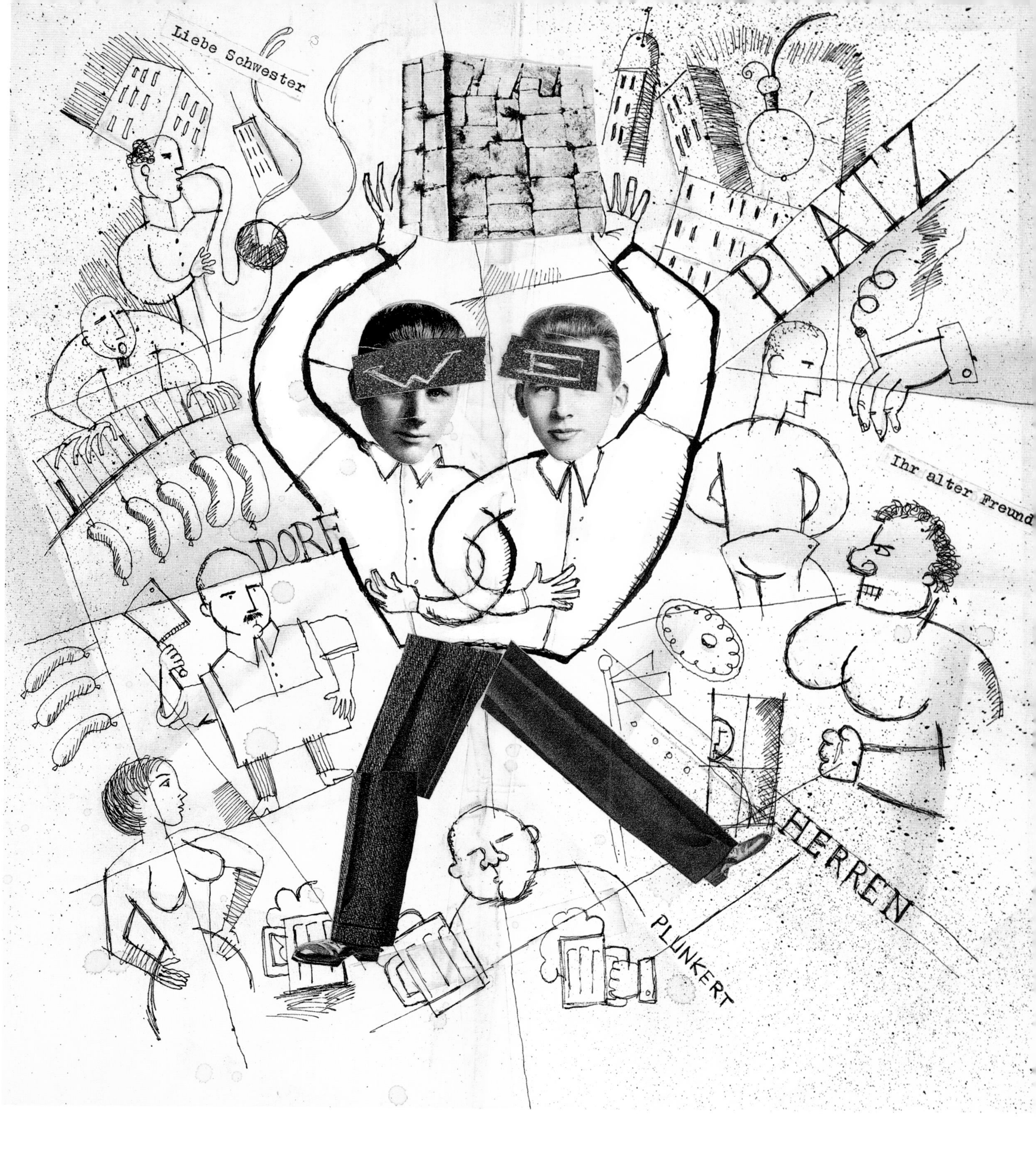

David Plunkert

Art Director) Mark Evans Editor) **Jim Duffy** Writer) **Kevin** Whitehead Publication) City Paper
Date) February 12, 1993 Publisher) Scr**anton Times** Medium) Collage, pen and ink, graphite and coffee
"Joined at the Hip, Berlin Does Believe in **Tears," an article about** German reunification, featured this image.

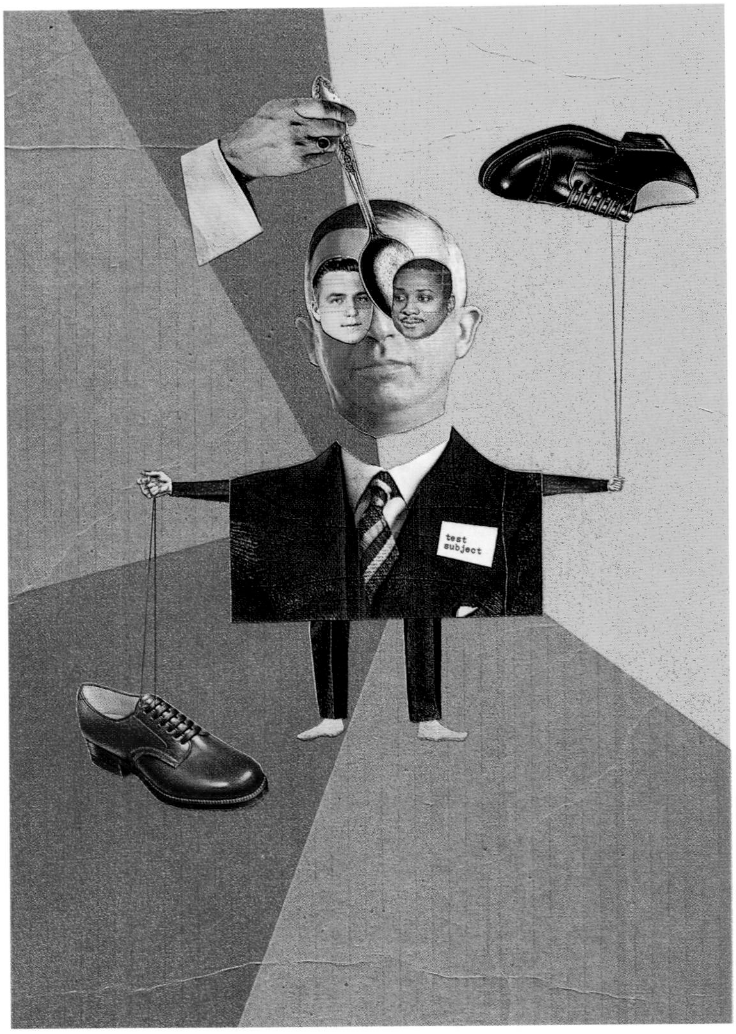

David Plunkert

Art Director) Leigh Caruso Writer) Patricia A. Galagan Publication) Training and Development Magazine
Date) March 1993 Publisher) American Society for Training and Development Medium) Collage
Race role reversal at a chemical plant was the subject of the article "Trading Places at Monsanto."

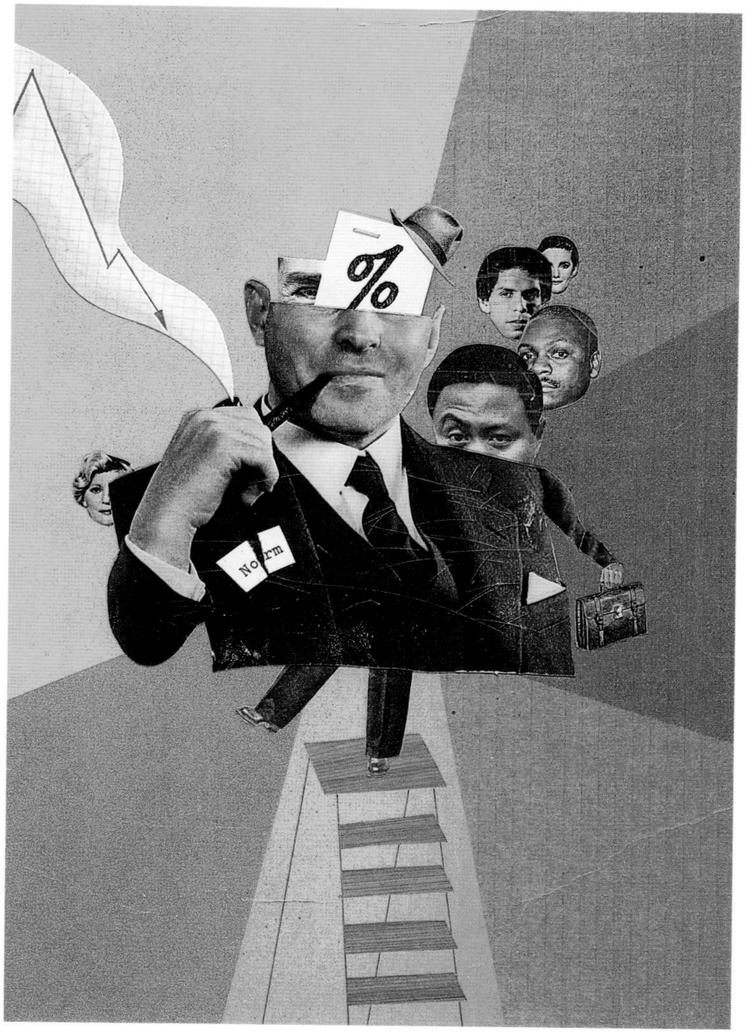

David Plunkert

Art Director) Leigh Caruso Writer) Patricia A. Galagan Publication) Training and Development Magazine
Date) March 1993 Publisher) American Society for Training and Development Medium) Collage
One of three illustrations for the feature "Navigating the Differences/Special Report on Diversity."

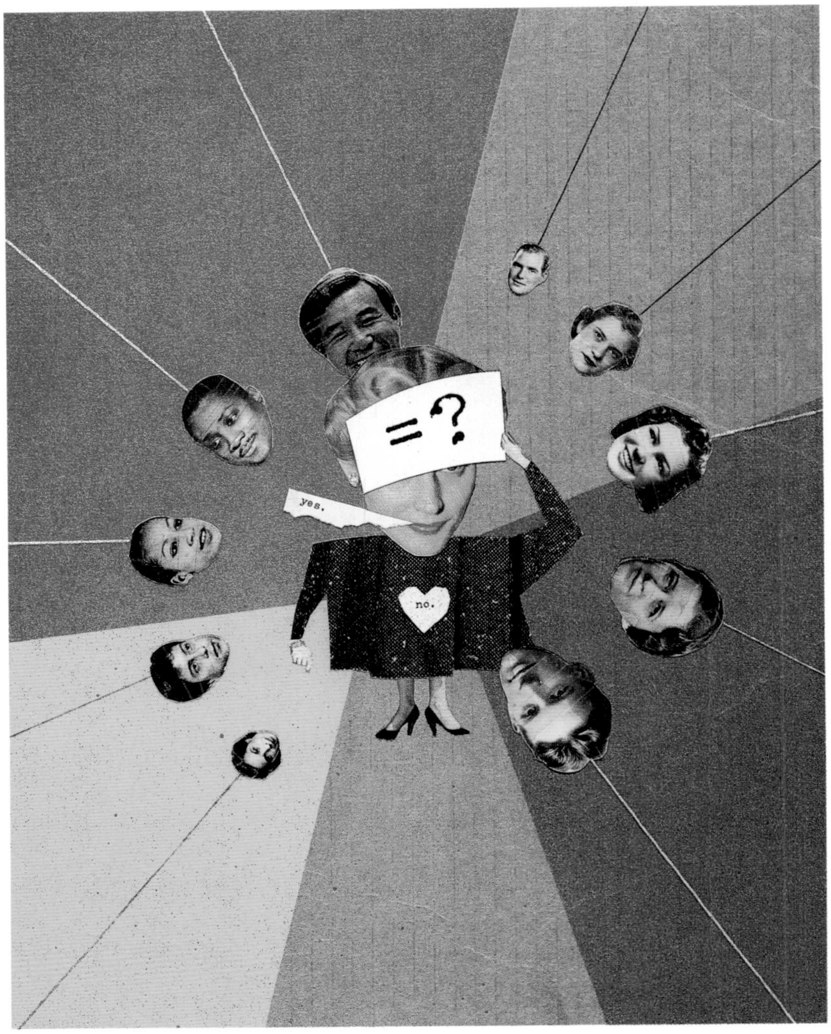

David Plunkert

Art Director) Leigh Caruso Writer) John Dovidio Publication) Training and Development Magazine Date) March 1993 Publisher) American Society for Training and Development Medium) Collage The article "Denying Racism" inspired this collage.

Art Director) Jane Palecek Editor) Eric Schrier Writer) Edward Dolnick Publication) Health
Date) July/August 1992 Publisher) Hippocrates Partners Medium) Mixed media
The characteristics of pathological liars inspired this illustration for the article "The Great Pretender."

Josh Gosfield and Nola Lopez

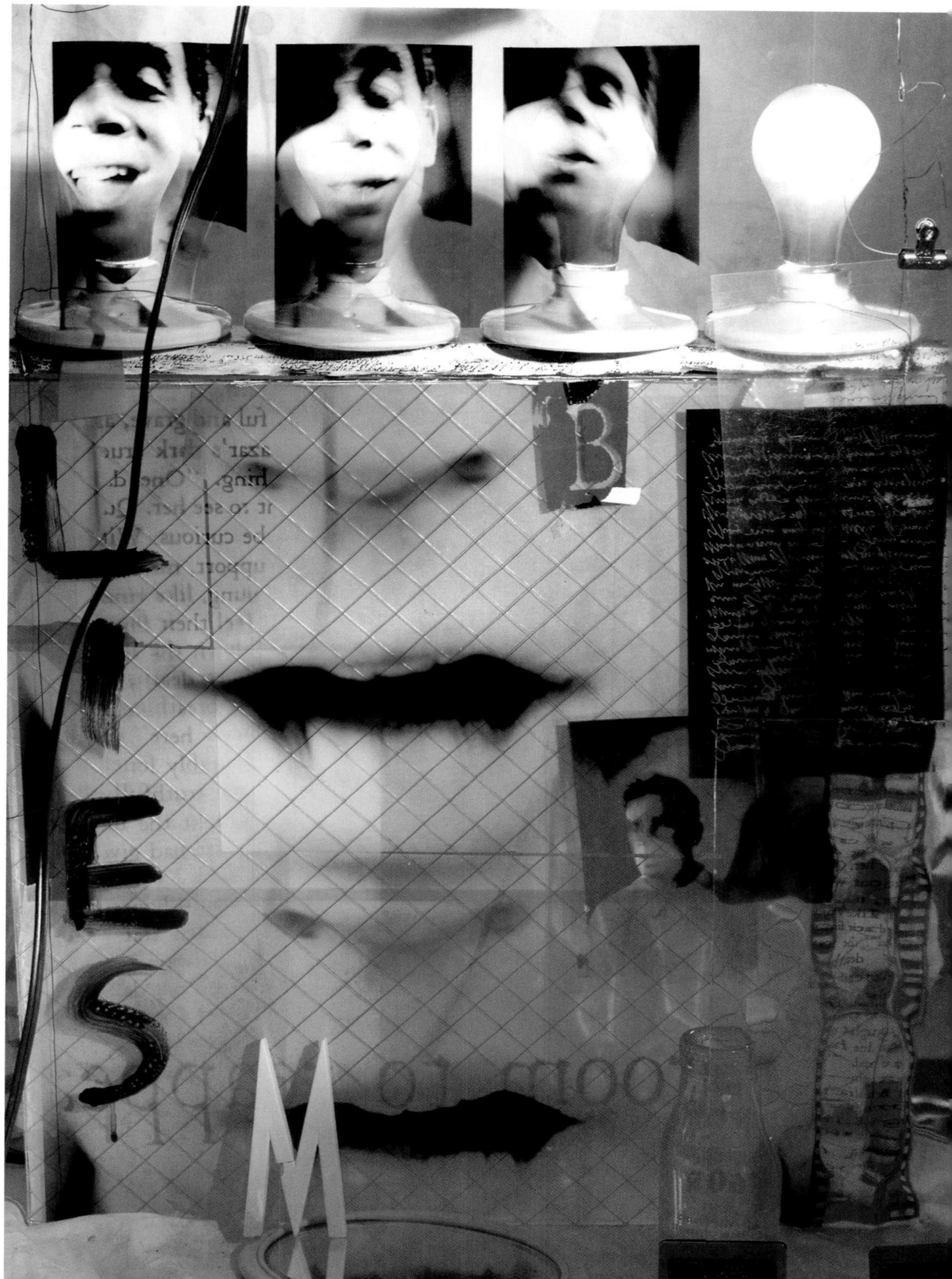

Art Director) Laura N. Frank Editor) Earl W. Foell Writer) Stephen H. Schneider Publication) World Monitor Magazine Date) April 1993 Publisher) Christian Science Publishing Society Medium) Mixed media Teaching children creative thinking was the subject of the article "A Better Way to Learn" featuring these two illustrations.

Christian Northeast

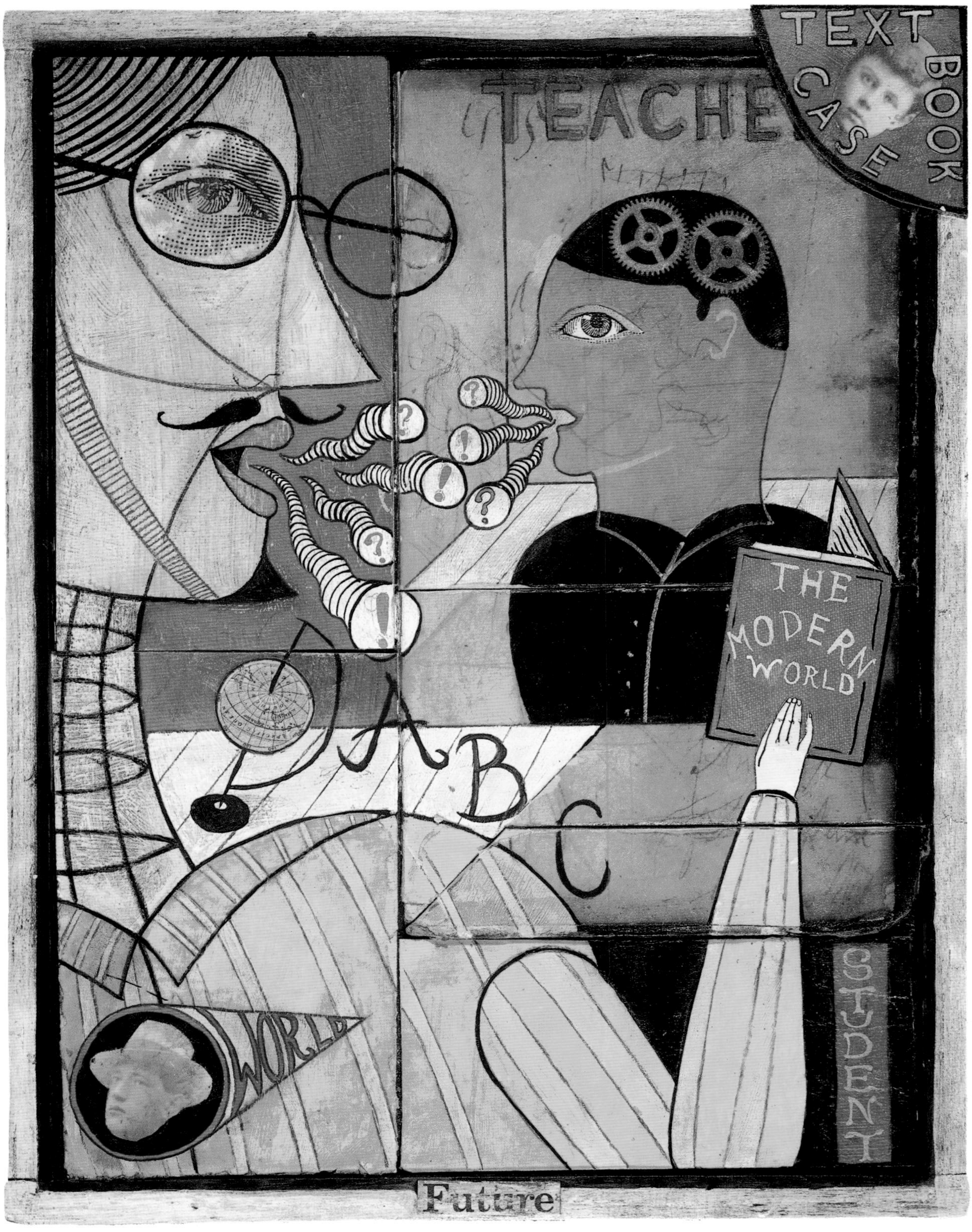

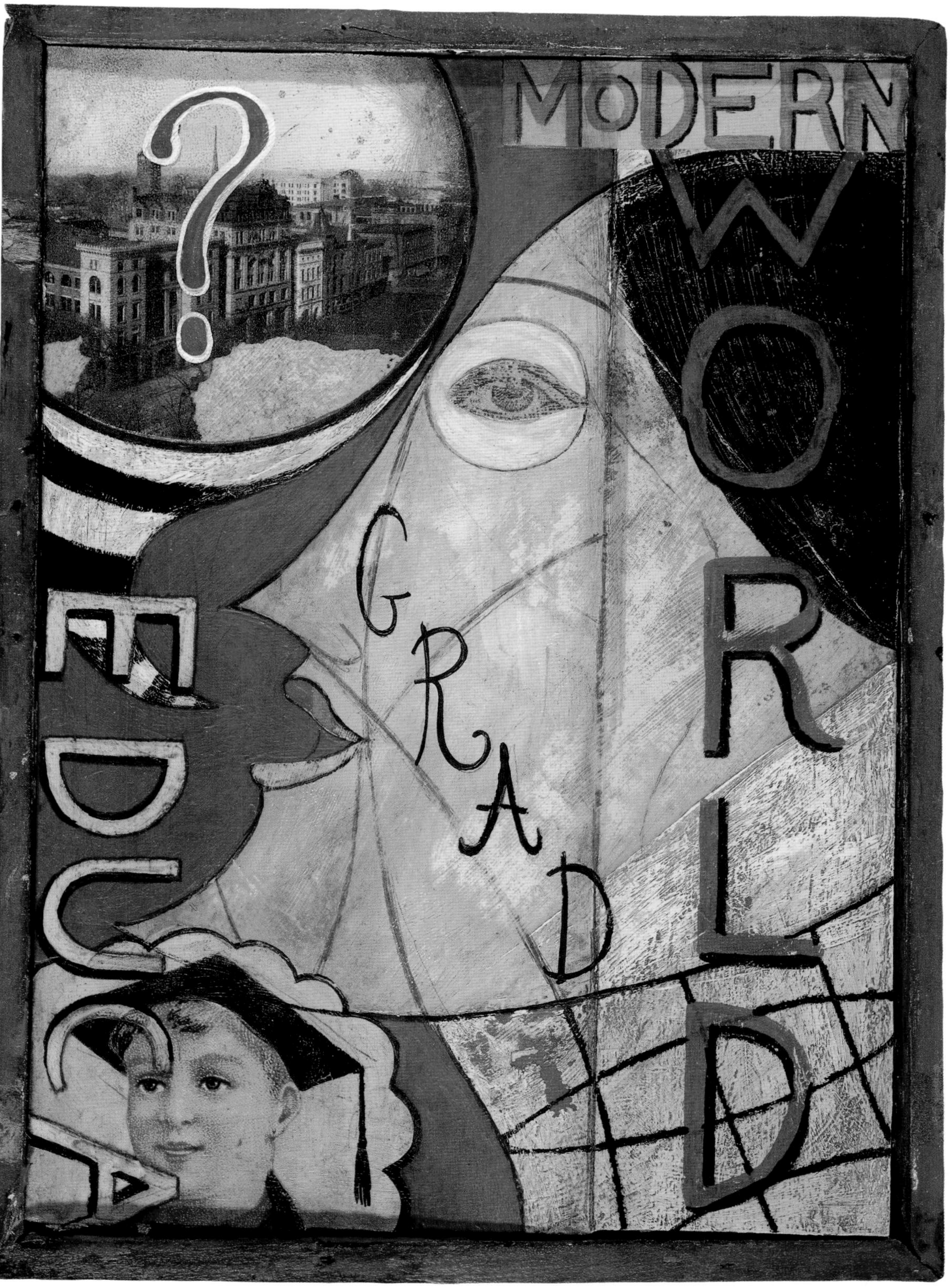
MODERN
WORLD
GRAD
EDUCA

Art Director) Pamela Berry Writer) Jeffrey Ressner Publication) US Magazine Date) March 1993 Publisher) Straight Arrow Publishers, Inc. Medium) Mixed media Hollywood's use of audience polling to predict the success of films was the subject of this illustration.

Christian Northeast

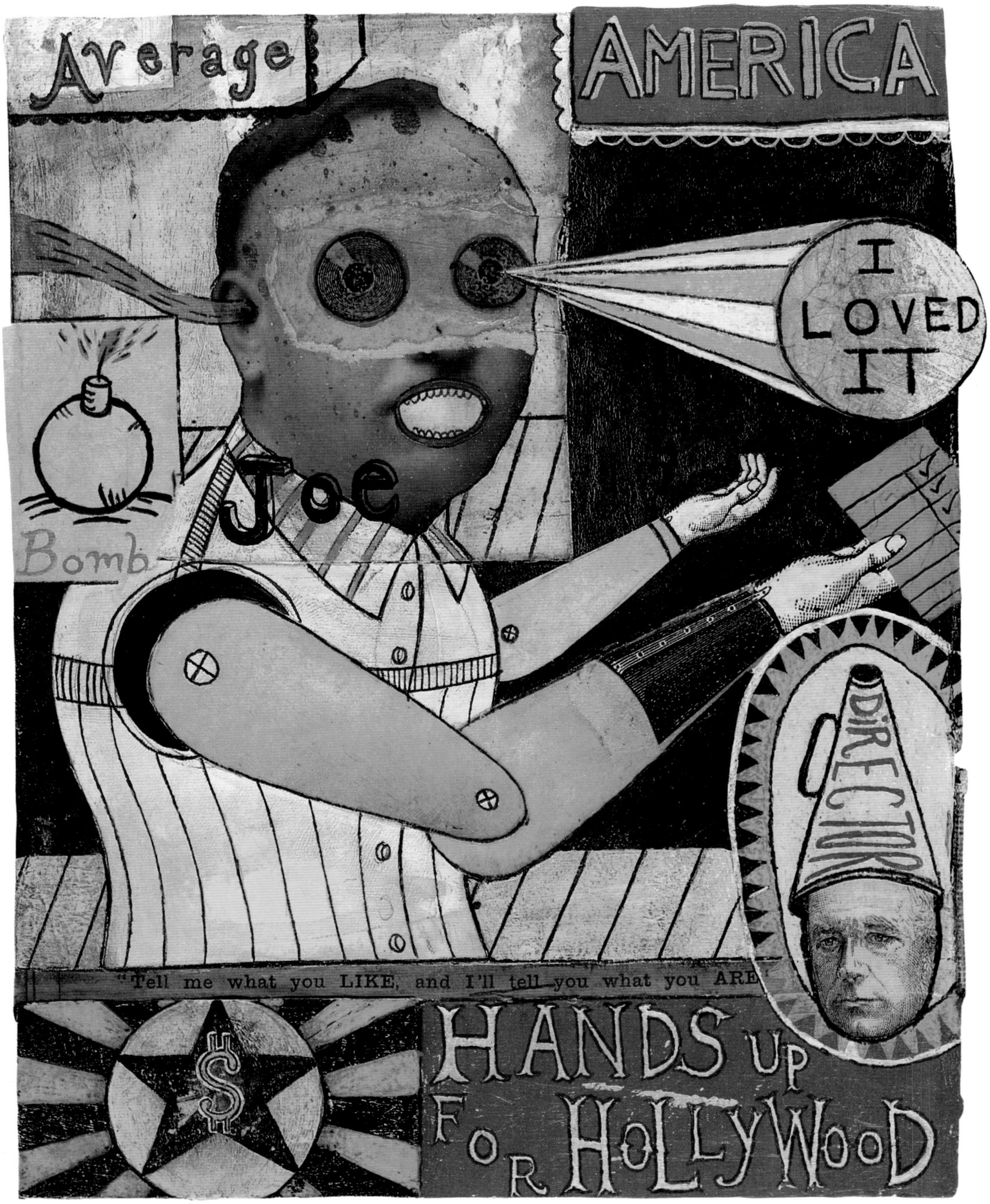

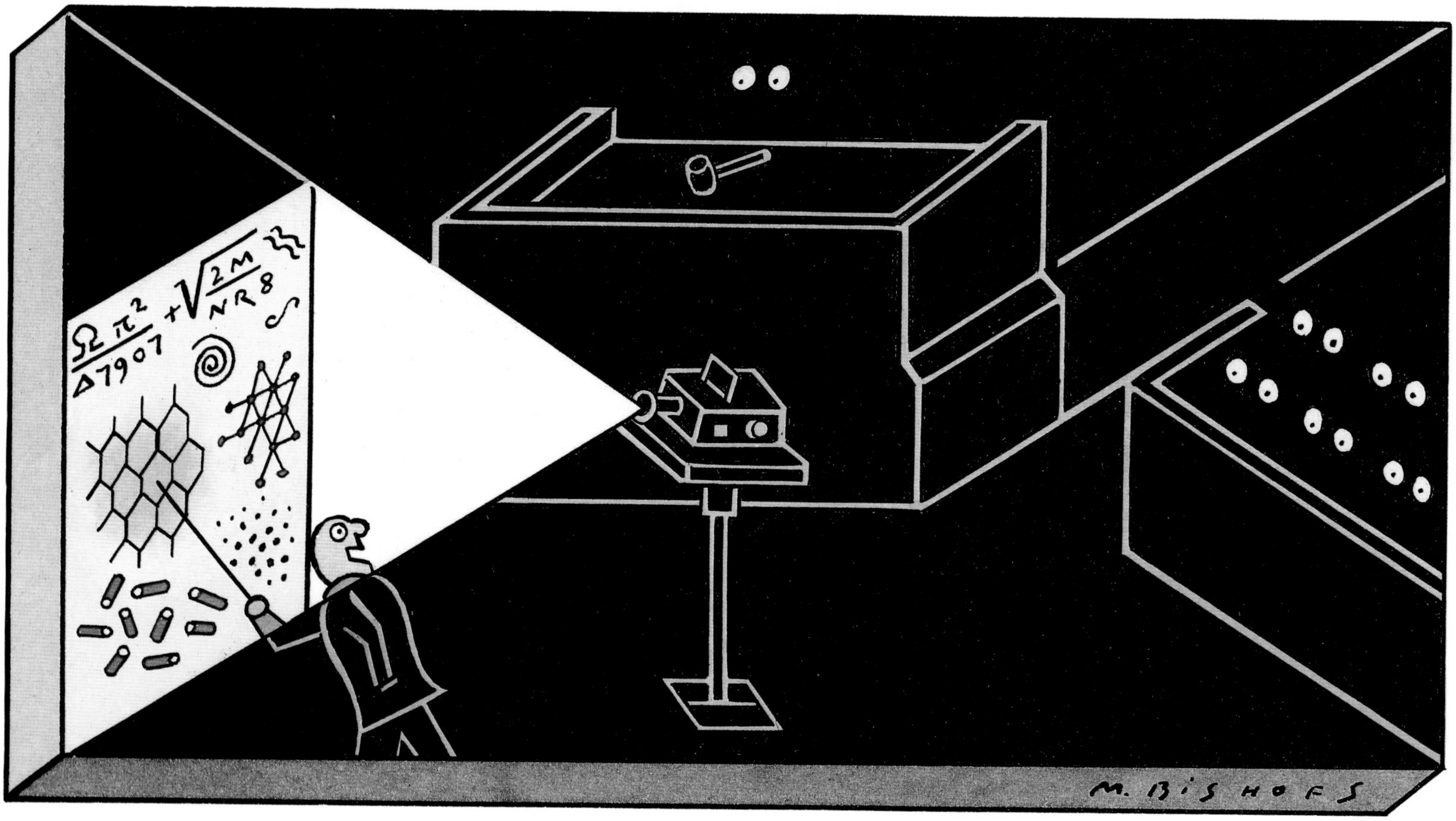

57

Maris Bishofs

Art Director) Michele Chu Editor) David Gergen Writer) Steve Anderson Publication) U.S. News & World Report Date) October 26, 1992 Publisher) World Color Press Medium) Ink and watercolor The problems that judges and juries face struggling with complex scientific testimony gave rise to this illustration.

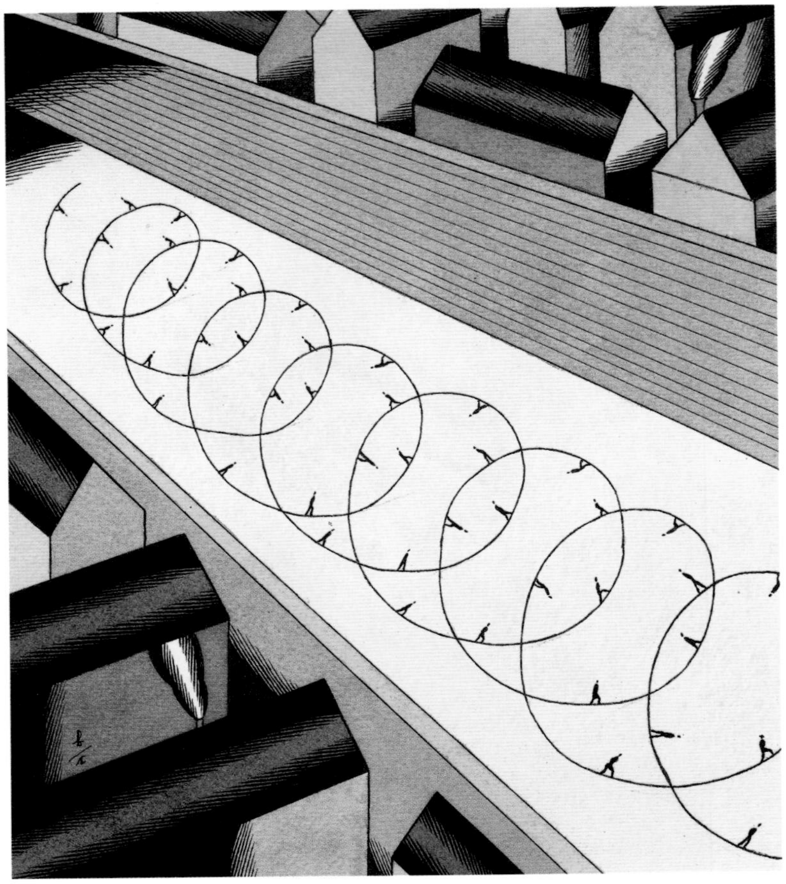

Brian Cronin

Art Director) Martin Colyer Editor) **Steve Weinman** **Writers)** Eric Waugh, Keith Graves, Jon Devitt, Charles Scanlon and Fergal Keane **Publication)** BBC Worldwide Date) January 1993 Medium) Pen and ink, watercolor The BBC **Worldwide Report article** "Borders" gave rise to this illustration.

Art Director) Joseph Dizney Editor) Stuart Emmrich Writer) James Lyons Publication) Smart Money Date) April 1993
Publisher) Hearst & Dow Jones Medium) Watercolor The article "Is Your Bank Ripping You Off?" featured this illustration.

Jeffrey Fisher

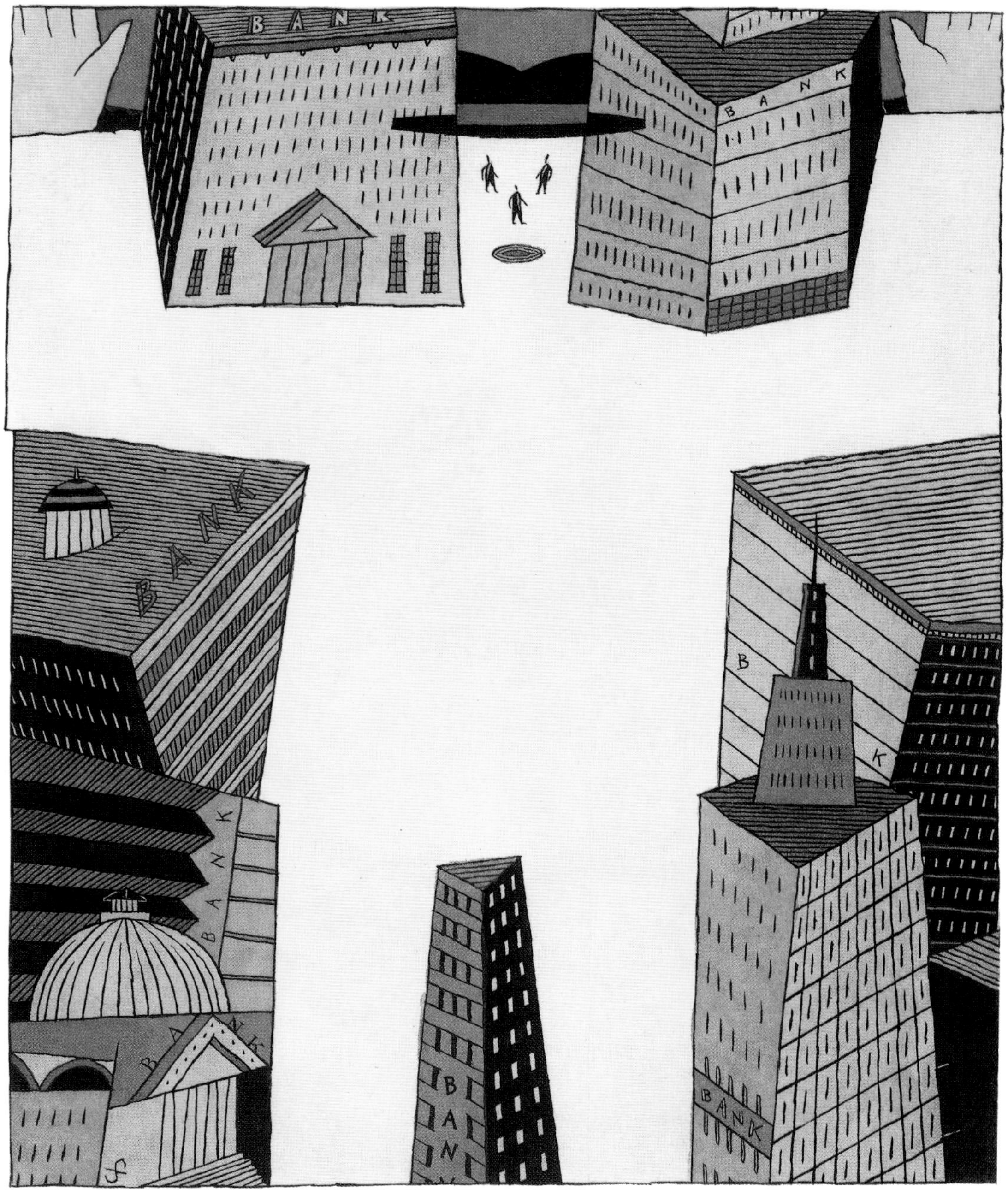

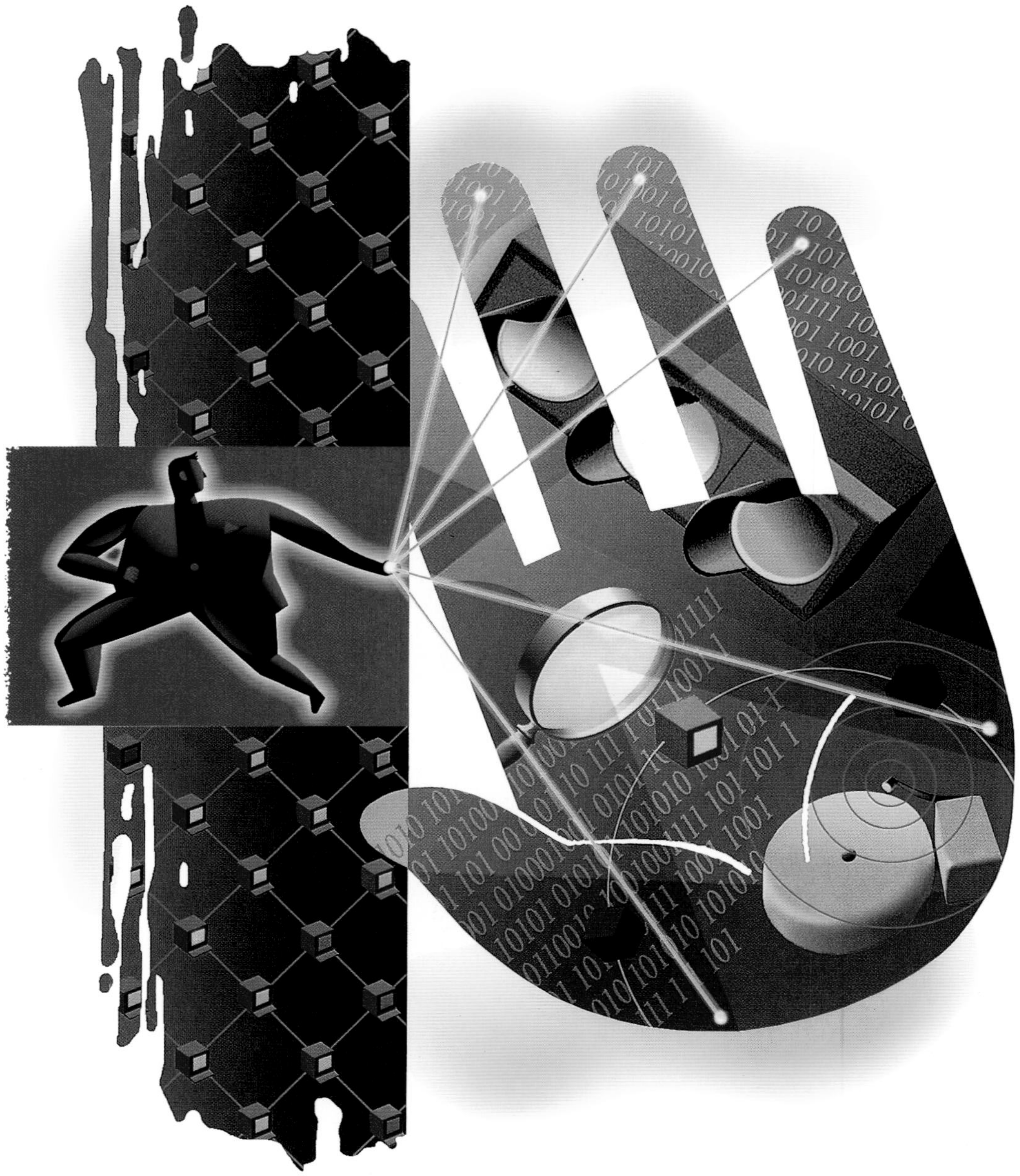

Mick Wiggins

Art Director) Joanne Hoffman Writer) Shelly Brisbin Publication) Macworld Date) February 1993
Publisher) Macworld Communications, Inc. Medium) Computer This illustration accompanied the article "Network Utilities," a guide to the best tools for diagnosing and solving computer network problems.

Art Director) David Armario Writer) Spyros Andreopoulos Publication) Stanford Medicine
Date) Fall 1992 Publisher) Stanford University Medical Center Office of Communications Medium) Gouache
Peptic ulcers were discussed in the article "The Internal Flame," featuring this image.

Terry Allen

61

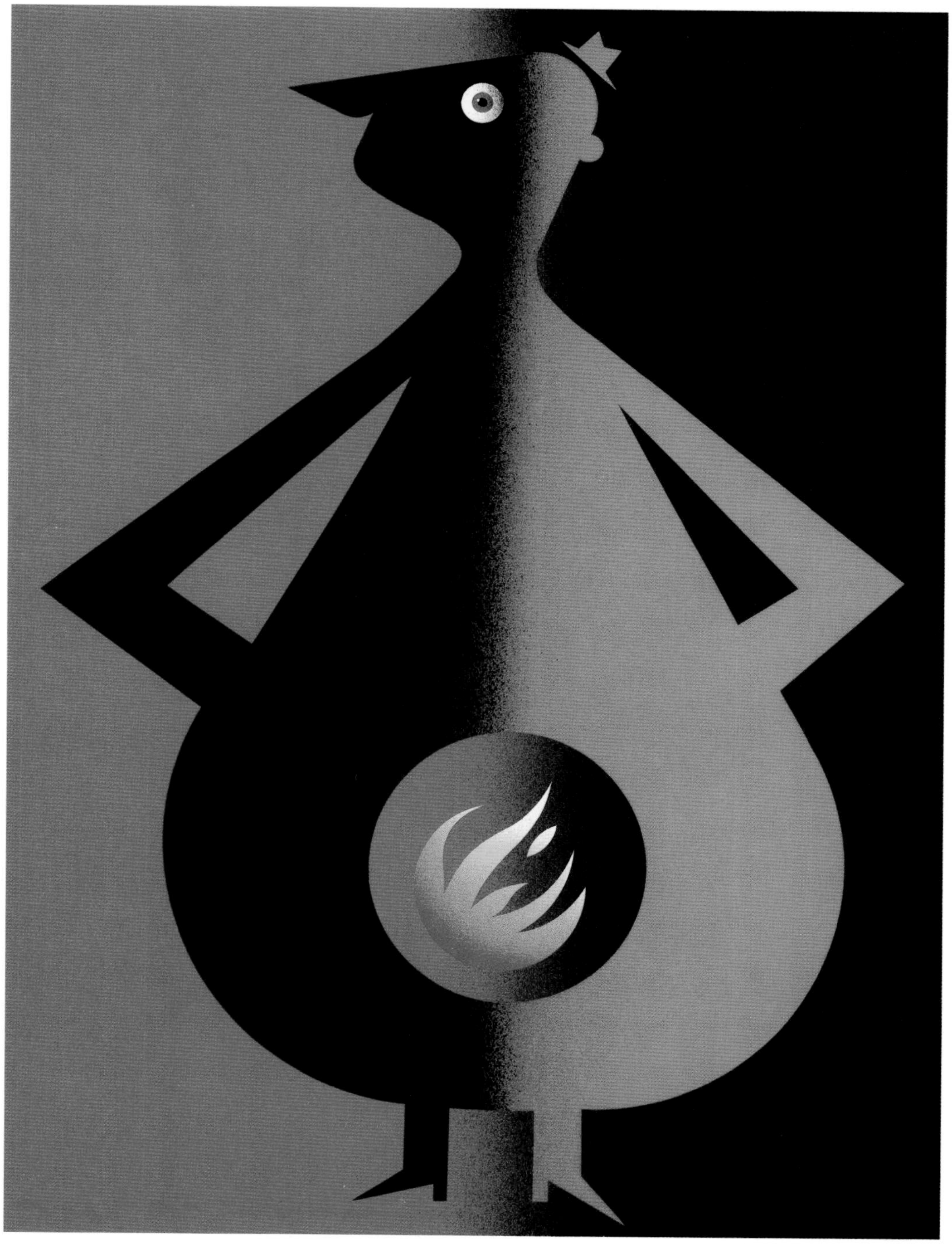

Hanoch Piven

Art Director) Chris Curry Editor) Tina Brown Publication) The New Yorker Date) March 29, 1993 Publisher) Condé Nast Publications, Inc. Medium) Gouache and sandpaper This caricature of pop singer Prince was included in the feature "Goings on About Town" (below).

∞

Art Directors) Fred Woodward and Gail Anderson Writer) Peter Travers Publication) Rolling Stone Date) February 4, 1993 Publisher) Straight Arrow Publishers, Inc. Medium) Collage "Madonna's Come-On," a review of her movie "Body of Evidence," included this caricature (right).

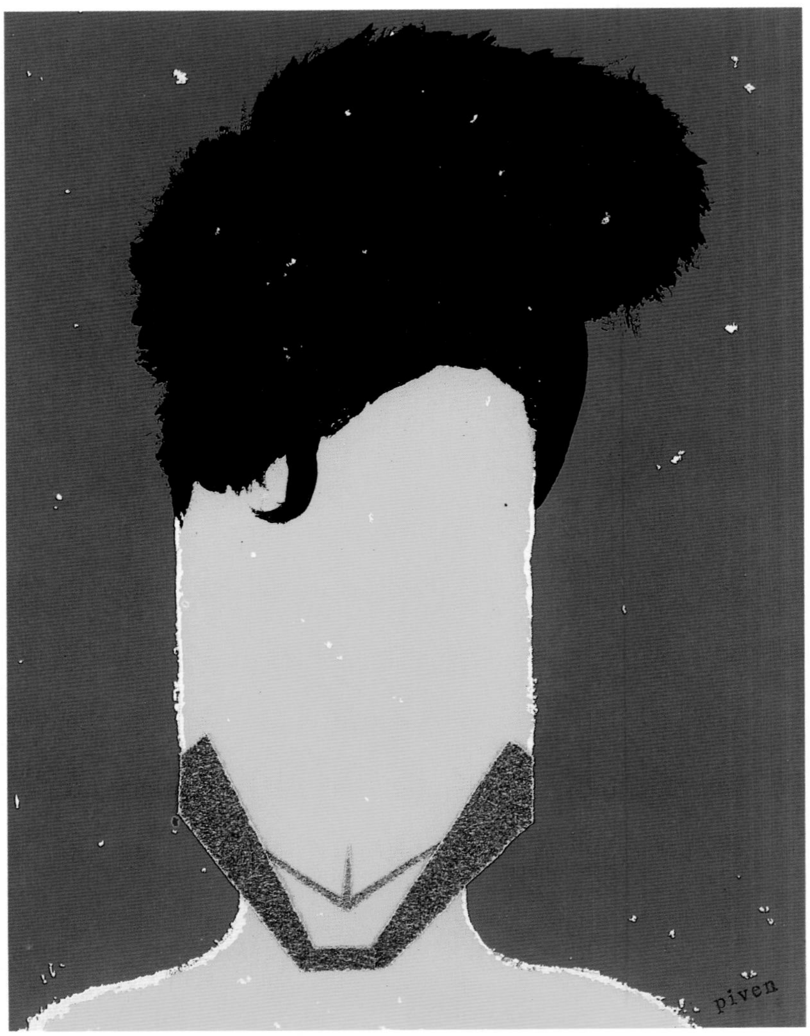

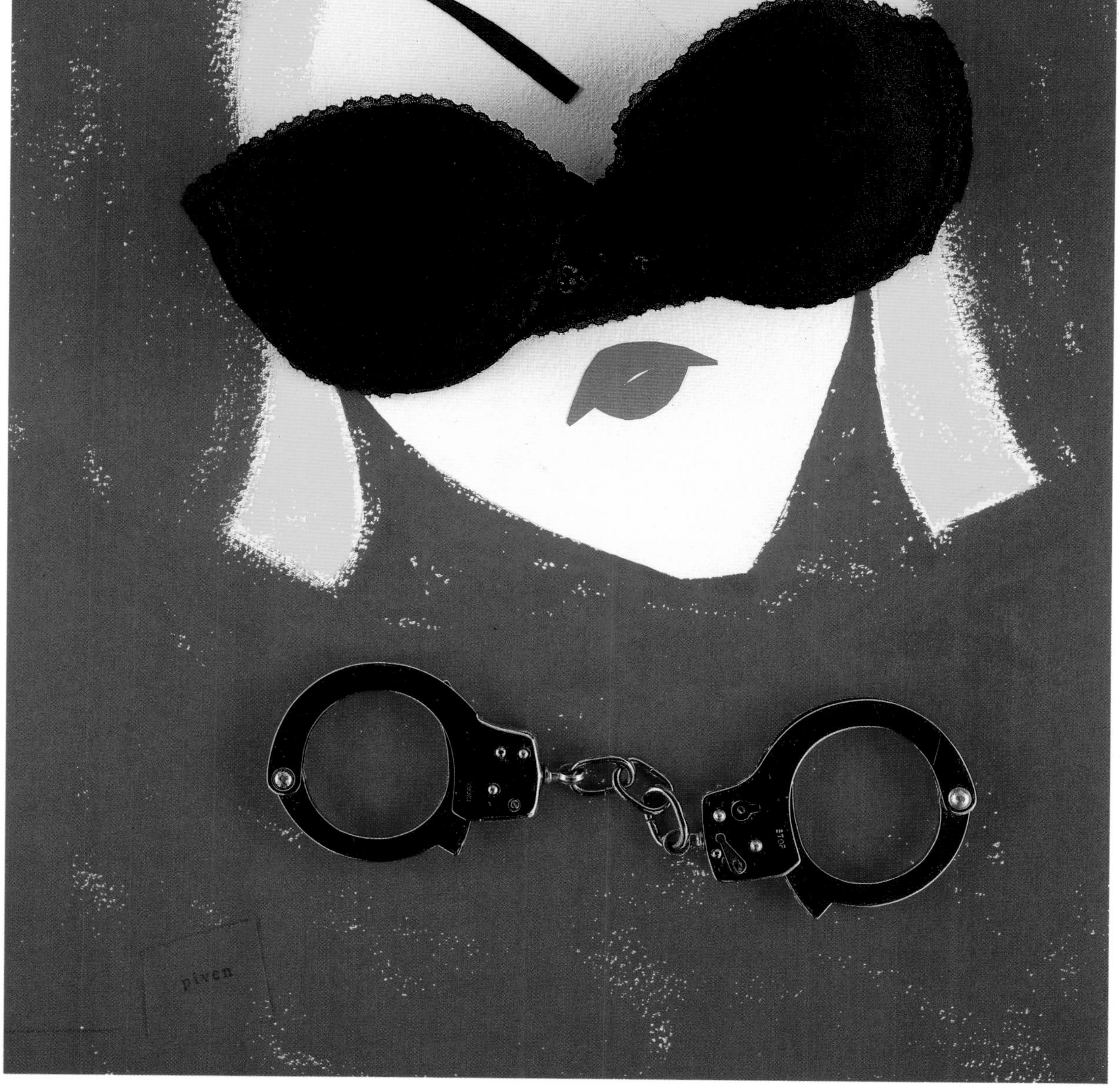
piven

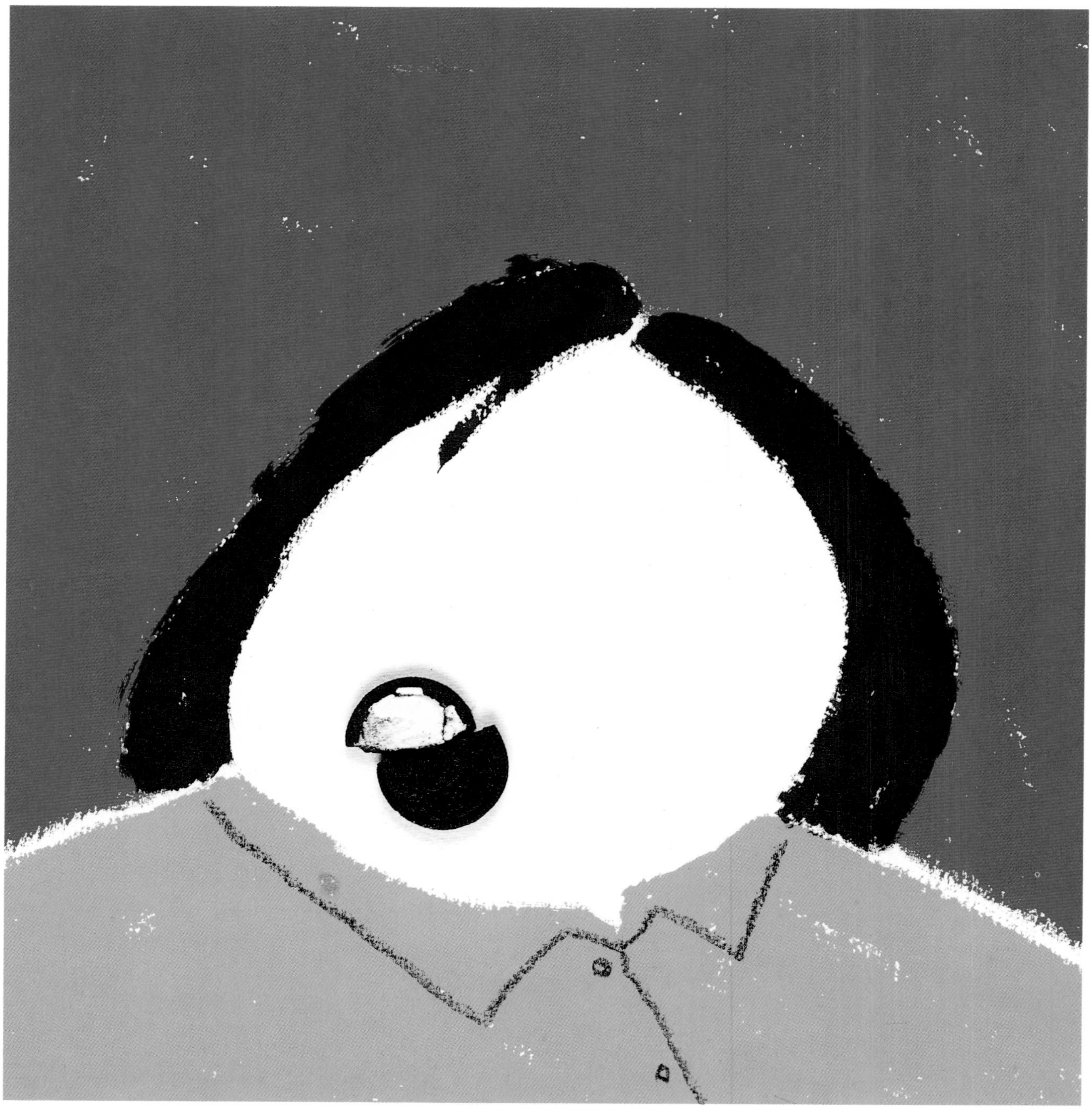

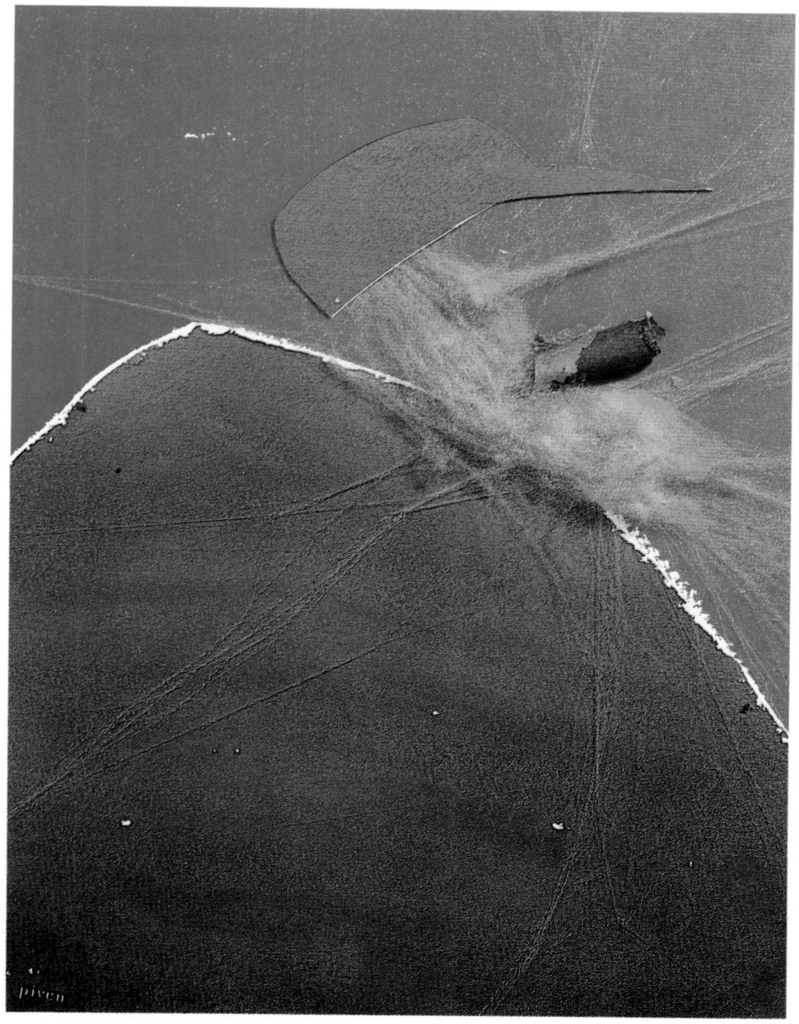

Hanoch Piven

Medium) Collage This caricature of Fidel Castro previously unpublished (above).

∞

Design Director) Michael Grossman Art Director) Elizabeth Betts Writer) Ken Tucker Publication) Entertainment Weekly
Date) January 7, 1993 Publisher) The Time Inc. Magazine Company Medium) Gouache and Oreos
This caricature of Roseanne Arnold is from the "1992 Best and Worst" feature in Entertainment Weekly (left).

Art Director) Fred Woodward Writer) Grant Alden Publication) Rolling Stone
Date) January 21, 1993 Publisher) Straight Arrow Publishers, Inc. Medium) Collage, pencil, acrylic and photo transfer
This illustration accompanied a review of rock music entitled "The Remains of Grunge."

Brian Krueger

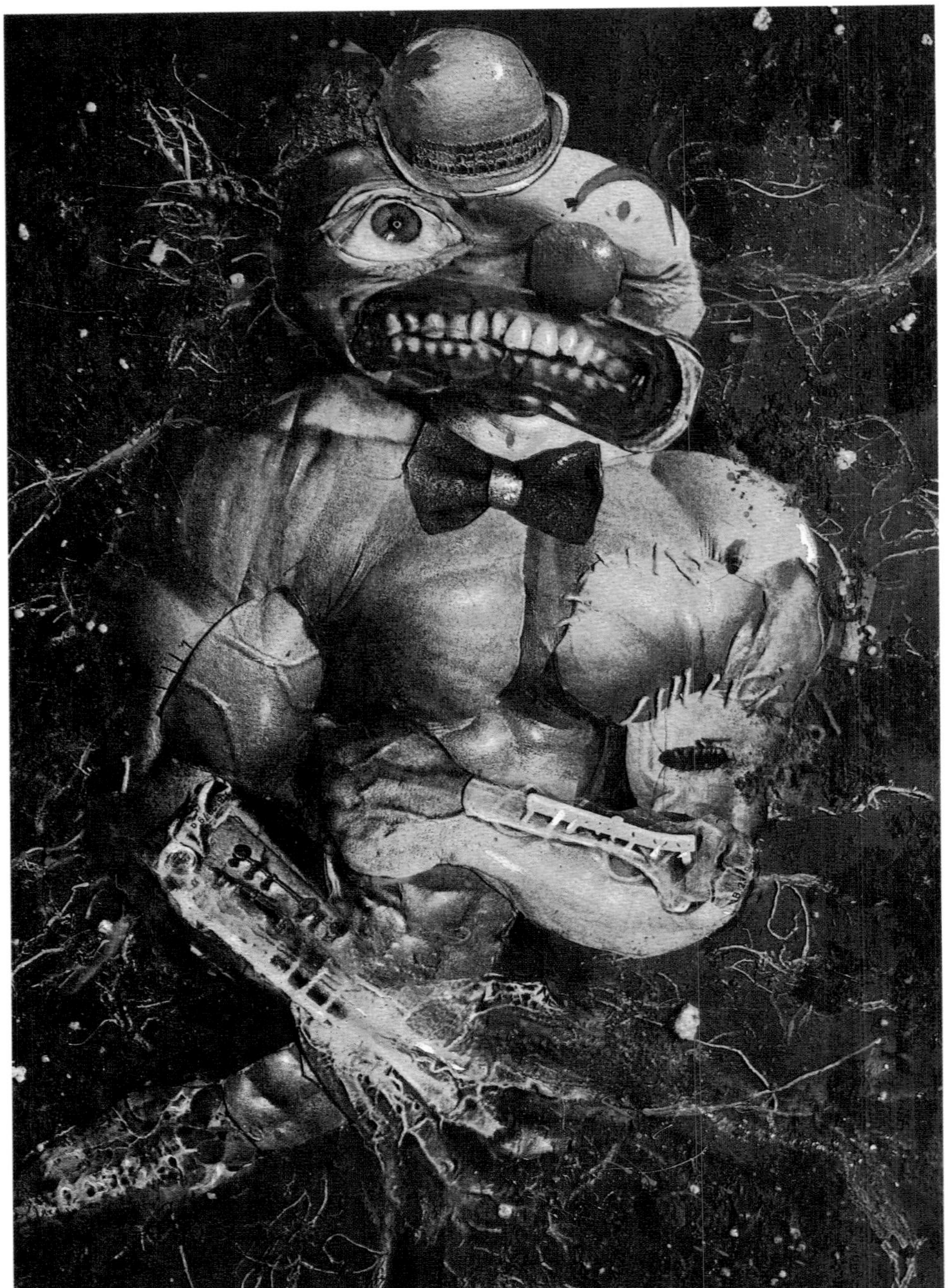

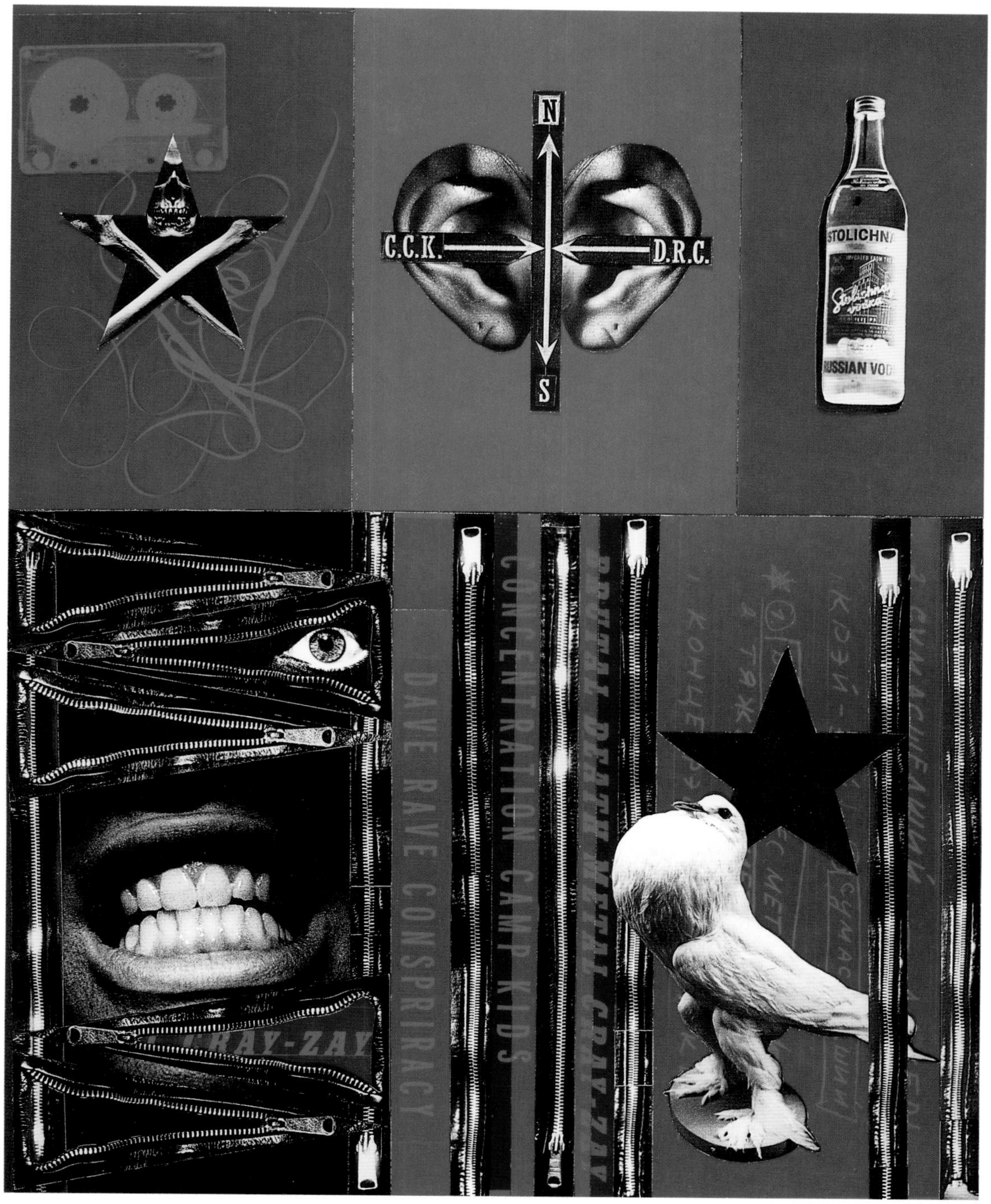

Amy Guip

Art Director) David **Carson** **Editor)** Marvin **Scott Jarrett** **Writer) Lauren Agnelli** **Publication) Ray Gun** Date) March 1993
Publisher) Ray Gun Pub**lishing, Inc.** **Medium) Collage** **This illustration was created for the article "Recordi**ng in Soviet Dis-Union."

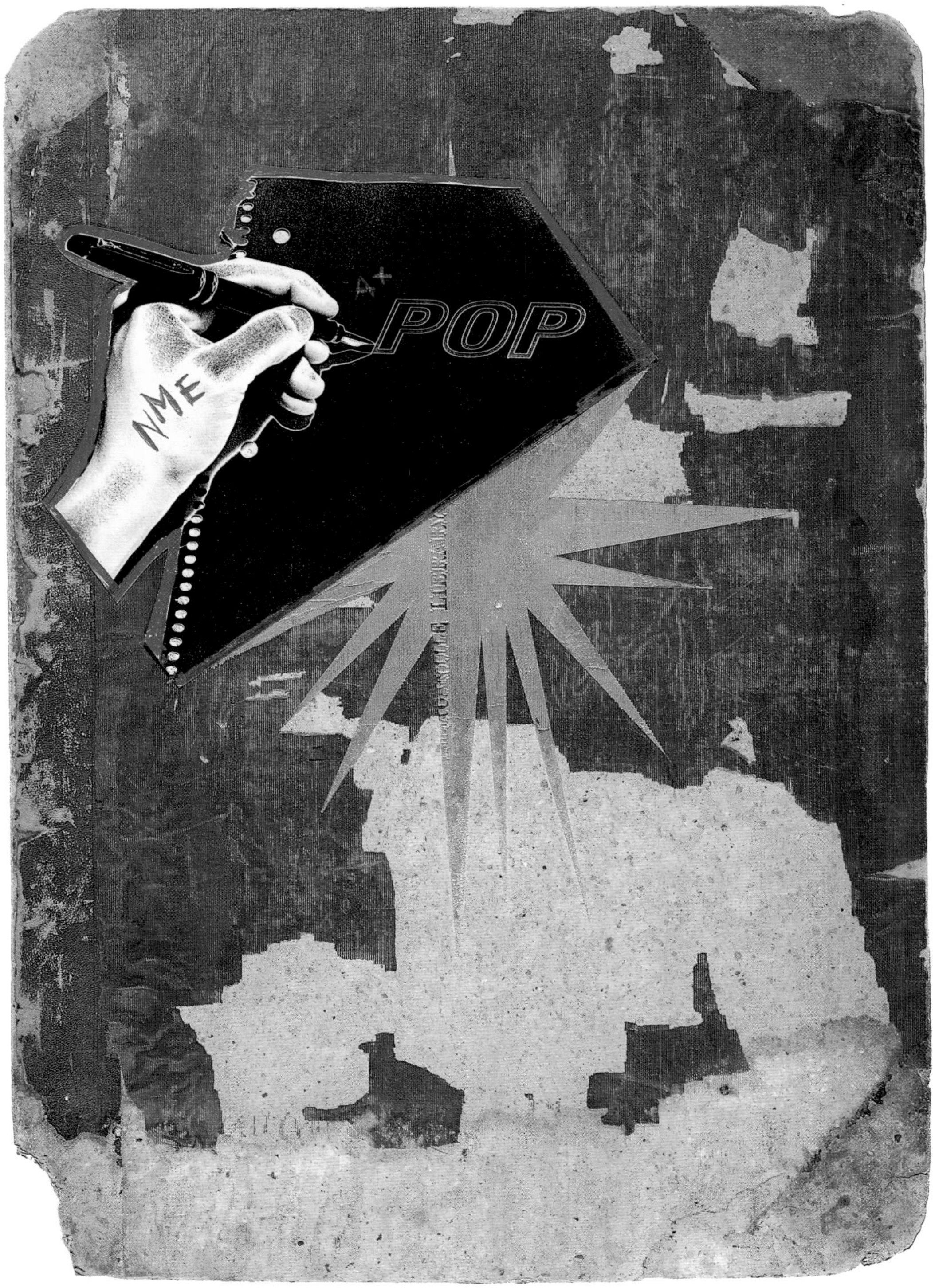

Amy Guip

Art Director) David Carson Editor) Marvin Scott Jarrett Writer) Dave Allen Publication) Ray Gun Date) April 1993
Publisher) Ray Gun Publishing, Inc. Medium) Mixed media The Ray Gun feature "Pop Smear" included these two illustrations.

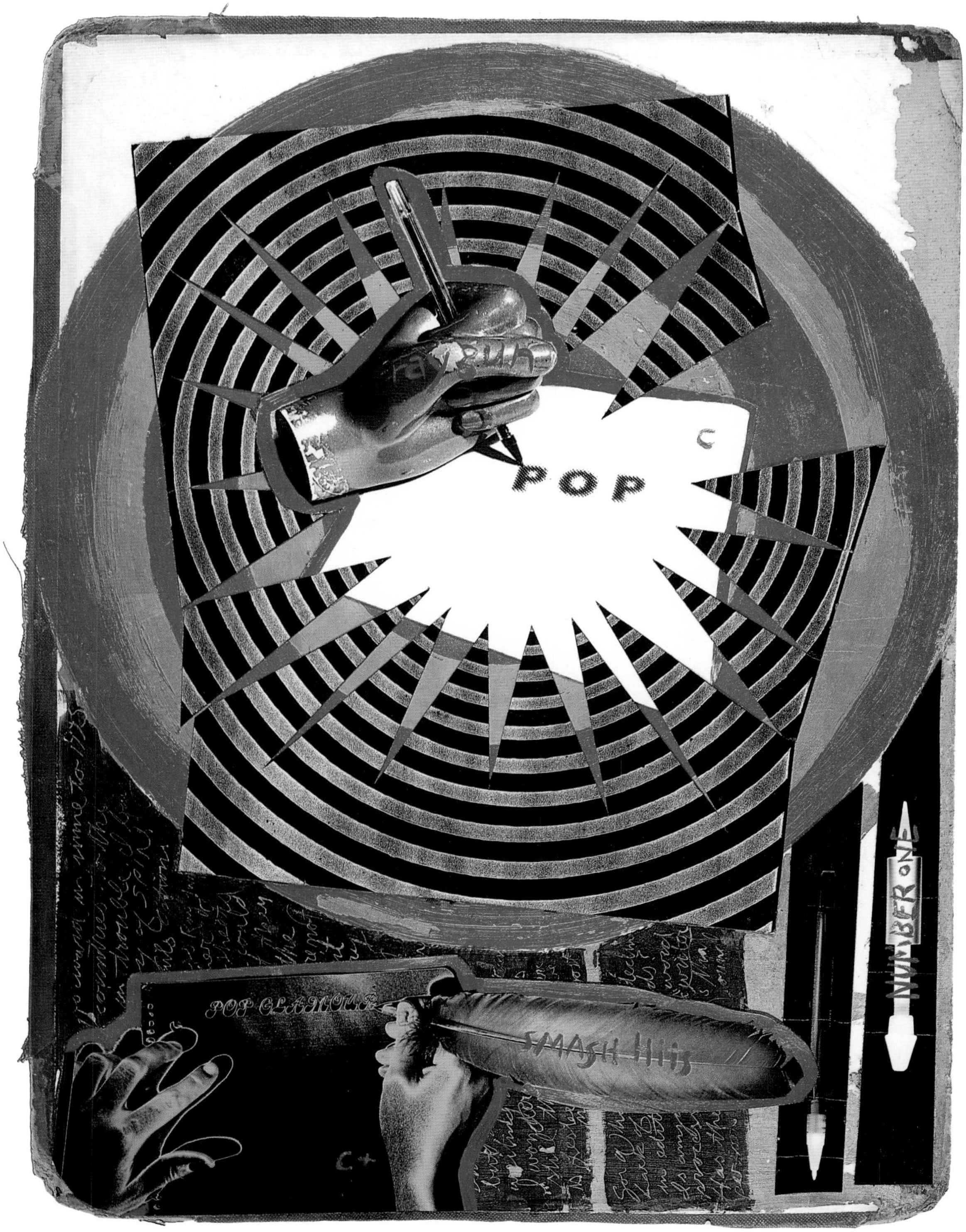
POP
NUMBER ONE
SMASH HITS
C+

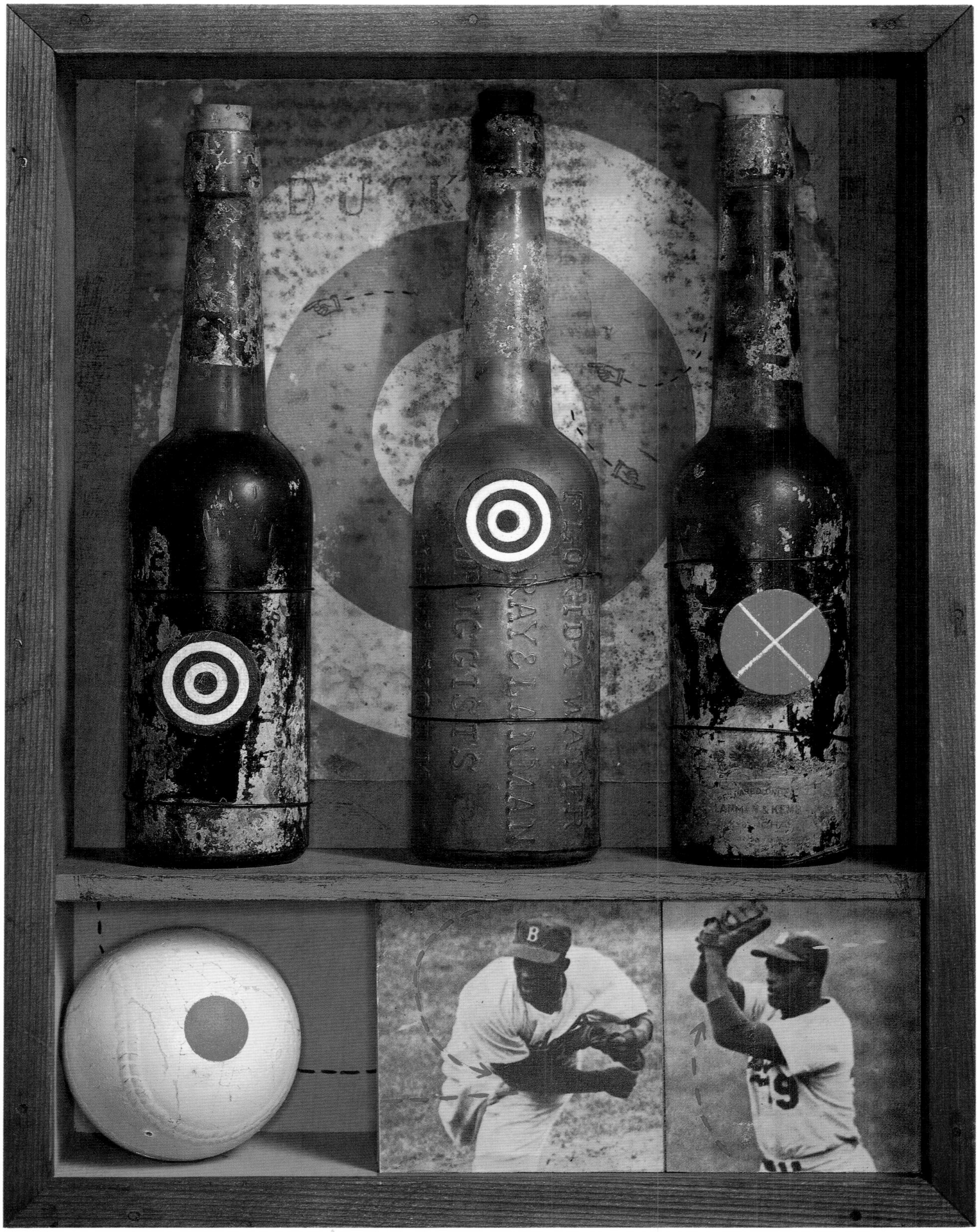

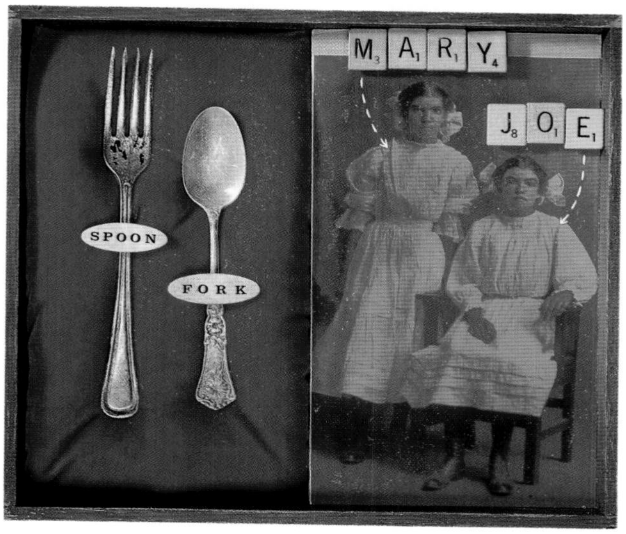

Gary Tanhauser

Art Director) Jane Palecek Editor) Eric Schrier Writer) Bonnie Wach Publication) Health Date) September 1992 Publisher) Hippocrates Partners Medium) Mixed media The task of choosing a unique name for your child was the subject of "What's In a Name," featuring this illustration (above).

∞

Art Director) Pat Mitchell Writer) Bill Breen Publication) Garbage Magazine Date) December/January 1993 Publisher) Dovetale Publishers Medium) Mixed media This image was created for an editorial about consumer product packaging (left).

Art Director) Claude Skelton Editor) Jim Rice Writer) Robert Heilbroner Publication) Washington Monthly Date) February 1993 Publisher) Capital City Publications Medium) Collage This collage ran with the article "Waiting for Change, What Can We Expect From the Clinton Administration?"

David Plunkert

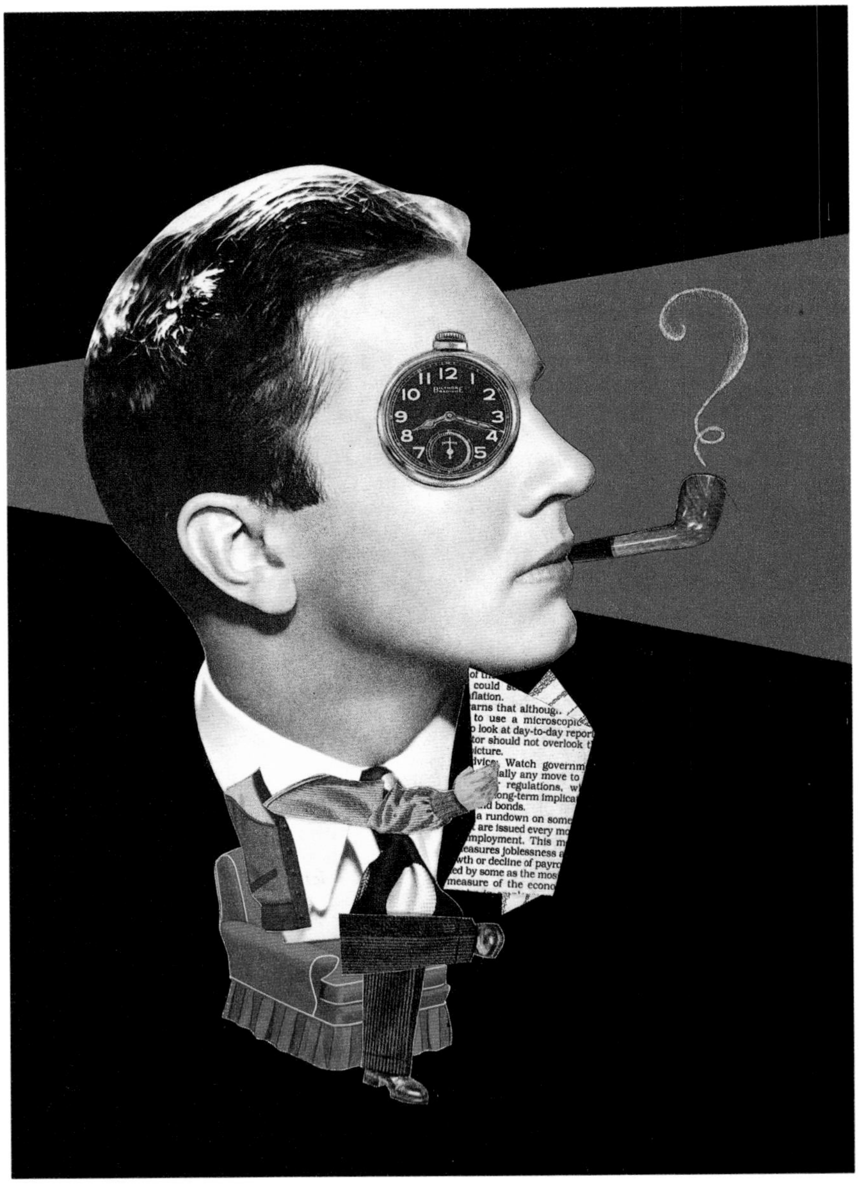

Art Director) Roger **Black** **Editor)** **Terry** McDonell **Writer) Jim Harrison** **Publication)** **Esquire Sportsman** Date) Autumn 1992 Publisher) The Hearst **Corporation** **Medium) Oil** **This illustration accompanied the article "A New Map of** the Sacred Territory."

Benoît

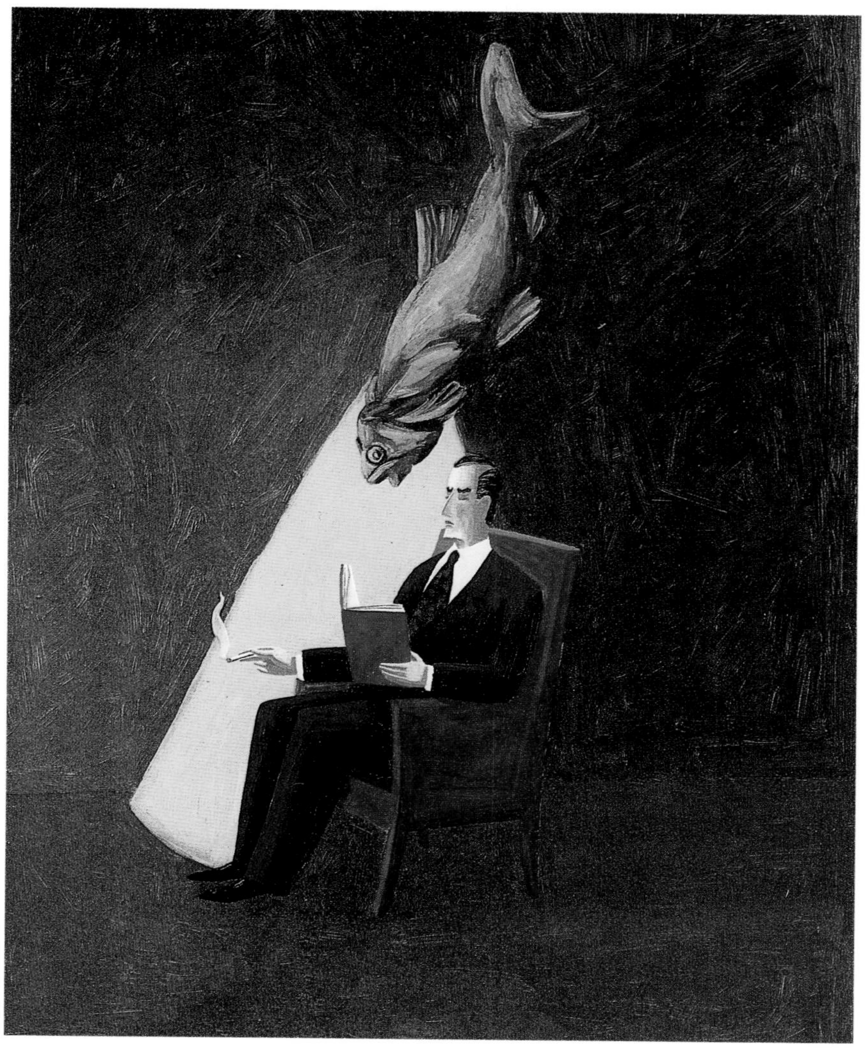

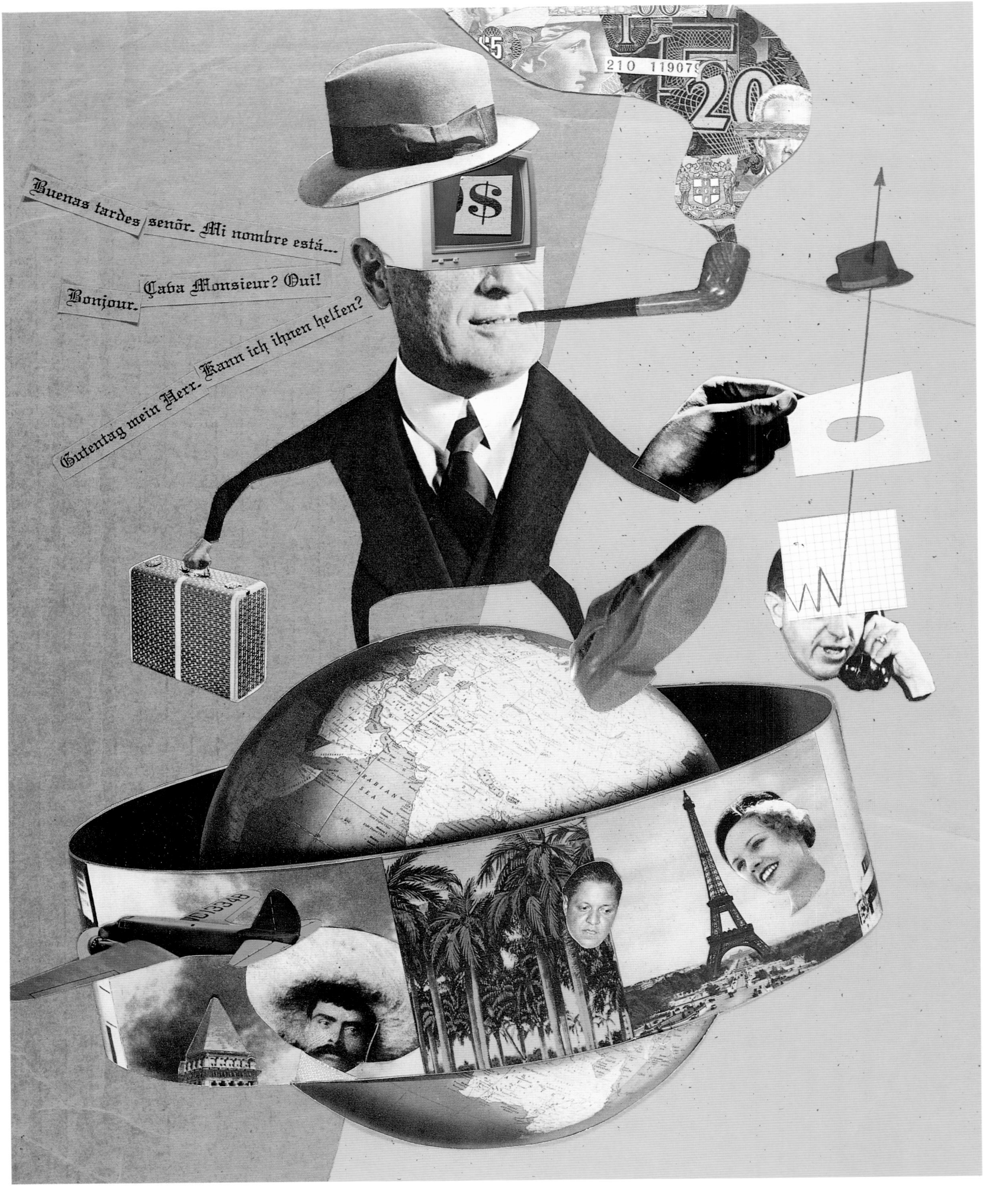
Buenas tardes senõr. Mi nombre está...
Bonjour. Çava Monsieur? Oui!
Gutentag mein Herr. Kann ich ihnen helfen?

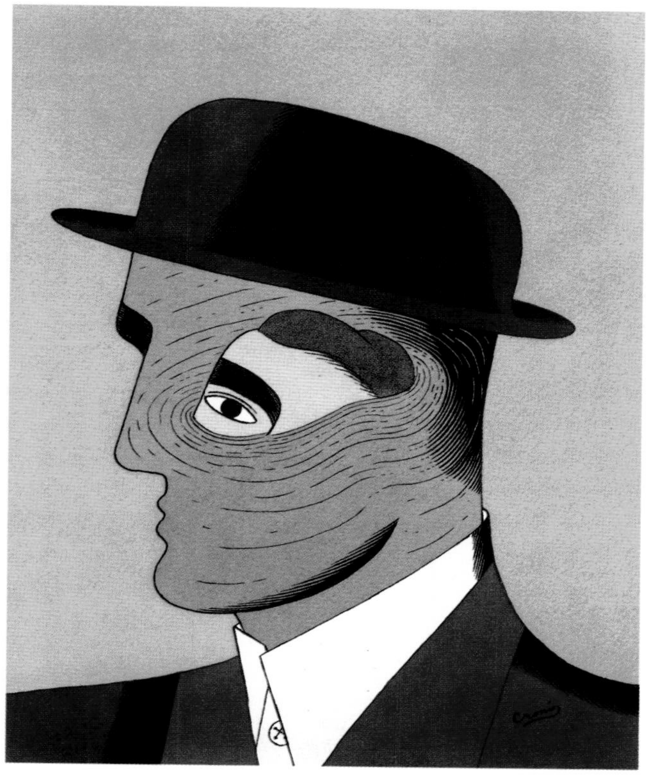

Brian Cronin

Art Director) Lucy Bartholomay Editor) Ande Zellman Writer) Anita Diamant Publication) The Boston Globe Magazine Date) March 14, 1993 Publisher) Affiliated Publications, Inc. Medium) Pen and ink and watercolor The cover illustration for the feature "What's the Matter with Men?" (above).

∞

Art Director) David Loewy Editor) Florence Lazar Publication) Varbusiness Date) February 1993 Publisher) CMP Publications Medium) Collage This interpretation of the global salesman was used for the article "Sales Around the World" (left).

David Plunkert

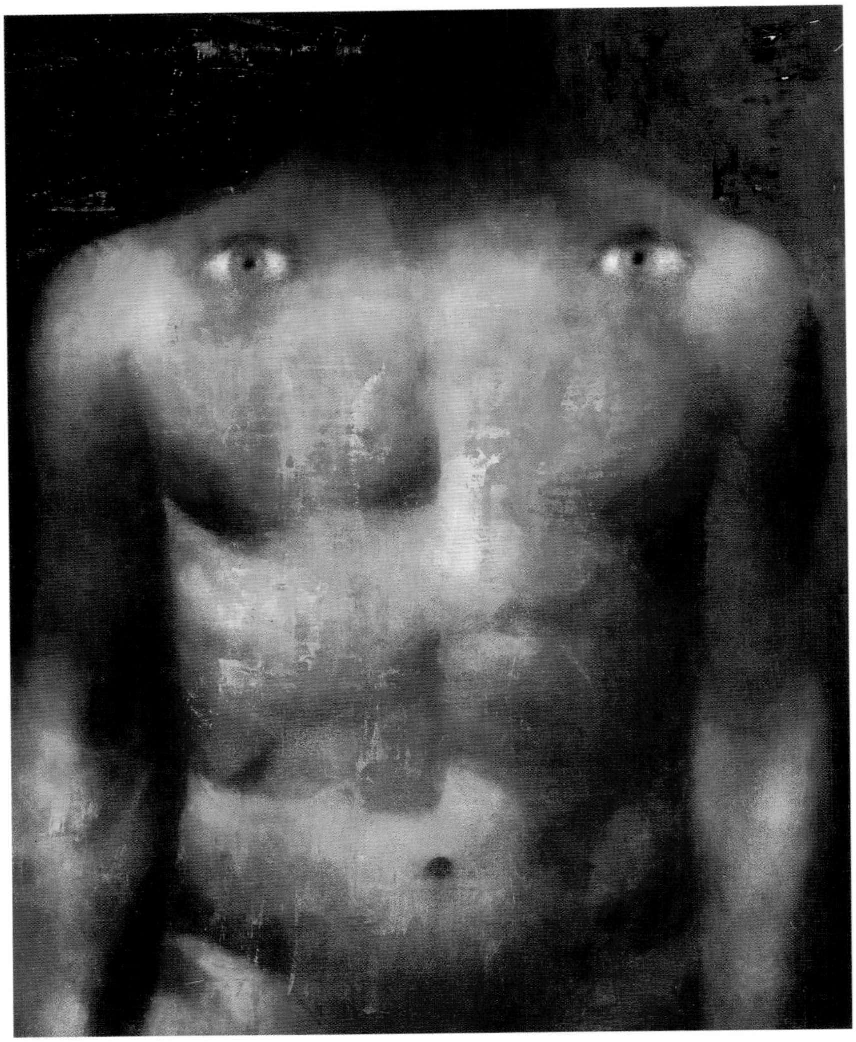

Brad Holland

Art Director) John Sanford Publication) TLC Monthly Date) January 1993 Publisher) Discovery Communications Medium) Acrylic This image was used as the cover for the feature "Body and Soul, Between Synapse and Psyche."

Art Director) Chuck Routhier **Editor) Daniel Ruby** **Writer) Eliot Bergson** **Publication)** NeXTWORLD **Date) Fall 1992** Publisher) Integrated Media
Medium) Collage This image **illustrates NeXT's approach to build-it-yourself programming for the automation** of business processes.

Malcolm Tarlofsky

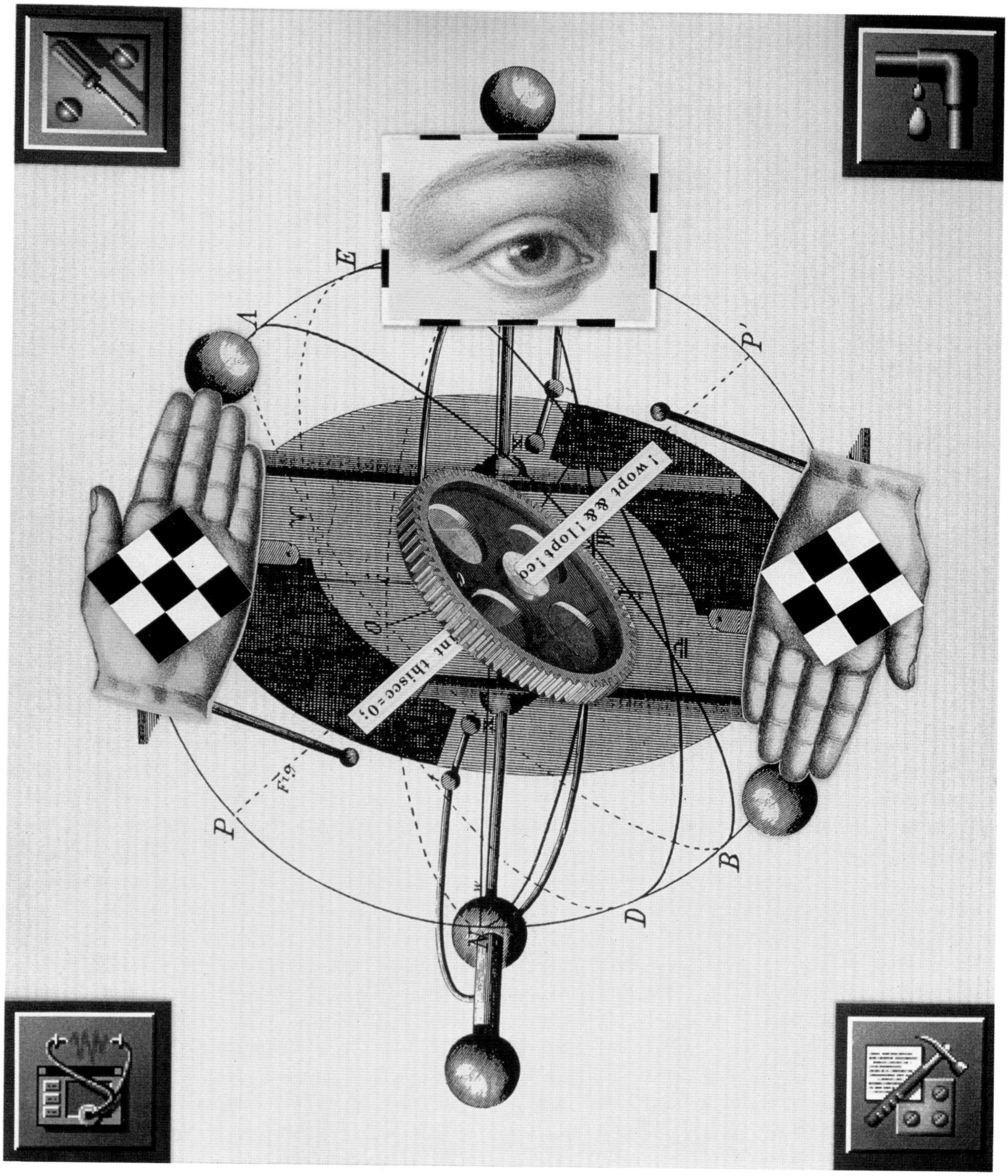

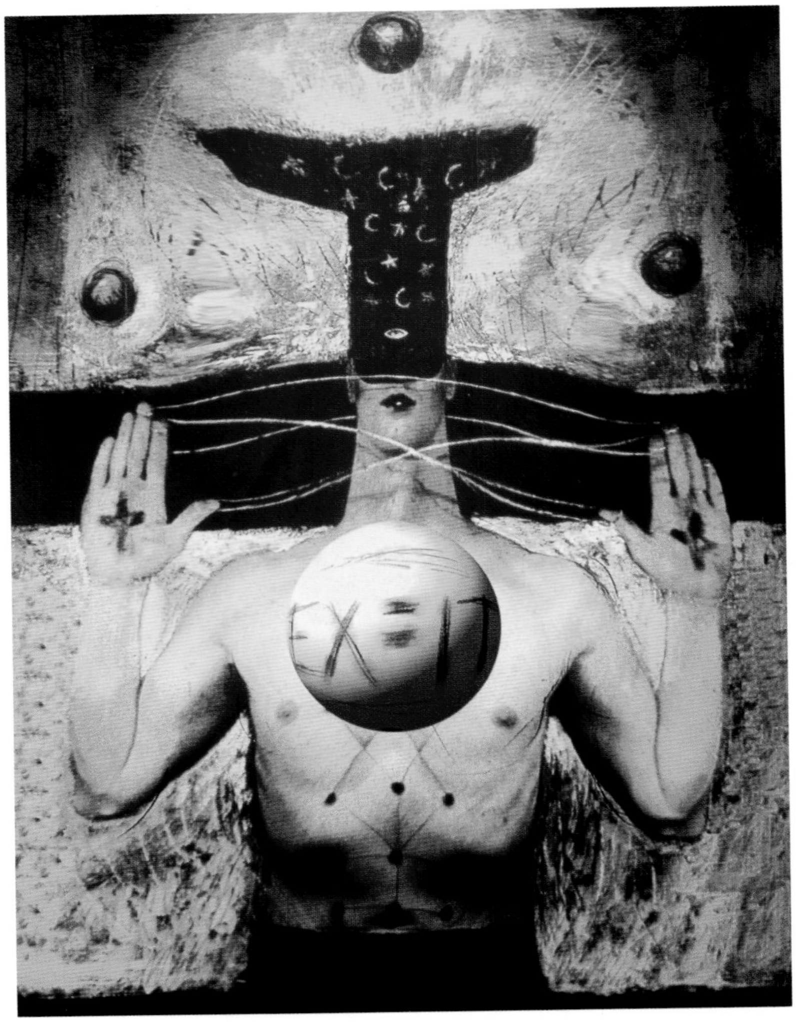

Eric Dinyer

Art Director) David Carson Editor) Marvin Scott Jarrett Publication) Ray Gun Date) March 1993
Publisher) Ray Gun Publishing, Inc. Medium) Paint, photography and computer manipulation
Evan Lurie's song "Alfredo's Response" was interpreted for the Ray Gun feature "Sound in Print."

Art Director) Jane Palecek Editor) Eric Schrier Writer) Edward Dolnick Publication) Health Date) July/August 1992 Publisher) Hippocrates Partners Medium) Photograph This illustration was created for the article "The Great Pretender," an examination of pathological liars.

Matt Mahurin

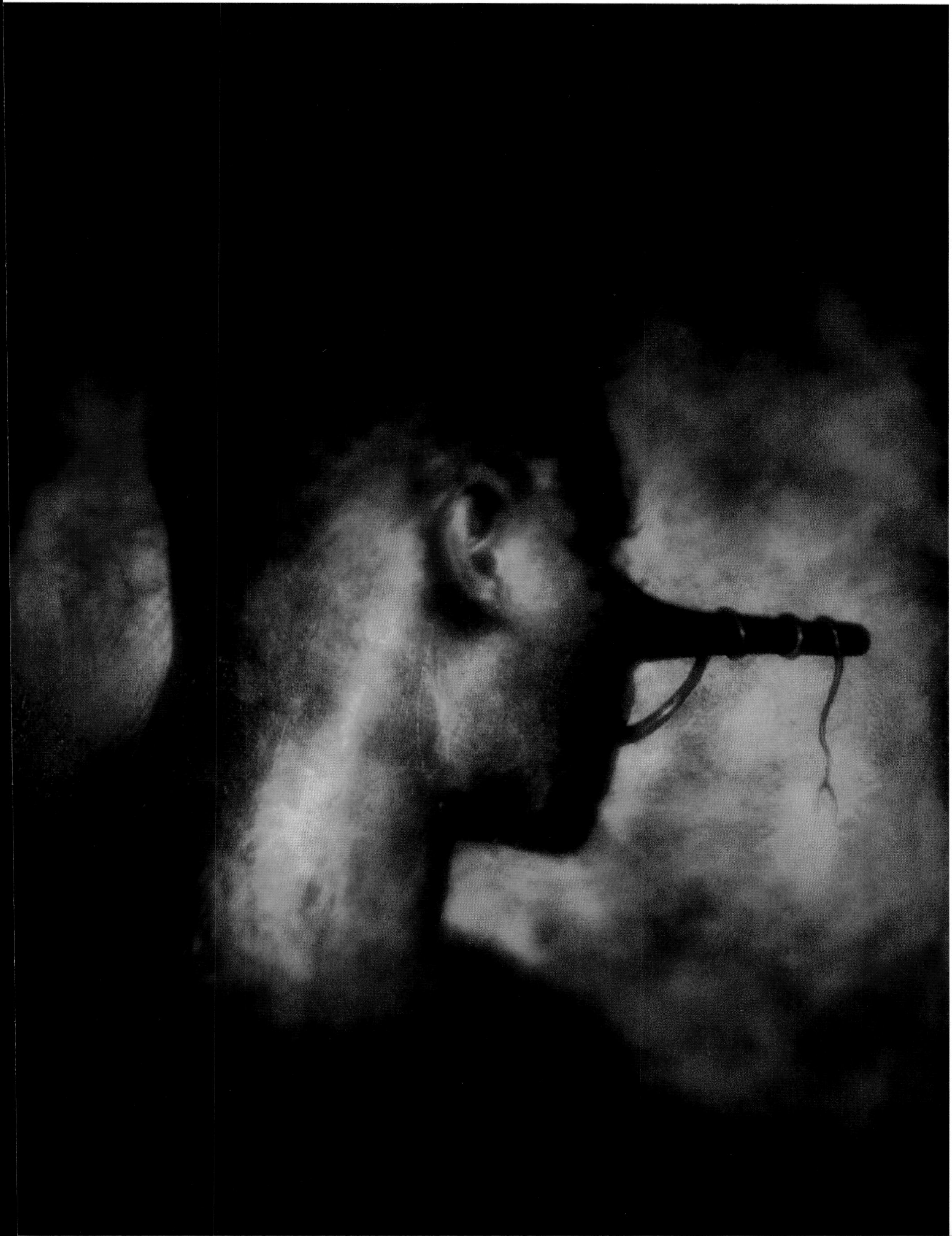

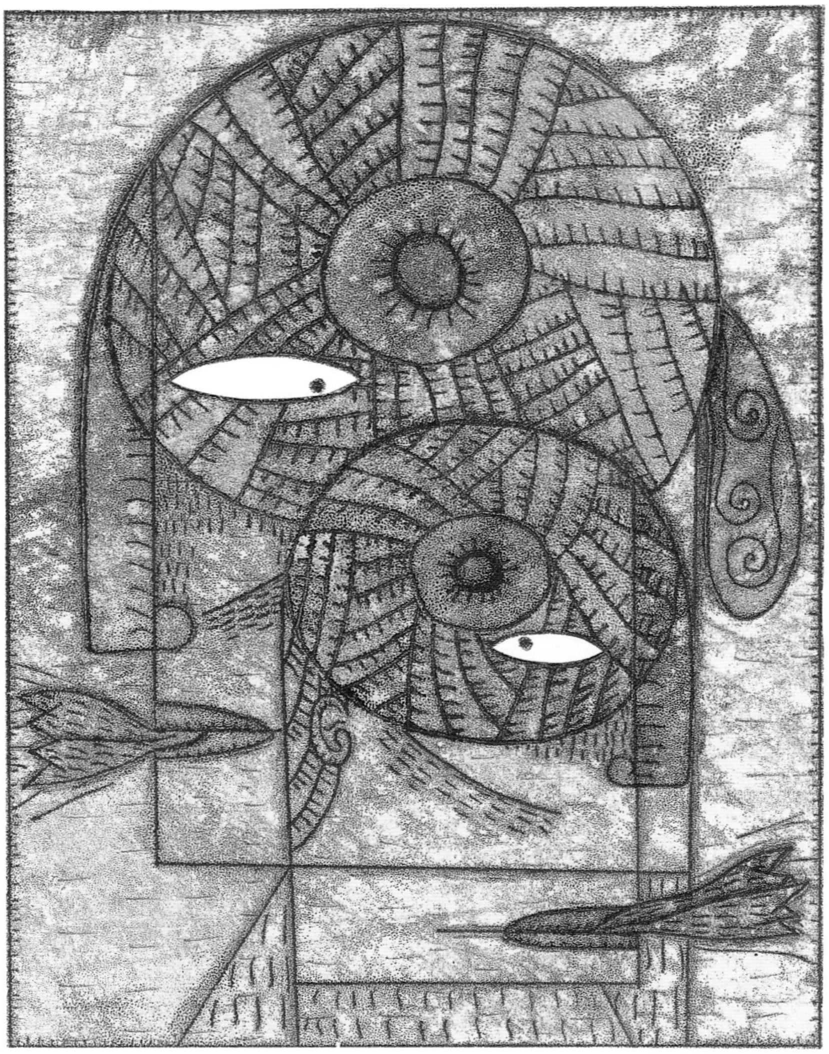

Richard Downs

Art Directors) Fred Woodward and Gail Anderson Writer) Scott Isler Publication) Rolling Stone
Date) February 4, 1993 Publisher) Straight Arrow Publishers, Inc. Medium) Mixed media
A review of Stiff and Chiswick's recent CD containing early punk music was accompanied by this illustration.

Editors) Sandy Jimenez, Sabrina Jones and Seth Tobocman Writer) José Ortega
Publication) World War Three Date) January 1993 Medium) Scratchboard and copier "Invasion!!!," a study of the European and North American invasion of Latin America from 1492 to 1992, featured this illustration.

José Ortega

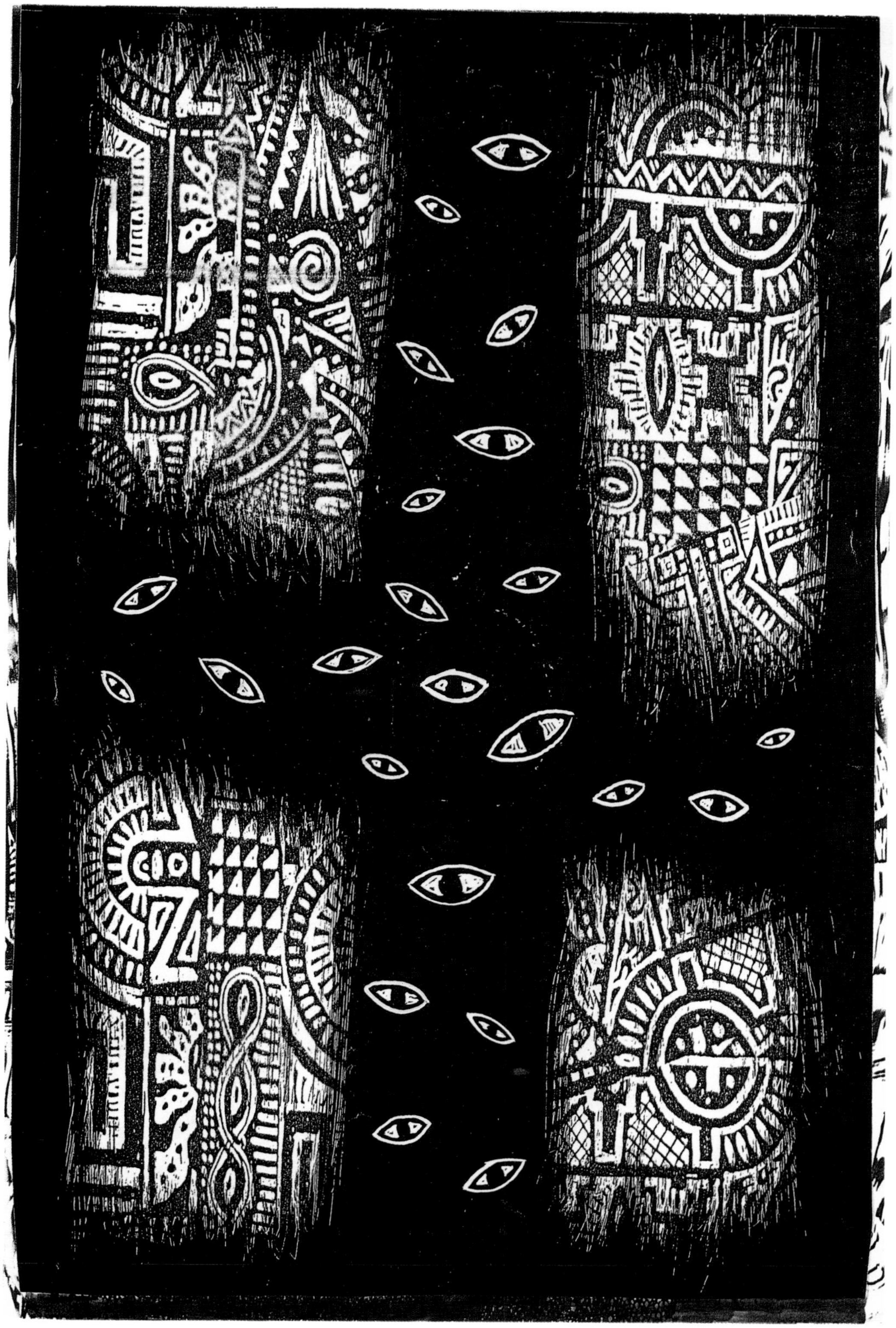

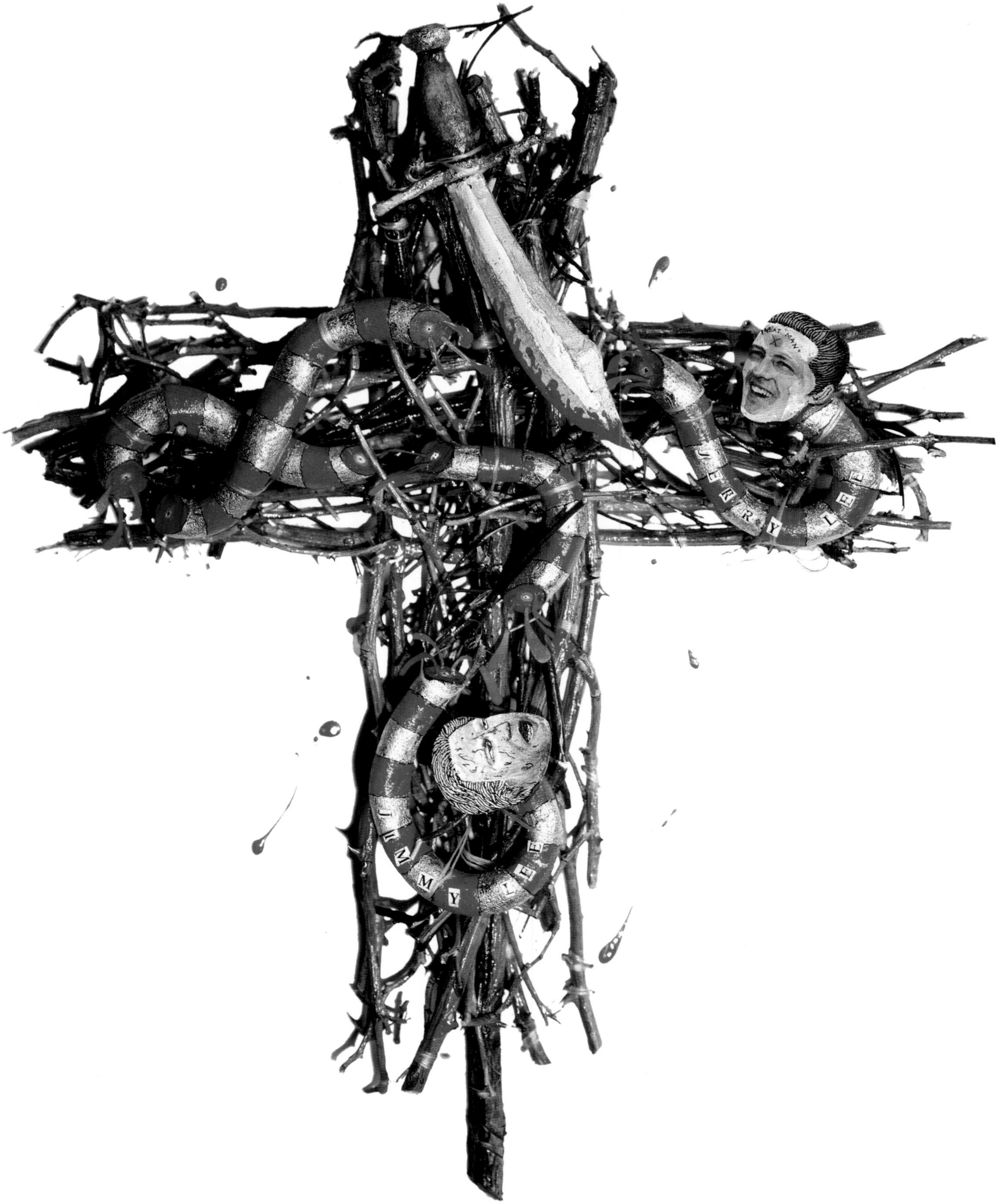

Henrik Drescher

Art Director) Fred Woodward Writer) Lawrence Wright Publication) Rolling Stone Date) June 11, 1992 Publisher) Straight Arrow Publishers, Inc. Medium) Mixed media The article "False Messiah," a look at Jimmy Swaggart, featured this illustration.

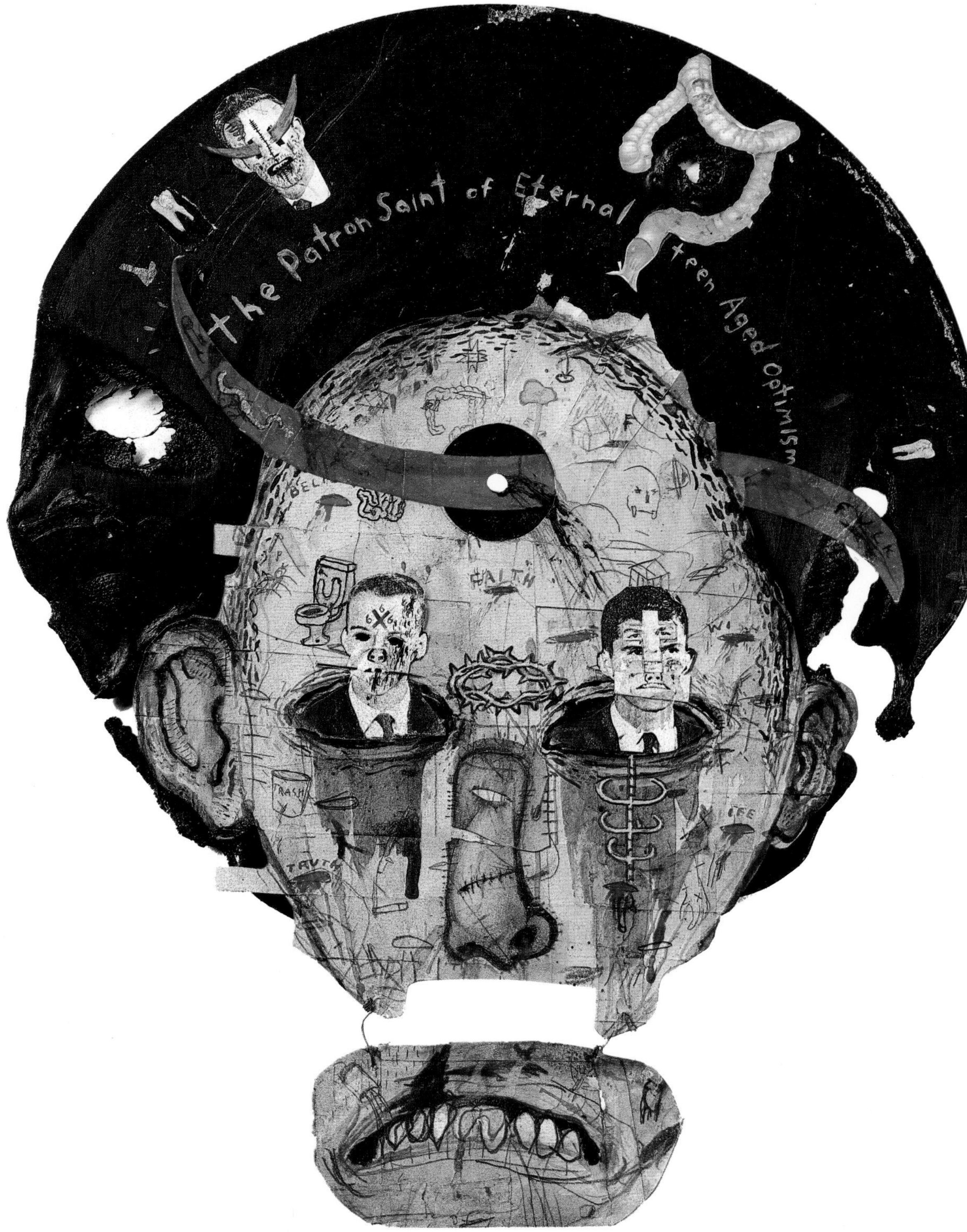

Jason Holley

Art Director) Tom Fillebrown Editor) Marc Weidenbaum Writer) Mike Gitter Publication) Pulse! Date) October 1992 Publisher) MTS Inc. Medium) Mixed media "Everything You Ever Wanted to Know About Death Metal, but Were Afraid to Ask," was the title of the article featuring this illustration.

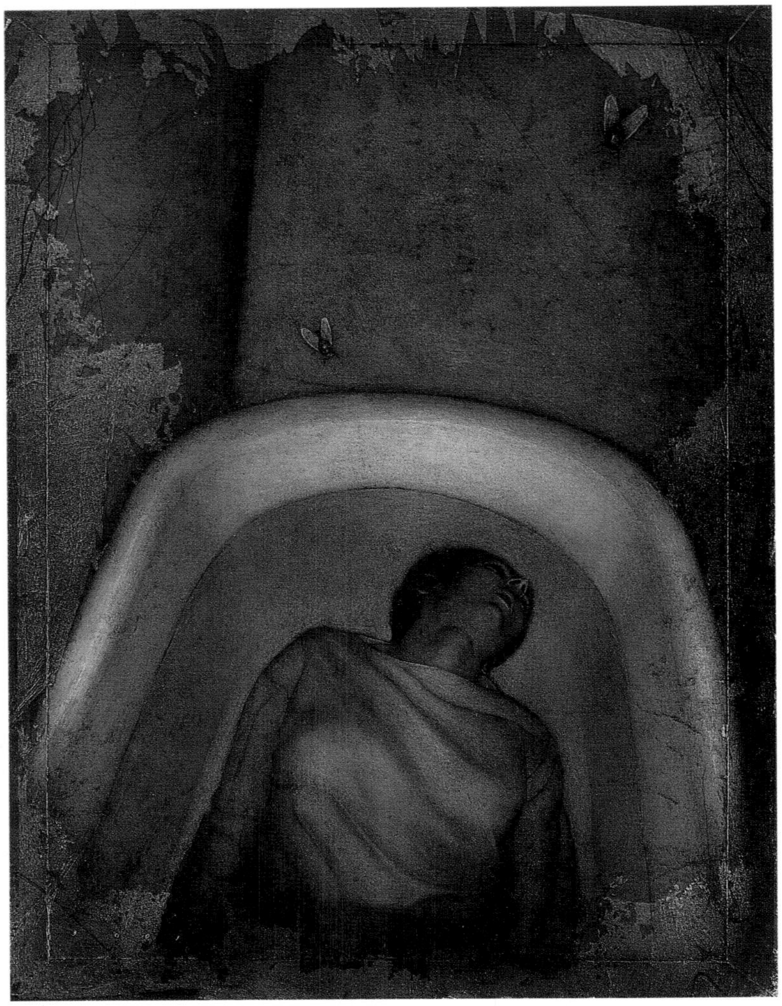

84

Joel Peter Johnson

Art Directors) Dwayne Flinchum and Suzette Ruys Editor) Bob Guccione Writer) Marc Laidlaw Publication) Omni Magazine Date) May 1993 Publisher) General Media Publication Group Medium) Acrylic and oil The quote "It's wonderful to see darkness again," taken from "The Diane Arbus Suicide Portfolio," is the basis for this haunting illustration.

Art Director) **Kerry Tremain** Writer) **Veronique Vienne** **Publication)** Mother Jones Magazine Date) March 1993
Publisher) Foundation for **National Progress** Medium) **Acrylic** **A mother searches for her son in the article** "Iron John: A Love Story."

Brad **Holland**

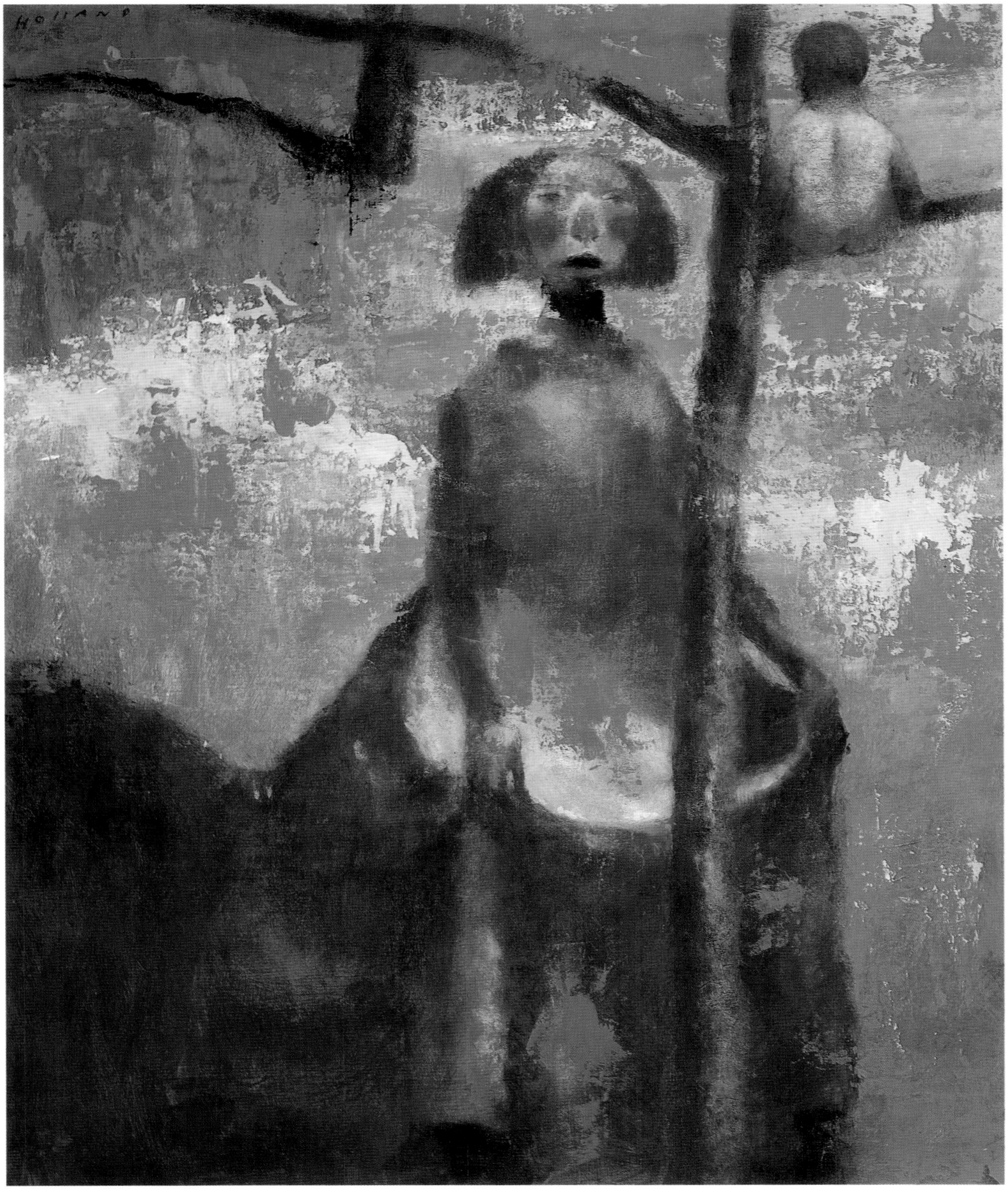

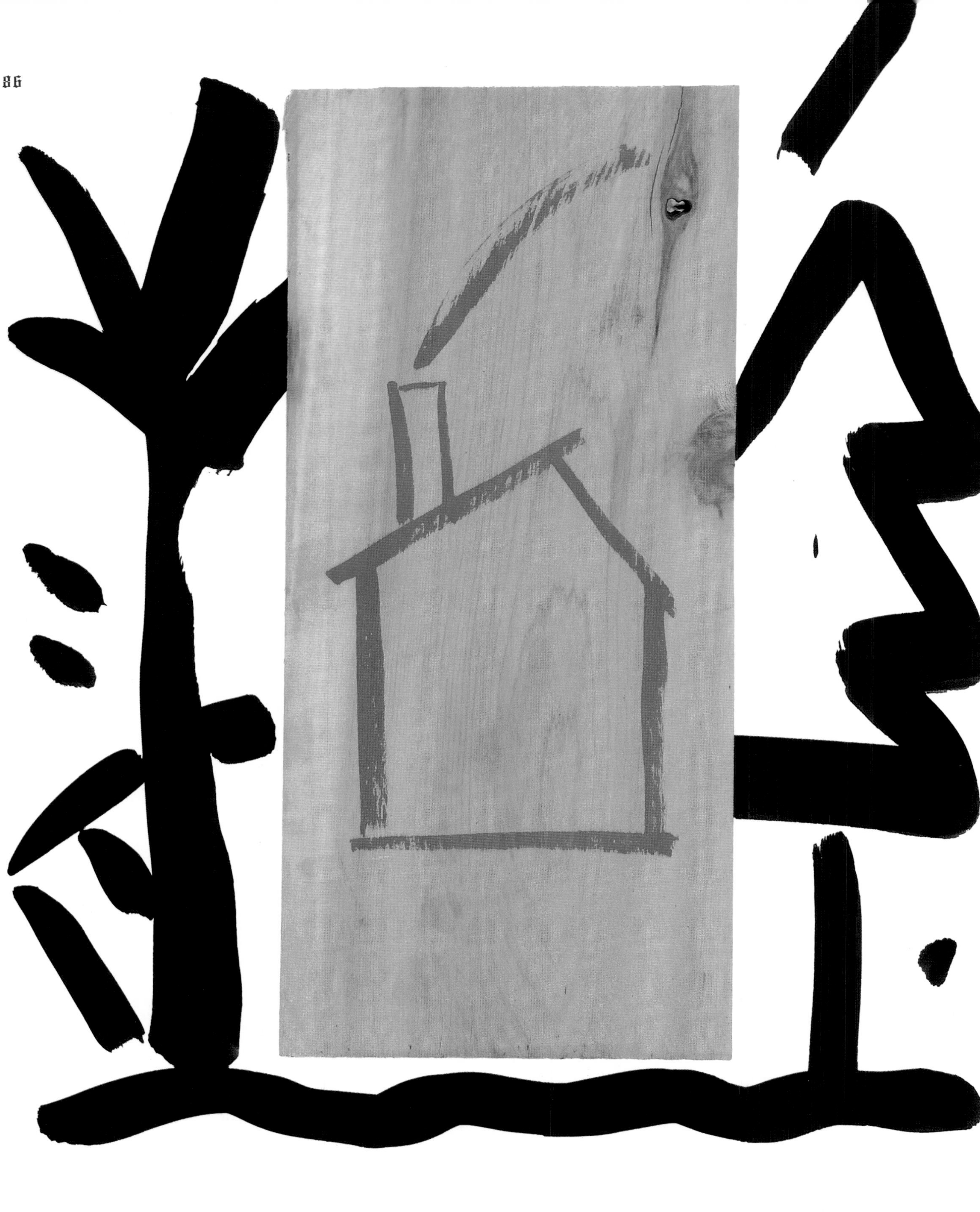

Patrick Blackwell

Art Director) Lucy Bartholomay Editor) Ande Zellman Writer) John R. Stilgoe
Publication) The Boston Globe Magazine Date) July 5, 1992 Publisher) Affiliated Publications, Inc. Medium) Wood, ink and gouache
This illustration accompanied the article "Wood Stock," a history and appreciation of the New England building shingle.

Art Director) Rhonda Rubinstein Editor) Terry McDonell **Writer) Peter Maas Publication)** Esquire Date) January 1992 Publisher) Hearst Corporation Medium) **Acrylic "Lawyers, Guns, and Money" featured this illustration** in Esquire's Dubious Achievement issue.

Jeffrey Fisher

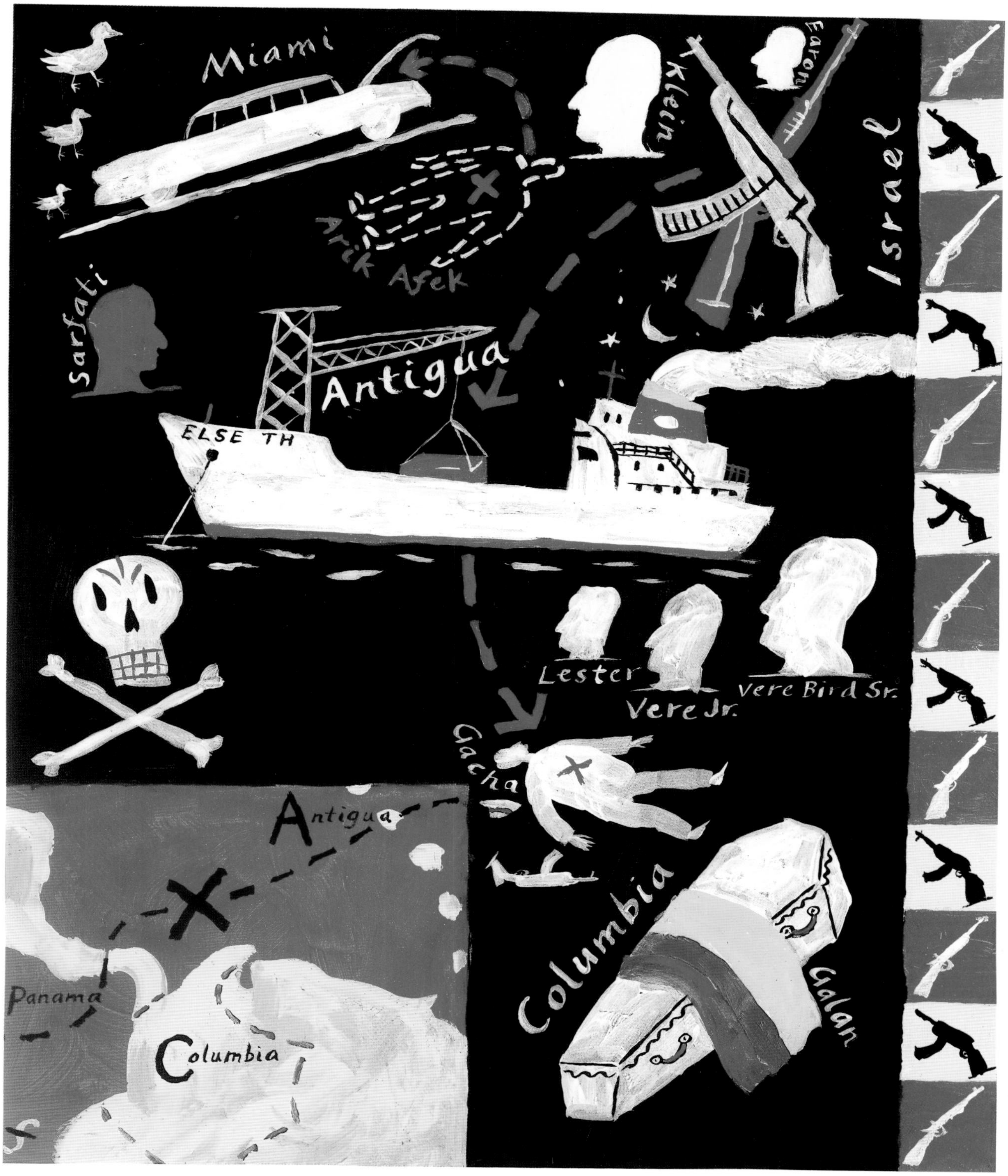

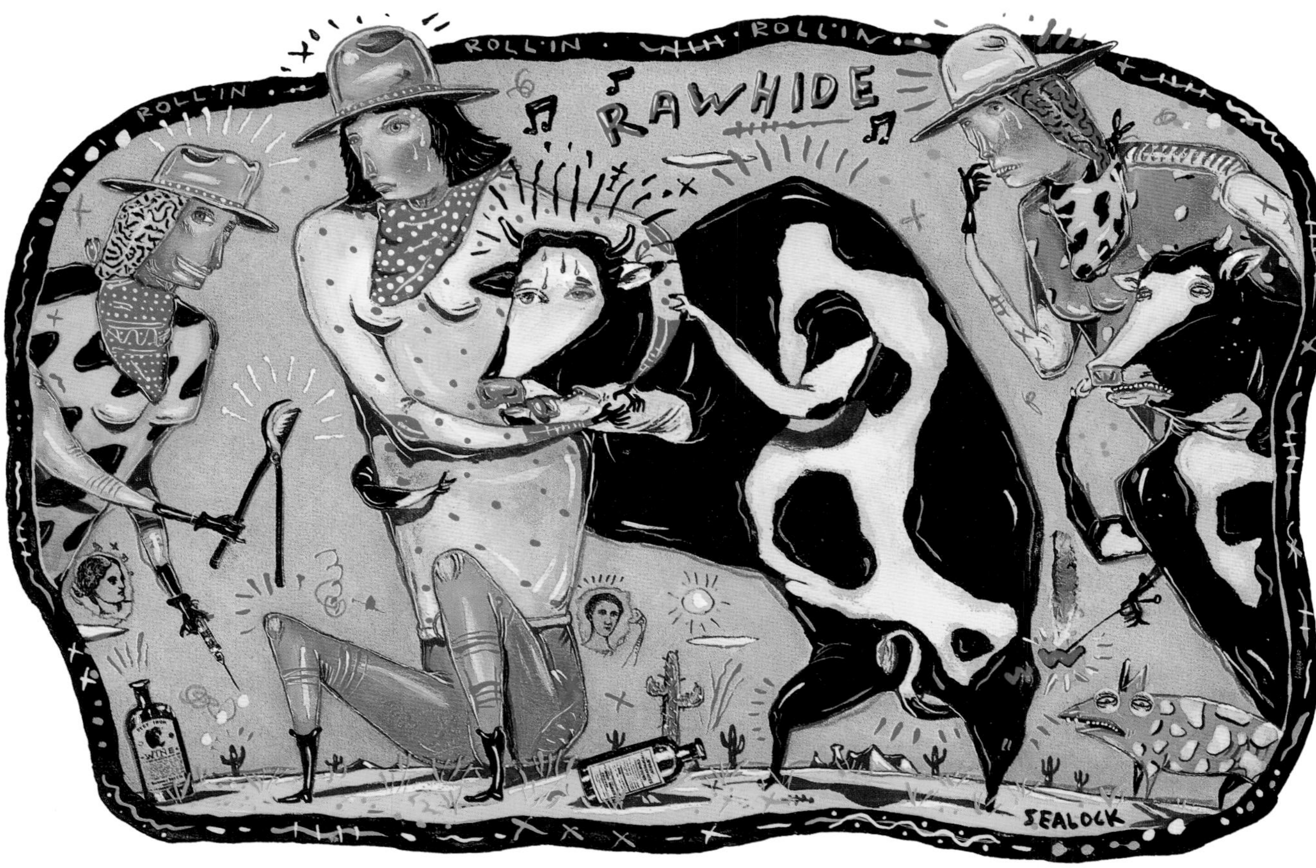

Rick Sealock

Art Director) Claire Innes Editor) Rick Sylvain **Writer) Melinda Beck Publication)** Detroit Free Press Date) August 16, 1992 Publisher) Knight-Ridder Medium) Watercolor, acrylic, **pastel and collage This illustration was created for** the Sunday Travel Section article "At Home on the Range," **a story about an all-wo**men, out-west vacation ranch.

Art Director) David Carson **Editor) Marvin Scott Jarrett** **Publication) Ray Gun** **Date) November 1992** **Publisher)** Ray Gun Publishing, Inc.
Medium) Mixed media For **the feature "Sound in Print" this image represents the illustrator's favorite song,** "Ring of Fire" by Johnny Cash.

Christian Clayton

89

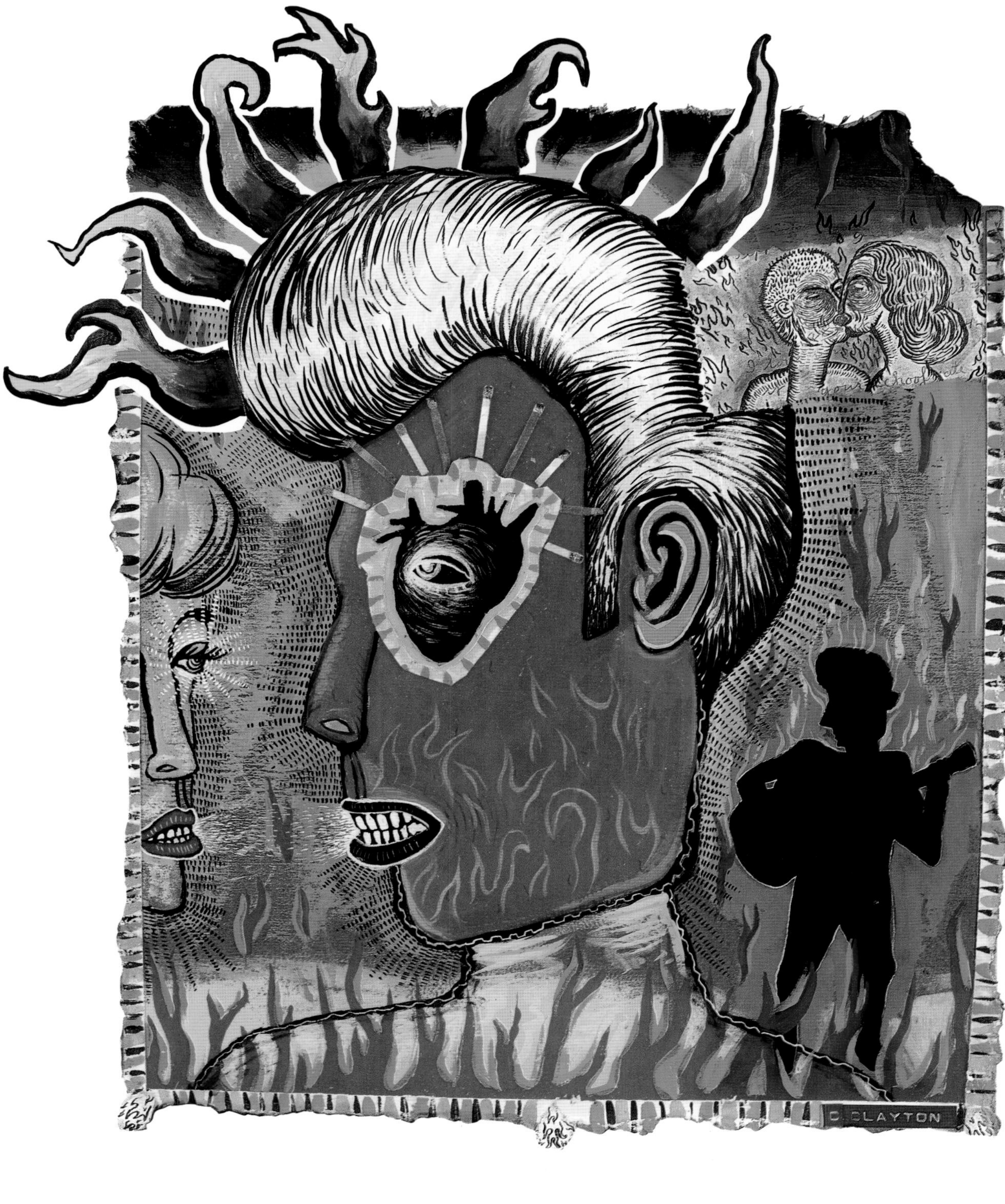

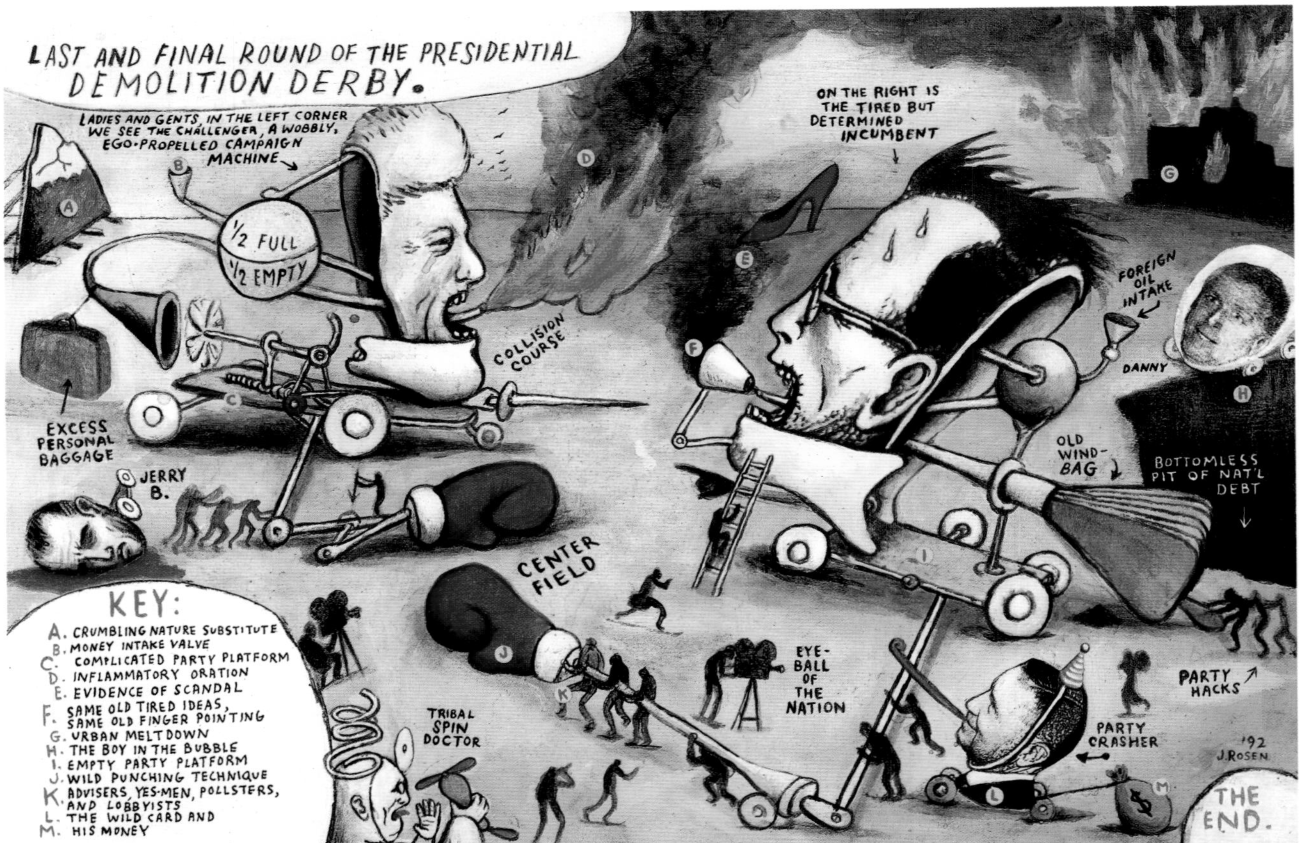
LAST AND FINAL ROUND OF THE PRESIDENTIAL DEMOLITION DERBY.
LADIES AND GENTS, IN THE LEFT CORNER WE SEE THE CHALLENGER, A WOBBLY, EGO-PROPELLED CAMPAIGN MACHINE
ON THE RIGHT IS THE TIRED BUT DETERMINED INCUMBENT
1/2 FULL
1/2 EMPTY
COLLISION COURSE
FOREIGN OIL INTAKE
DANNY
EXCESS PERSONAL BAGGAGE
JERRY B.
OLD WIND-BAG
BOTTOMLESS PIT OF NAT'L DEBT
CENTER FIELD
EYE-BALL OF THE NATION
TRIBAL SPIN DOCTOR
PARTY HACKS
PARTY CRASHER
'92 J. ROSEN
THE END.
KEY:
A. CRUMBLING NATURE SUBSTITUTE
B. MONEY INTAKE VALVE
C. COMPLICATED PARTY PLATFORM
D. INFLAMMATORY ORATION
E. EVIDENCE OF SCANDAL
F. SAME OLD TIRED IDEAS, SAME OLD FINGER POINTING
G. URBAN MELTDOWN
H. THE BOY IN THE BUBBLE
I. EMPTY PARTY PLATFORM
J. WILD PUNCHING TECHNIQUE
K. ADVISERS, YES-MEN, POLLSTERS, AND LOBBYISTS
L. THE WILD CARD AND
M. HIS MONEY

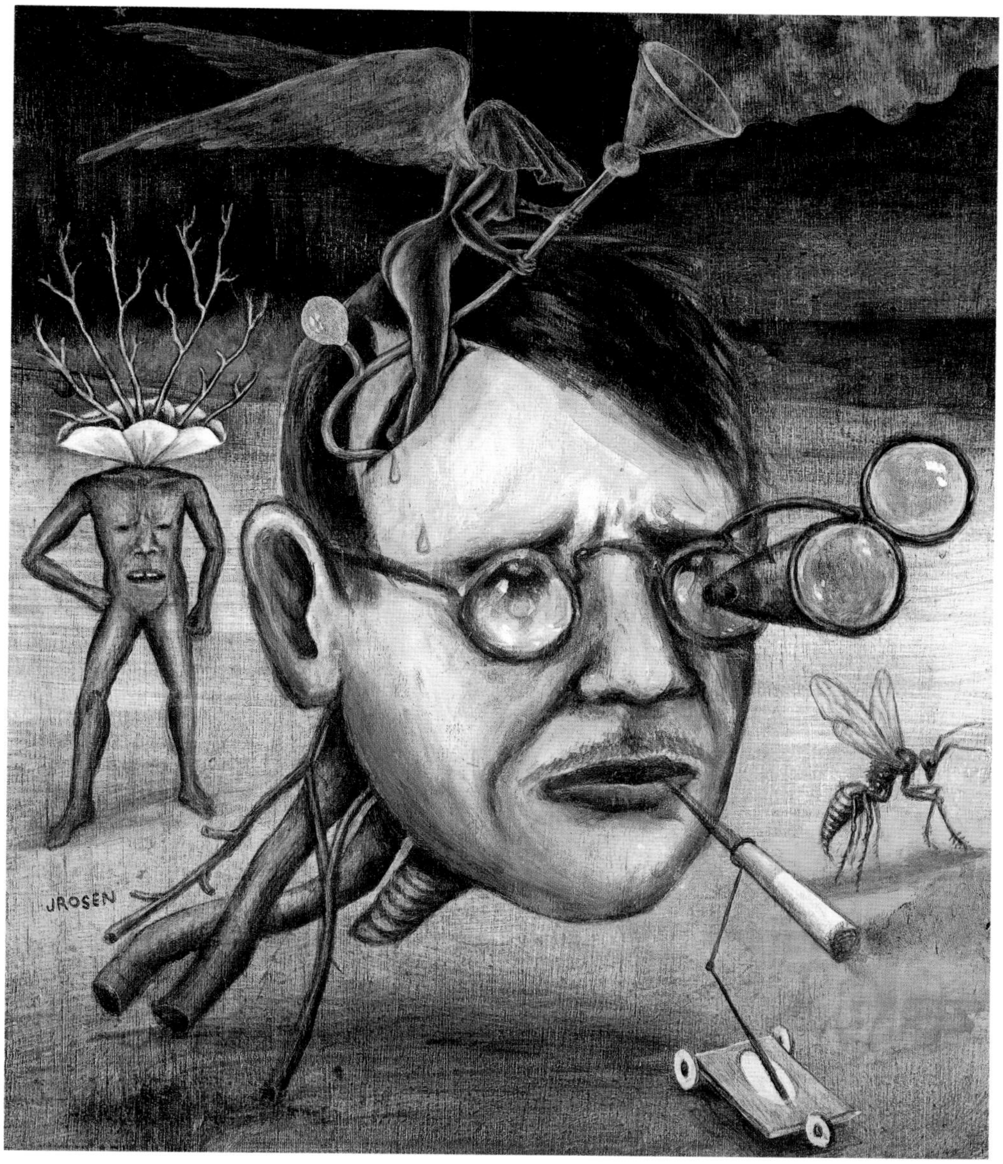

Jonathon Rosen

Art Director) David Carson Editor) Marvin Scott Jarrett Publication) Ray Gun Date) Fall 1992 Publisher) Ray Gun Publishing, Inc. Medium) Acrylic An interpretation of the song "Love's Secret Domain" by the group Coil (above).

∞

Art Director) B.W. Honeycutt Publication) Details Date) August 1993 Publisher) Condé Nast Publications, Inc. Medium) Acrylic The pre-presidential election battle is depicted in this illustration (left).

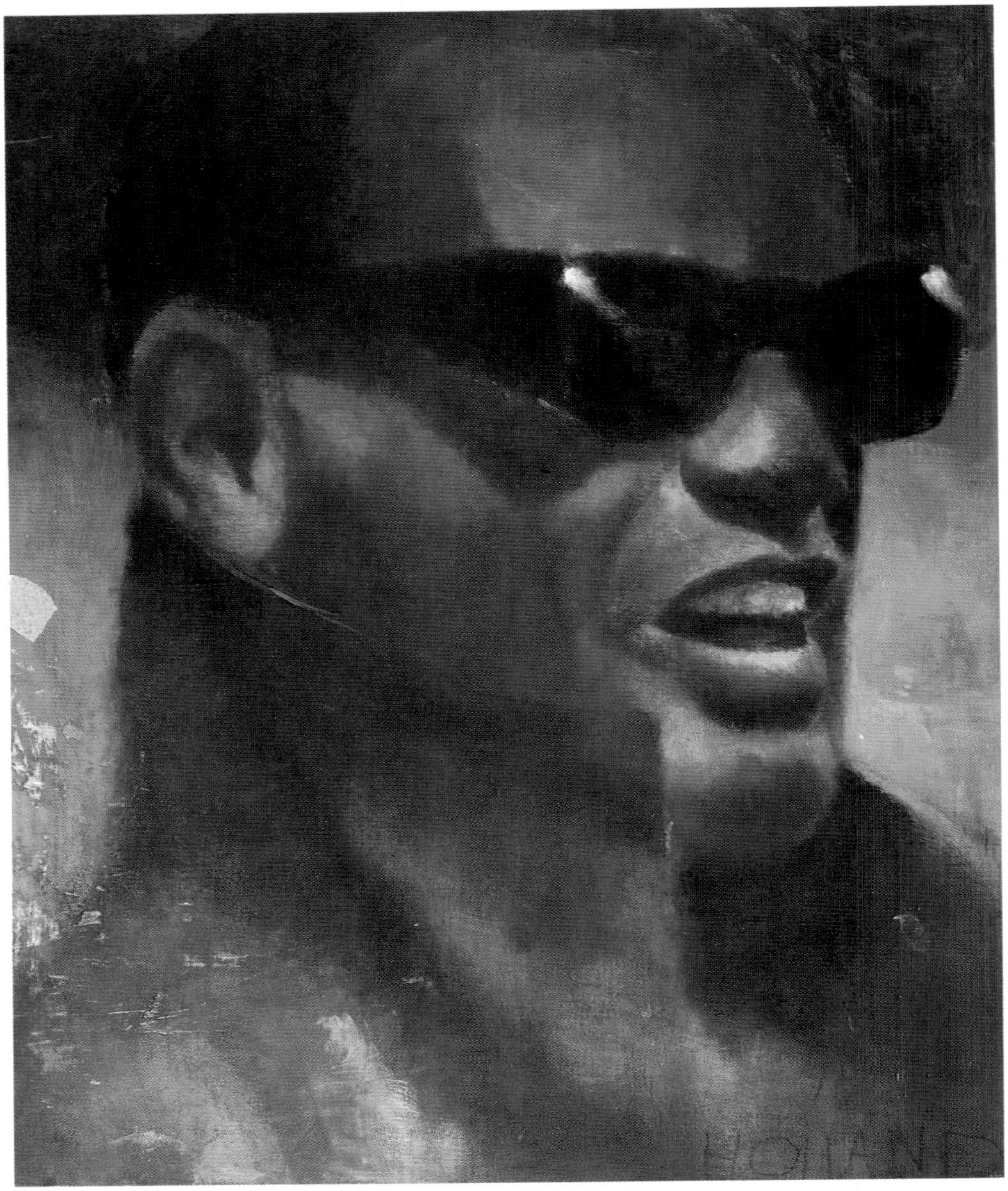

Brad **Holland**

Art Director) Fred Woodward Publication) Rolling Stone Date) October 15, 1992 Publisher) Straight Arrow Publishers, Inc. Medium) Acrylic on masonite This portrait of Ray Charles was included in the 25th anniversary issue article "The Interviews."

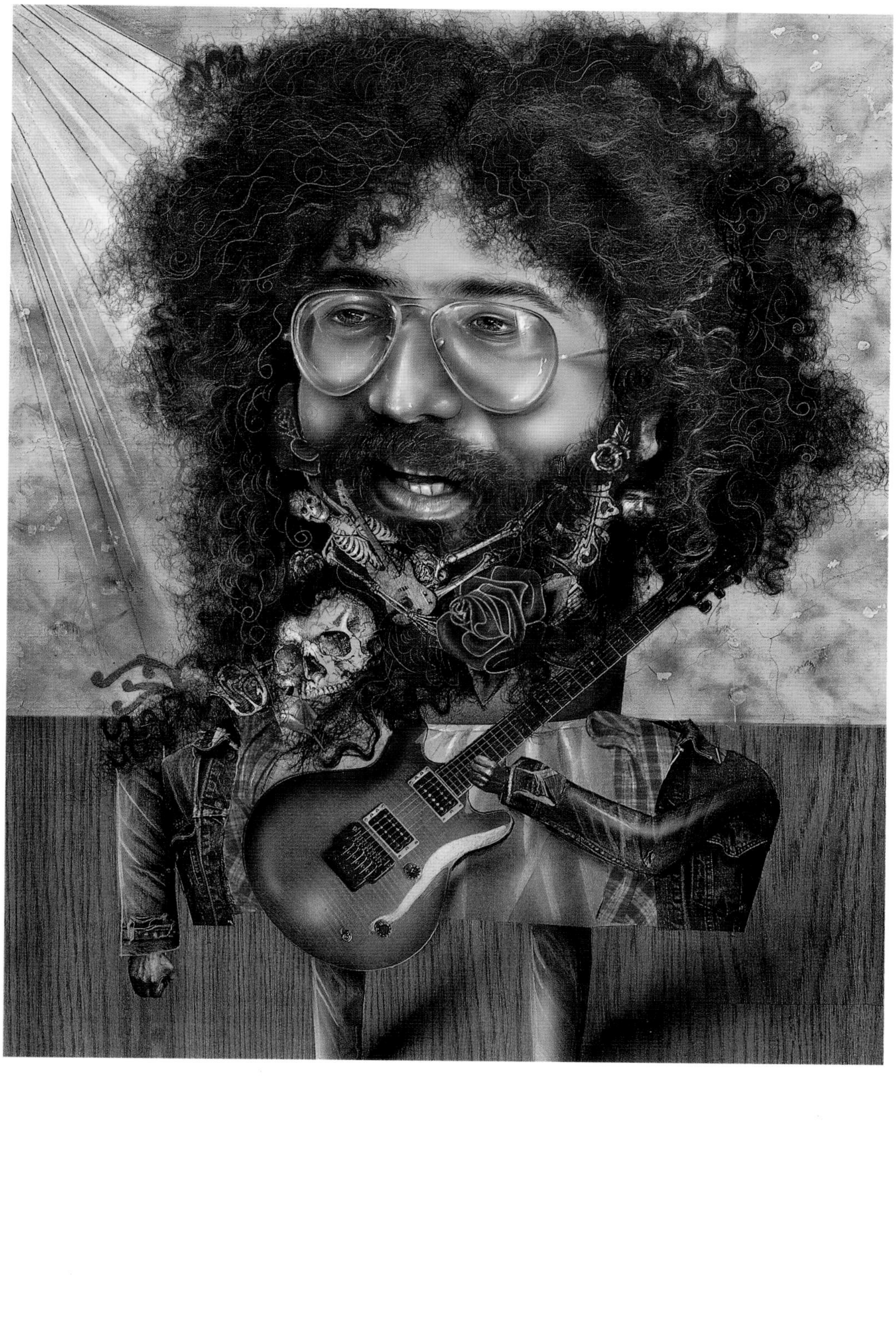

Janet Woolley

Art Director) Fred Woodward Publication) Rolling Stone Date) October 15, 1992 Publisher) Straight Arrow Publishers, Inc.
Medium) Mixed media This portrait of Jerry Garcia appeared in the 25th anniversary issue article "The Interviews."

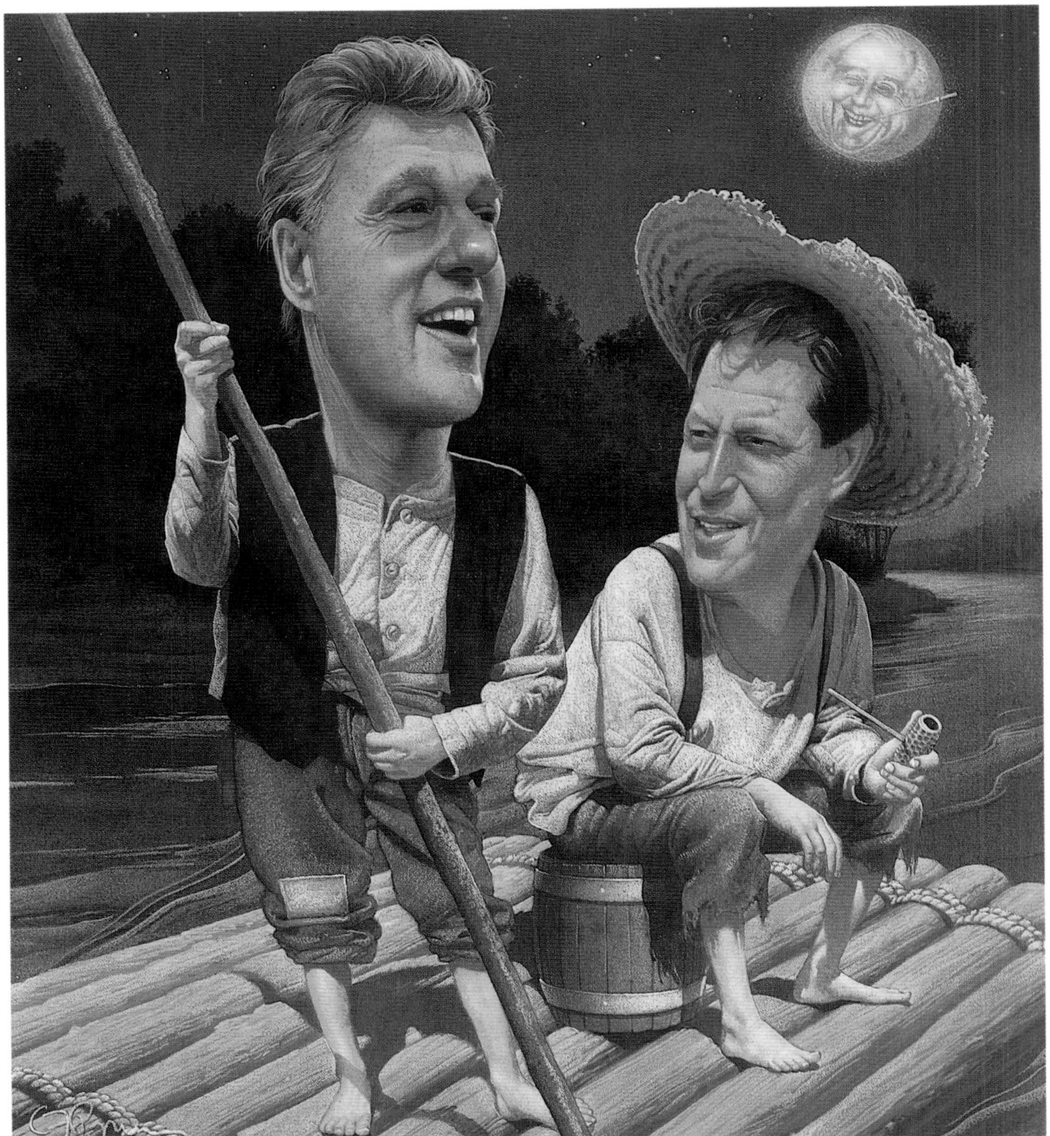

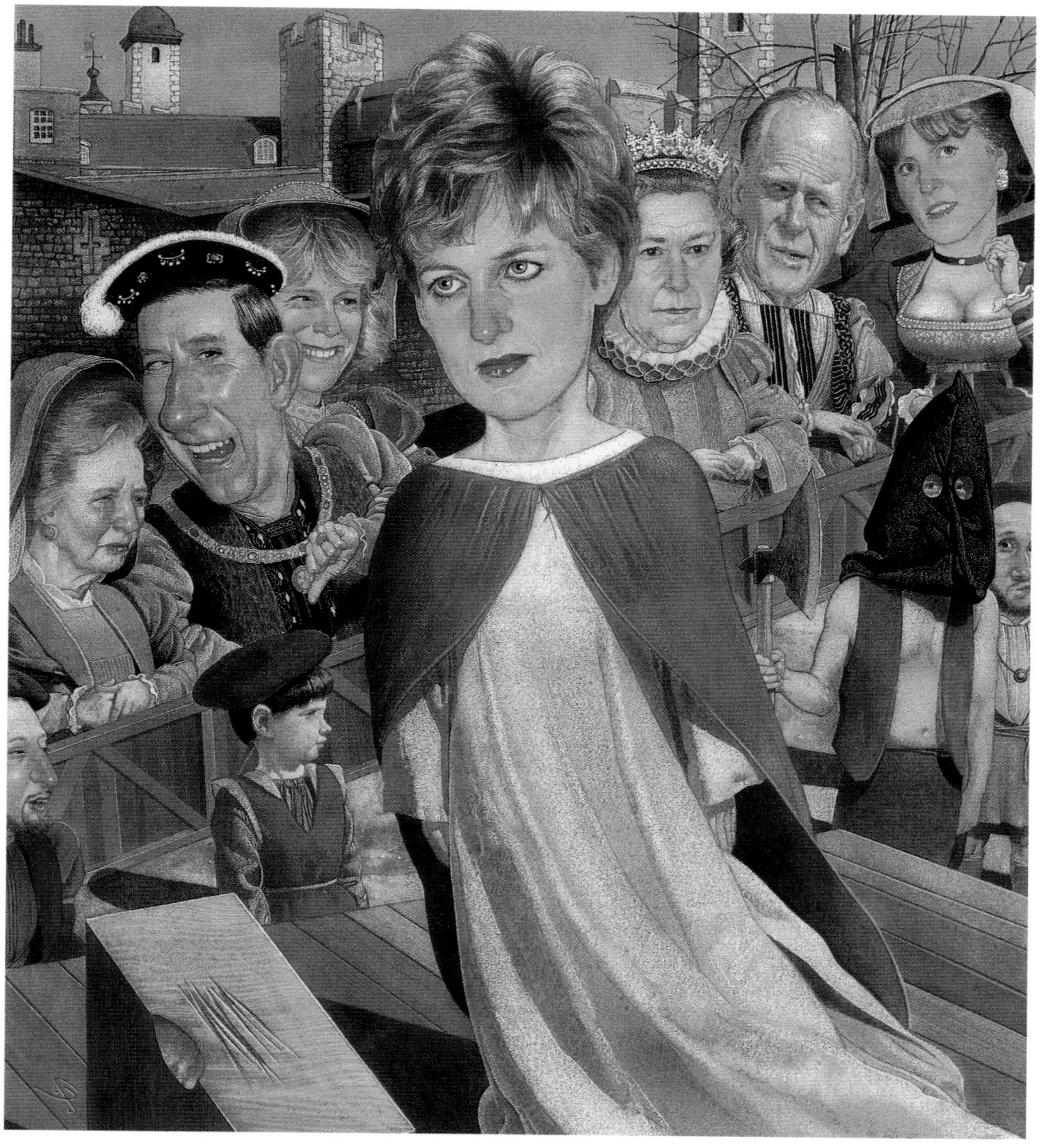

C.F. Payne

Art Director) Robert Priest Writer) John Mortimer Publication) GQ Magazine Date) April 1993 Publisher) Condé Nast Publications, Inc. Medium) Mixed media The perplexities of being Princess Di were dicussed in the article "Noblesse Besieged" (above).

Art Director) Robert Priest Writer) Gore Vidal Publication) GQ Magazine Date) November 1992 Publisher) Condé Nast Publications, Inc. Medium) Mixed media Clinton and Gore are depicted here for the article "Goin' South" (left).

Warren Linn

Art Directors) Victoria Maddocks and Jaime Ferrand Editor) Katherine Arthaud Writer) Stan Gibilisco Publication) South Beach Magazine Date) February 1993 Publisher) South Beach Magazine, Inc. Medium) Collage and acrylic on wood A family at home with a polluted ocean was created for the article "Earthwatch: Seawise" (below).

∞

Art Director) Nancy Duckworth Editor) Bret Israel Publication) The Los Angeles Times Magazine Date) April 18, 1993 Publisher) Times Mirror Medium) Oil and acrylic A portrait of African American men and women was created for the article "Shades of Black" (right).

Calef Brown

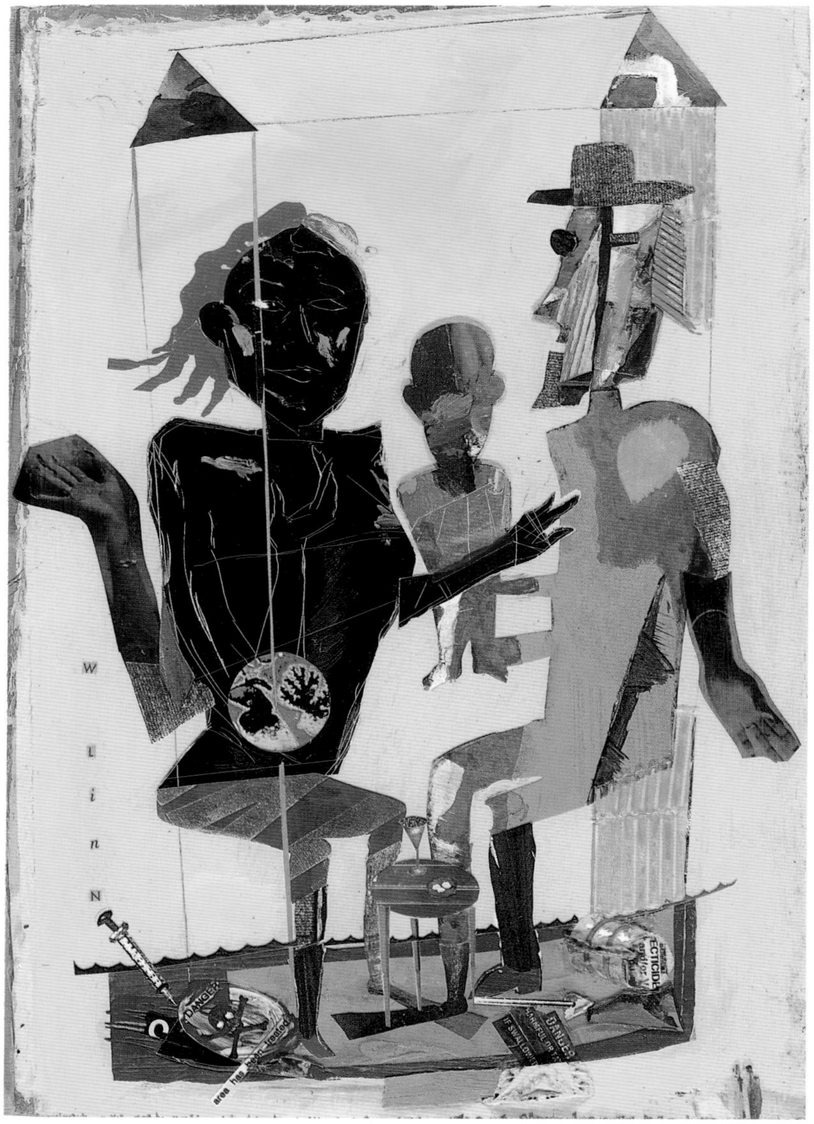

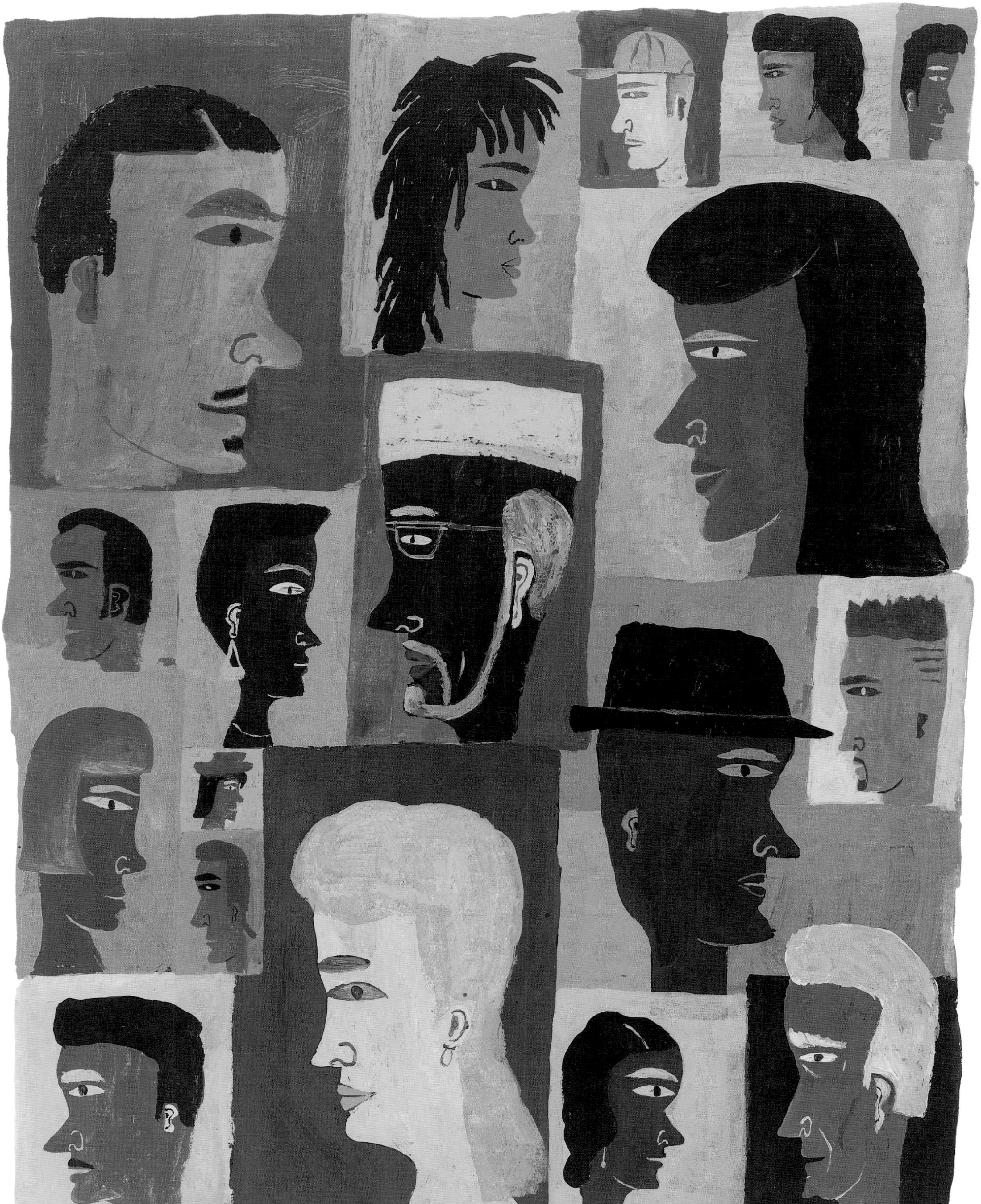

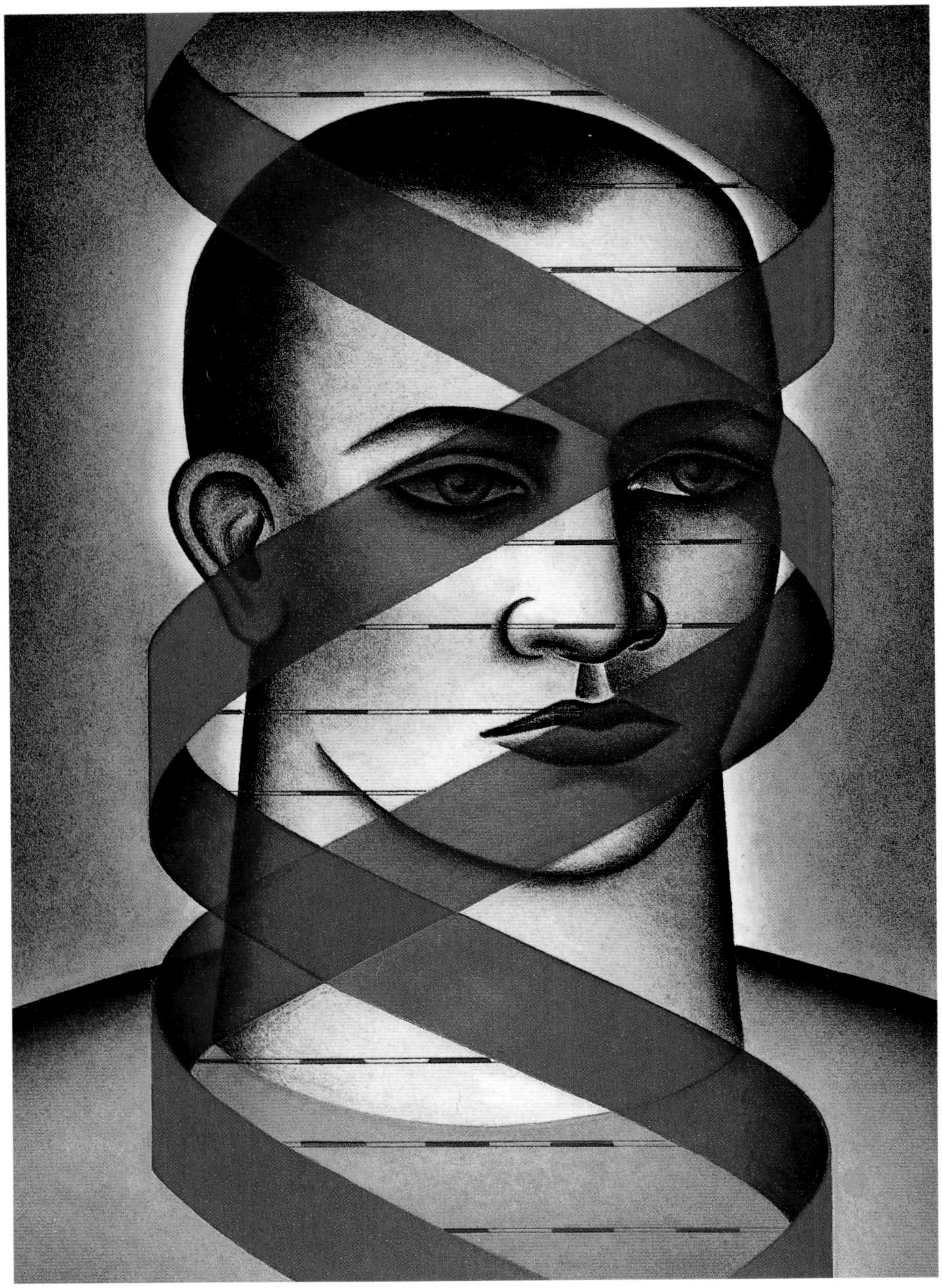

Sandra Dionisi

Art Director) Tom Suzuki Designer) Tim Cook Writers) William E. Winter and Mark A. Atkinson Publication) Diabetes Forecast Date) May 1992 Publisher) American Diabetes Association, Inc. Medium) Acrylic This illustration depicts the connection between diabetes and DNA.

Art Director) Tom Suzuki Designer) Tim Cook Writer) Leslie R. Schover Publication) Diabetes Forecast Date) August 1992 Publisher) American Diabetes Association Medium) Oil on wood The article "Women, Sexual Health and Diabetes" inspired this illustration.

Stefano Vitale

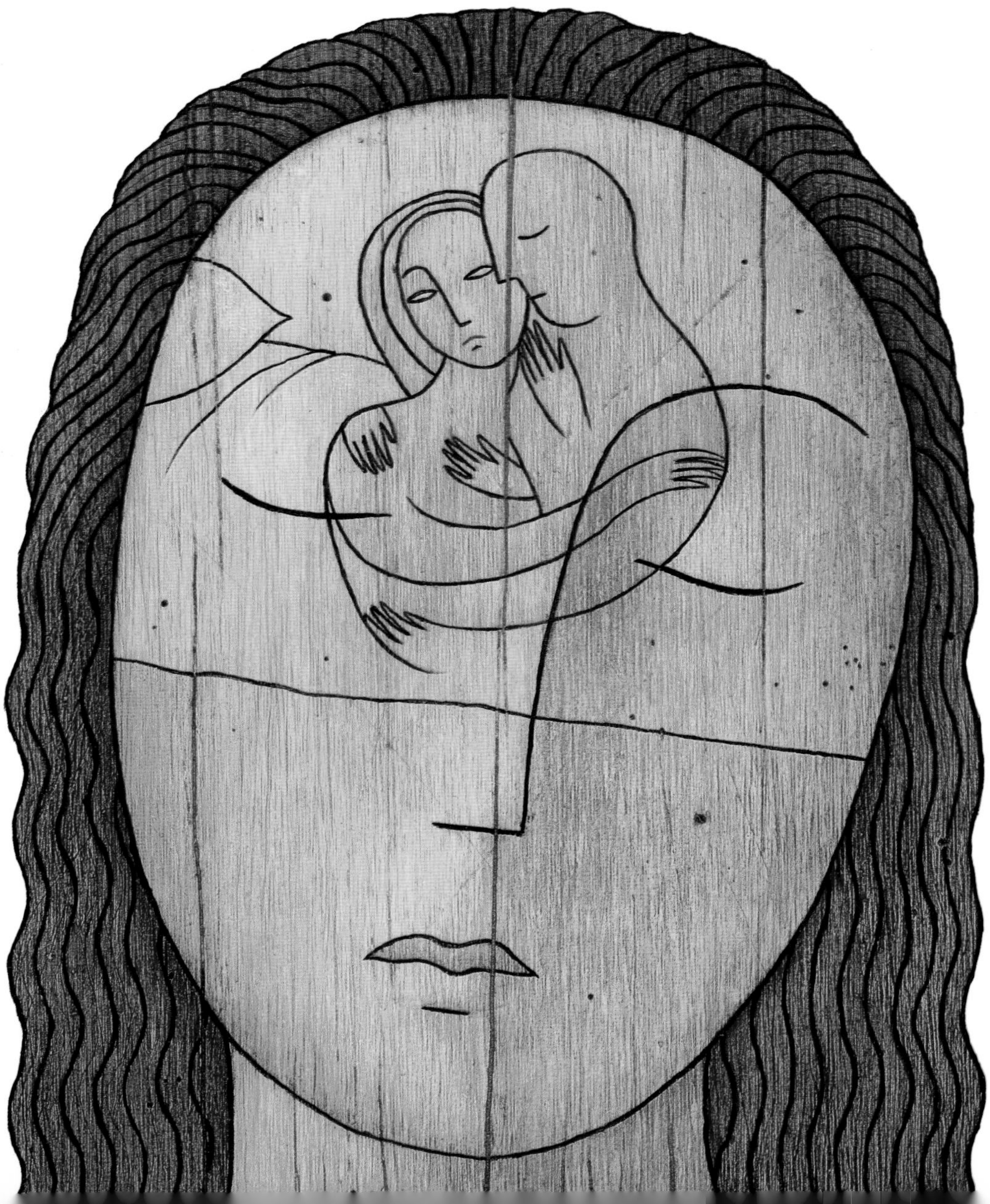

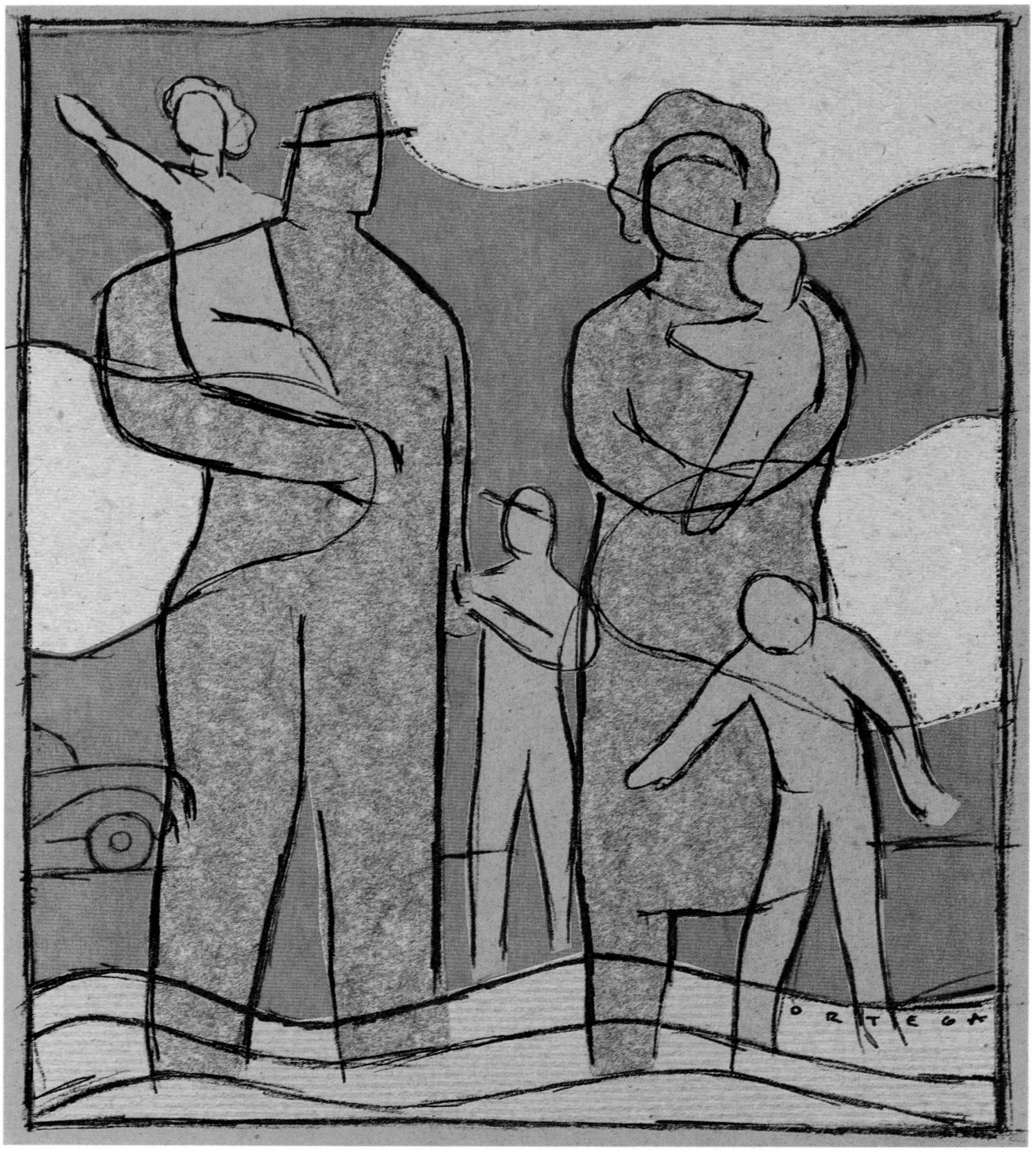

José Ortega

Art Director) Jessica Helfand Editor) Avery Rome Writer) Louis J. Rodriguez Publication) Philadelphia Inquirer Magazine Date) February 21, 1993 Publisher) Knight-Ridder Medium) Pencil, copier and cut paper This illustration accompanied the article "Trapped in the Land of the Free," about a Mexican family and their experiences in the United States.

Art Director) Sarah Stearns Editor) William Inman Writer) Douglas C. McGill Publication) Bloomberg Magazine
Date) November 1992 Publisher) Michael Bloomberg Publishing Medium) Ink and watercolor
"Japan's Newest Invention" was the title of an article featuring this image.

Philippe Lardy

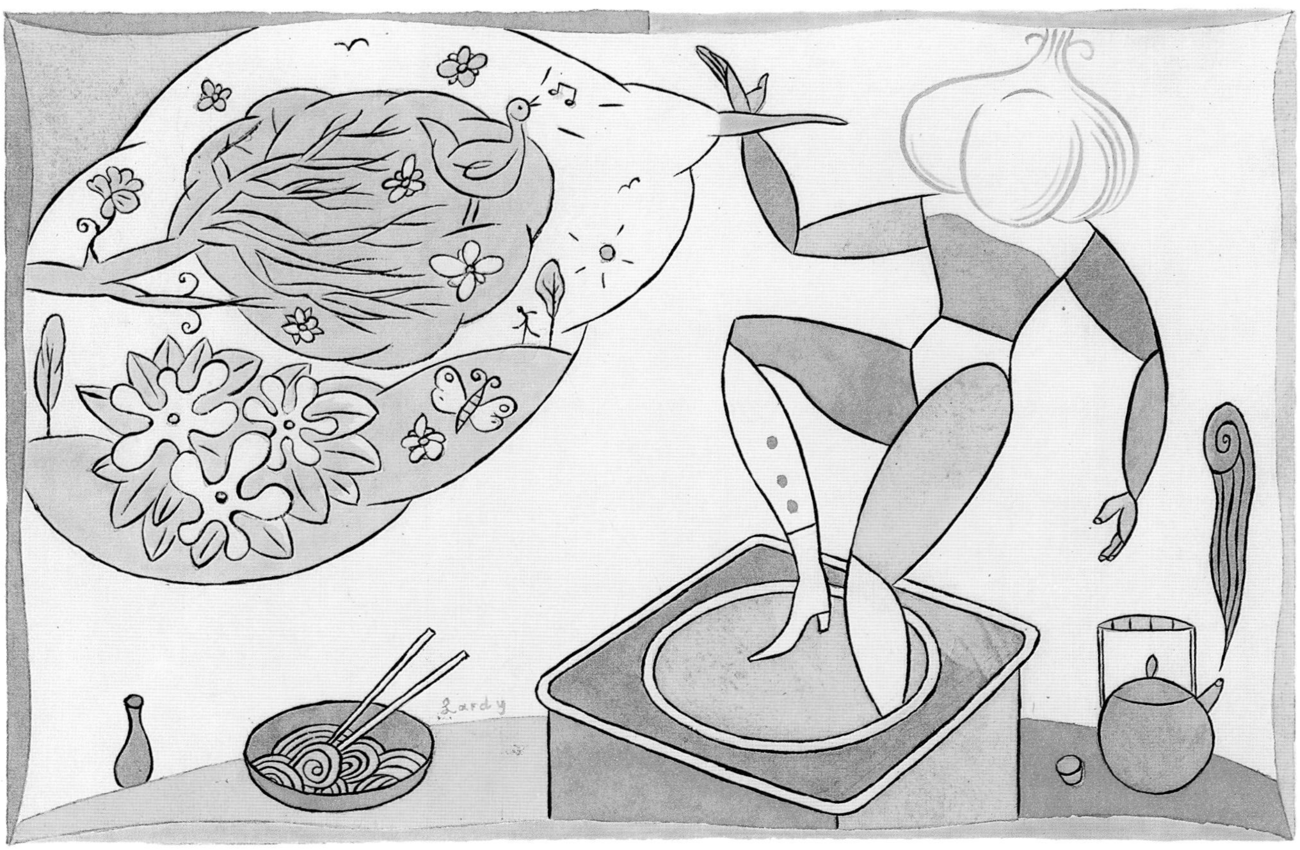

Art Director) Mark Koudys Editor) Betty Ewing-Pearse Publication) Digital News Date) Spring 1993
Publisher) Digital Equipment of Canada, Ltd. Medium) Pen and ink, watercolor, and collage
This illustration charts the evolution of the business enterprise, from supplier to business partner.

Barry Blitt

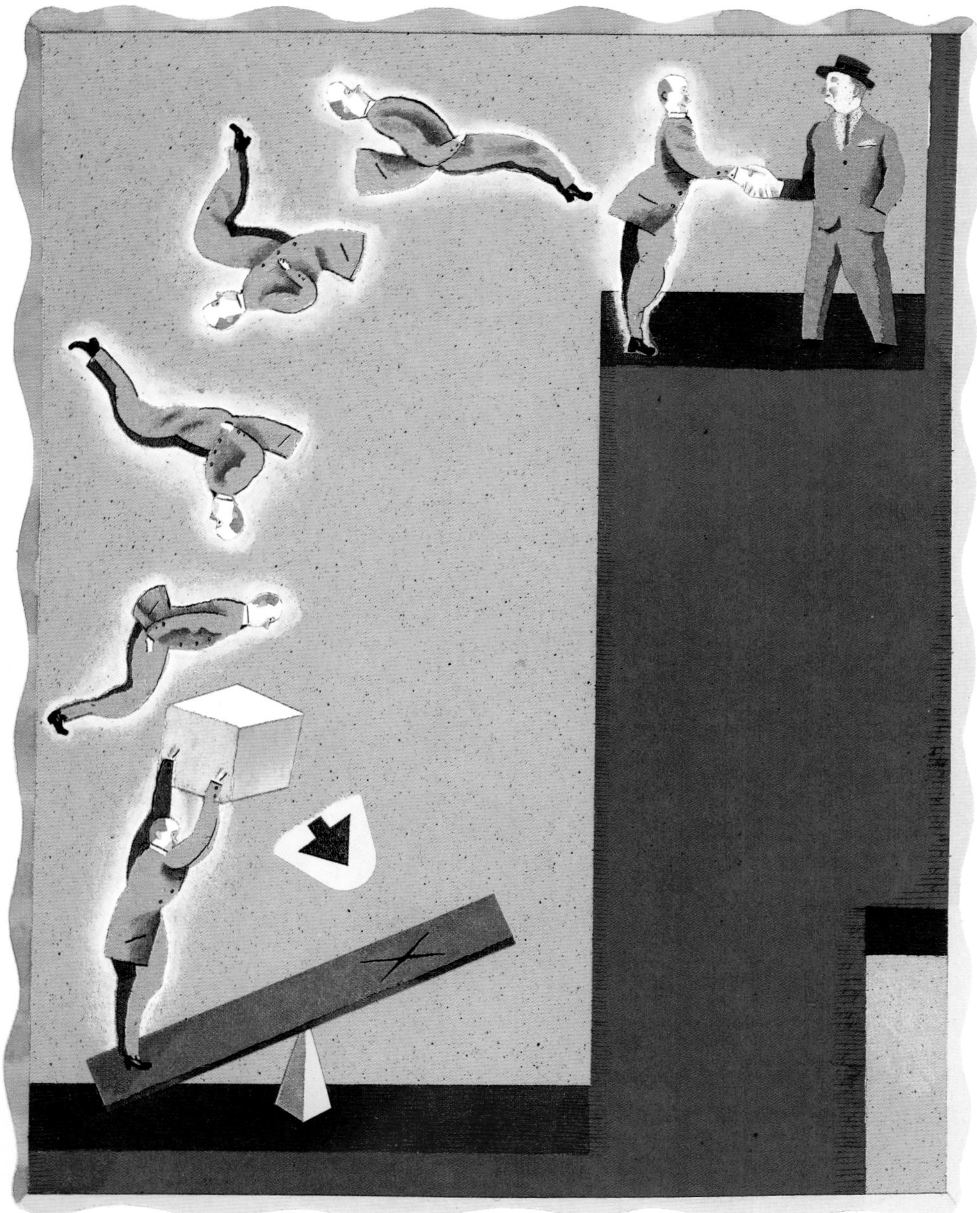

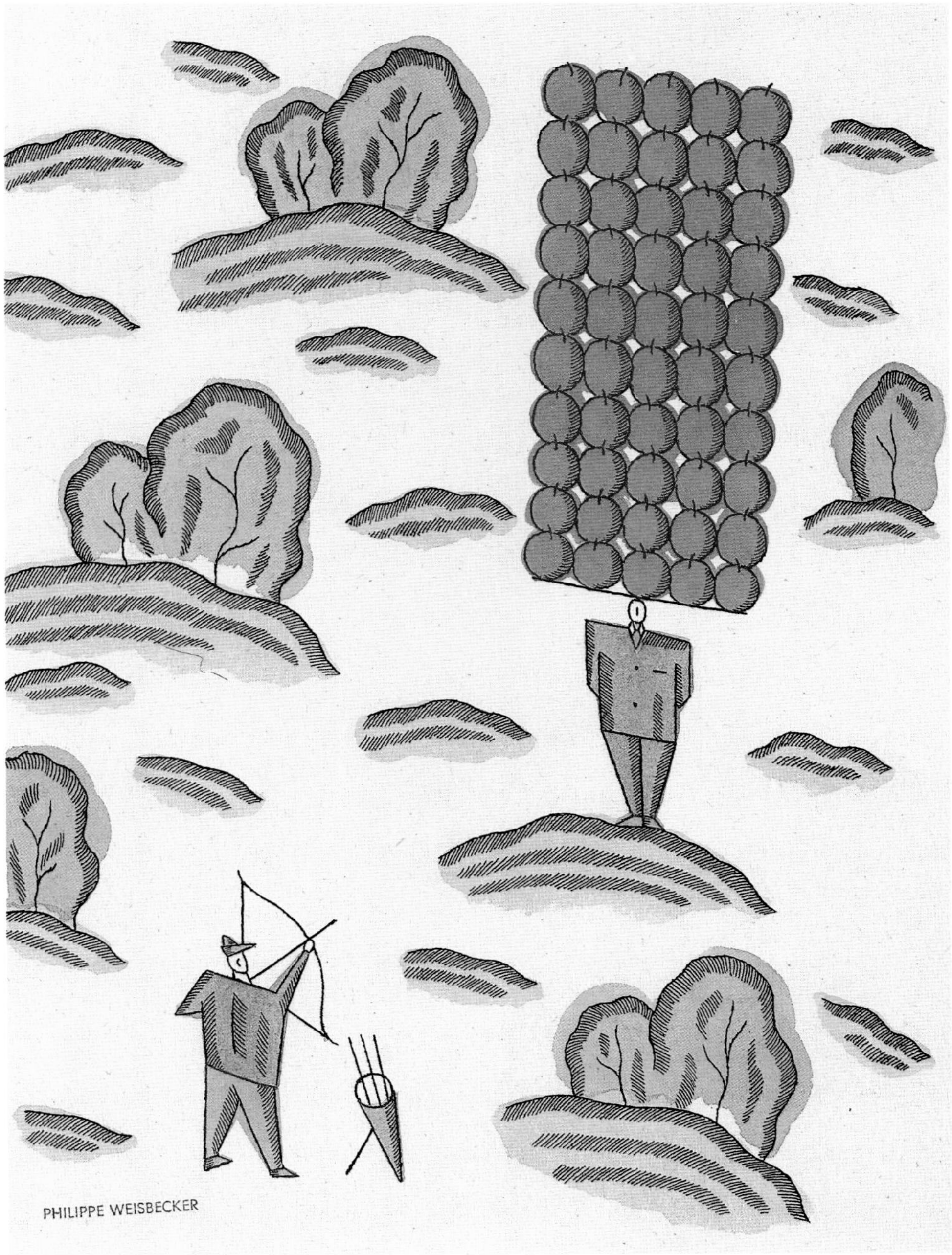

Philippe Weisbecker

Art Director) Chris Sloane Writer) Dan Moreau Publication) Kiplinger's Personal Finance Magazine Date) June 1992
Publisher) Kiplinger Washington Editors Medium) Watercolor The article "Investments That Won't Let You Down" featured this illustration.

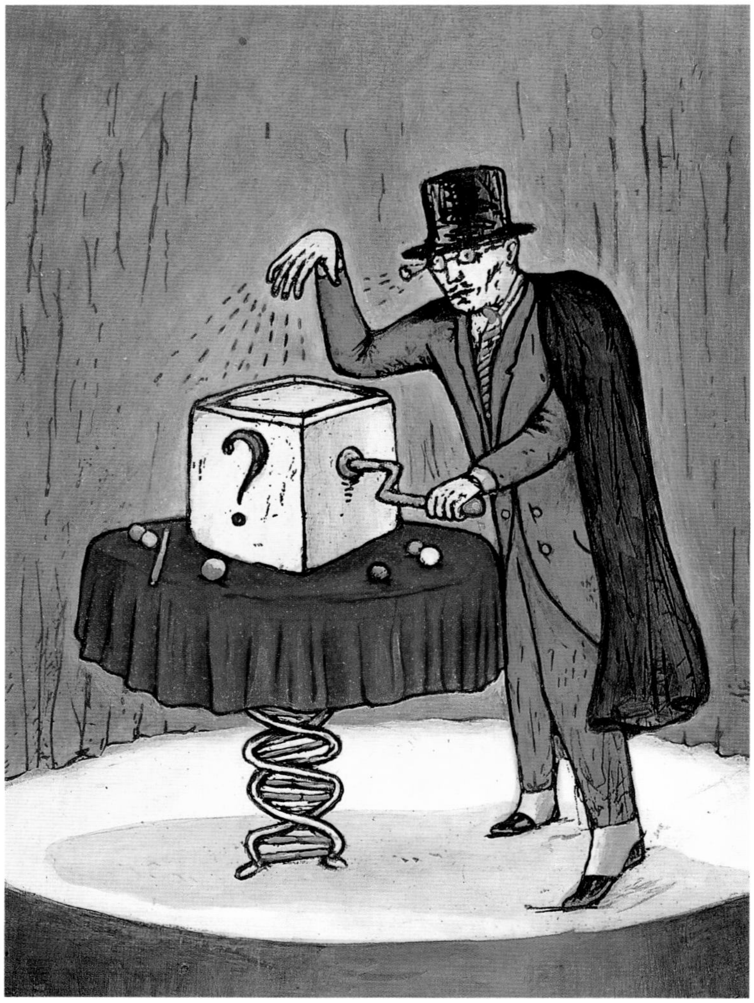

Jonathon Rosen

Art Directors) David Armario and James Lambertus **Editors) Paul Hoffman** and Patricia Gadsby Writer) Jerold M. Lowenstein
Publication) Discover Magazine Date) December 1992 **Publisher) Disney Magazine** Publishing, Inc. Medium) Acrylic and pen and ink
The seriously weird things that are popping out of our DNA were discussed in "Genetic Surprises," which featured these two illustrations.

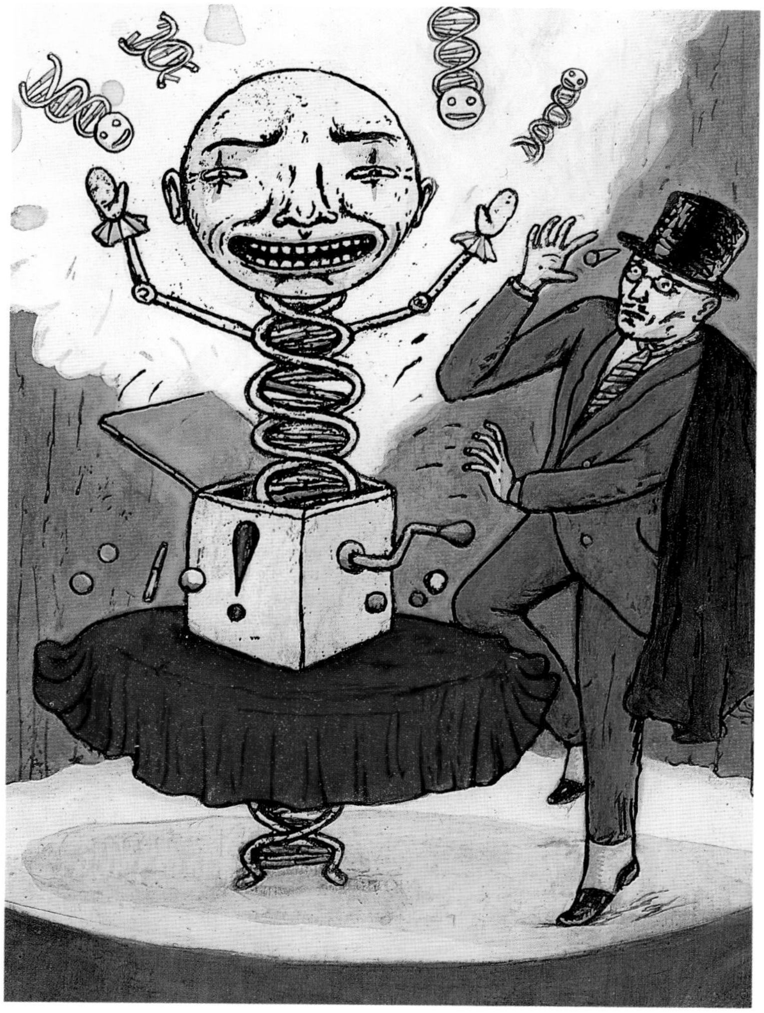

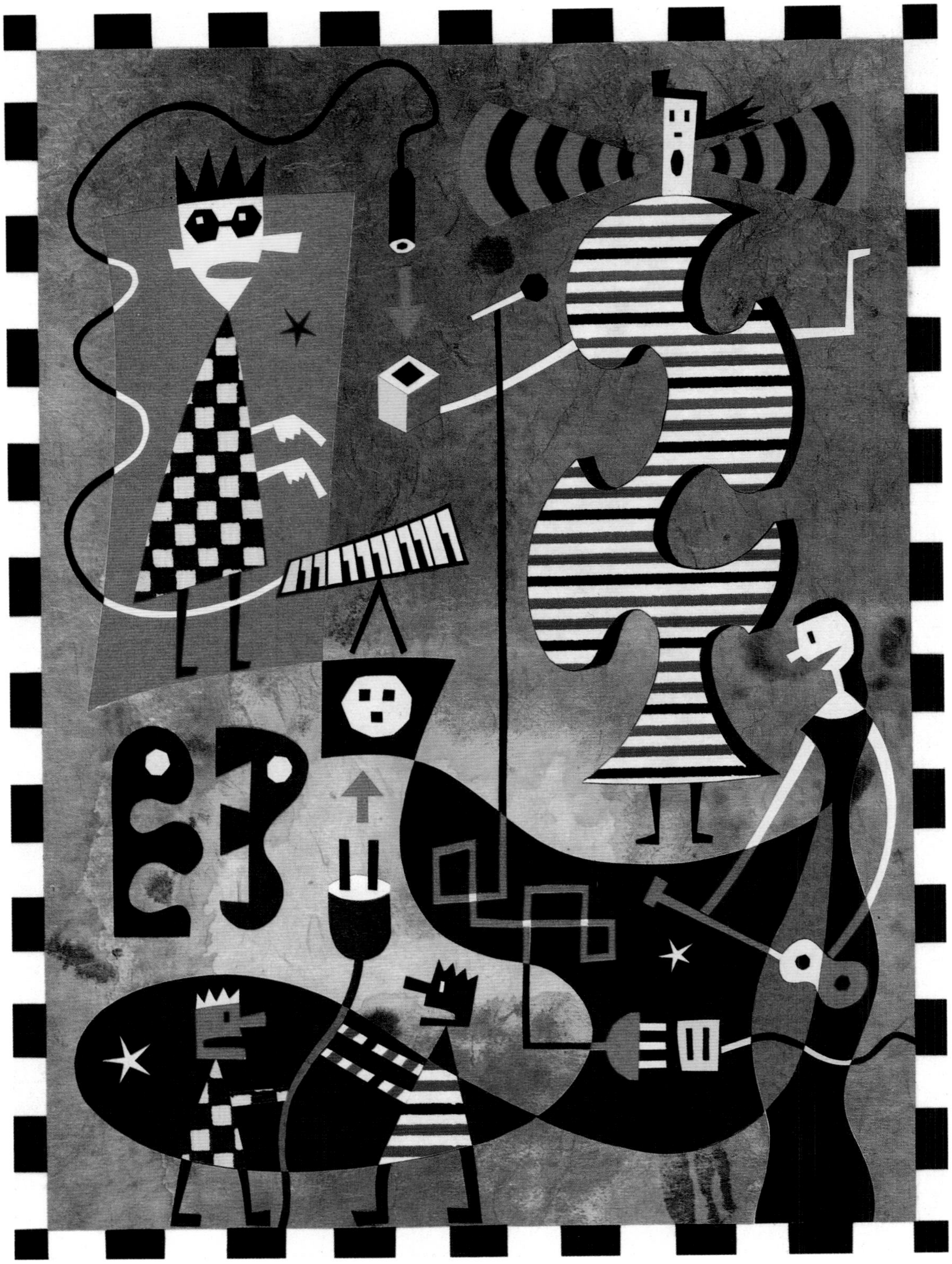

Michael Bartalos

Art Director) Linda Birch Editor) Bob O'Donnell Writers) Larry Oppenheimer and Scott Wilkinson Publication) Electronic Musician Date) March 1993 Publisher) Act III Publishing Medium) Cut paper This illustration was created for the article "The Digital Puzzle."

Art Director) **Cindy Hoffman** Editor) **Gail Ravgiala** Writer) **Ellen Steinbaum** Publication) **The Boston Globe**
Date) April 25, 1993 **Publisher) Affiliated Publications, Inc.** **Medium) Mixed media** **"The Resilient Ones,"** an article examining the factors **that allow children to survive dysfunctional upbringings,** was accompanied by this illustration.

Steven Guarnaccia

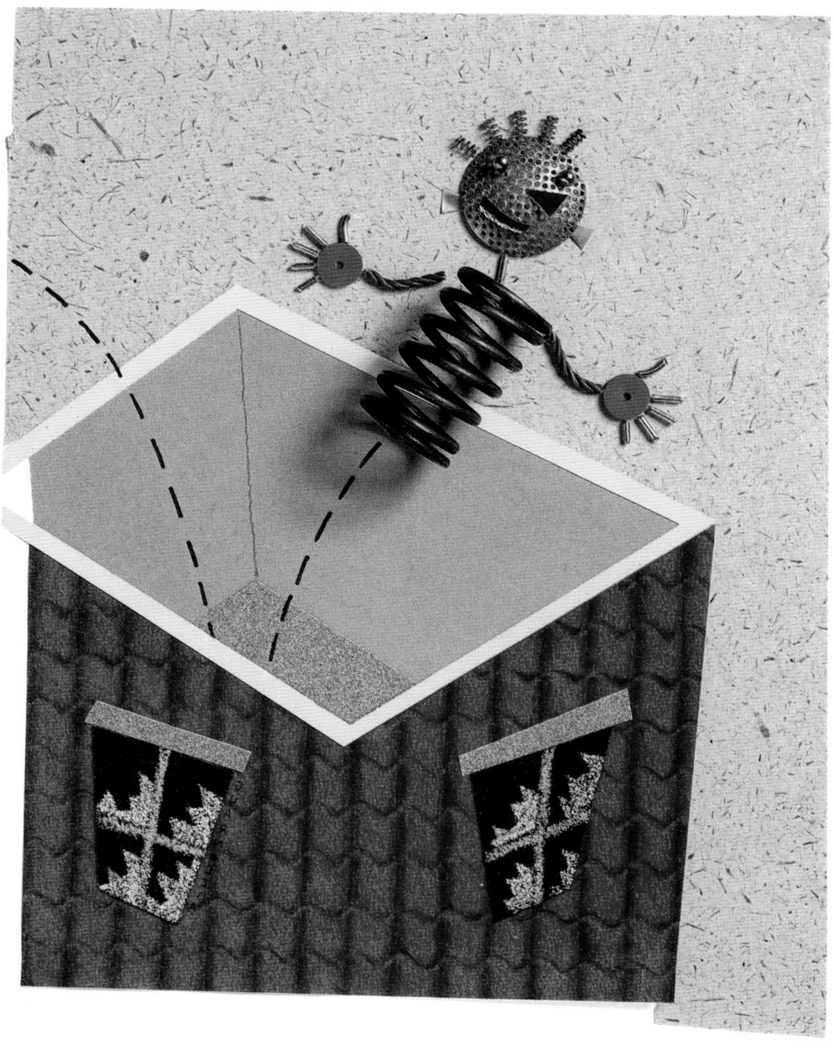

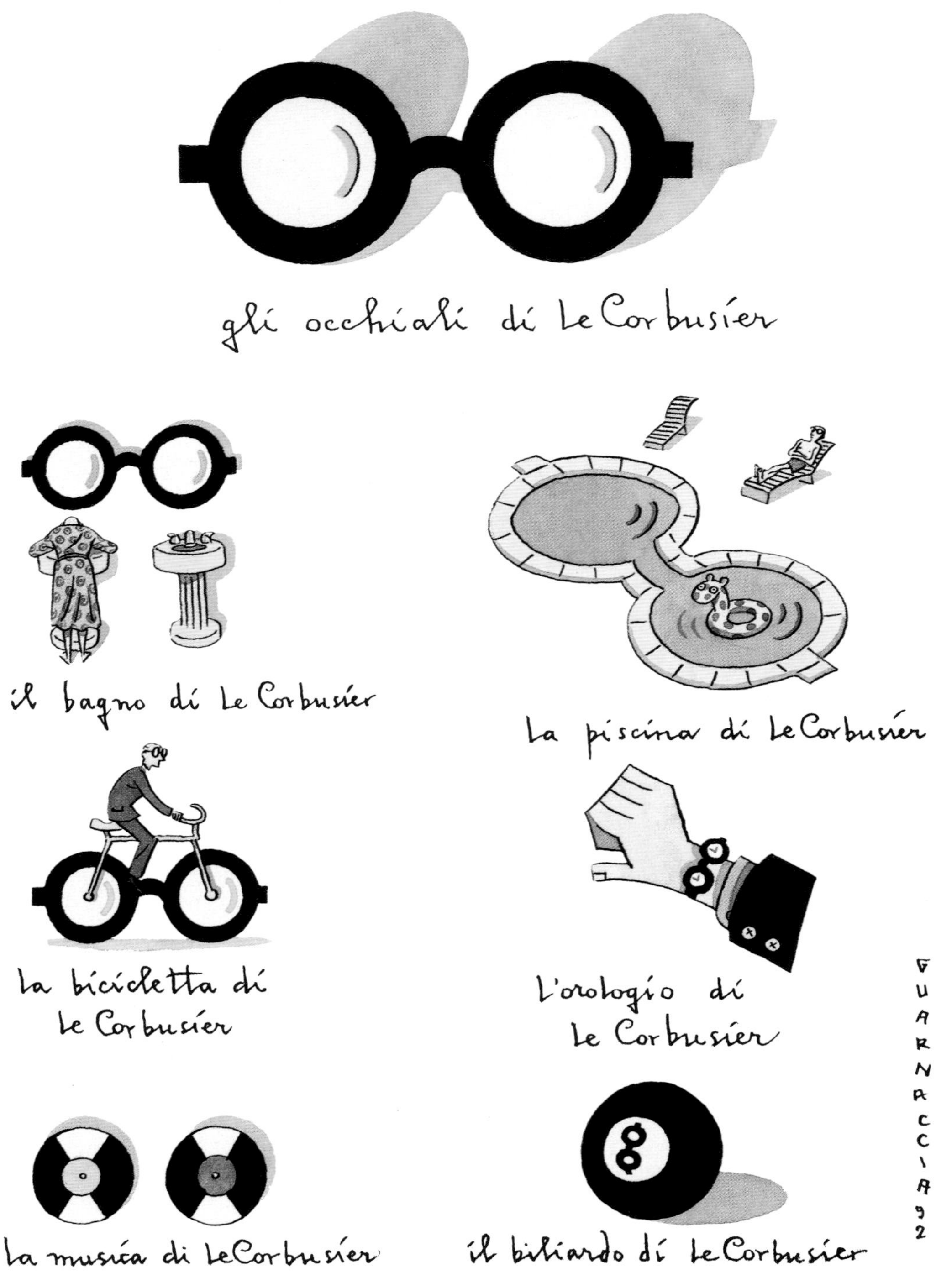

Steven Guarnaccia

Art Director) Silvia Latis Editor) Renato Minetto Publication) Abitare Date) May 1992 Publisher) Abitare Segesta Medium) Ink and water
This illustration, entitled "Le Corbusier's Eyeglasses," was commissioned for an Italian magazine.

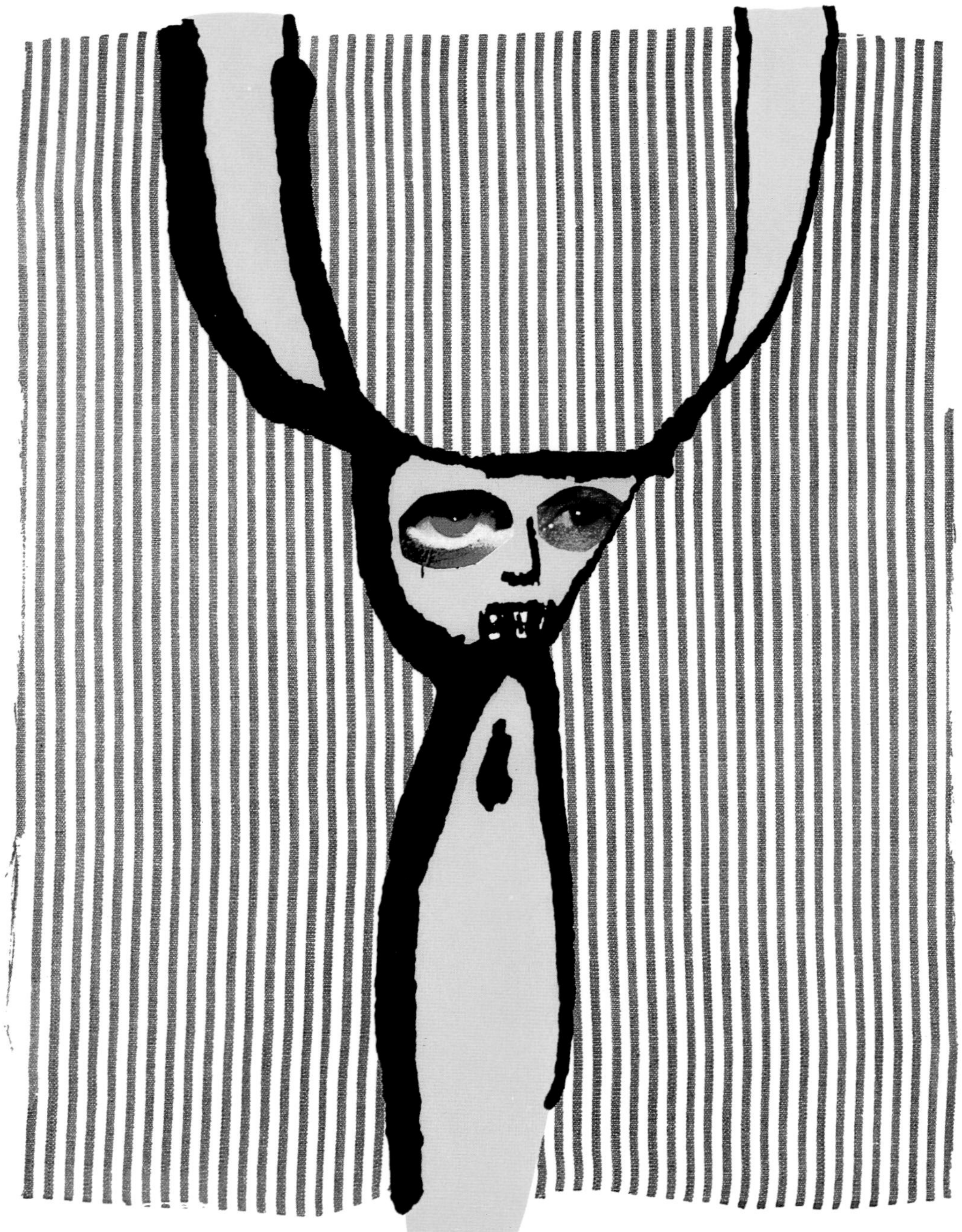

Scott Menchin

Art Director) Richard Baker Designer) Kelly Doe Editor) Bob Thompson Writer) Susan Cohen
Publication) The Washington Post Magazine Date) January 1993 Publisher) The Washington Post Company
Medium) Ink and collage "Tie Guy" accompanied the article entitled "White Collar Blues."

Art Director) Kate Thompson Writer) Henry Louis Gates Jr. Publication) The Village Voice Date) October 20, 1992 Publisher) VV Publishing Corporation Medium) Ink This illustration accompanied the article "Memoirs of an Anti-Anti-Semite."

Scott Menchin

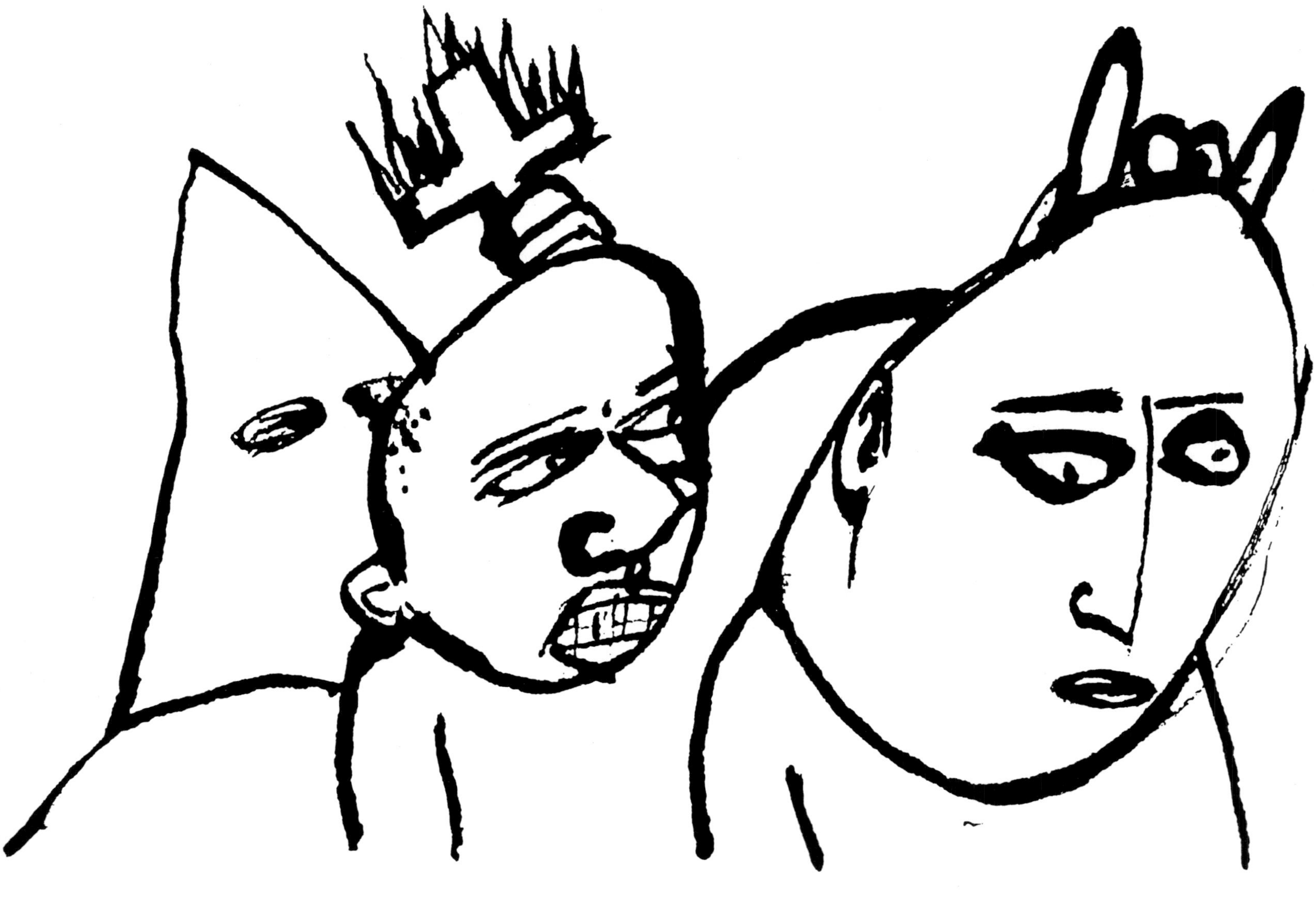

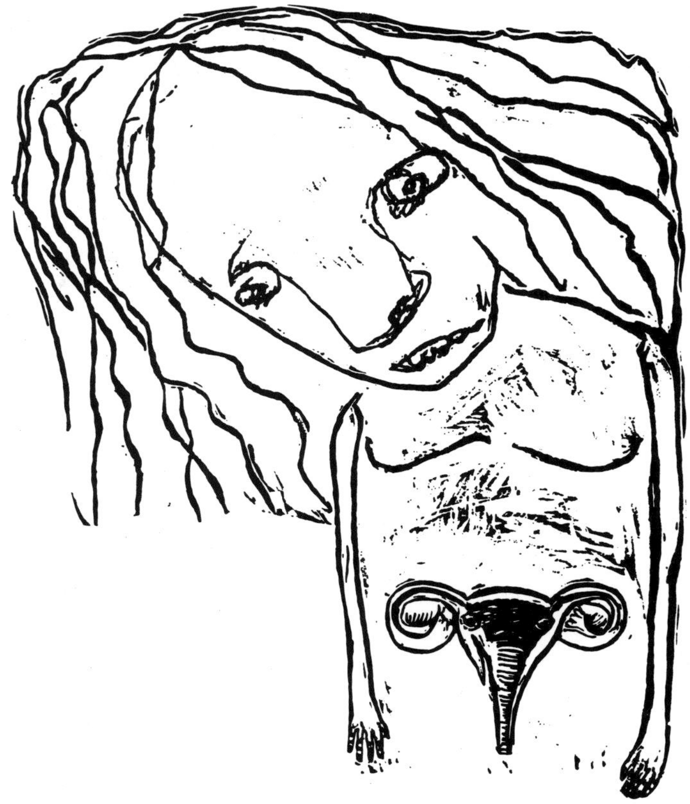

Frances Jetter

Art Director) Jennifer Gilman Writer) Elizabeth Ho Publication) The Village Voice Date) May 19, 1992 Publisher) VV Publishing Corporation Medium) Linoleum cut The debate over abortion rights was the subject of "Packaging Prochoice," which featured this illustration.

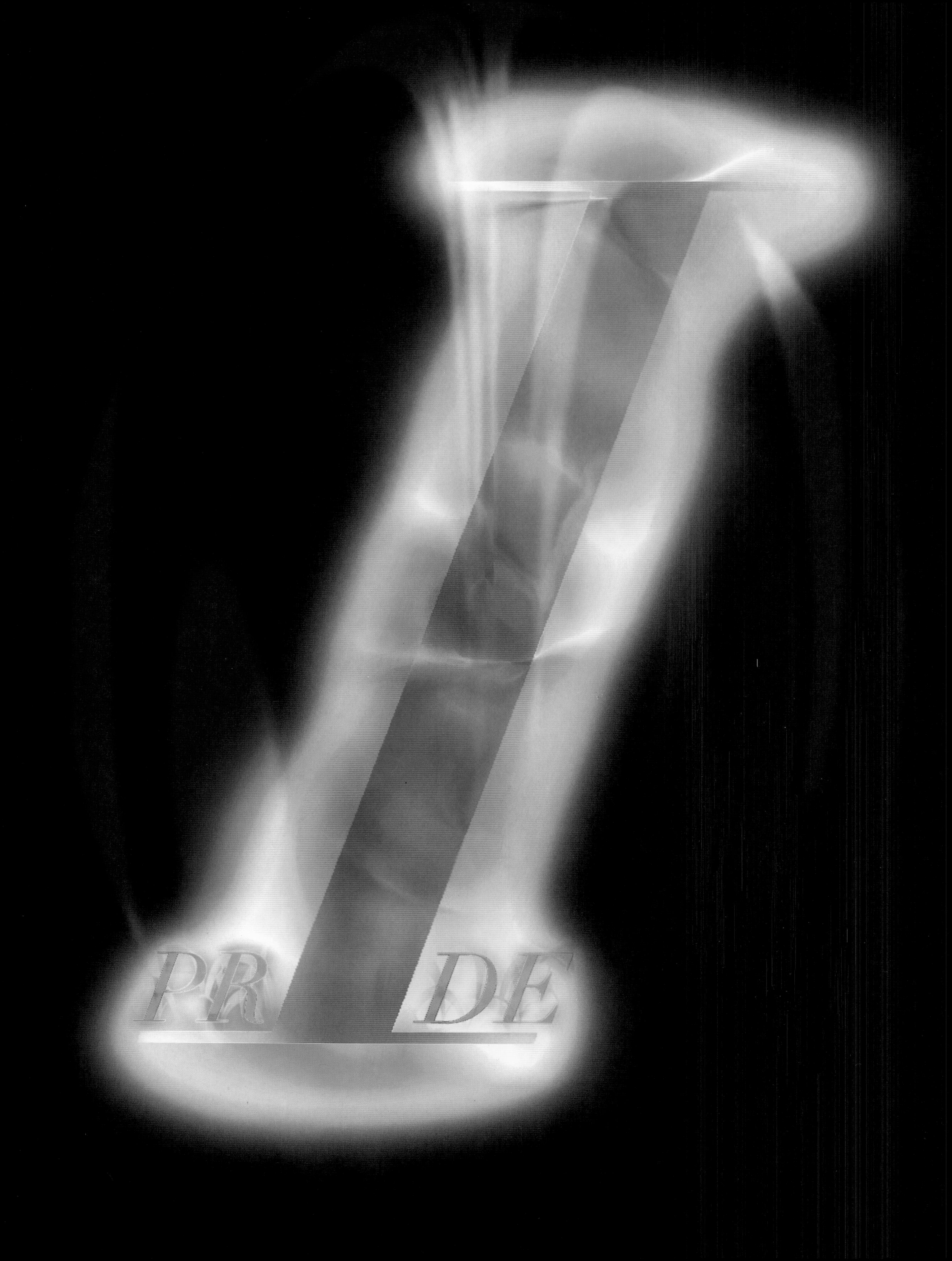
PRIDE

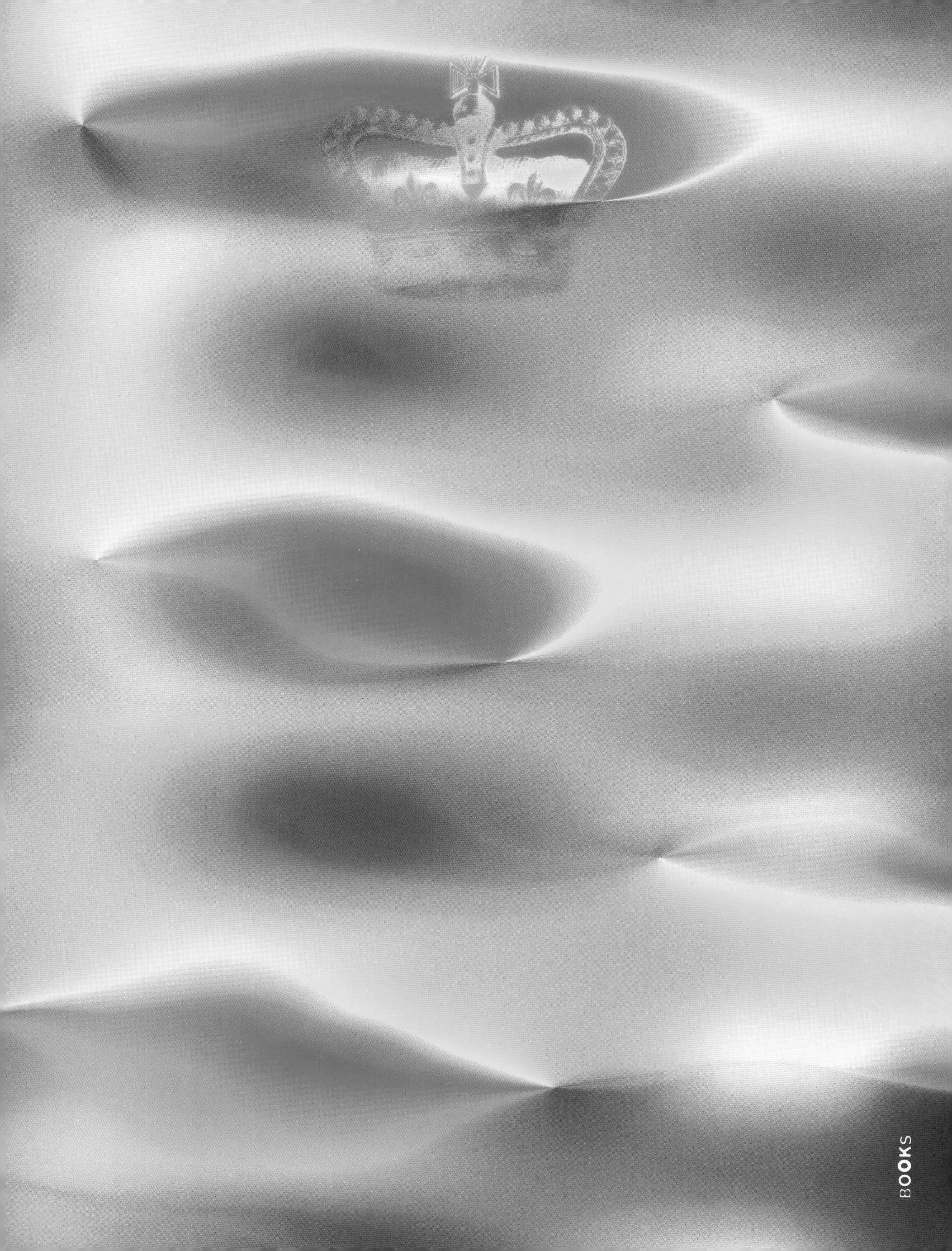
BOOKS

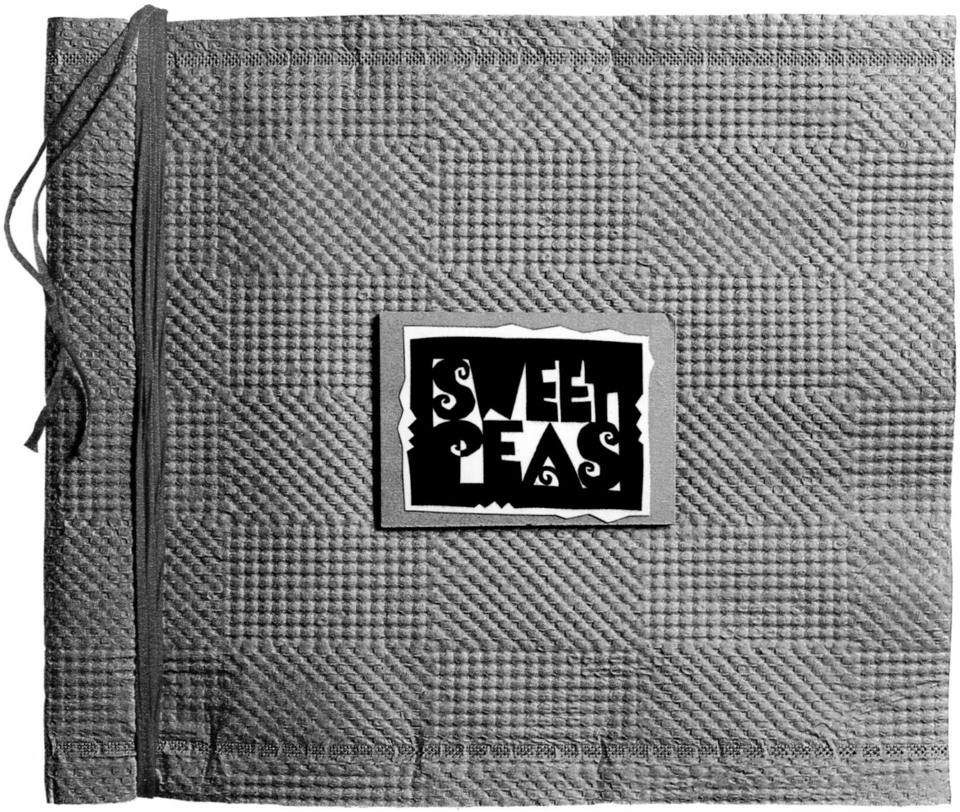

David Diaz

Art Director) Cecelia Diaz Designer) David Diaz Date) December 1992 Publisher) Icon Books Medium) Ink
This series of three-dimensional images was created for the book "Sweet Peas."

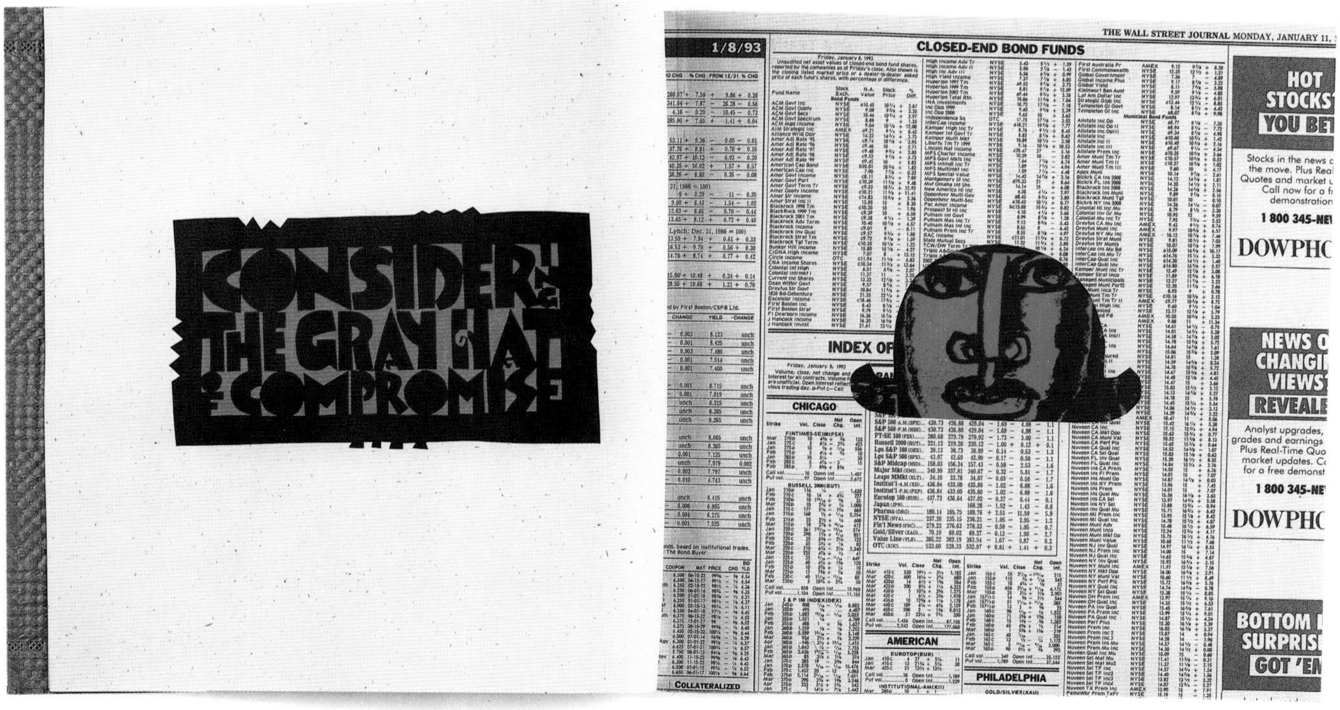
CONSIDER THE GRAY HAT OF COMPROMISE
THE WALL STREET JOURNAL MONDAY, JANUARY 11,
1/8/93
CLOSED-END BOND FUNDS
HOT STOCKS YOU BET
DOWPHO
INDEX OP
CHICAGO
AMERICAN
PHILADELPHIA
COLLATERALIZED
NEWS O CHANGI VIEWS REVEALE
1 800 345-NE
DOWPHO
BOTTOM SURPRISE GOT 'EM

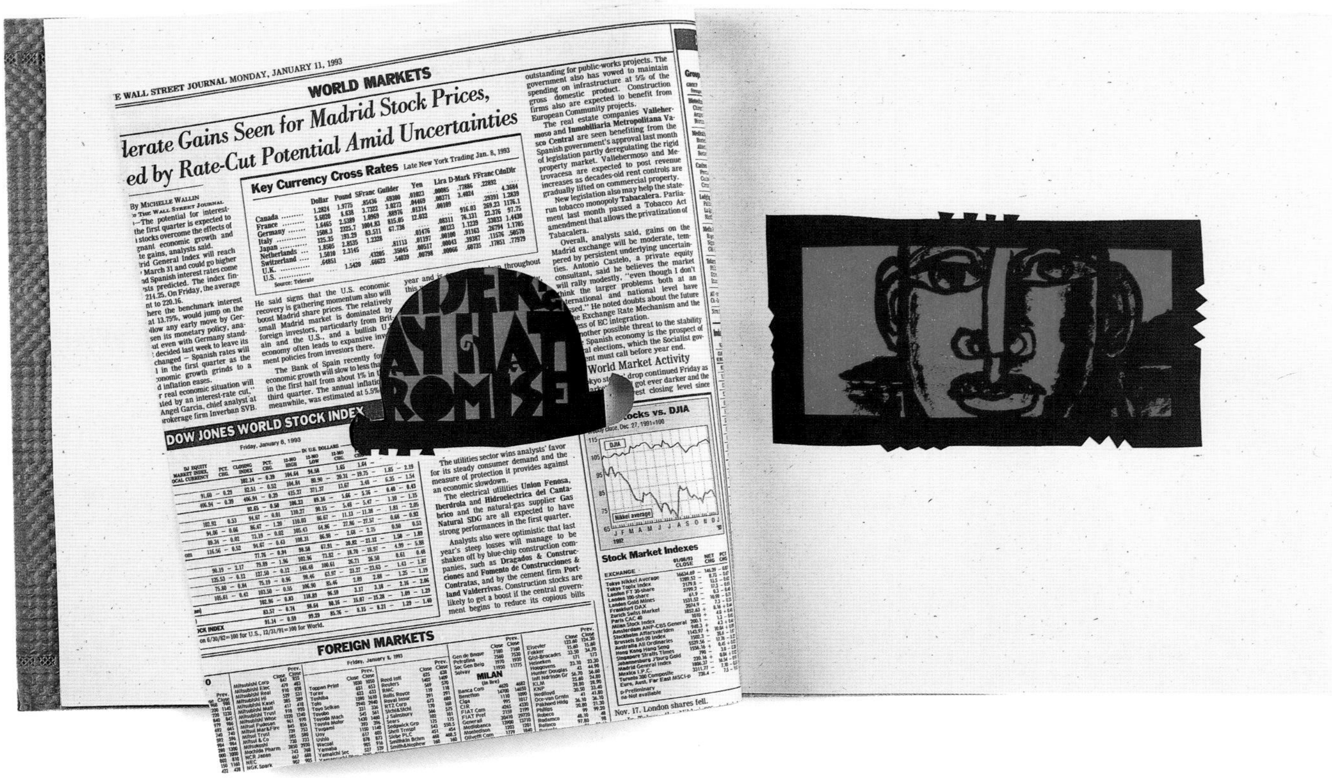
WALL STREET JOURNAL MONDAY, JANUARY 11, 1993
WORLD MARKETS
lerate Gains Seen for Madrid Stock Prices,
ed by Rate-Cut Potential Amid Uncertainties
Key Currency Cross Rates
DOW JONES WORLD STOCK INDEX
World Market Activity
Stock Market Indexes
FOREIGN MARKETS
MILAN

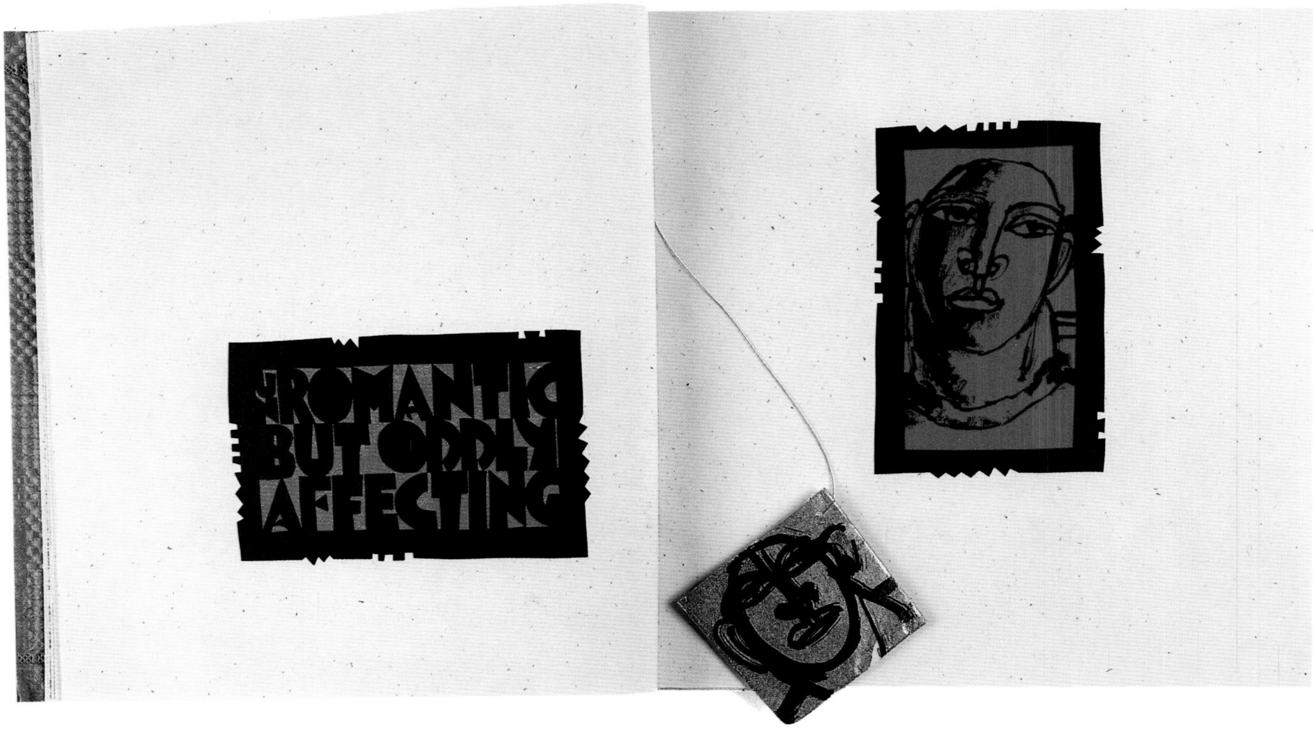
ROMANTIC
BUT ODDLY
AFFECTING

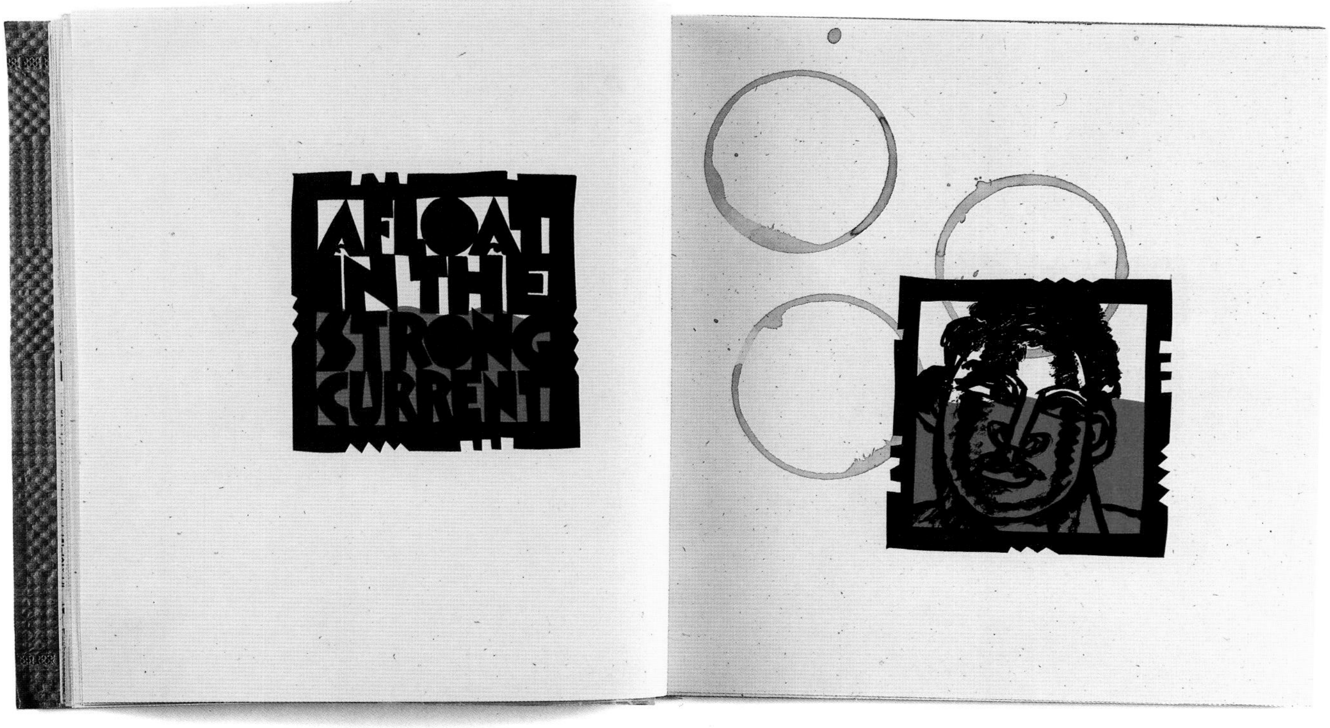
AFLOAT
IN THE
STRONG
CURRENT

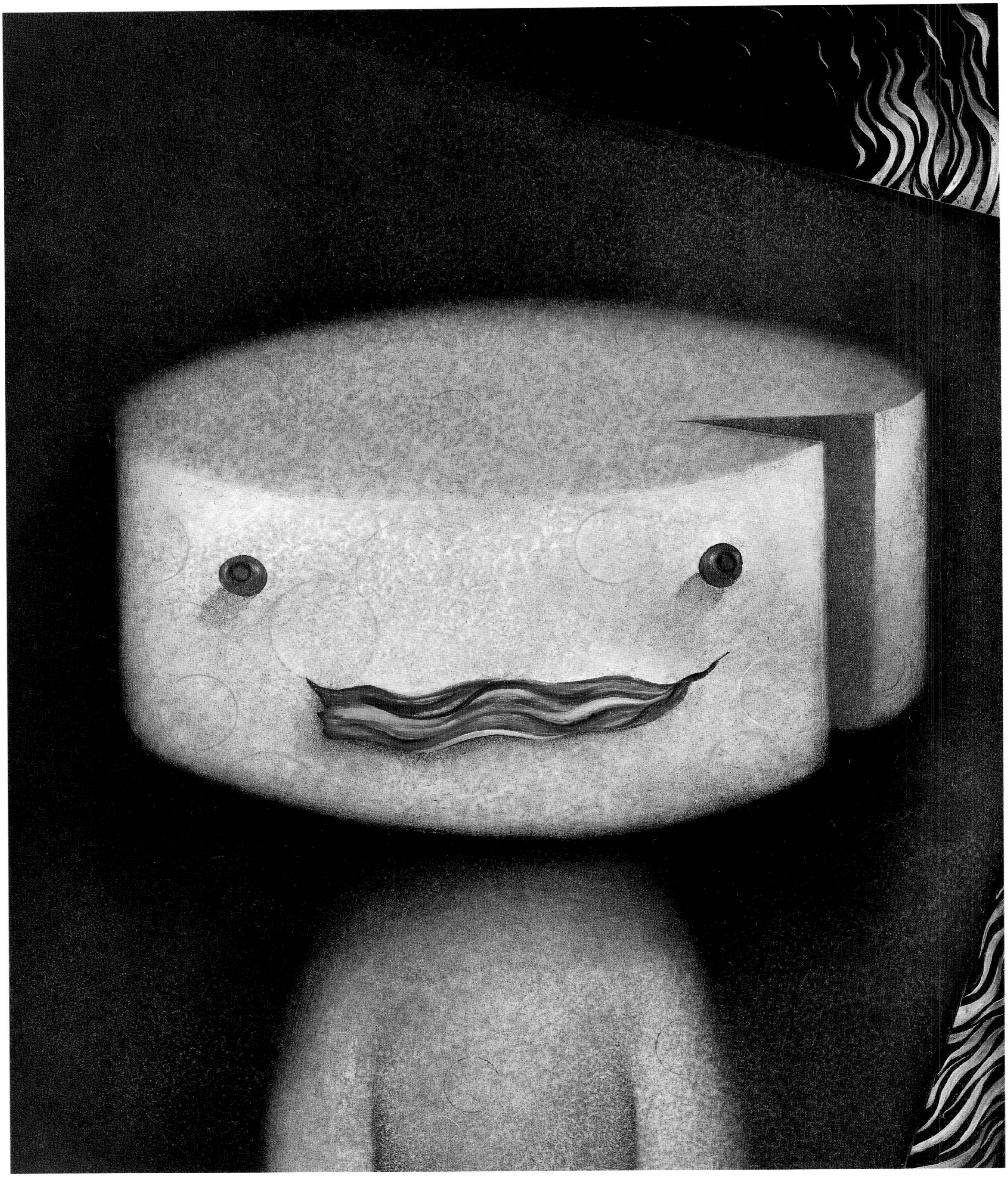

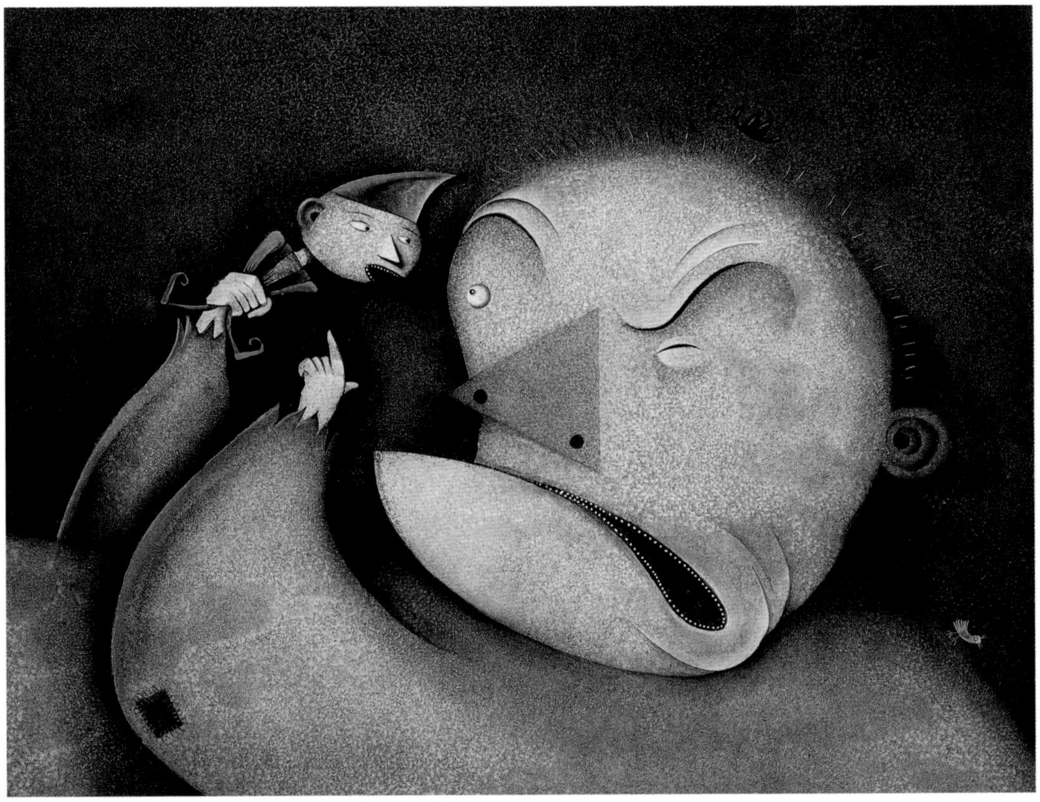

Lane Smith

Art Director) Molly Leach Editor) Regina Hayes Writer) **Jon Scieszka Date) 1993** Publisher) Viking Books Medium) Mixed media These four illustrations appear in the book **"The Stinky Cheese Man and Other Fairly Stupid Tales."** This one introduces "The Stinky Cheese Man" (left).

∞

"Jack's Story" (above).

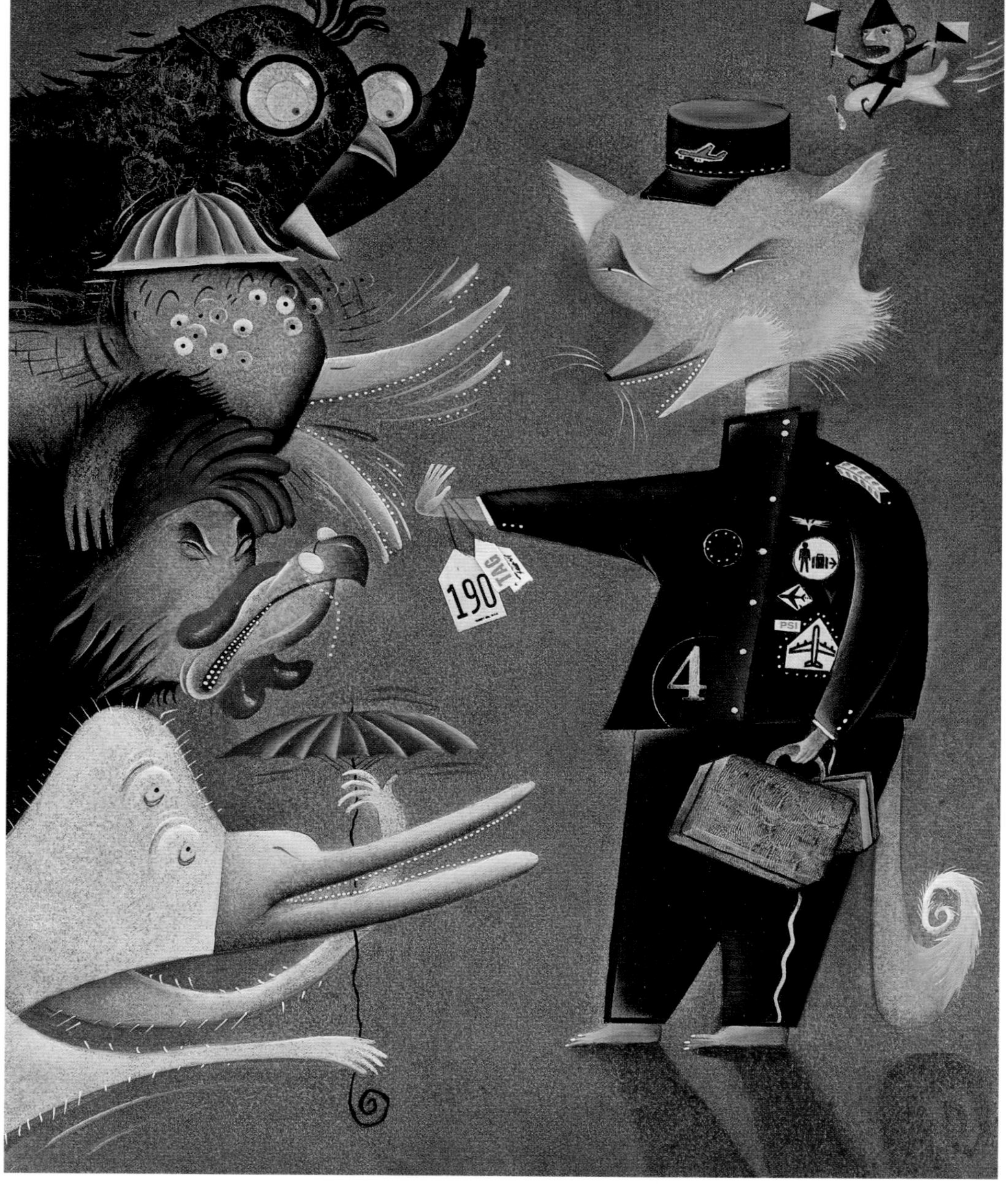

"Chicken Licken"

"The Really Ugly Duckling"

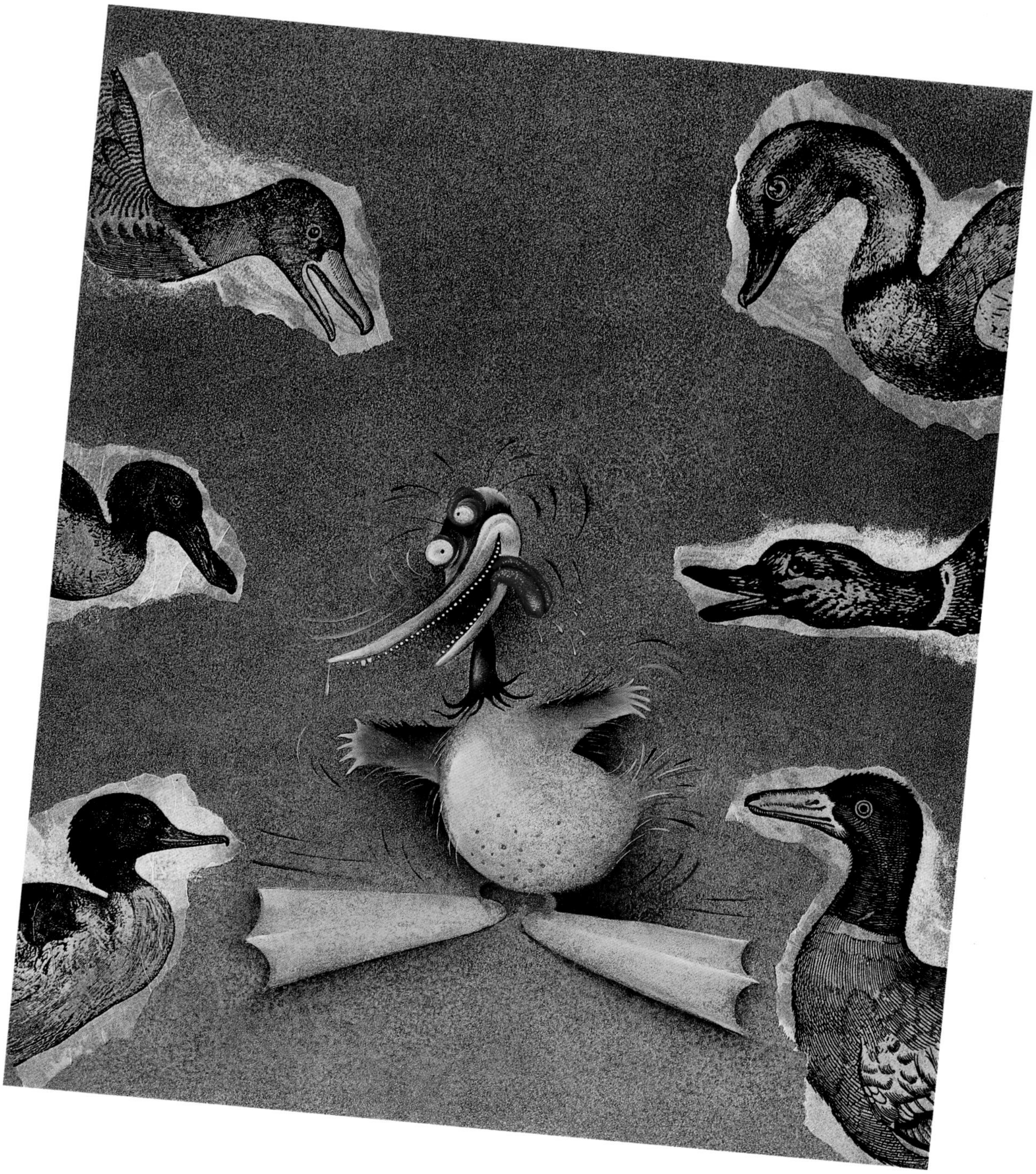

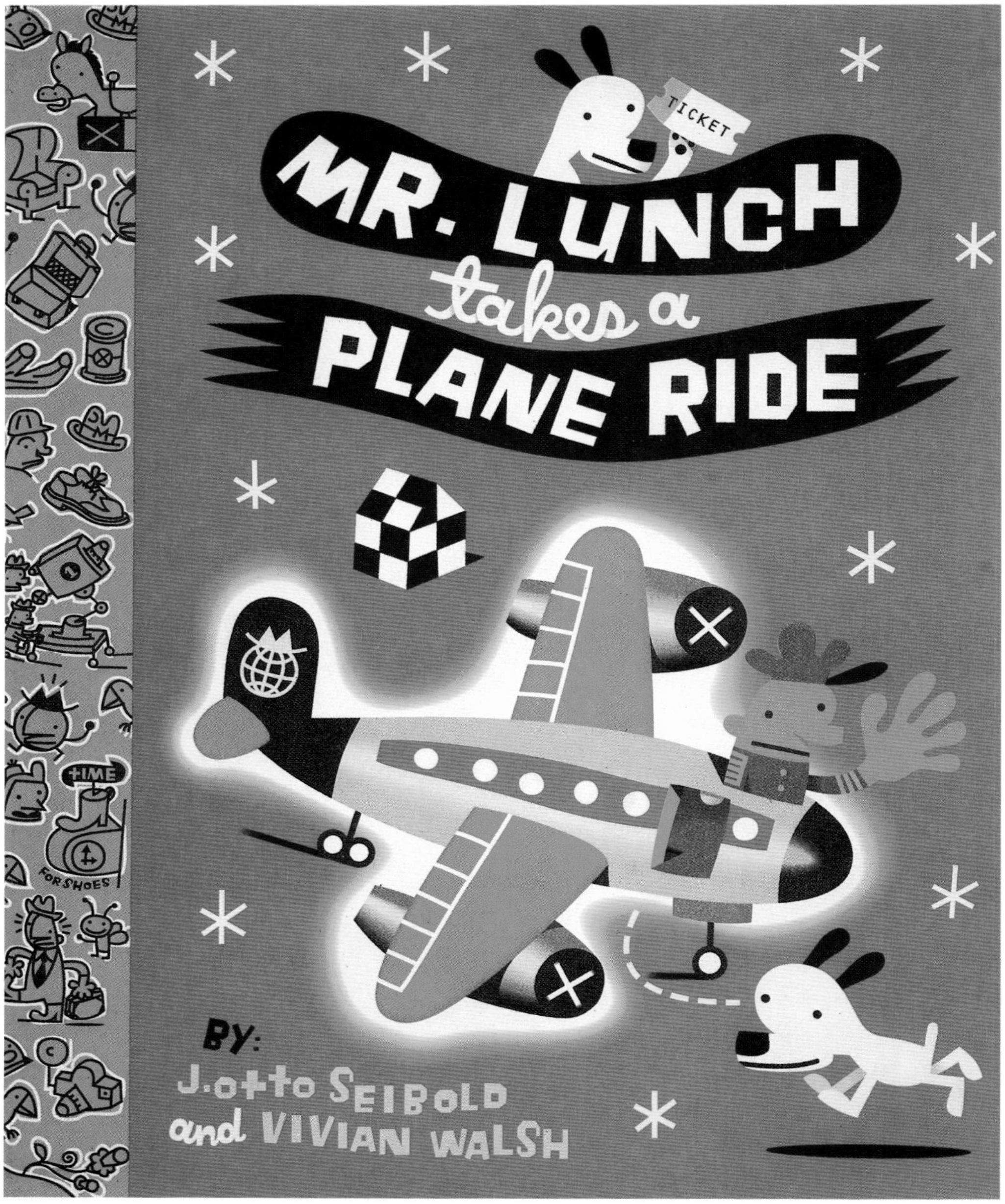

J. Otto Seibold

Writers) J. Otto Seibold and Vivian Walsh **Date) 1993 Publisher) Viking** Books Medium) Macintosh generated
The following illustrations appear **in the children's book** "Mr. Lunch Takes a Plane Ride."

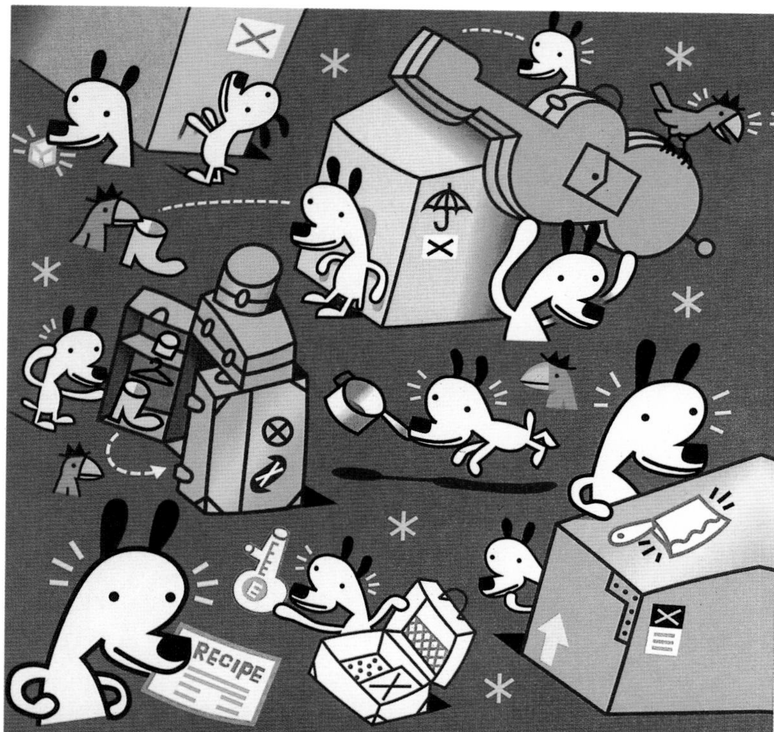

When Mr. Lunch woke up, he saw a terrible mess. If anyone else saw this his reputation could be ruined. With little time left he hurried to put things back, but it was hard to remember what went where.

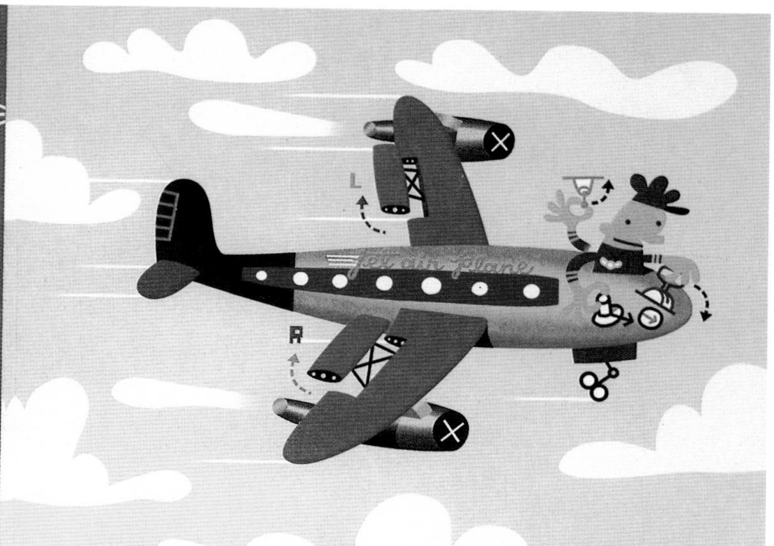

As the captain prepared for landing, Mr. Lunch forgot all about the bags. He realized that he would soon be on television.

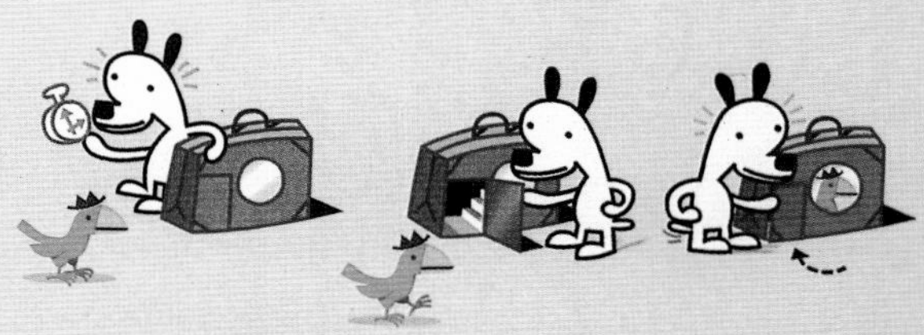

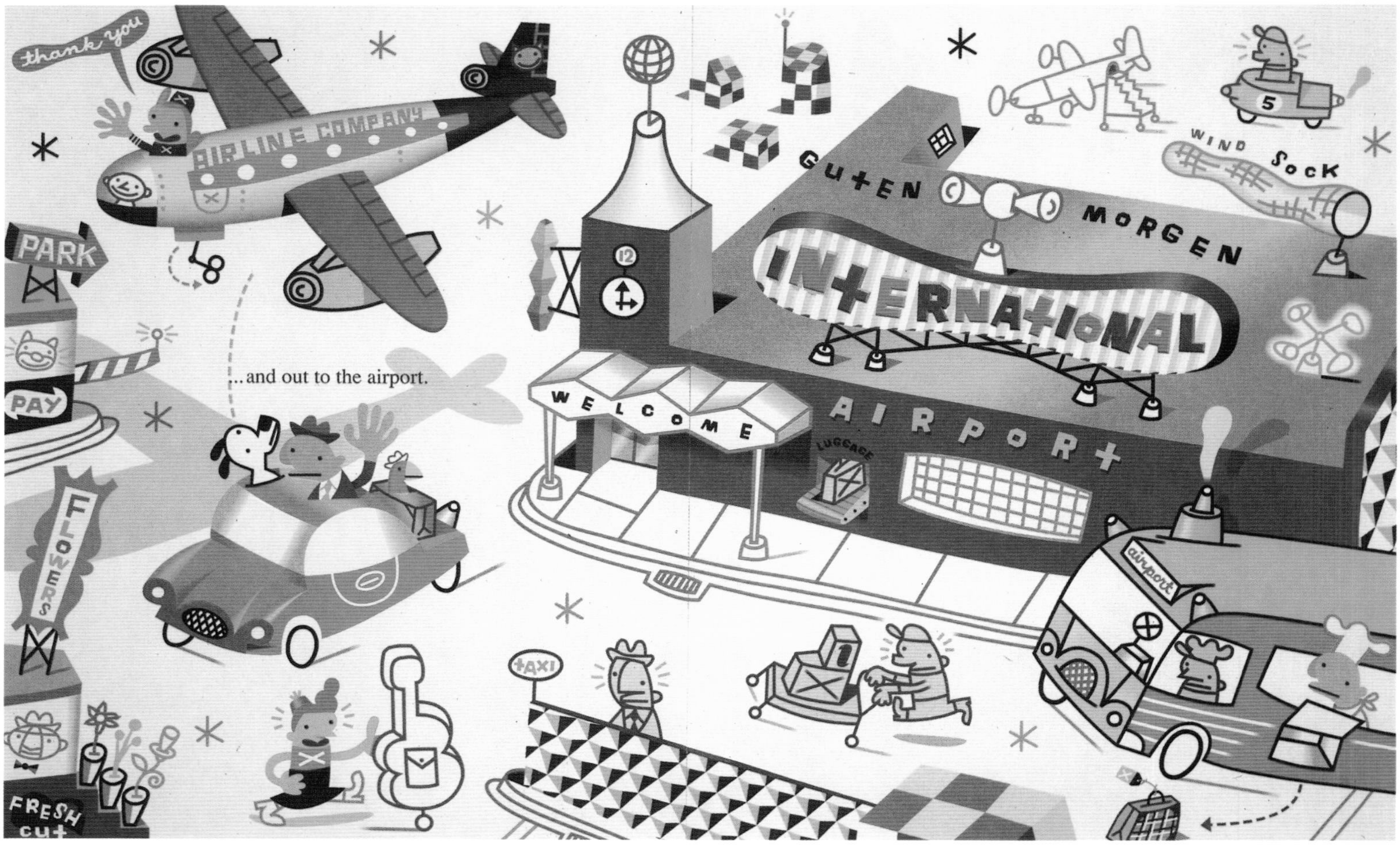

...and out to the airport.

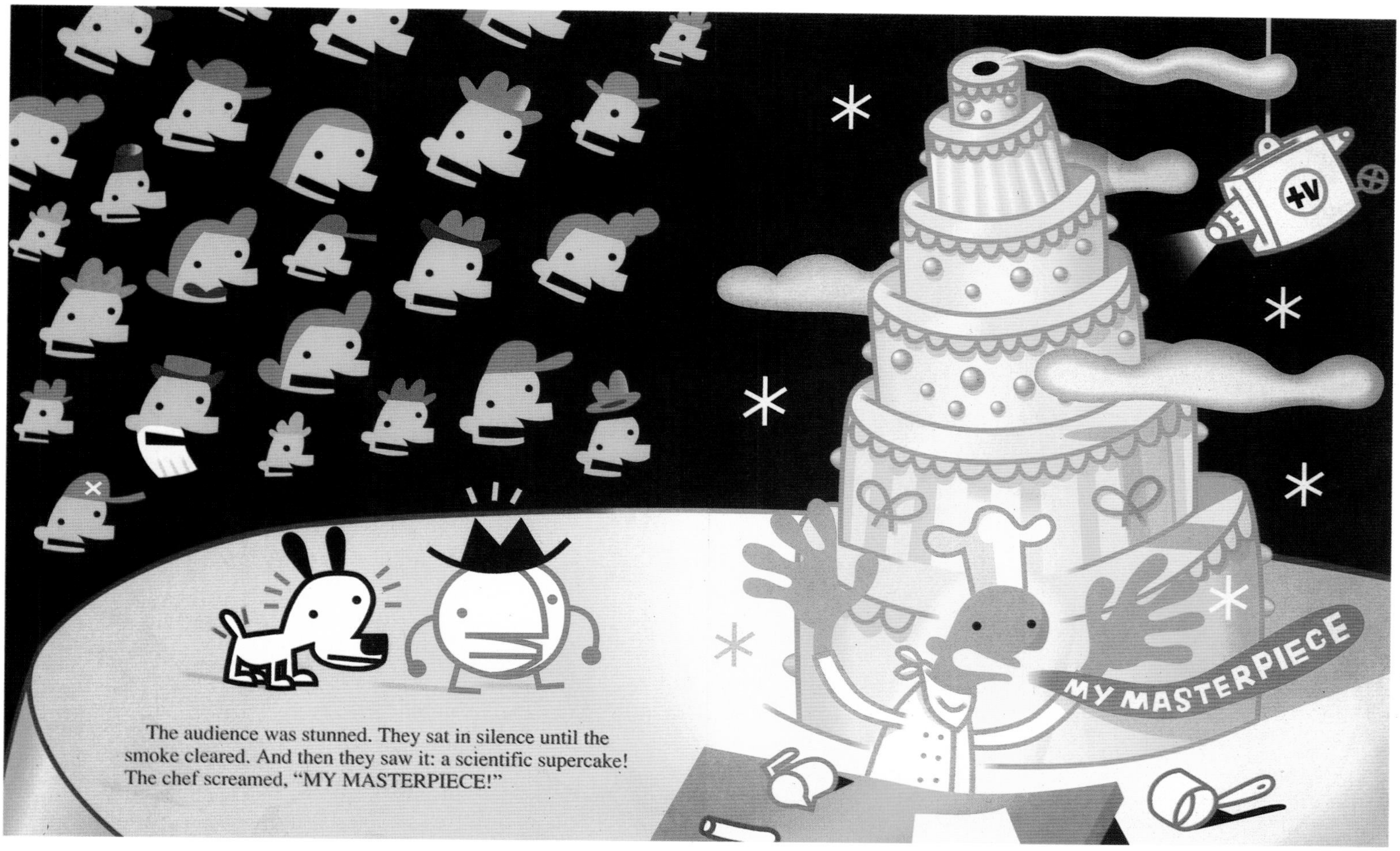

The audience was stunned. They sat in silence until the smoke cleared. And then they saw it: a scientific supercake! The chef screamed, "MY MASTERPIECE!"

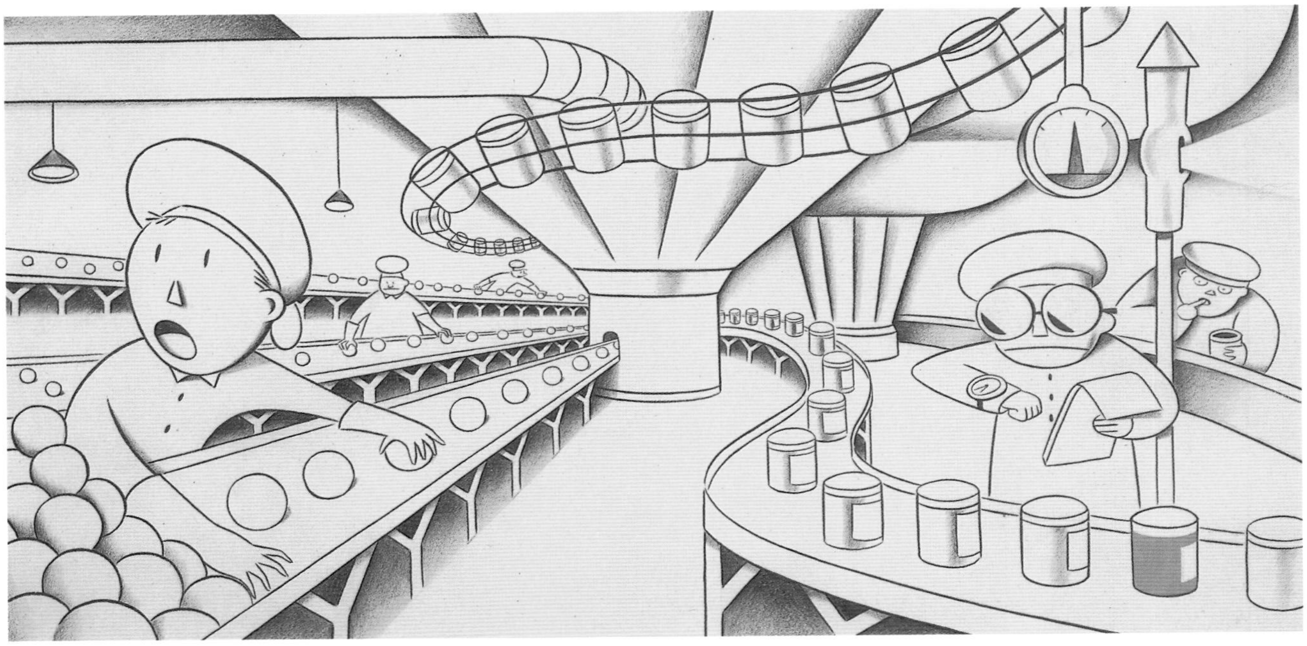

Richard McGuire

Editor) Howard Reeves Date) 1992 Publisher) Rizzoli International Publications, Inc. Medium) Gouache and pencil
This series of illustrations was created for the "Orange Book," which told the story of fourteen oranges after they had been picked and had gone their separate ways. This one's entitled "Six was used for marmalade."

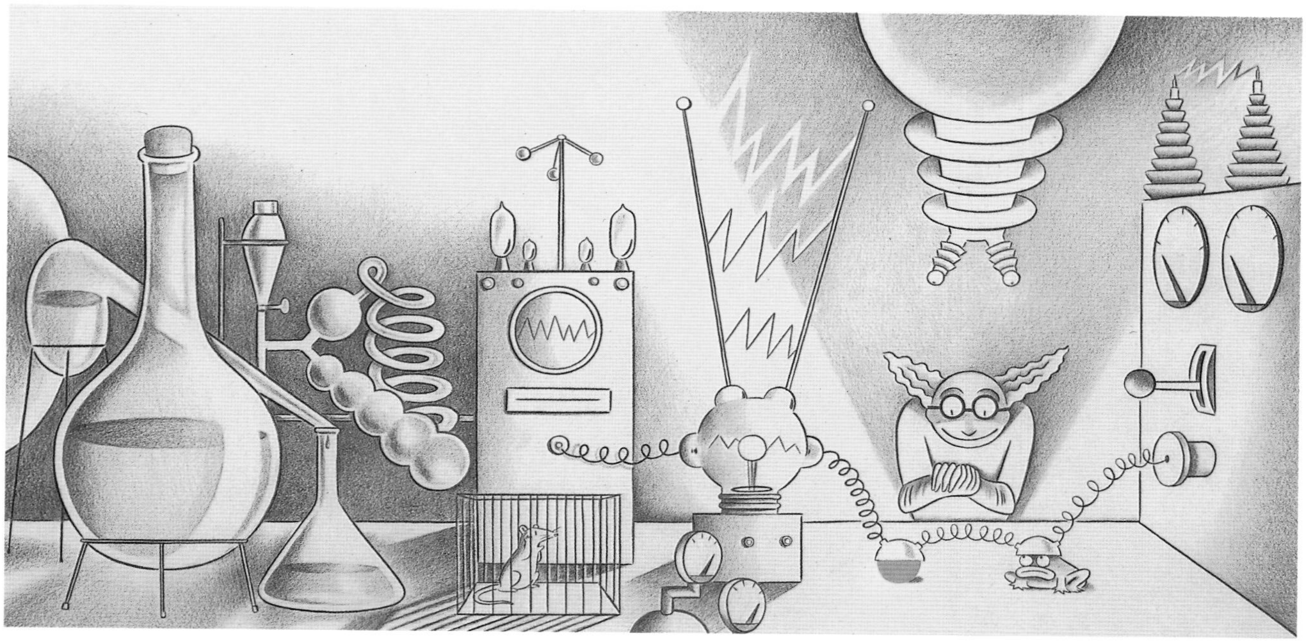

“Nine **was used in a strange experi**ment.”

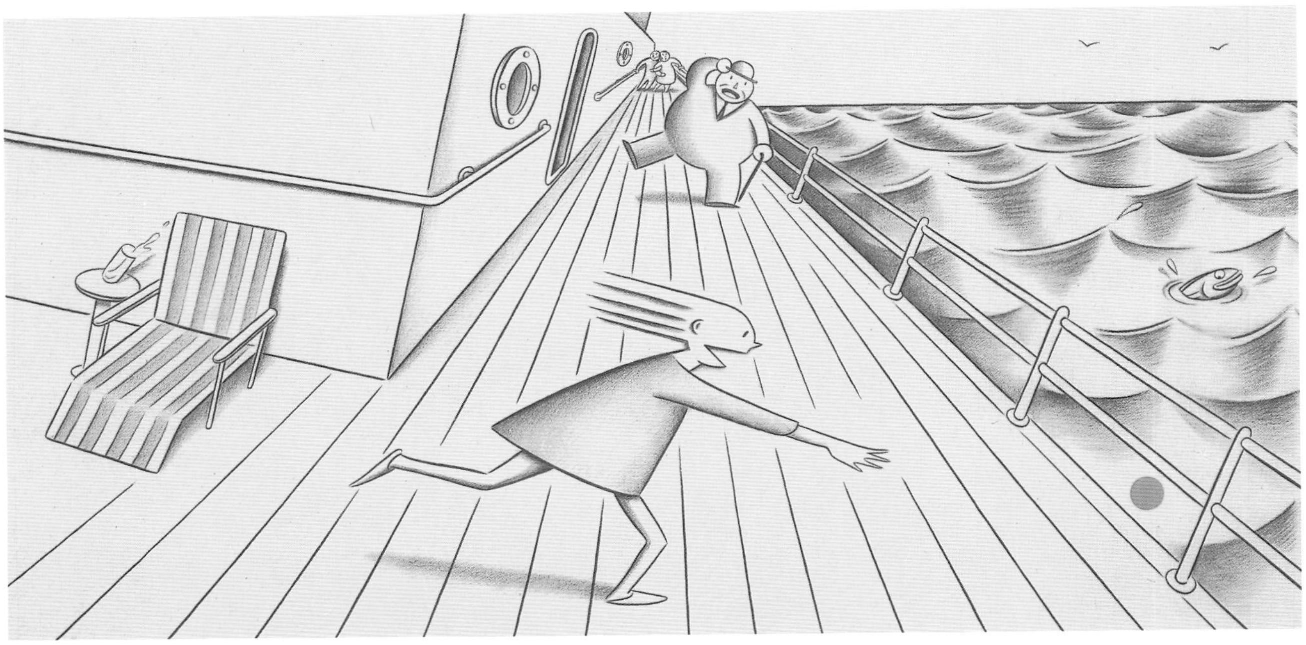

"Eight rolled overboard."

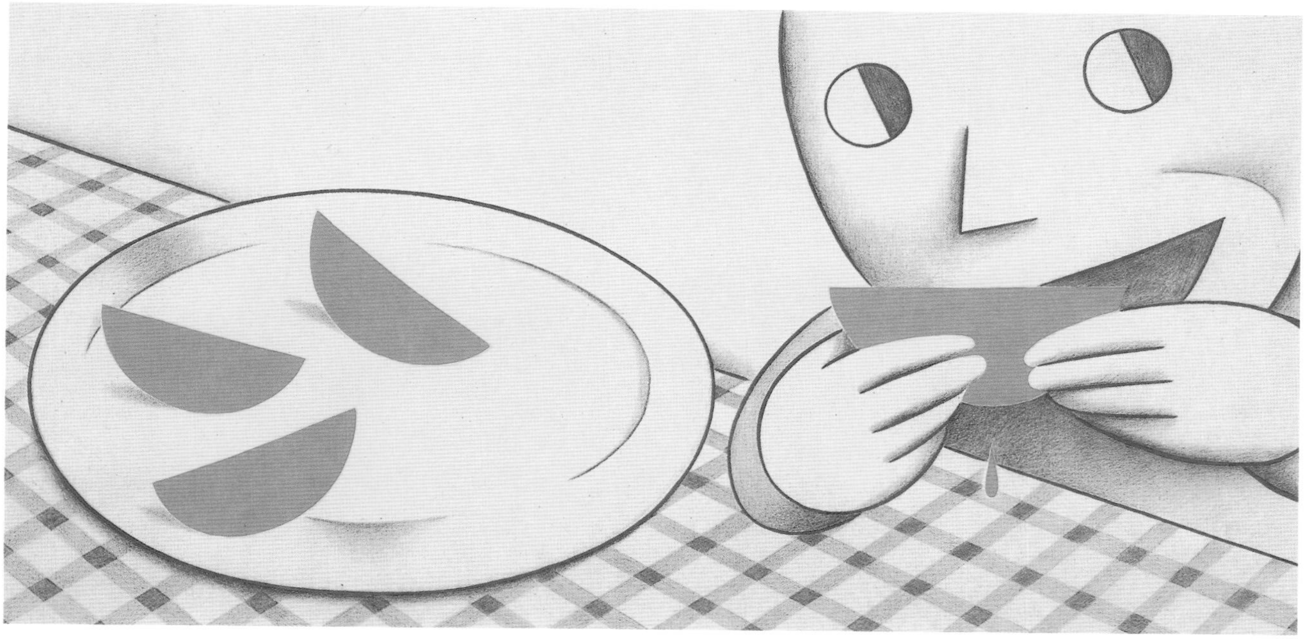

129

"...and **maybe the next one you** eat."

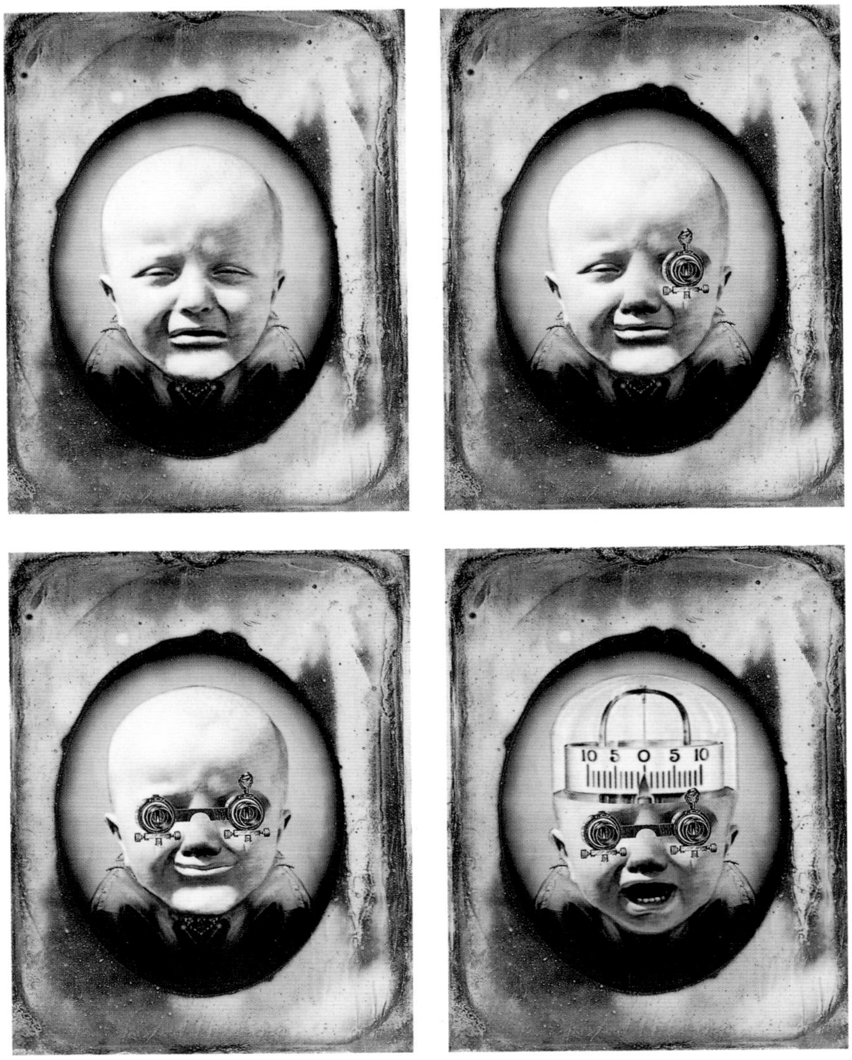

John Borruso

Art Director) Bart Nagel Editor) Rudy Rucker and Queen Mu Writer) R.U. Sirius Book Title) Mondo 2000 A User's Guide to the New Edge Date) November 1992 Publisher) Harper Collins Publishers, Inc. Medium) Collage Originally titled "Transformer," this illustration introduces the chapter "Evolutionary Mutations."

Date) December 1992 **Publisher) Brad Burkhart** Publishing Medium) Oil
This **illustration appeared in the "Recording** Industry Sourcebook."

Mark Ryden

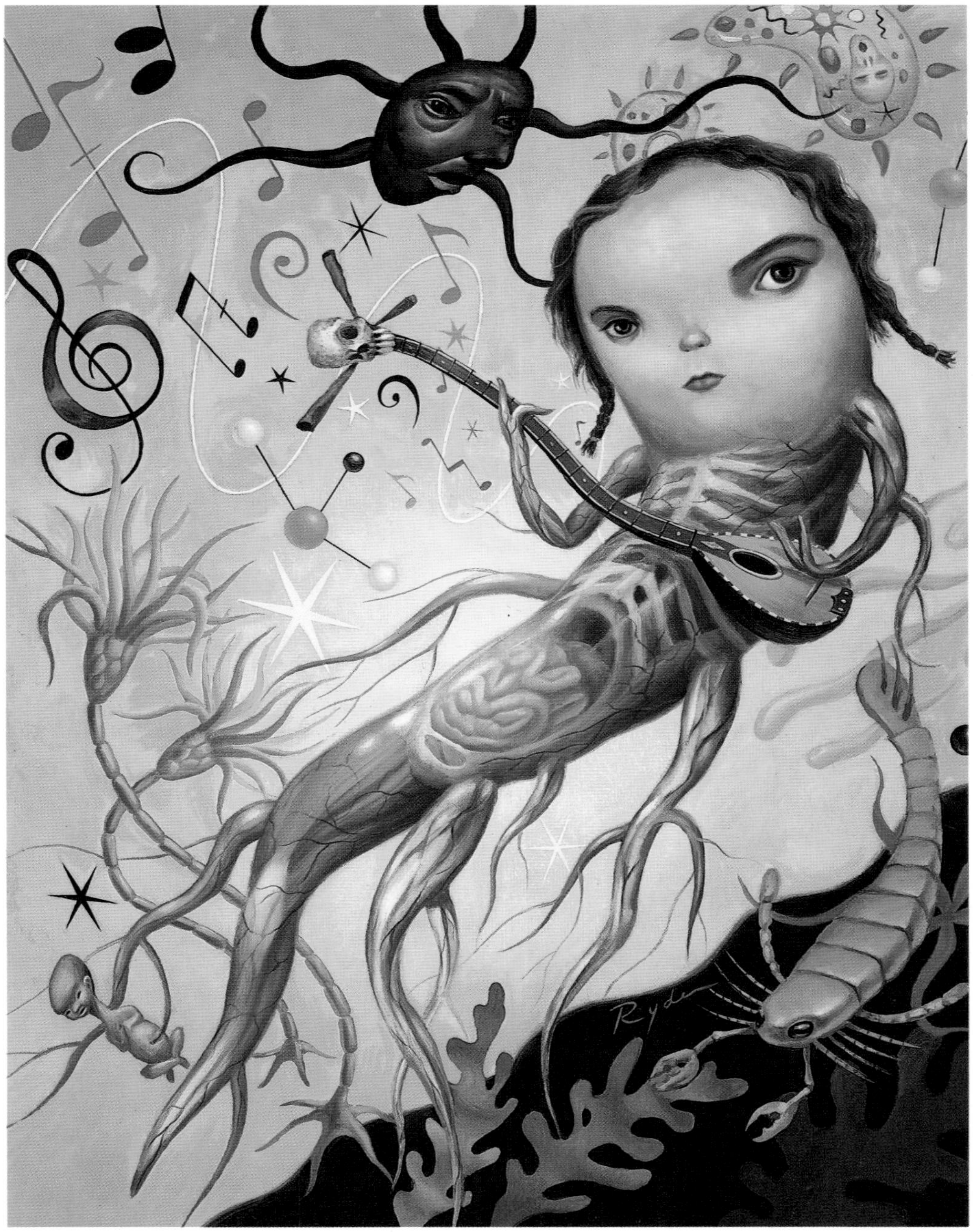

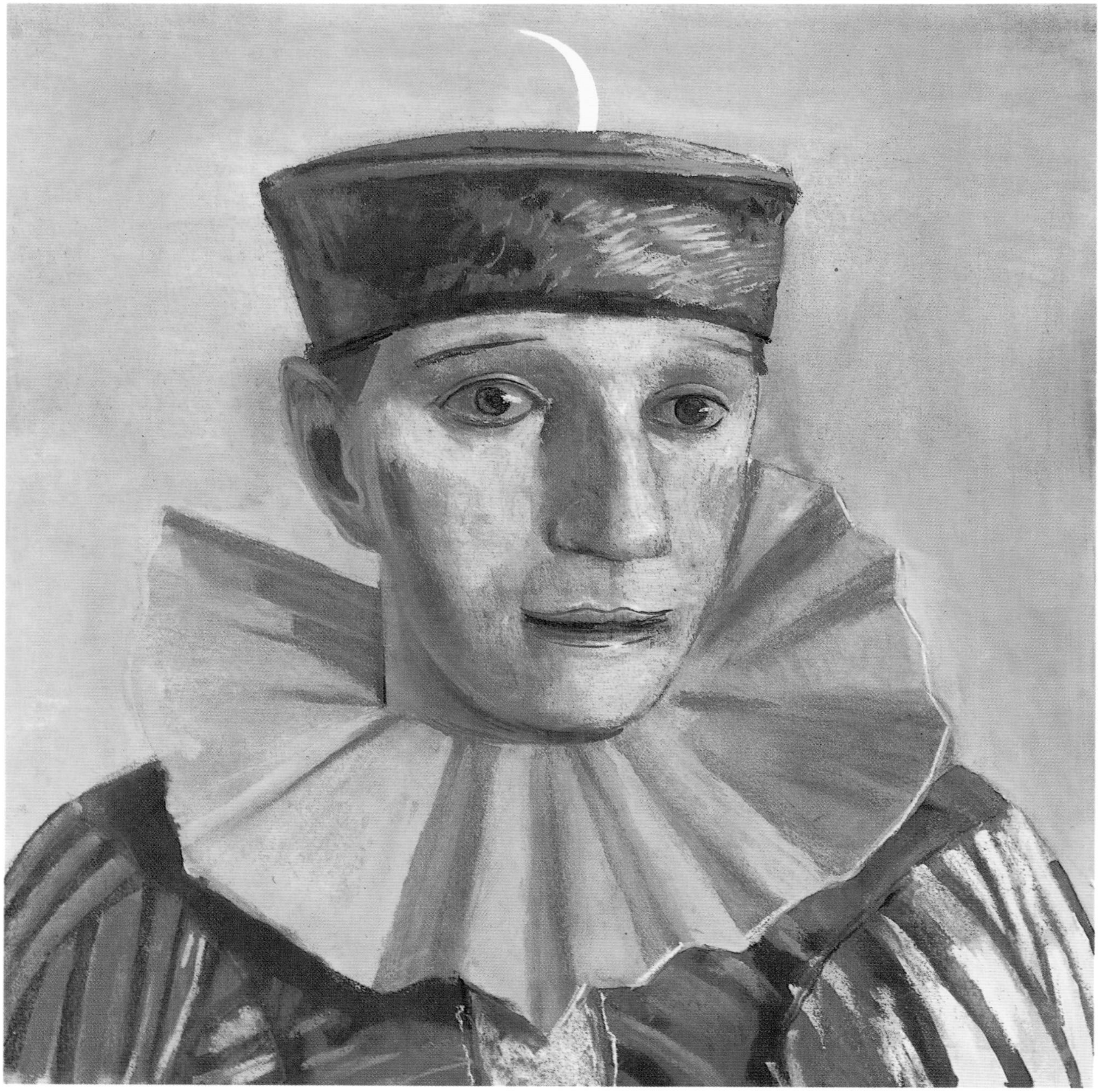

John Collier

Art Director) Alex Jay Editor) Gillian Bucky Writer) Vivian Werner Date) 1992 Publisher) Byron Preiss Visual Publications Medium) Pastel
This series was used as the cover and inside illustrations for the book "Petrouchka – The Story of the Ballet."

"Ballerina on Moor's Lap."

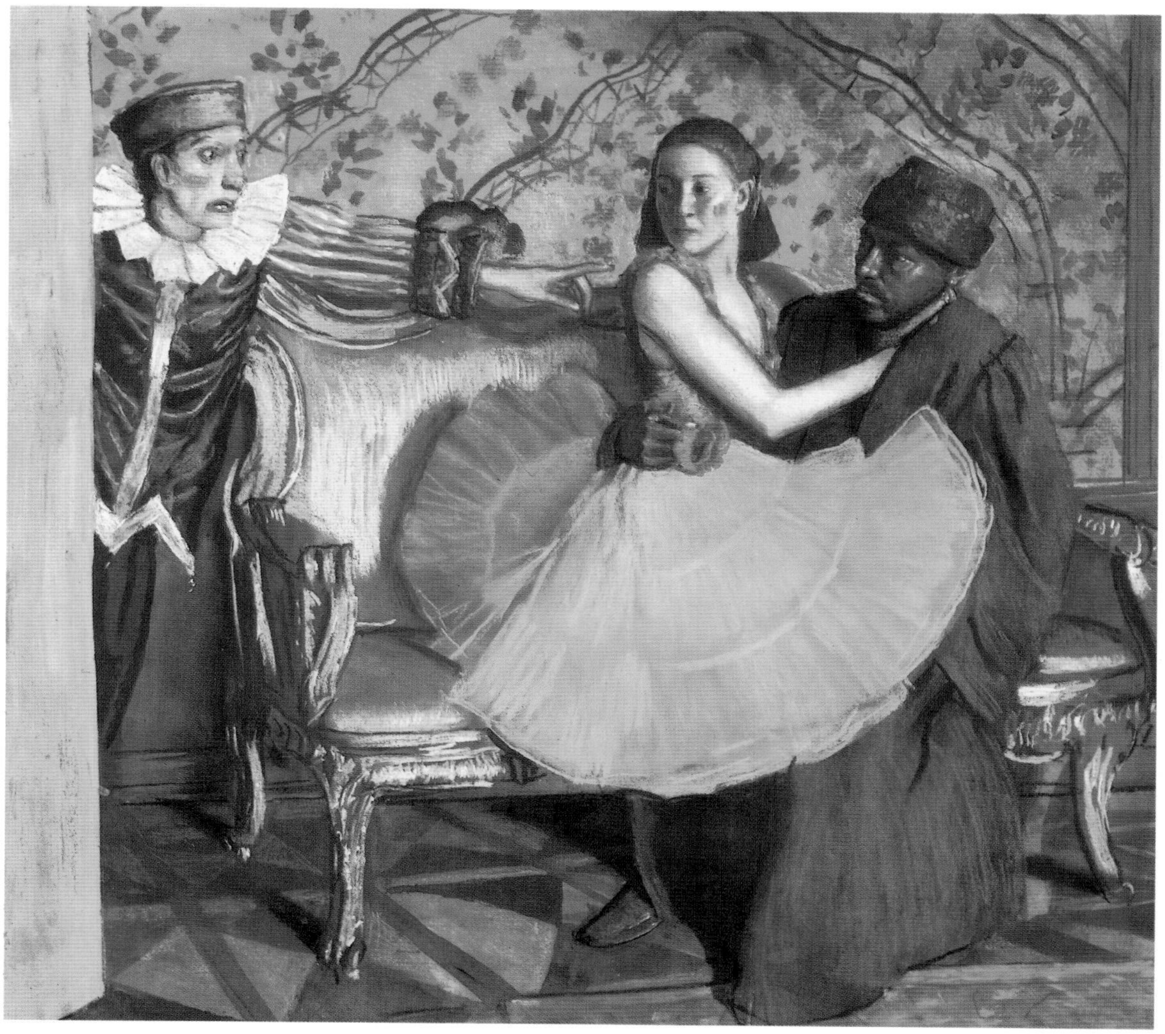

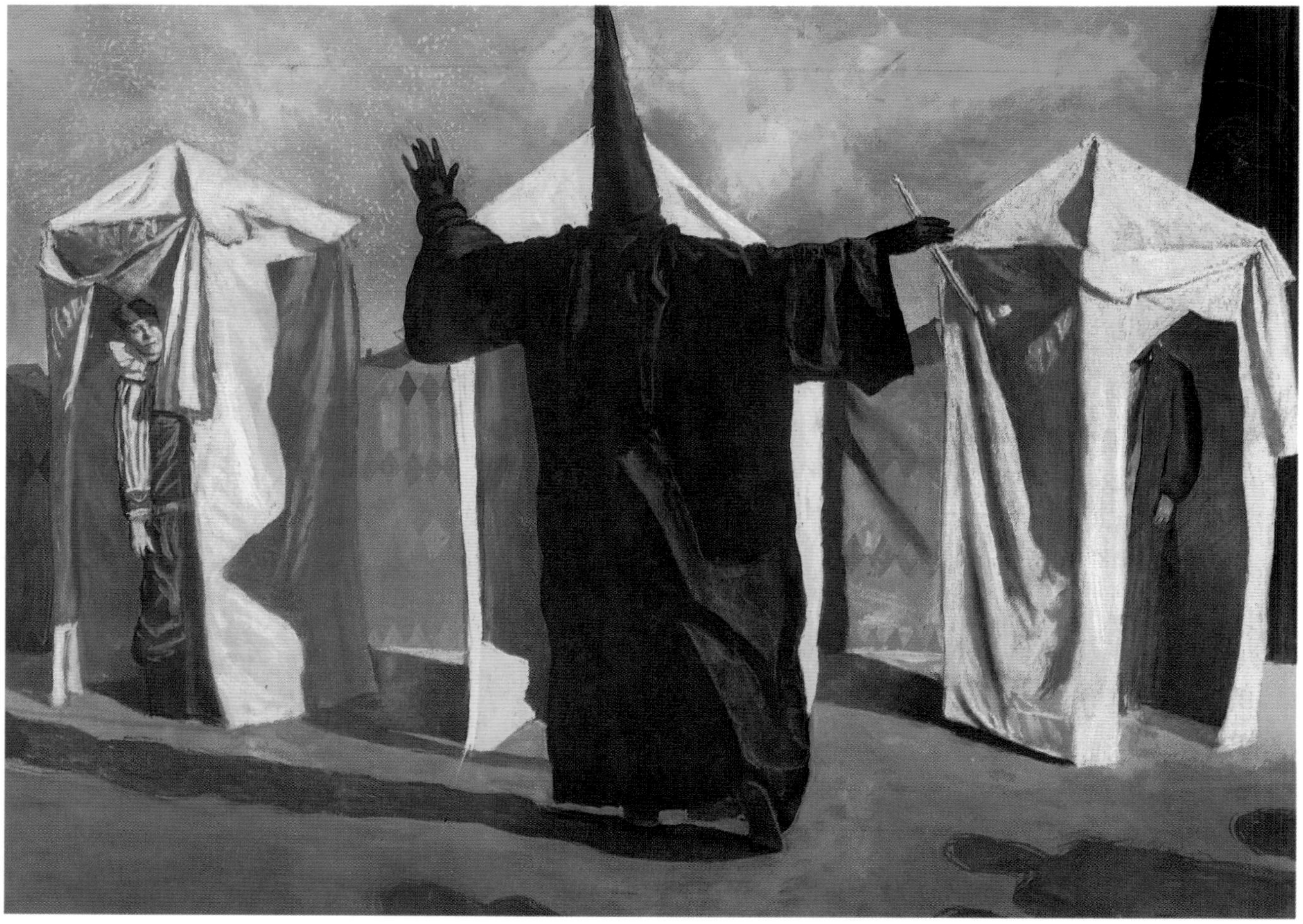

"The Magician."

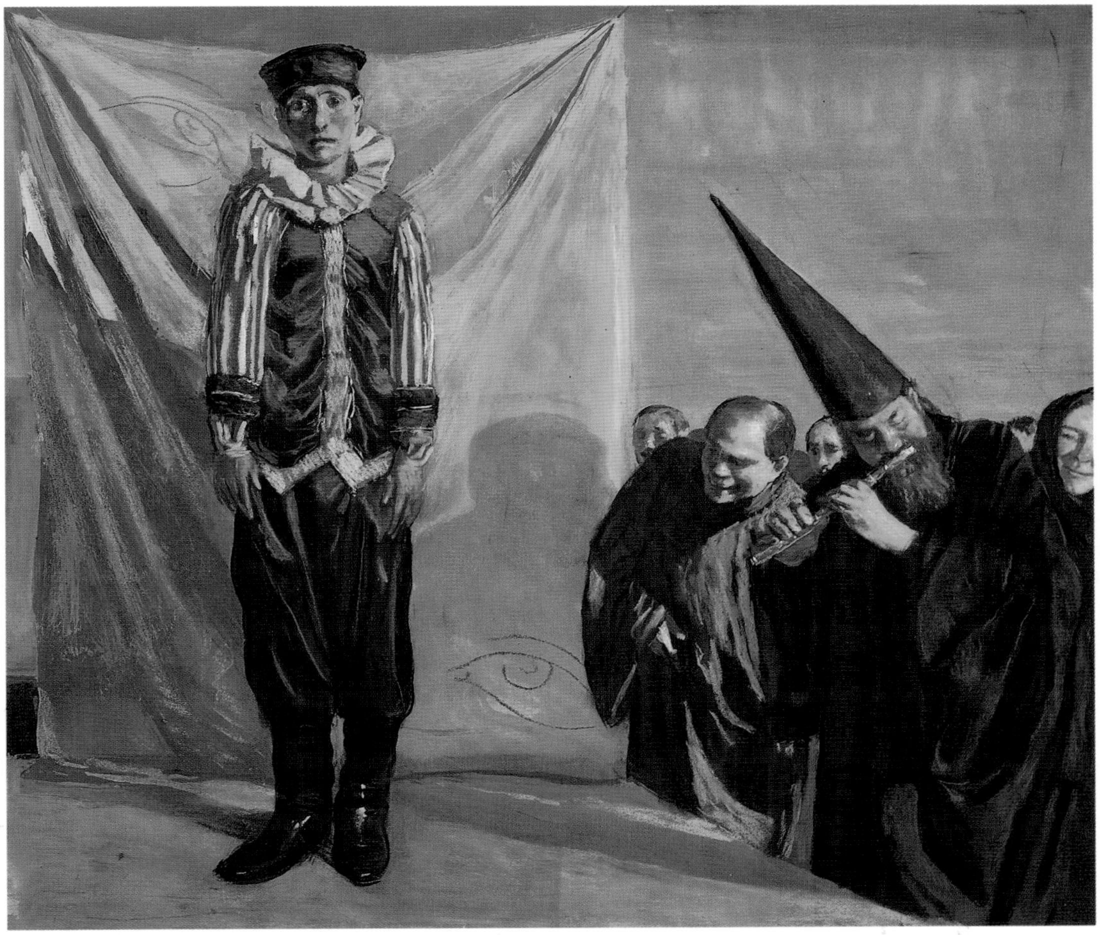

"Petrouchka and the Magician's Flute."

Lilla Rogers

Art Director) Tomoko Kochi Date) February 1993 Publisher) Fukutake Publishing Co., Ltd. Medium) Mixed media
This series of illustrations accompanied the story "The Rainbow Magicians," written for a children's book.

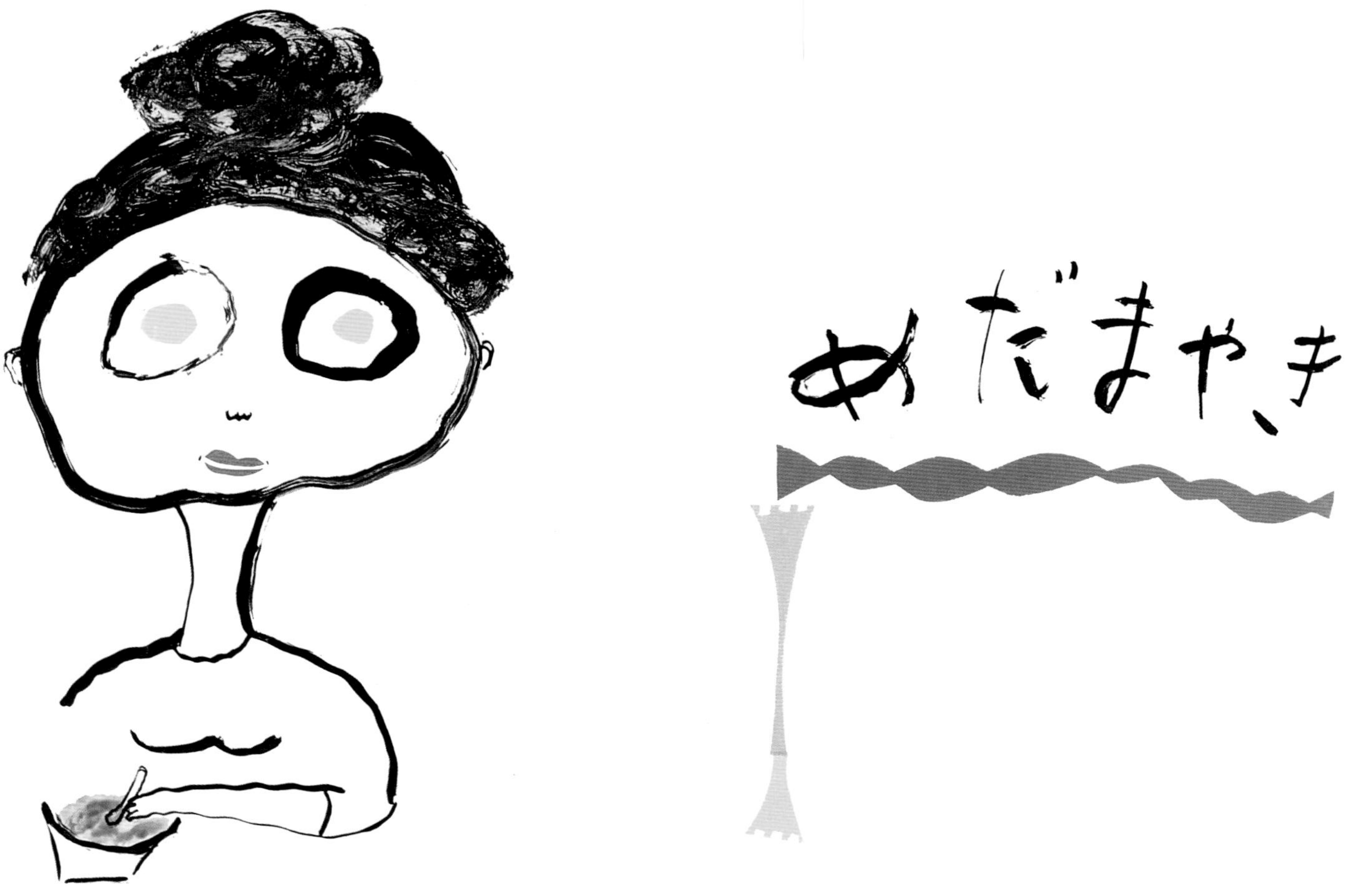

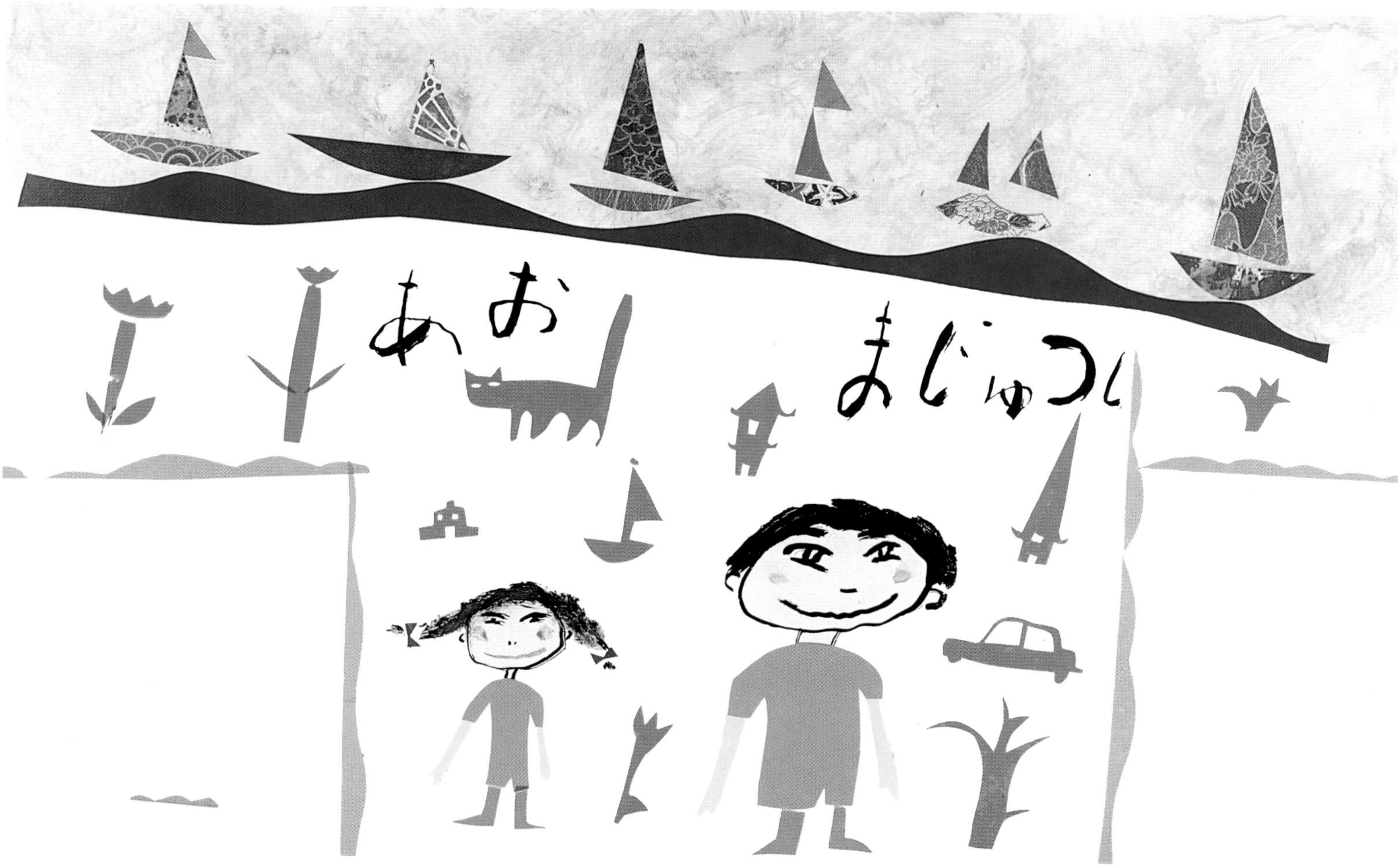
あお
まじゅつし

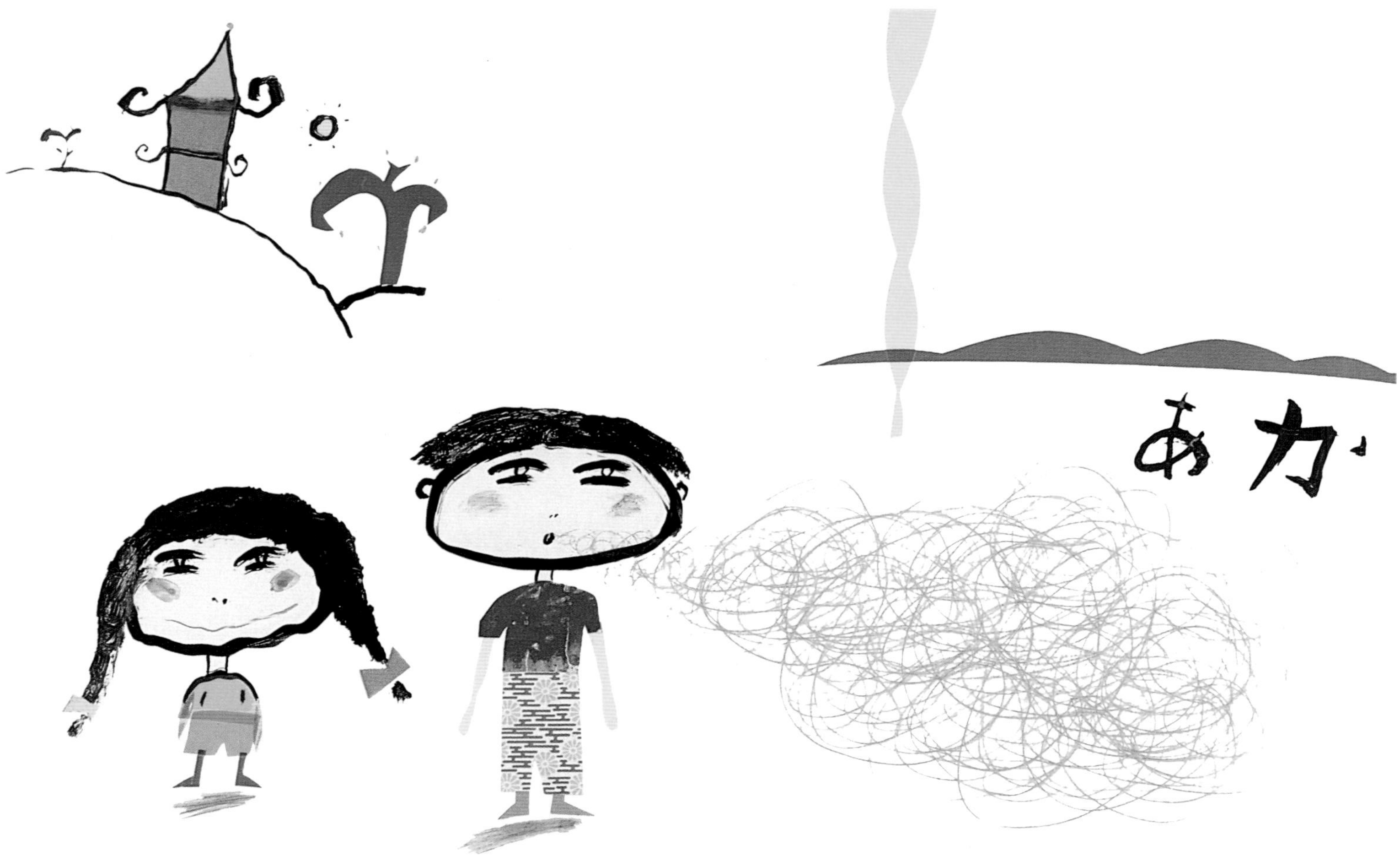
あか

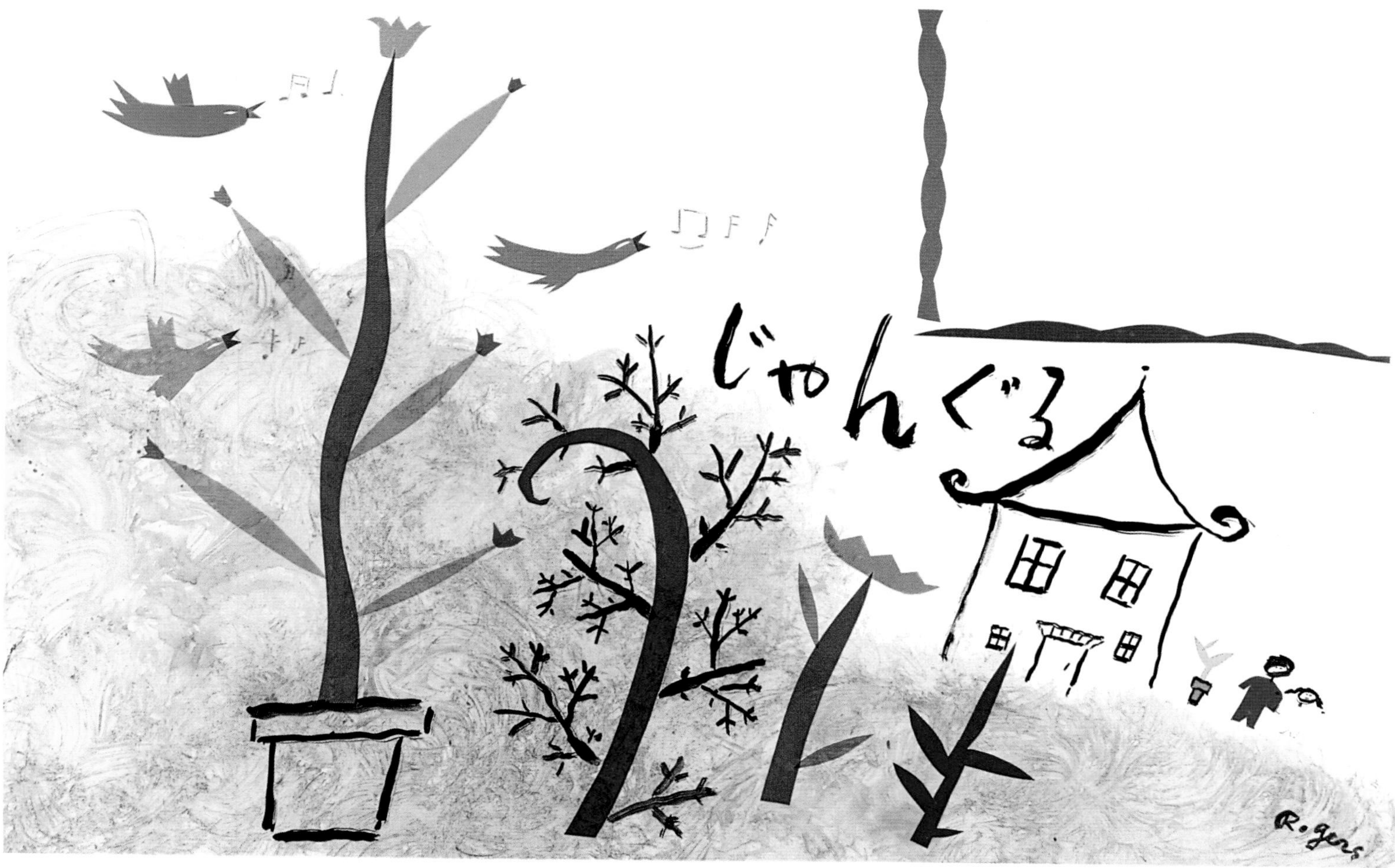
じゃんぐる

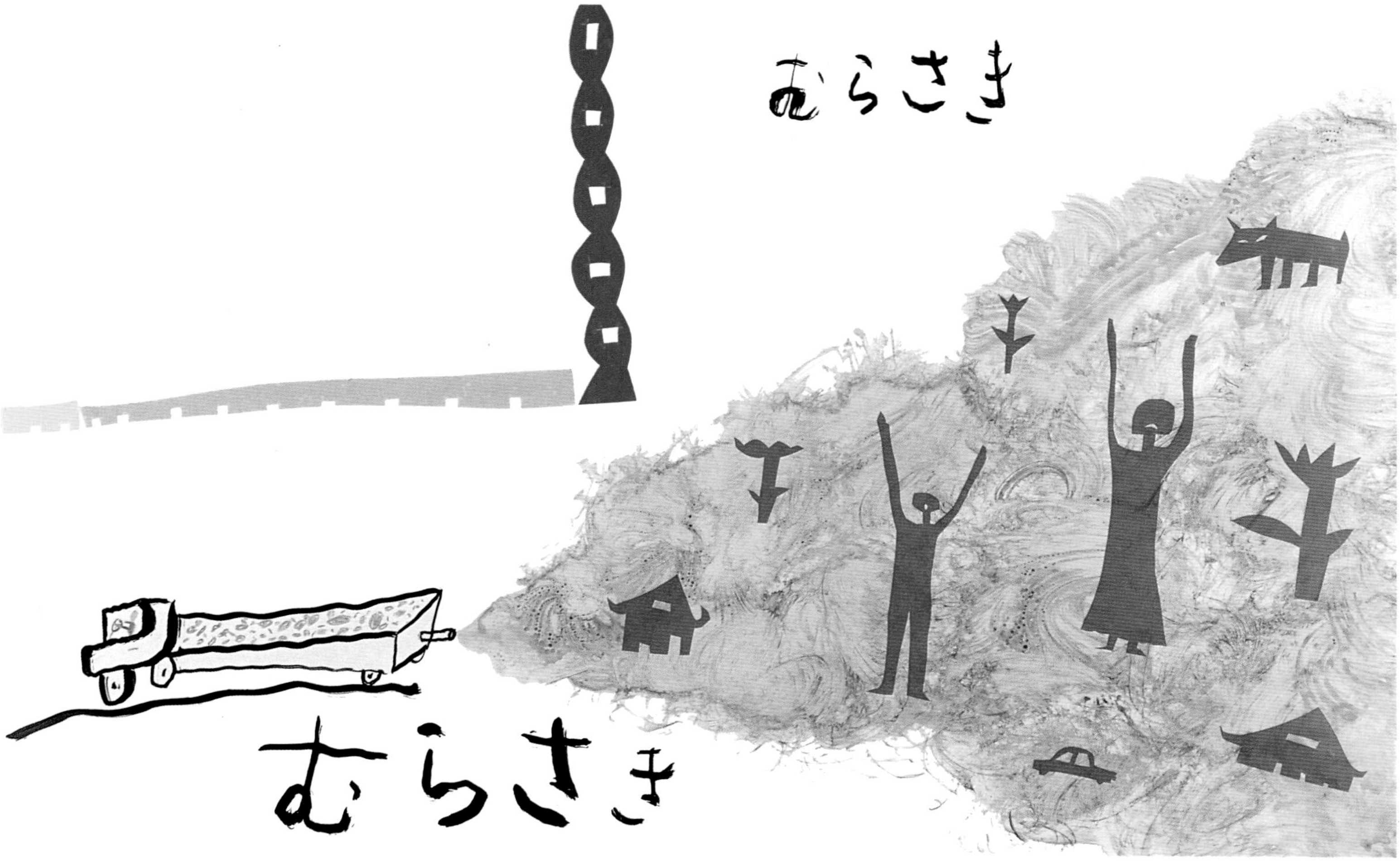
むらさき
むらさき

Editor) Gary Groth Date) March 1992 Publisher) Fantagraphics Medium) Stencil, enamel paint and colored pencils
In response to the Rodney King beating, this illustration appeared on the cover of the comic book "Bleeding Heart #2."

Peter Kuper

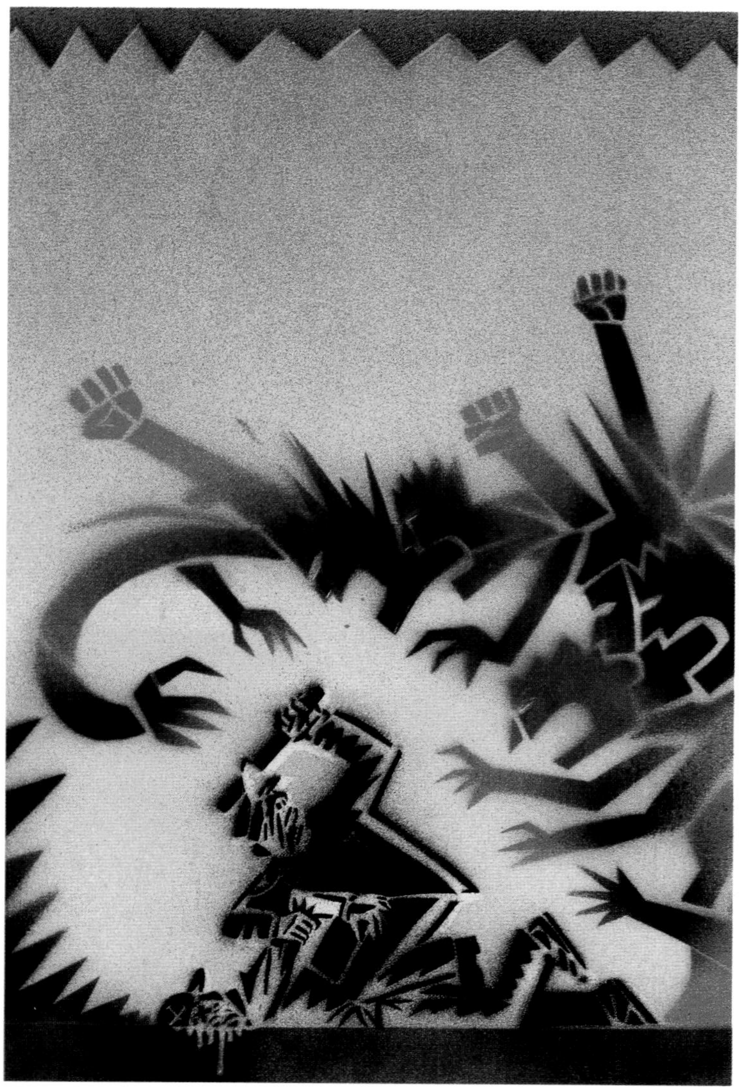

Art Director) Paul Elliot Writer) D.J. MacHale Date) Winter 1992 Publisher) Rabbit Ears Medium) Pastel
This image of two heads kissing appears in the children's book "East of the Sun, West of the Moon."

Vivienne Flesher

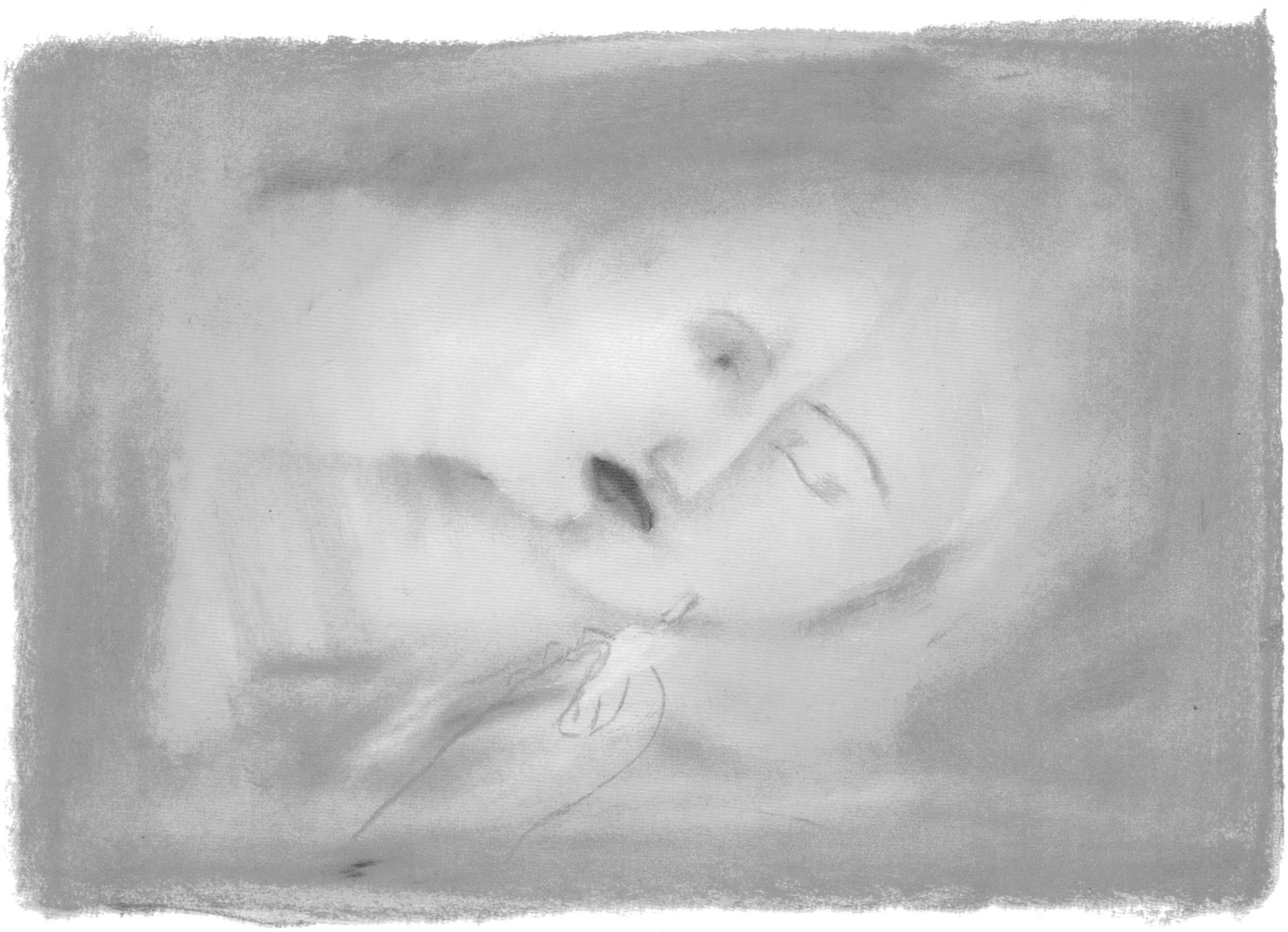

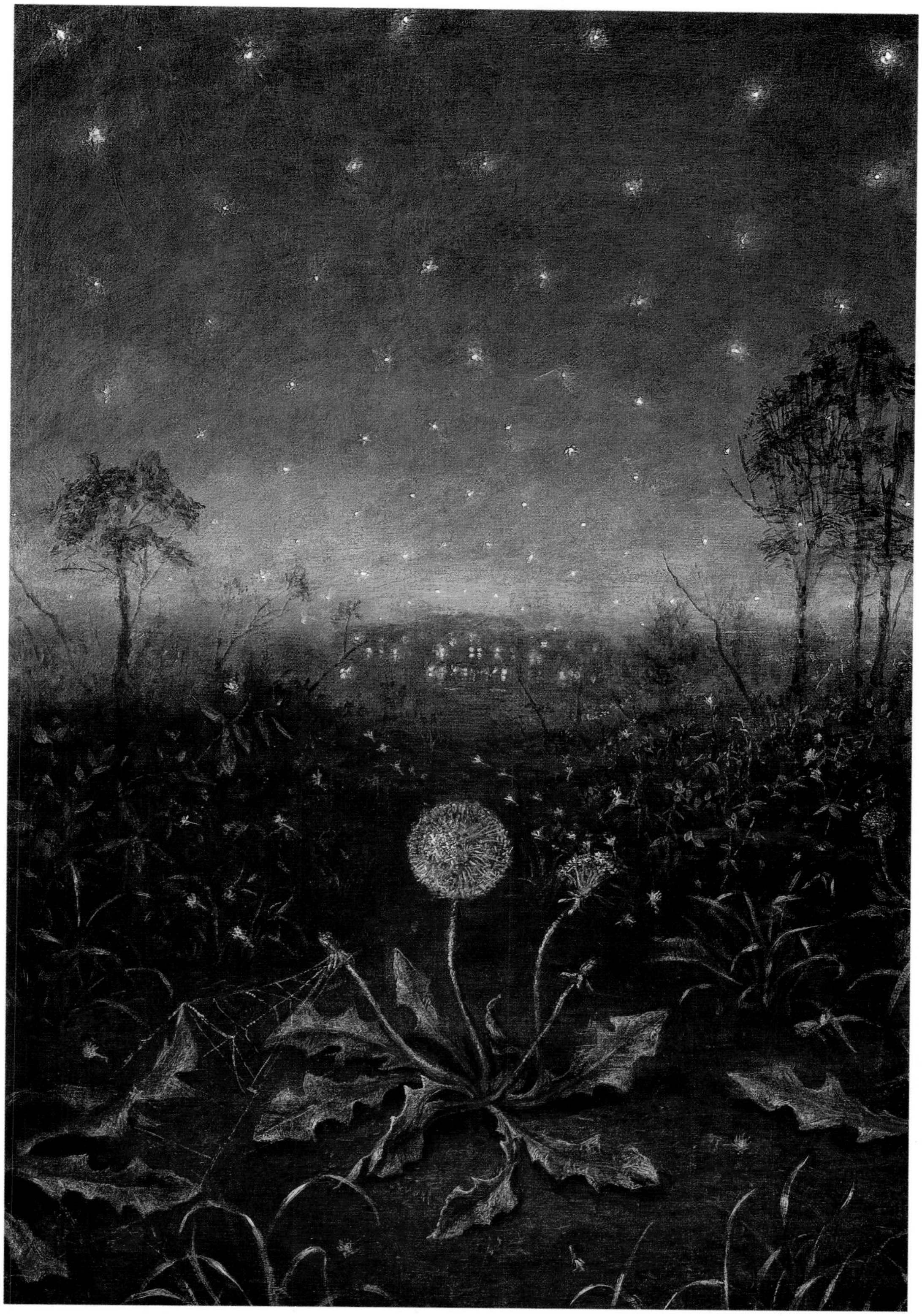

143

Thomas Woodruff

Art Director) Michaela Sullivan Editor) Richard Todd Author) Ann Patchett Date) 1992 Publisher) Houghton Mifflin Company Medium) Acrylic on linen This illustration appears as the cover for "The Patron Saint of Liars."

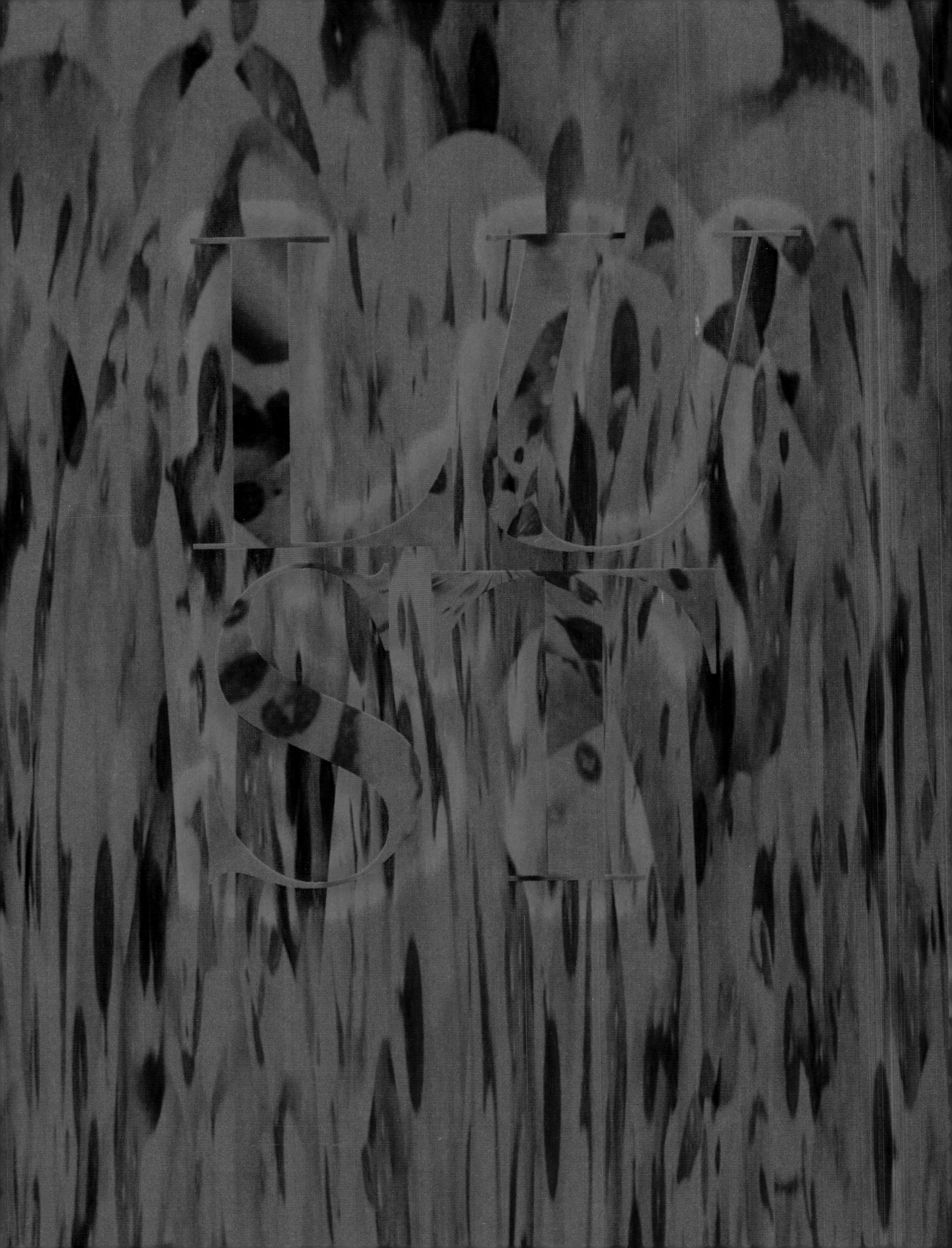
LU
ST

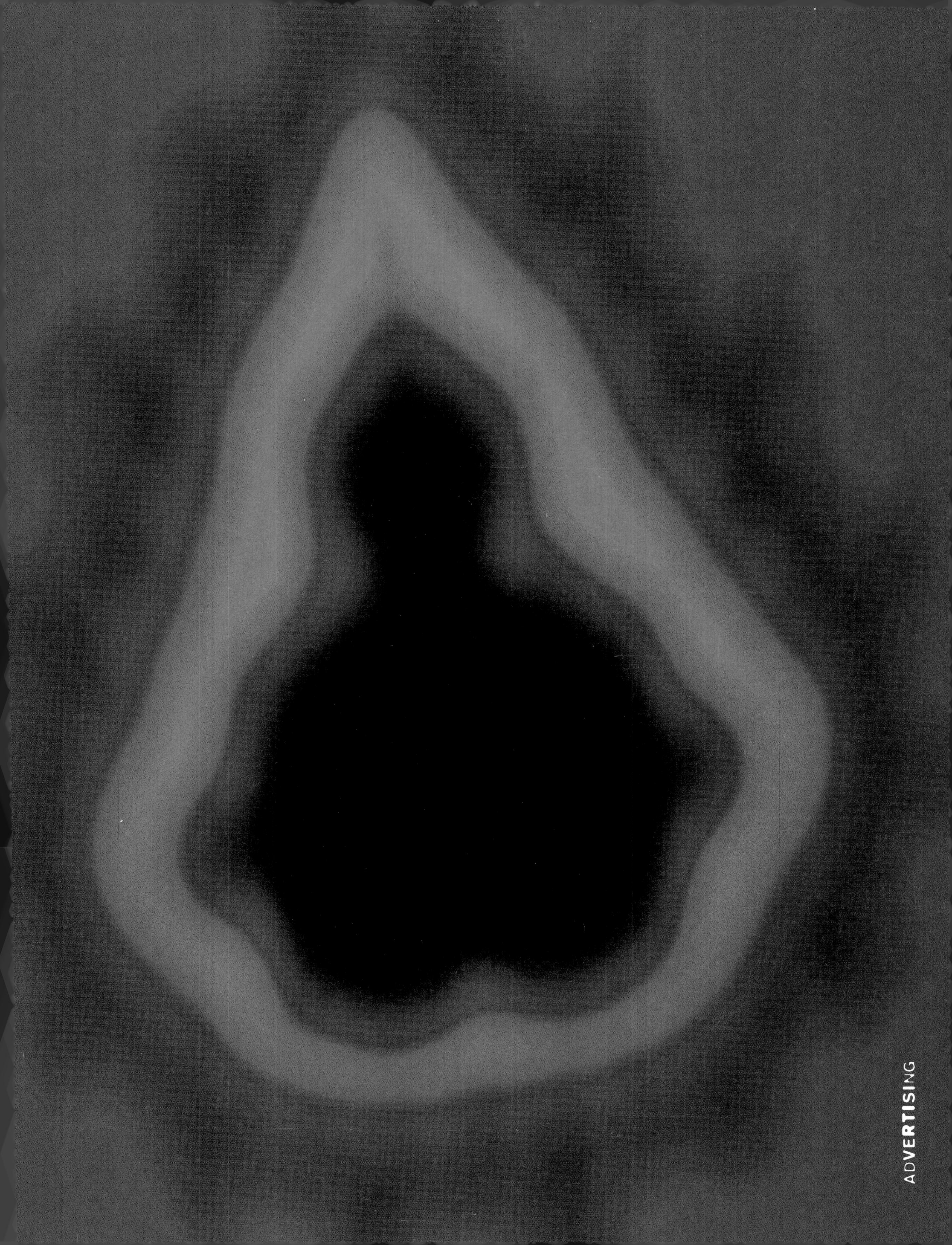

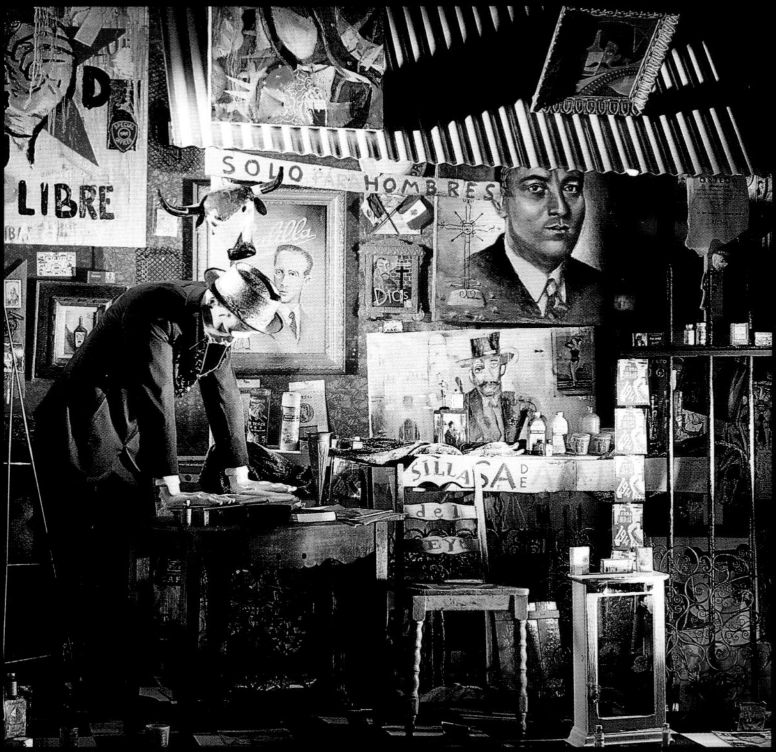

Josh Gosfield

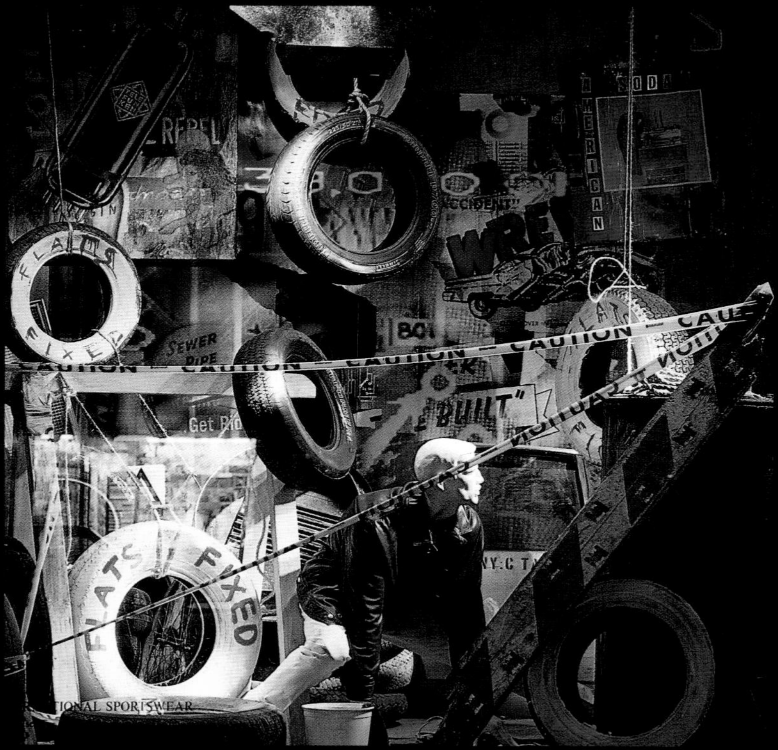

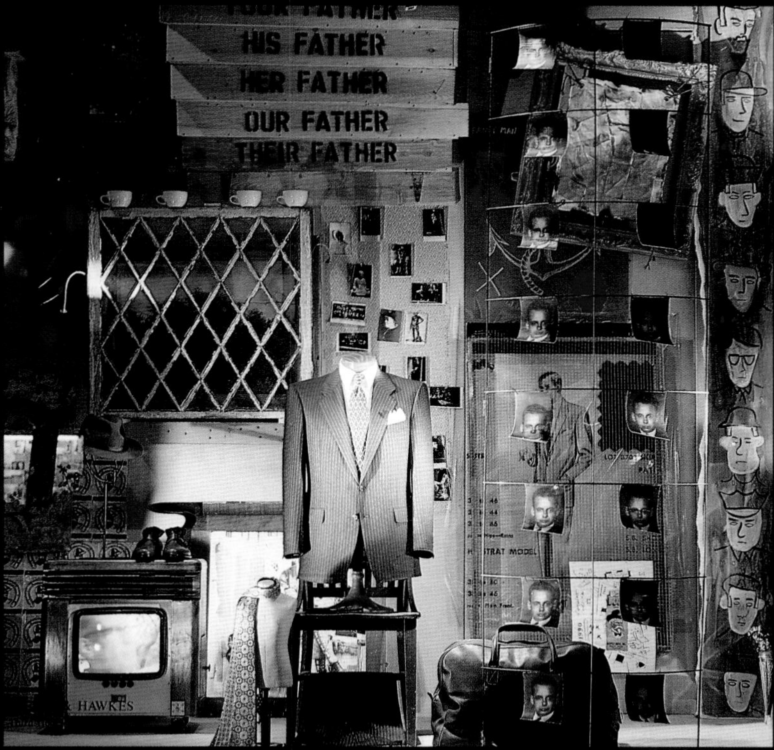

Art Directors) Simon Doonan, Tony Kushner and Josh Gosfield Client) Barneys New York Medium) Mixed media
This collection of window displays was created for Barneys New York, in celebration of Fathers Day, 1992.

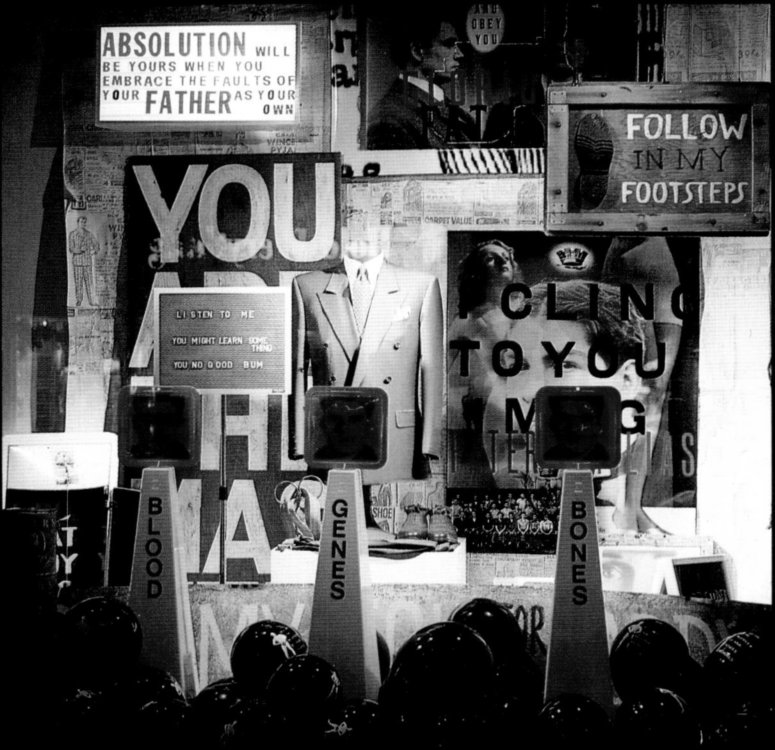

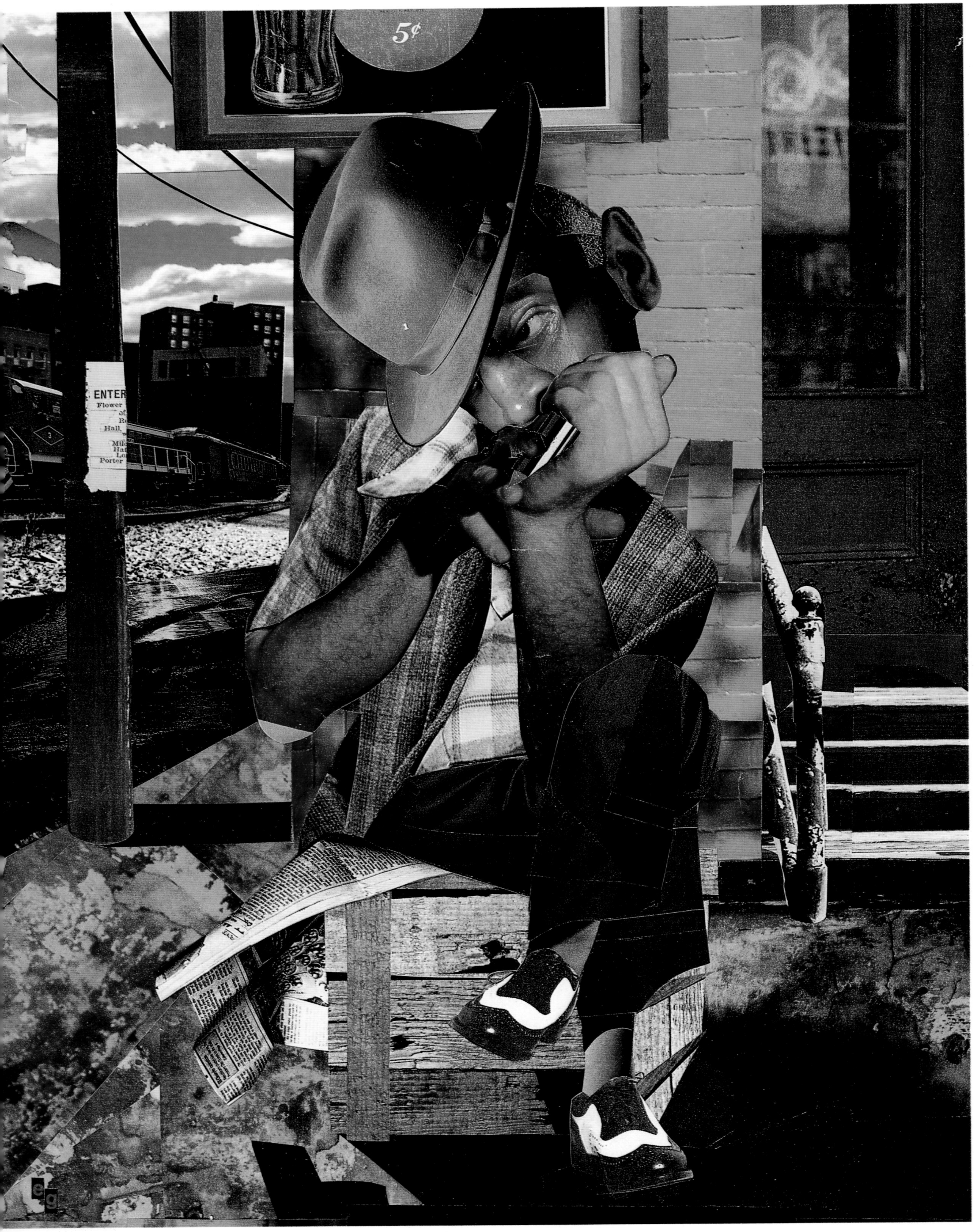
5¢
ENTER
Flower
Hall,
Porter

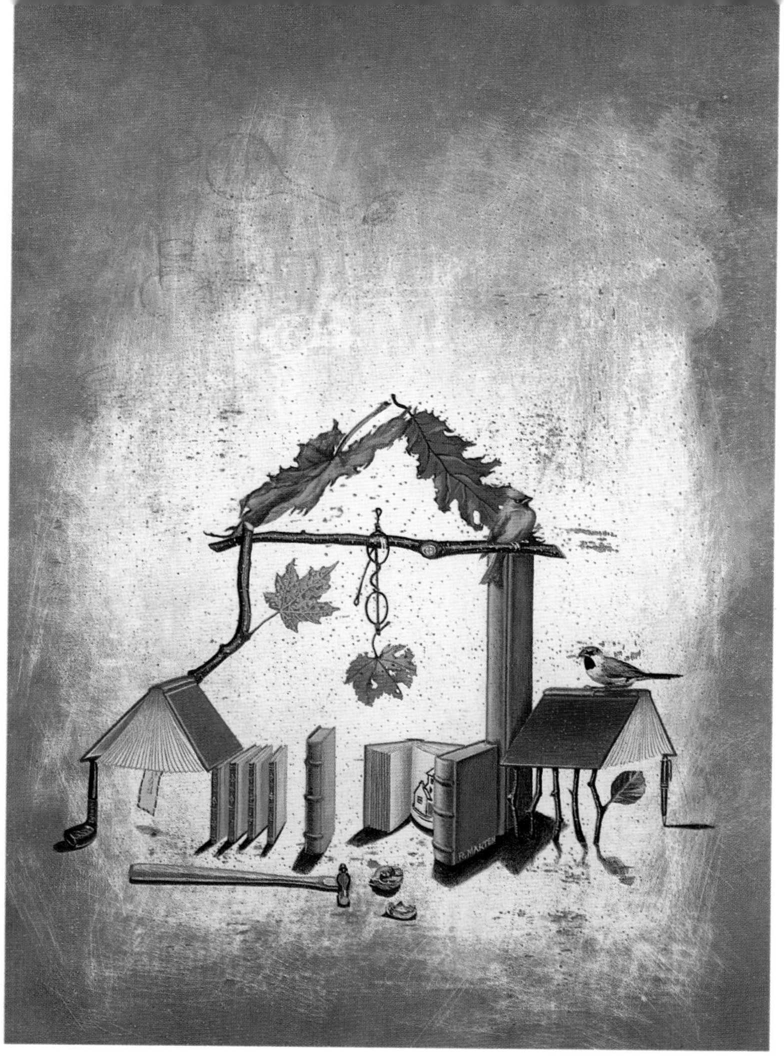

Ruth Marten

Art Director) Robin Schiff Publisher) Random House Medium) Egg tempera on wood
This illustration appeared in the Random House Autumn Catalogue, 1992 (above).

∞

Art Director) Melanie Nissen Publication) The Seventh Annual Soul Train Music Awards Date) March 9, 1993
Client) Atlantic Recording Corporation Medium) Collage This collage appeared in the award show's souvenir program book (left).

Edmund Guy

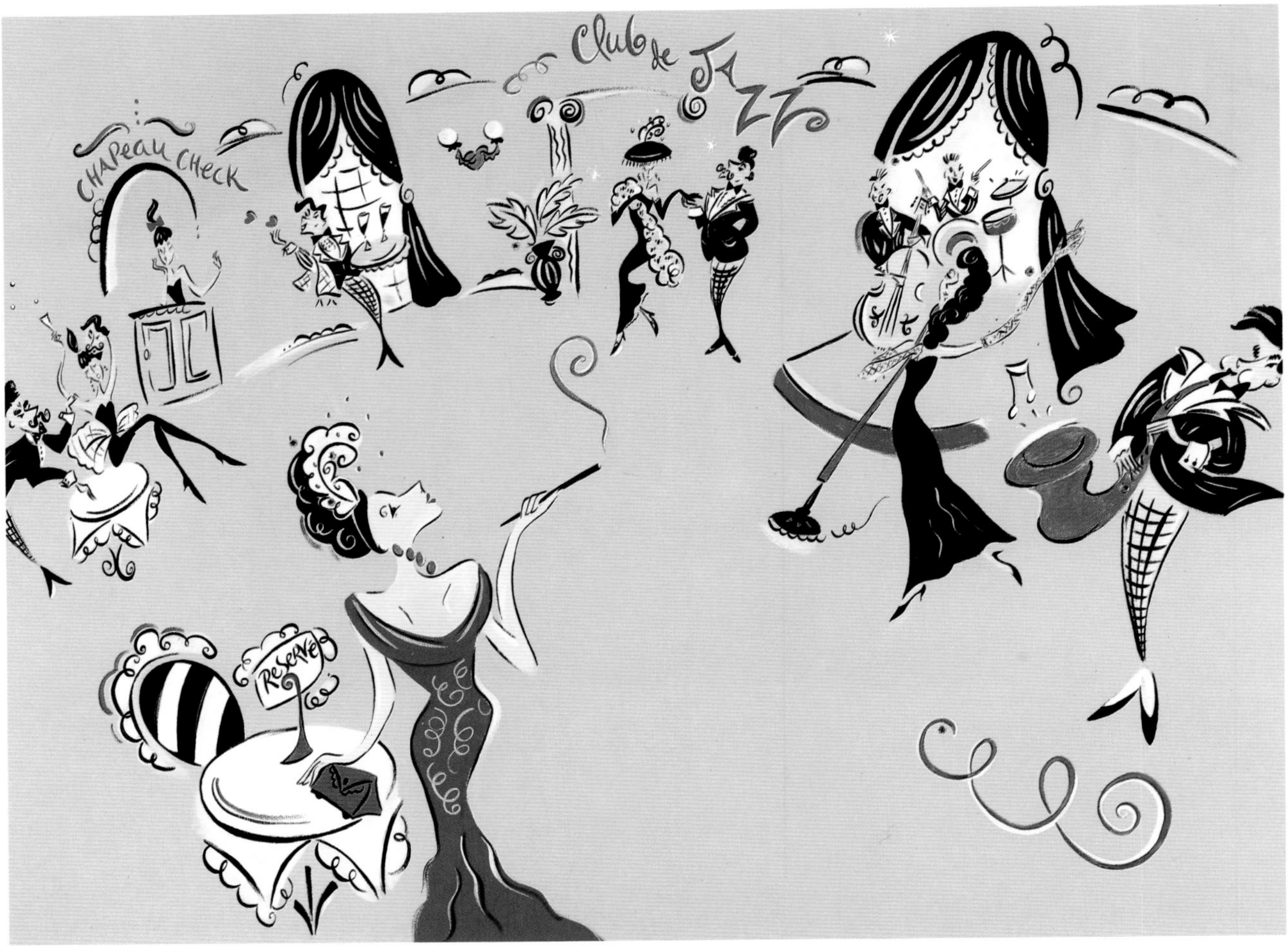

Chesley McLaren

Client) Prix Fixe Restaurant Medium) Acrylic on canvas
One in a series of murals entitled "Club de Jazz," created for a New York restaurant.

Art Director) Scott Wadler Designer) Laurie Hinzman and Jennifer Juliano
Client) Comedy Central Medium) Ink This illustration appeared on promotional t-shirts.

Scott Menchin

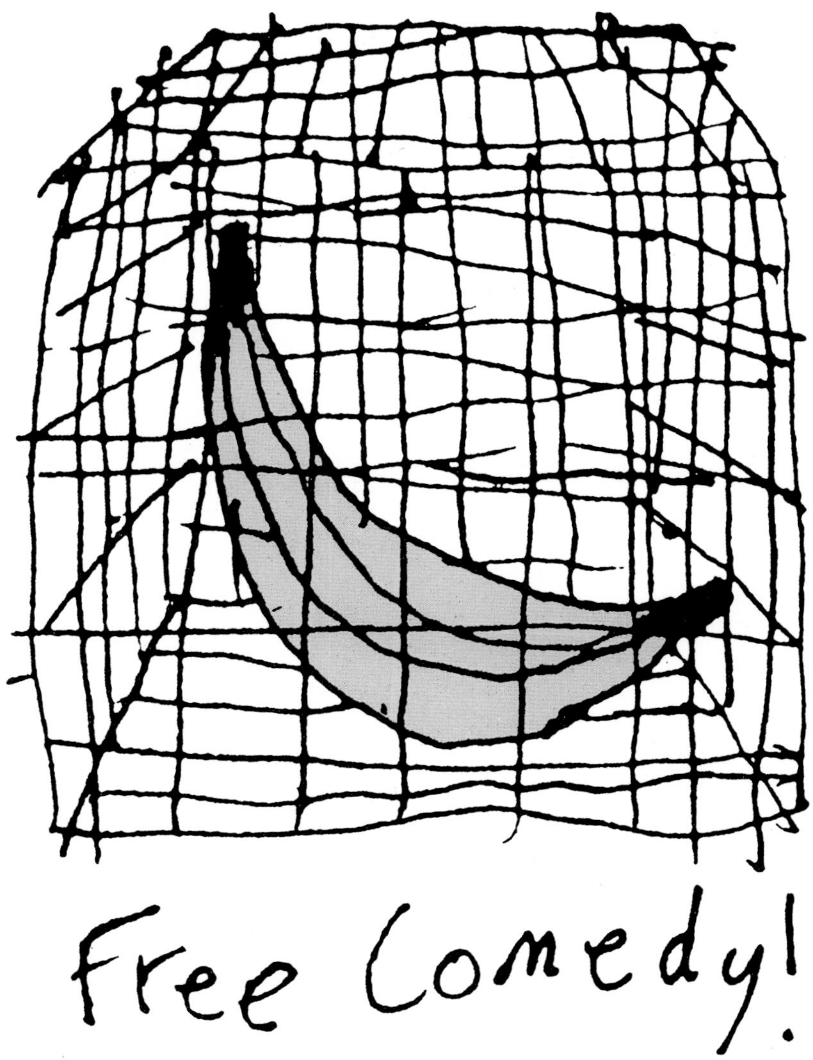

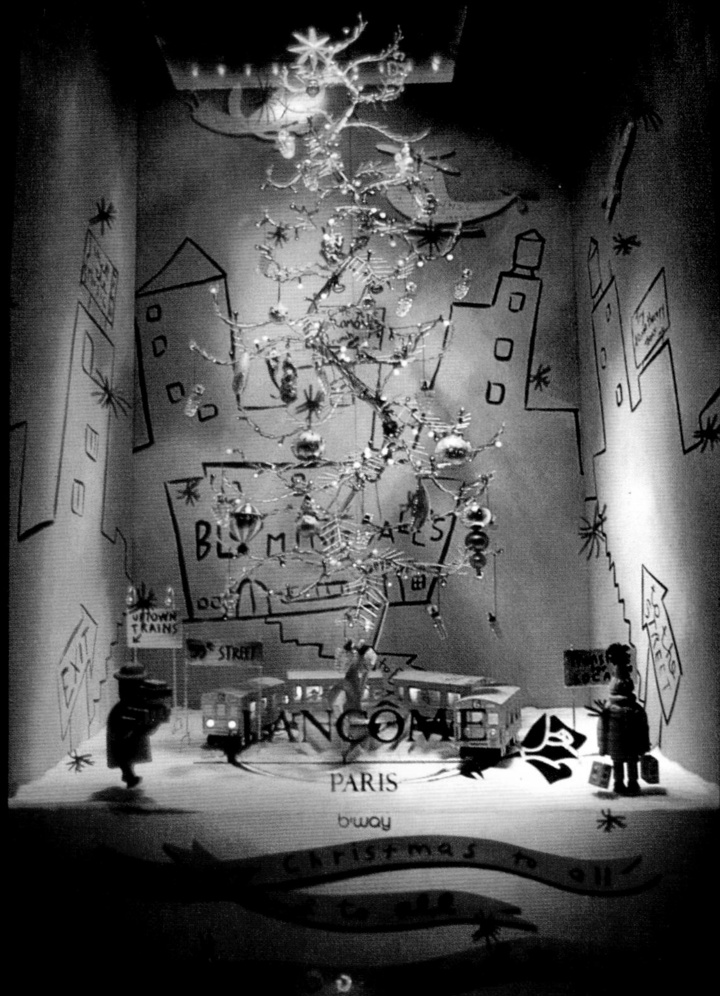
UPTOWN TRAINS
STREET
LANCÔME
PARIS
b'way
Christmas to all

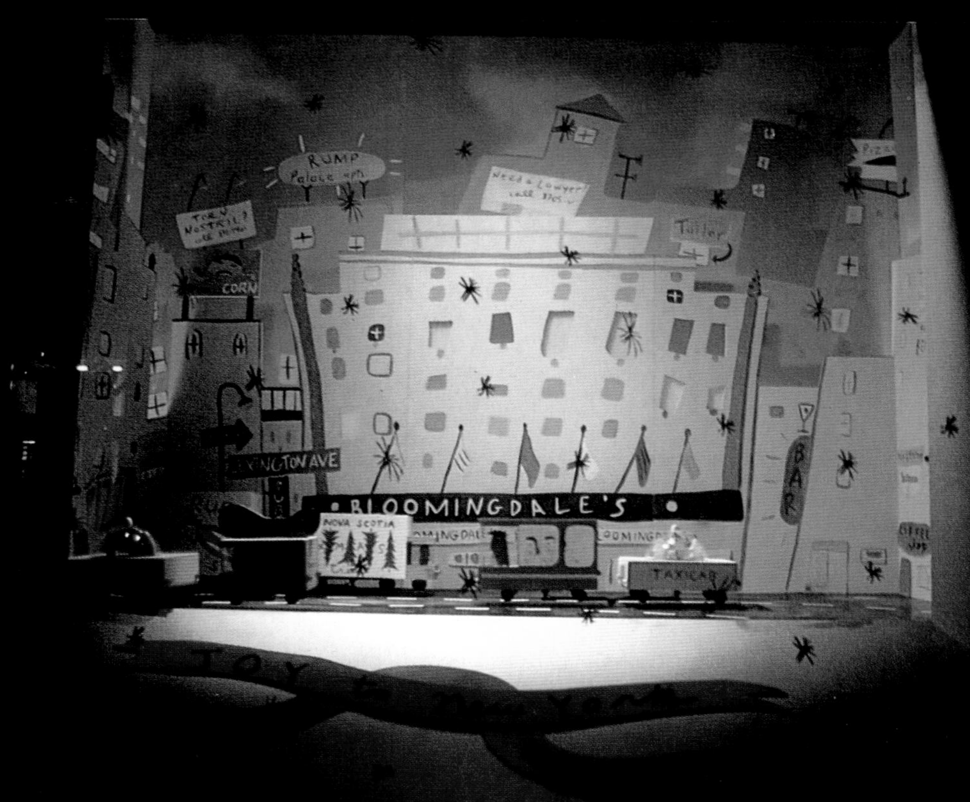
RUMP
Need a Lawyer
BLOOMINGDALE'S
NOVA SCOTIA
TAXICAB
BAR

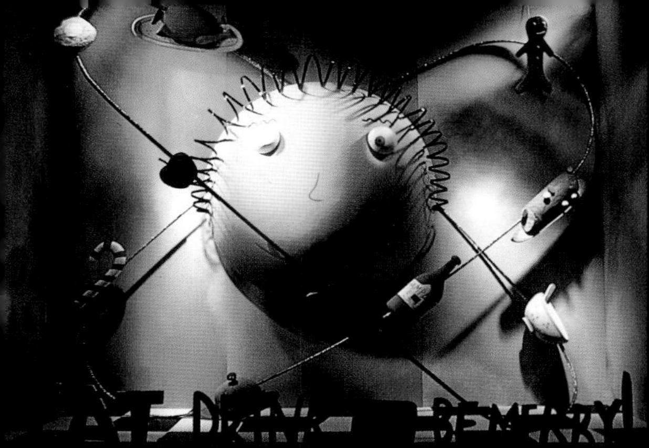

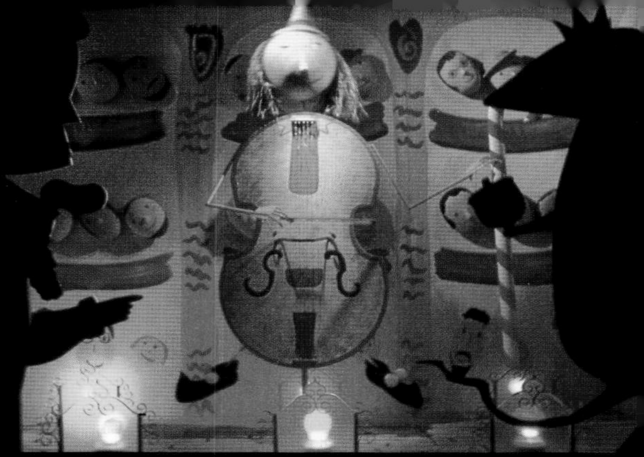

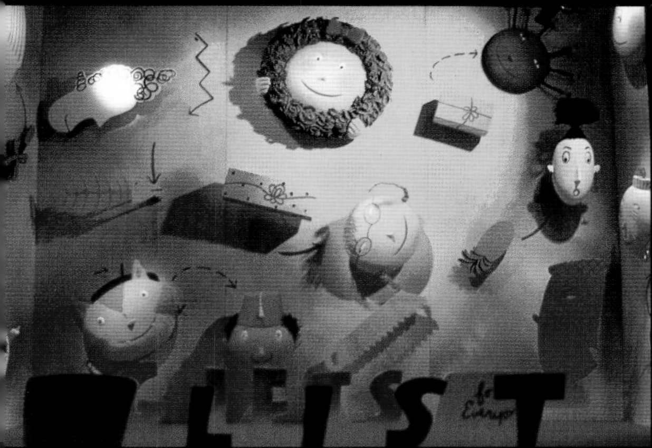

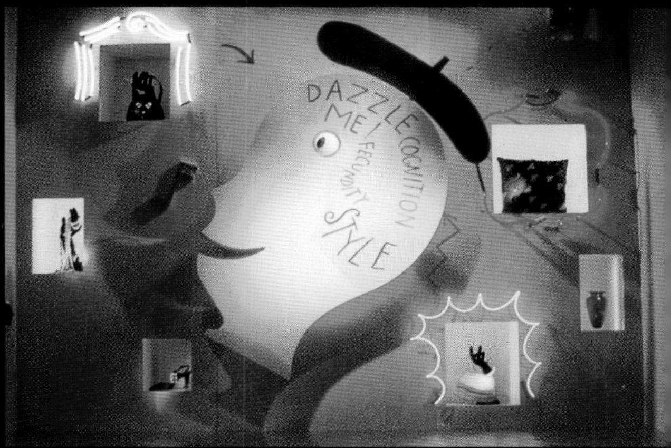

Jessie Hartland

Art Director) Robin M. Lauritano Client) Bloomingdale's Medium) Mixed media

This collection of window displays, celebrating Christmas at Bloomingdale's, featured objects that moved, spun and nodded

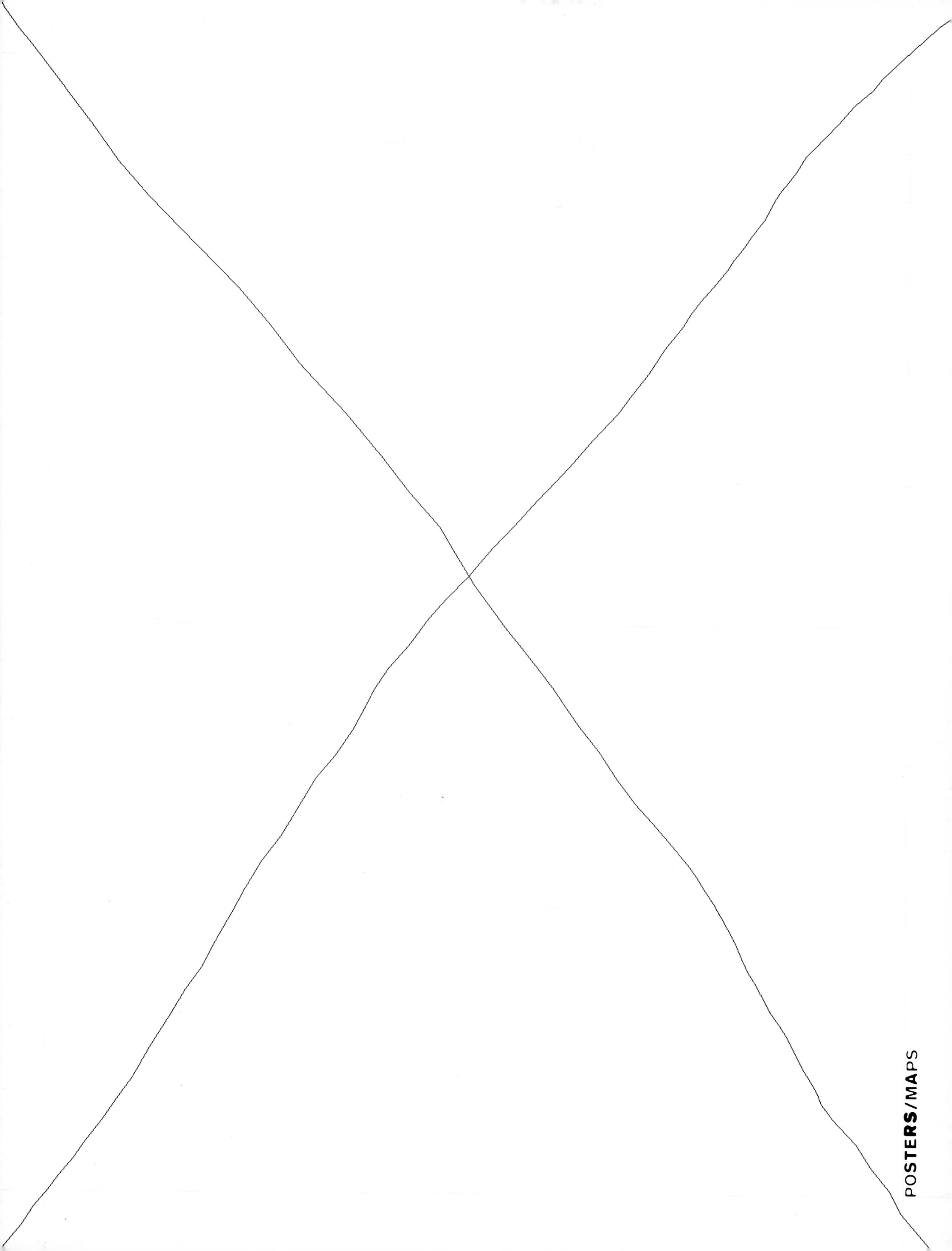

Medium) Ink and chalk on vellum **This poster was used as a** promotional piece for HBO/TVKO.

Jill **Buchan**an

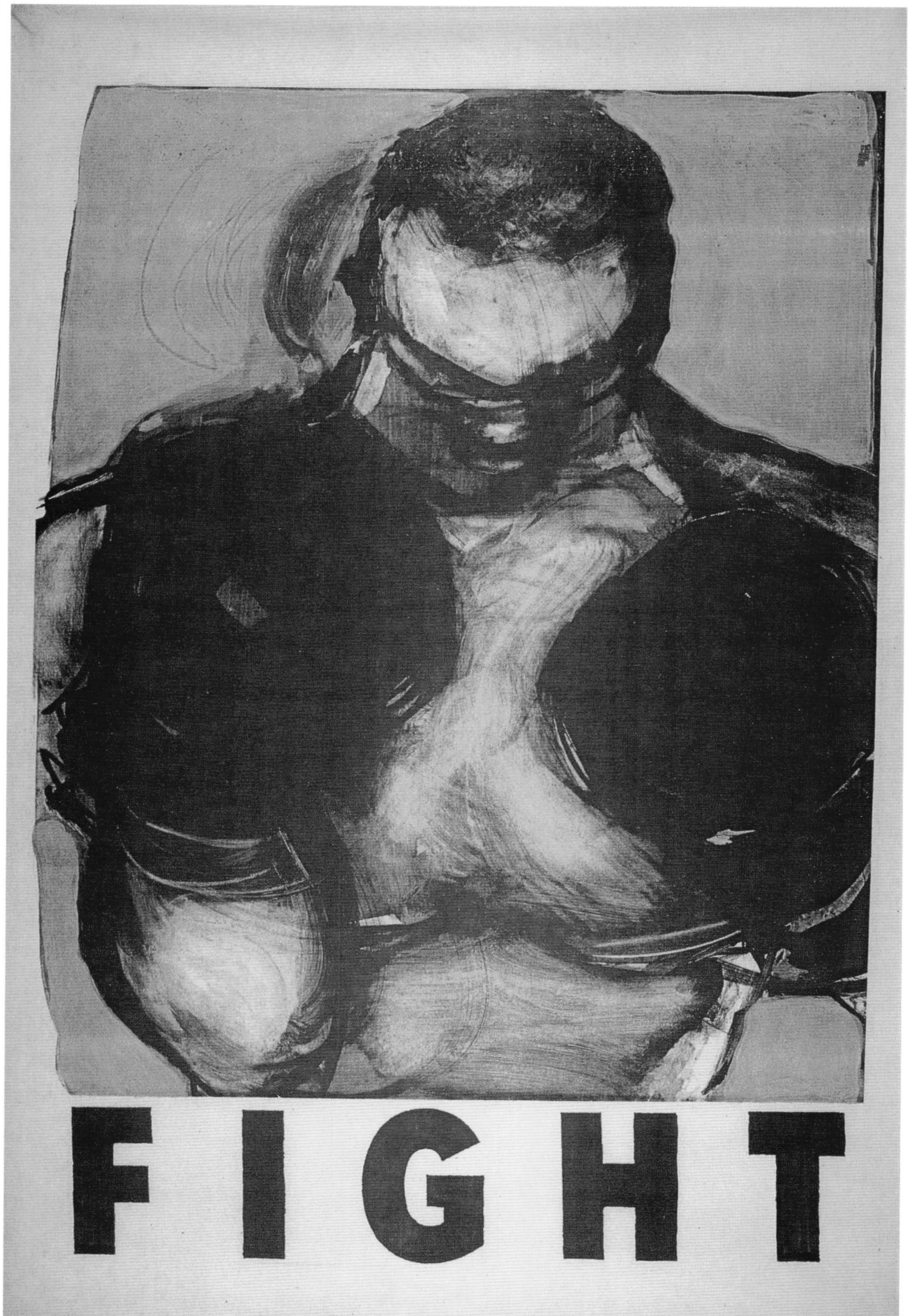

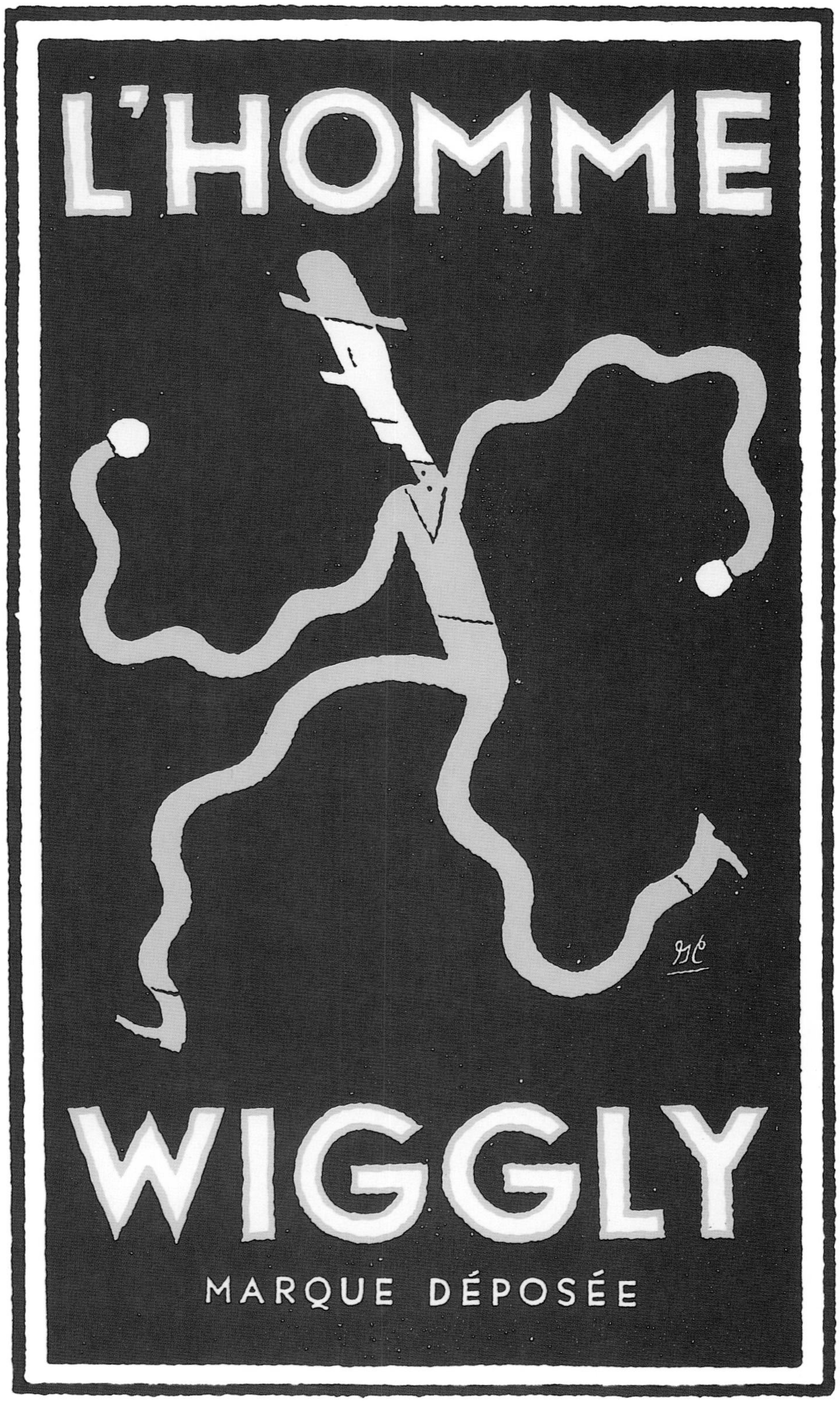

Greg Clarke

Medium) Limited edition silkscreen print on rag paper.
This poster was created for an exhibition called "Wisegeist" at the Clay Doyle Gallery in Los Angeles.

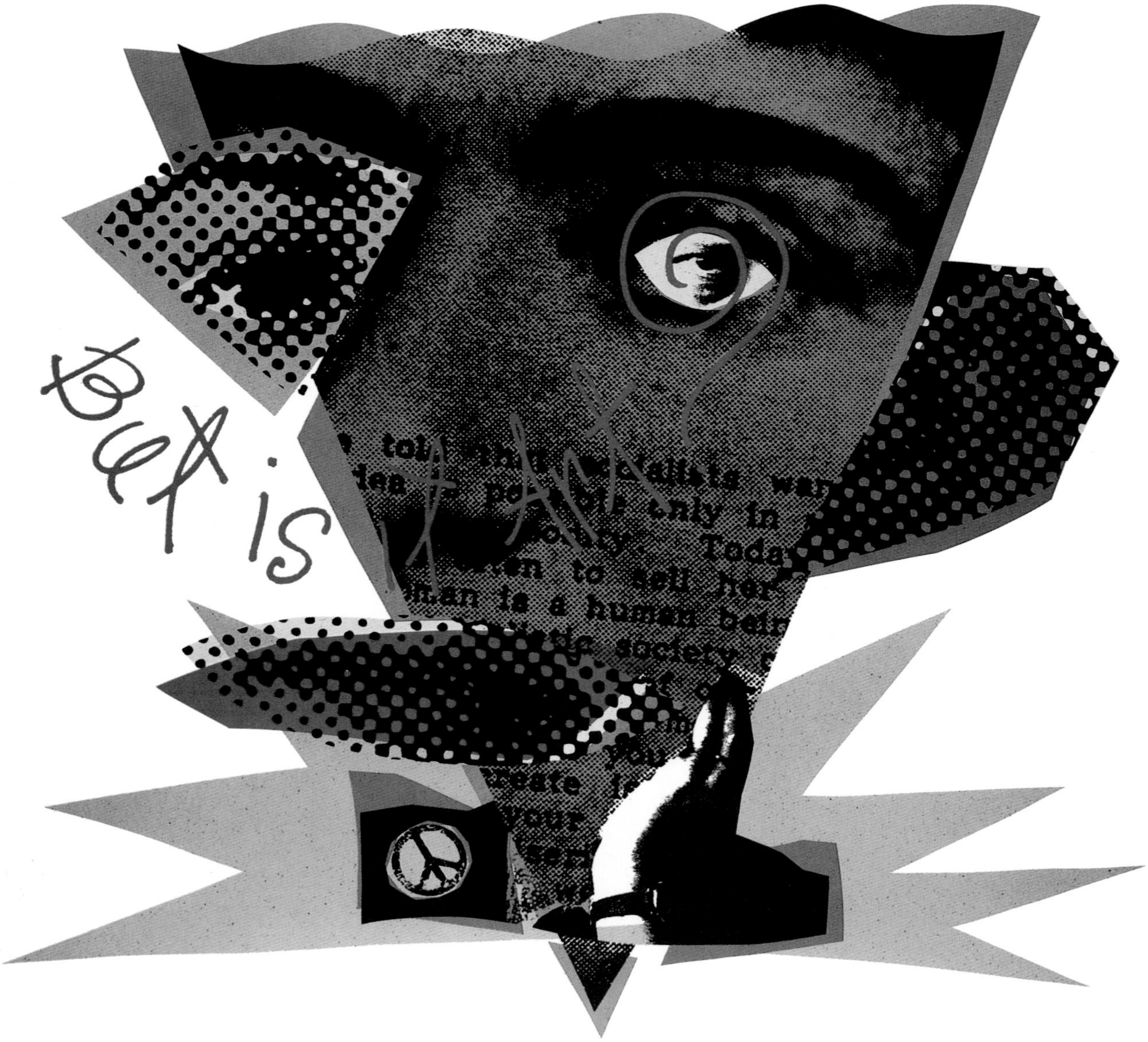

Art Garcia

Art Directors) Ron Sullivan and Art Garcia Writers) Mark Perkins and Priscilla Siegel Printer) Williamson Medium) Xerox collage and offset printing This poster was designed to announce the guest speaker, Art Chantry, at a Dallas Society of Visual Communications meeting.

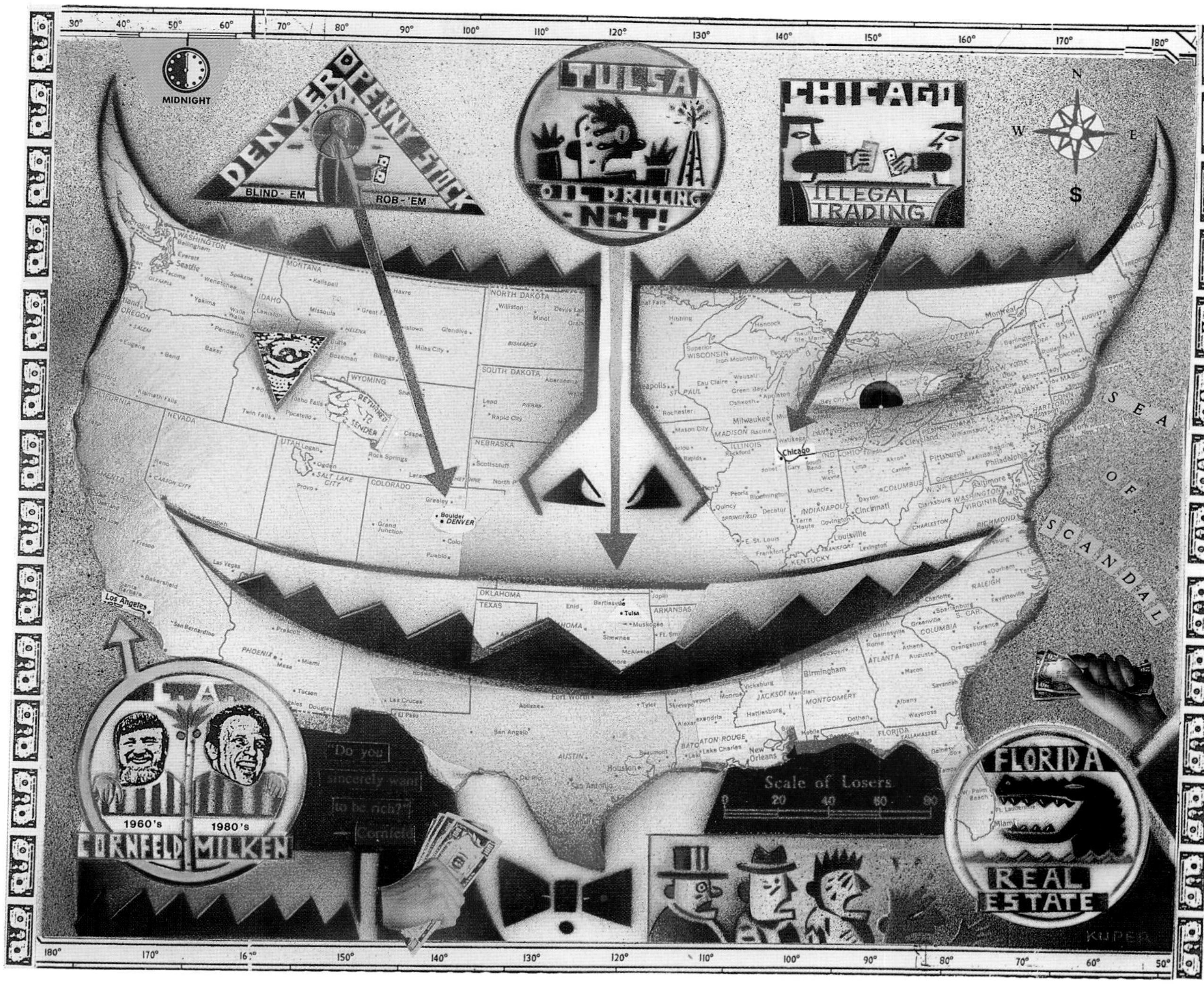

Peter Kuper

Art Director) Kelly McMurray Writer) John Strahinich Publication) Worth Date) March 1993 Publisher) Capital Publishing Medium) Mixed media Appearing with the article "Scams USA," this map is a guide to various American investment swindles, rip-offs and scams.

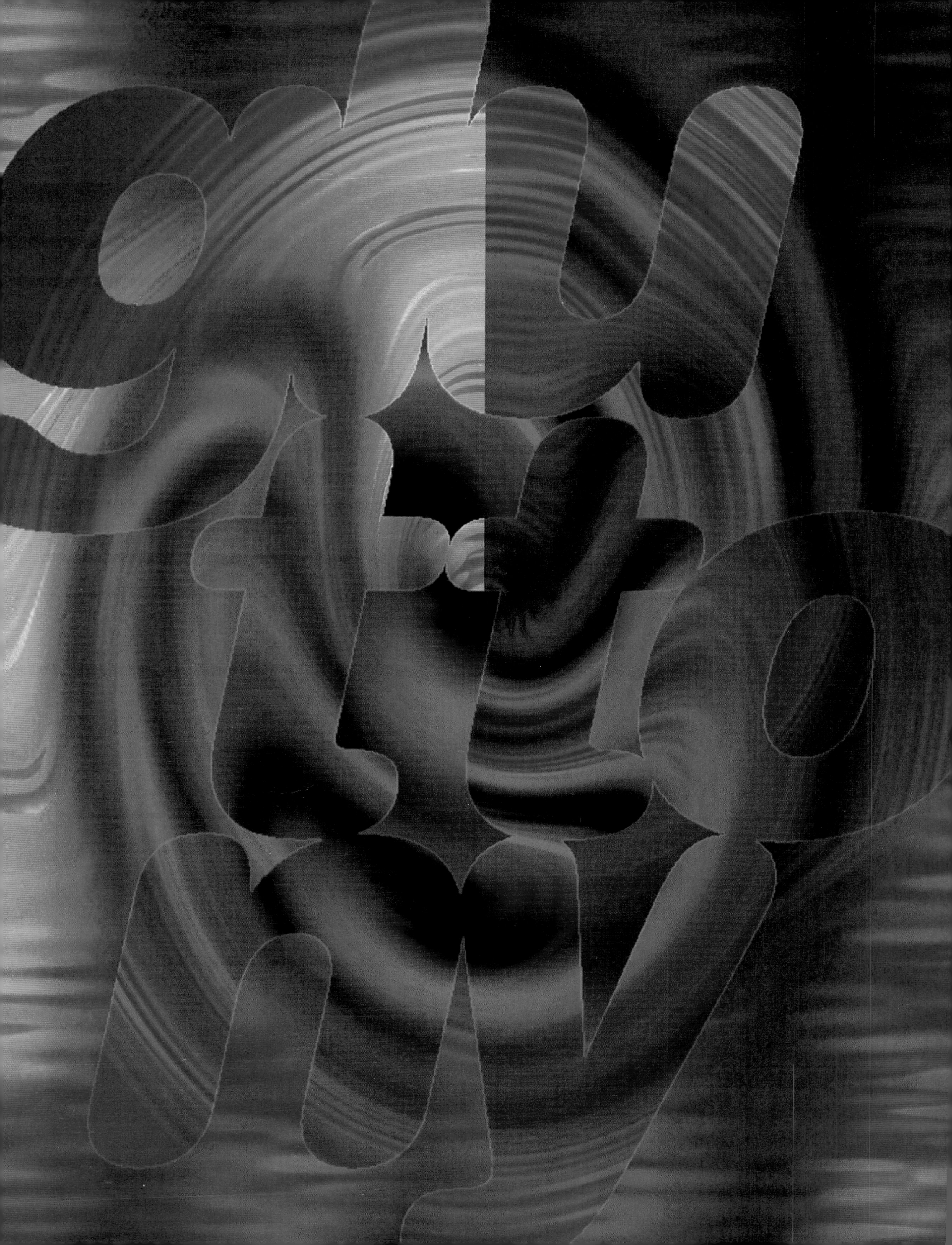

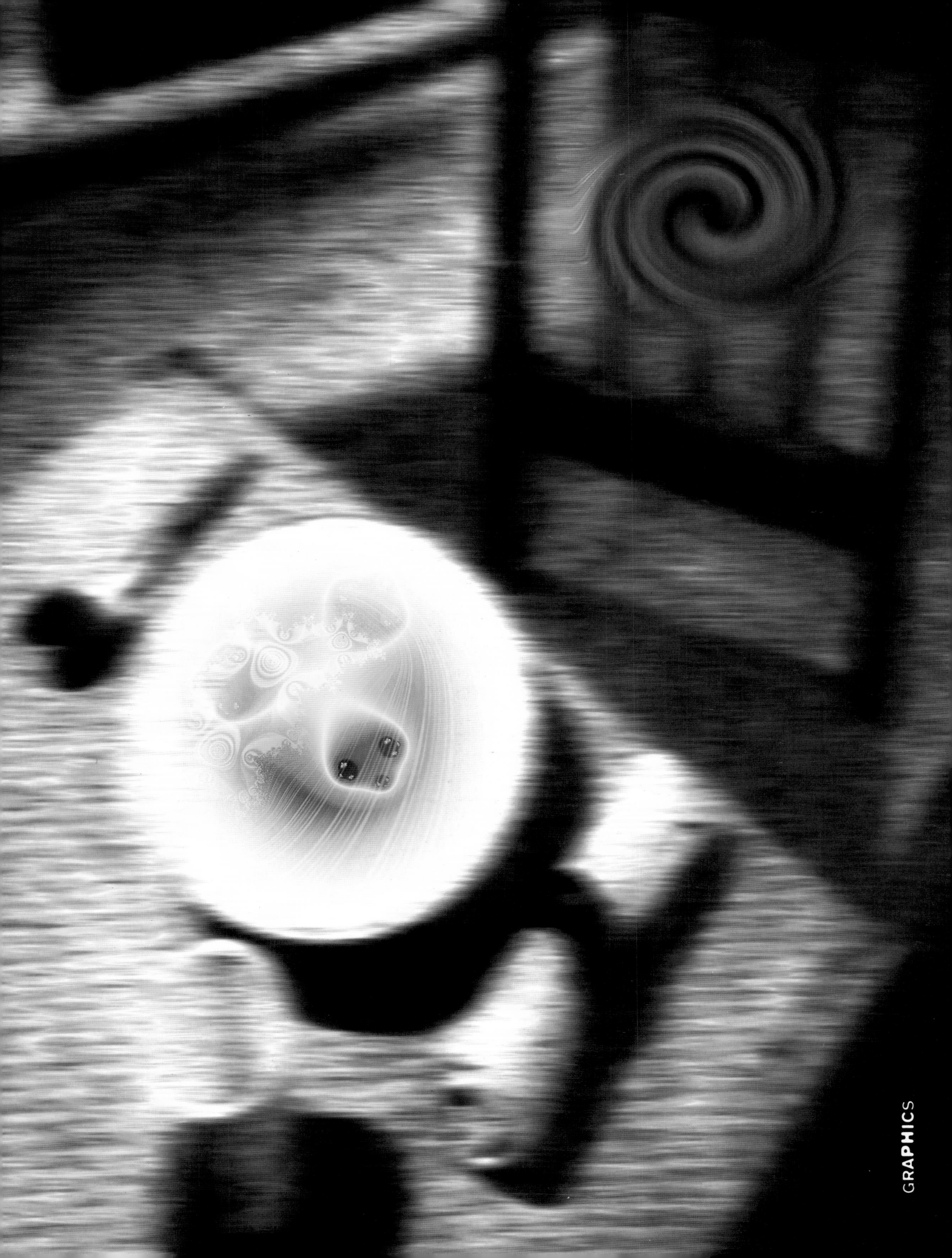

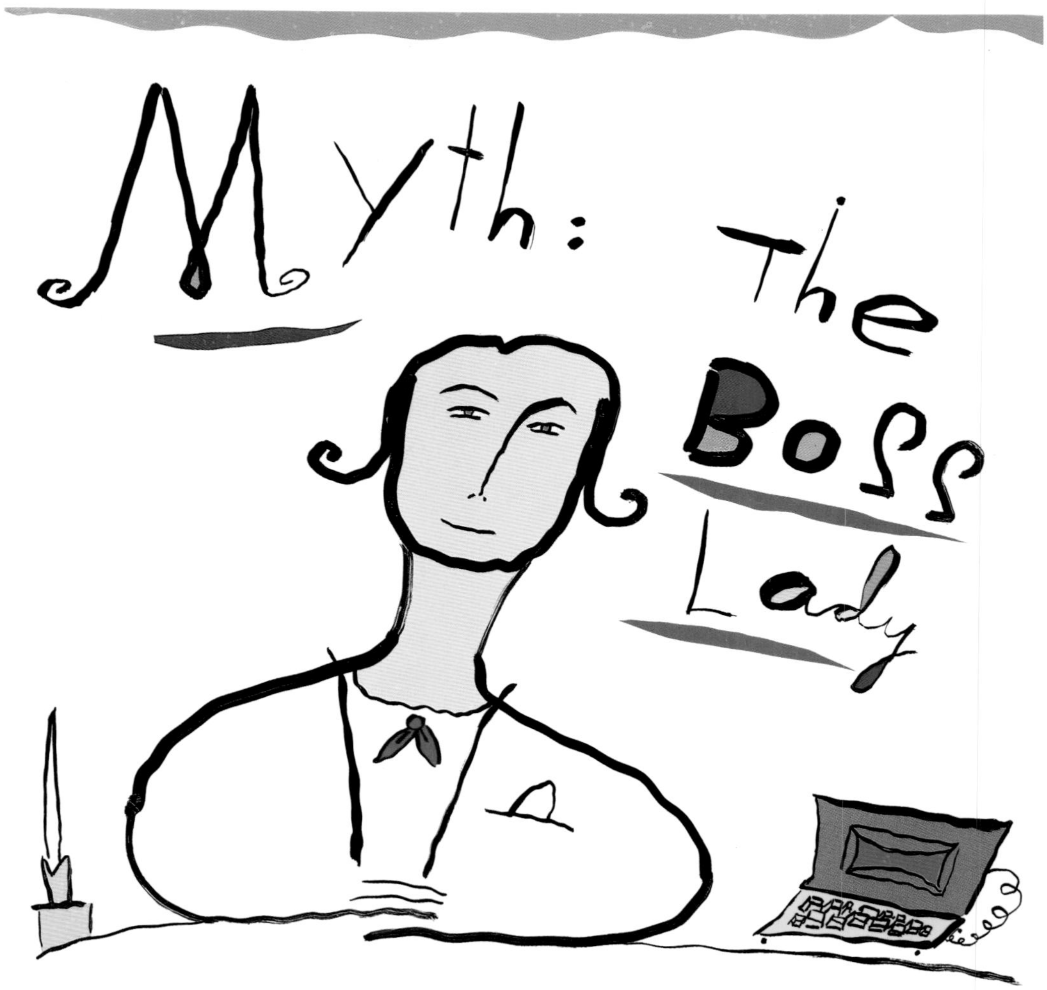

Lilla Rogers

Art Directors) **Chris Farley and Gina Russell** **Design Firm) Chermayeff and Geismar** Medium) **Ink** and cut paper
These **two illustrations appeared as a display for The Woman's** Rights Museum, **Seneca Falls**, NY.

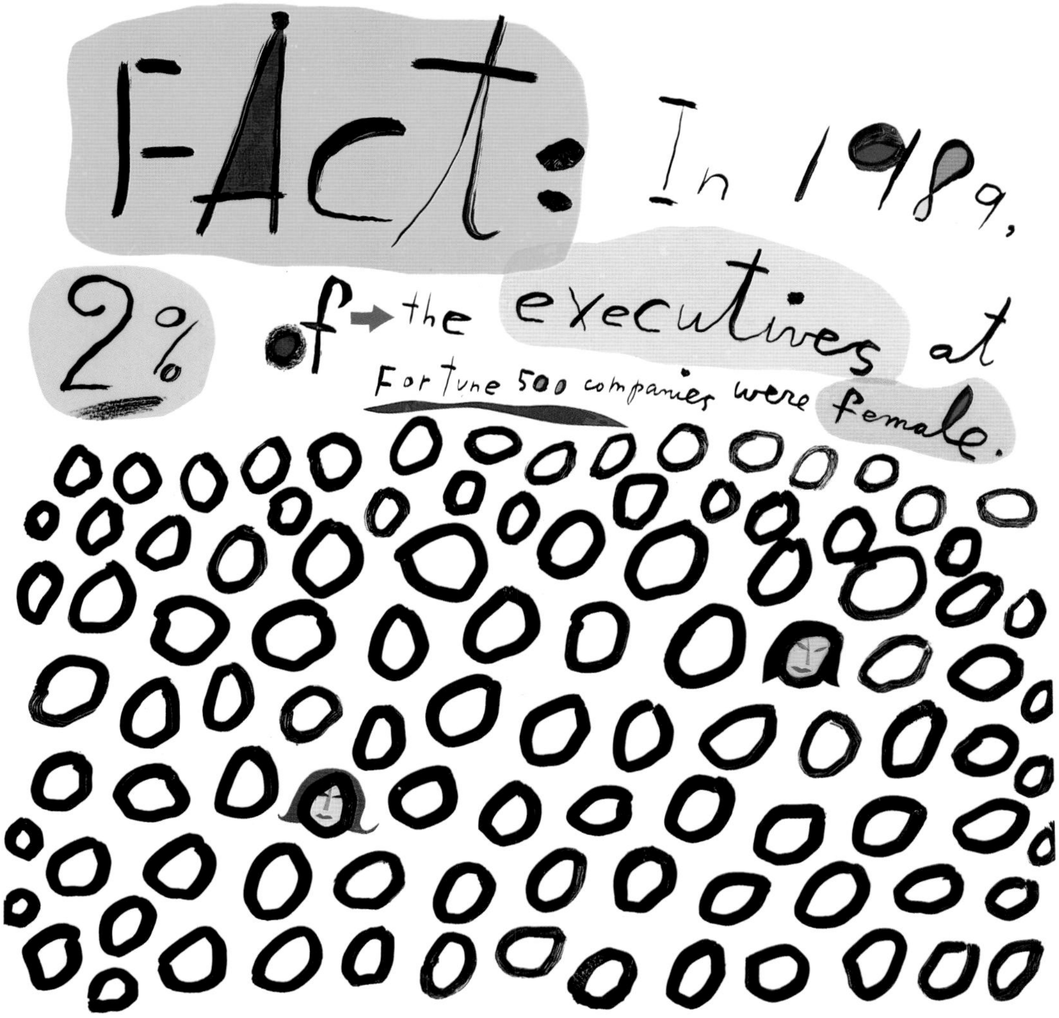
FACT: In 1989,
2% of the executives at
Fortune 500 companies were female.

Art Director) Hitoshi Himagawa Agency) Close World Collection Client) Sugar for Strawberry Fields and Bow Brand Date) Spring 1993 Medium) Brush and ink and color tints A promotional piece for a spring clothing line.

Isabelle Dervaux

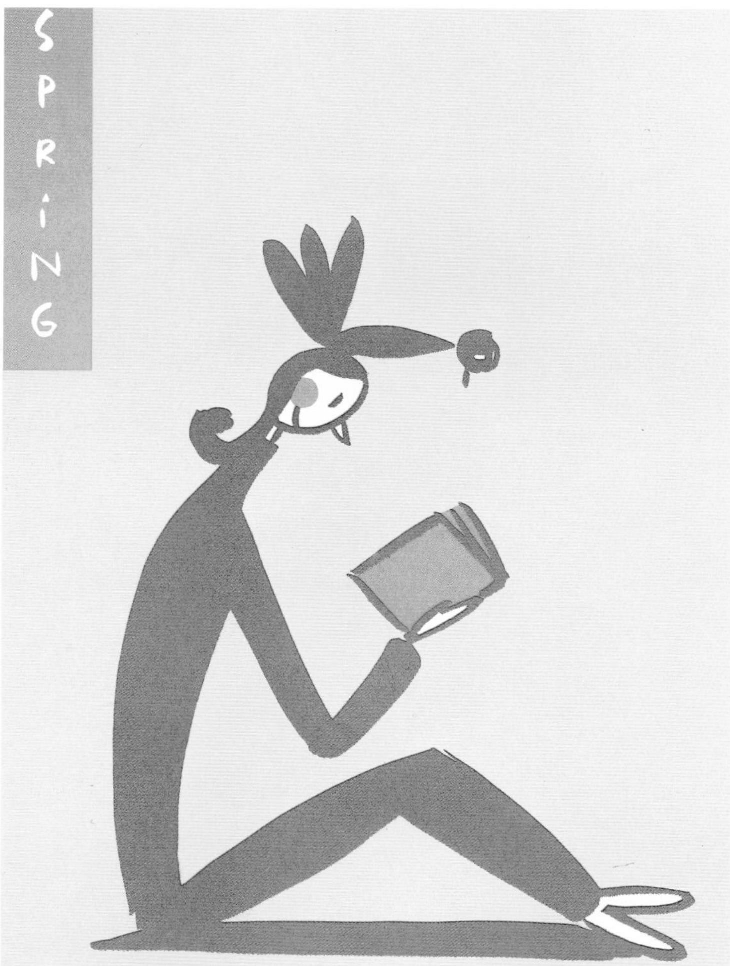

Client) Architects, Designers & Planners for Social Responsibility Medium) Ball point pen on corrugated cardboard
This illustration, entitled "Shelter ca 1990," is currently being sold as a postcard.

Kiyoshi Kanai

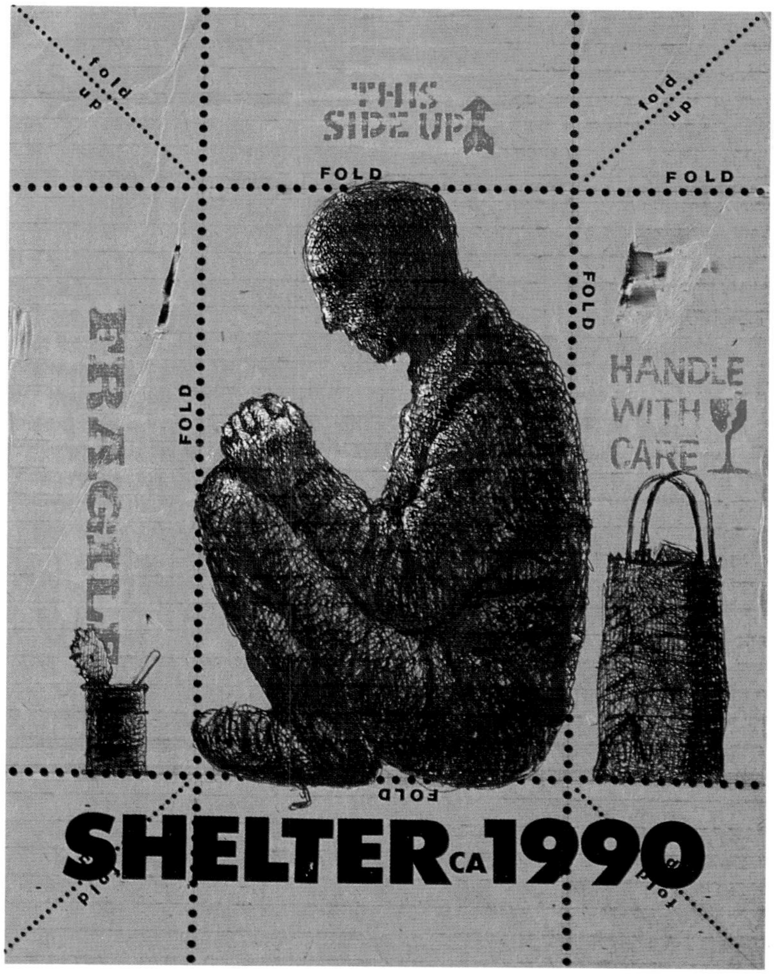

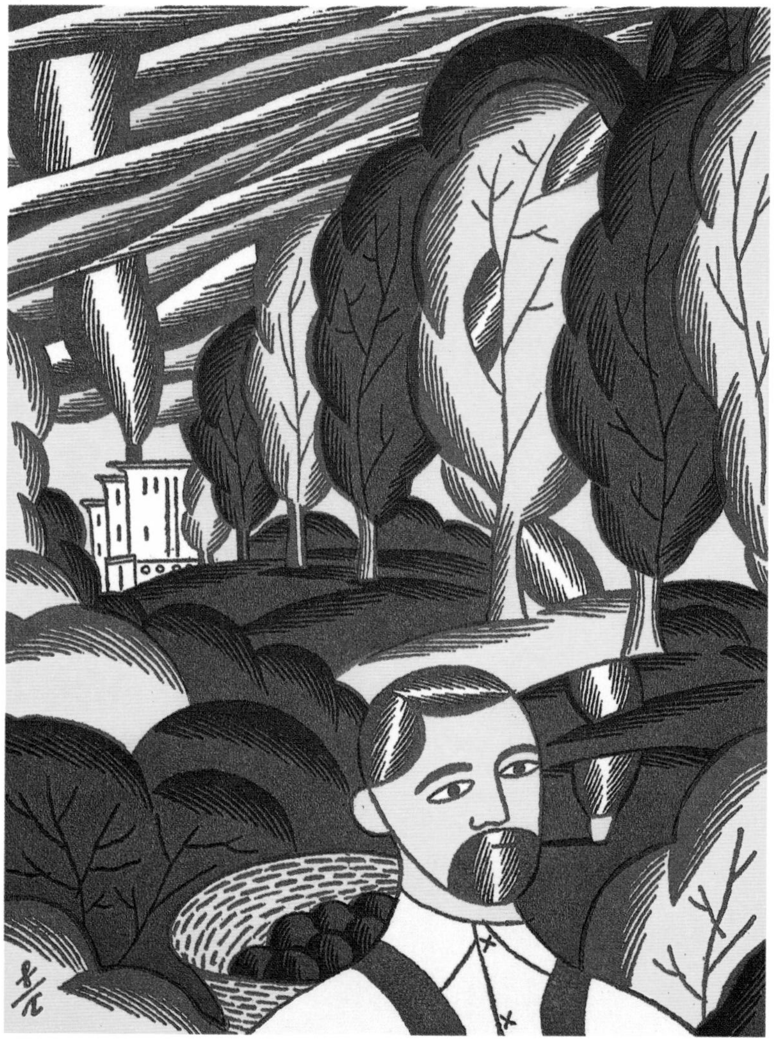

Brian Cronin

Medium) Pen and ink and letter press printing A self-promotional piece.

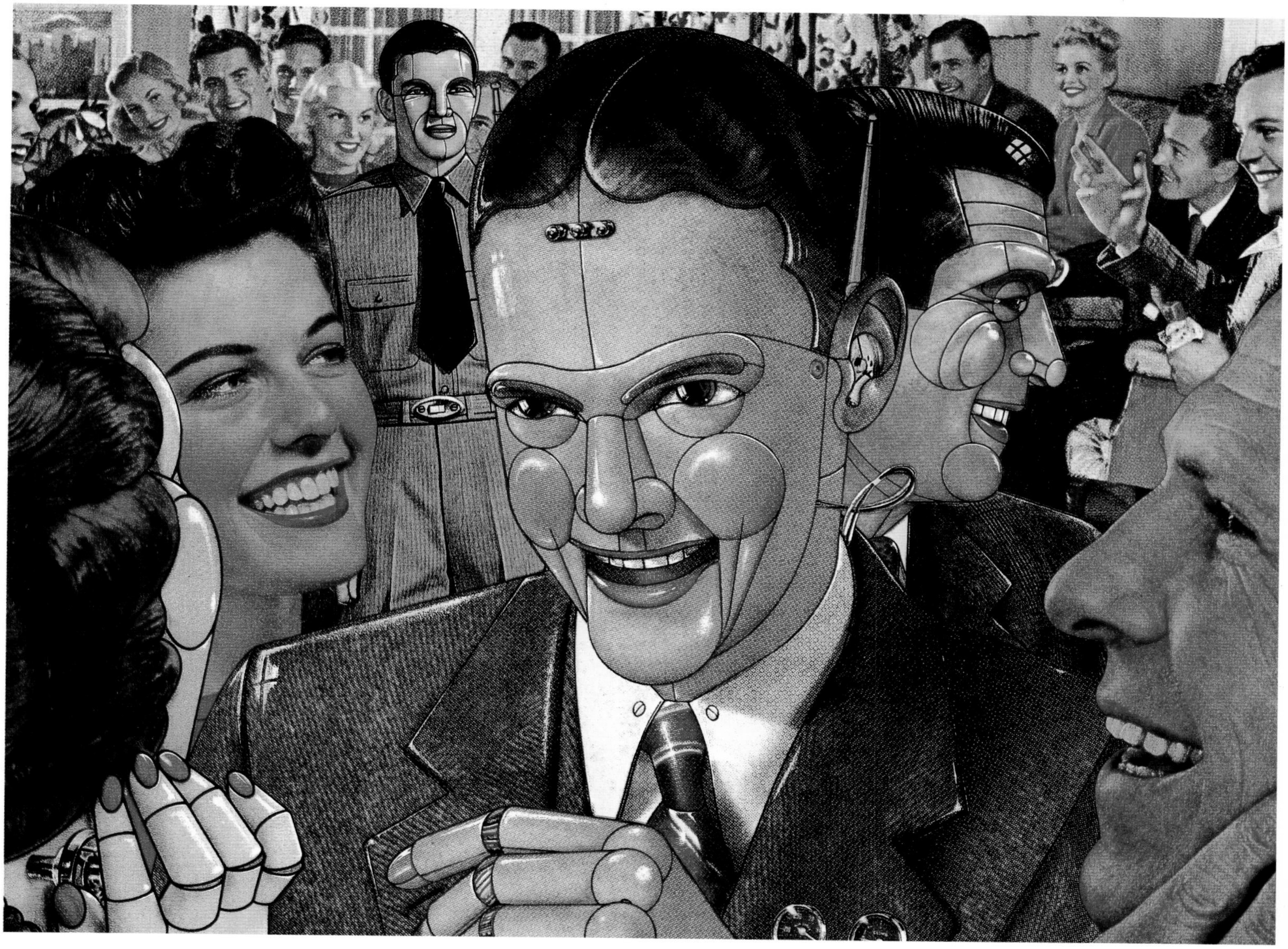

John Craig

Art Director) Gordon Mortensen Design Firm) Mortensen Design Publication) Harnessing Information
Date) Spring 1992 Client) Stanford University, Center for the Study of Languages and Information
Medium) Collage, ink and scratching An informational booklet on robotics and language included this illustration.

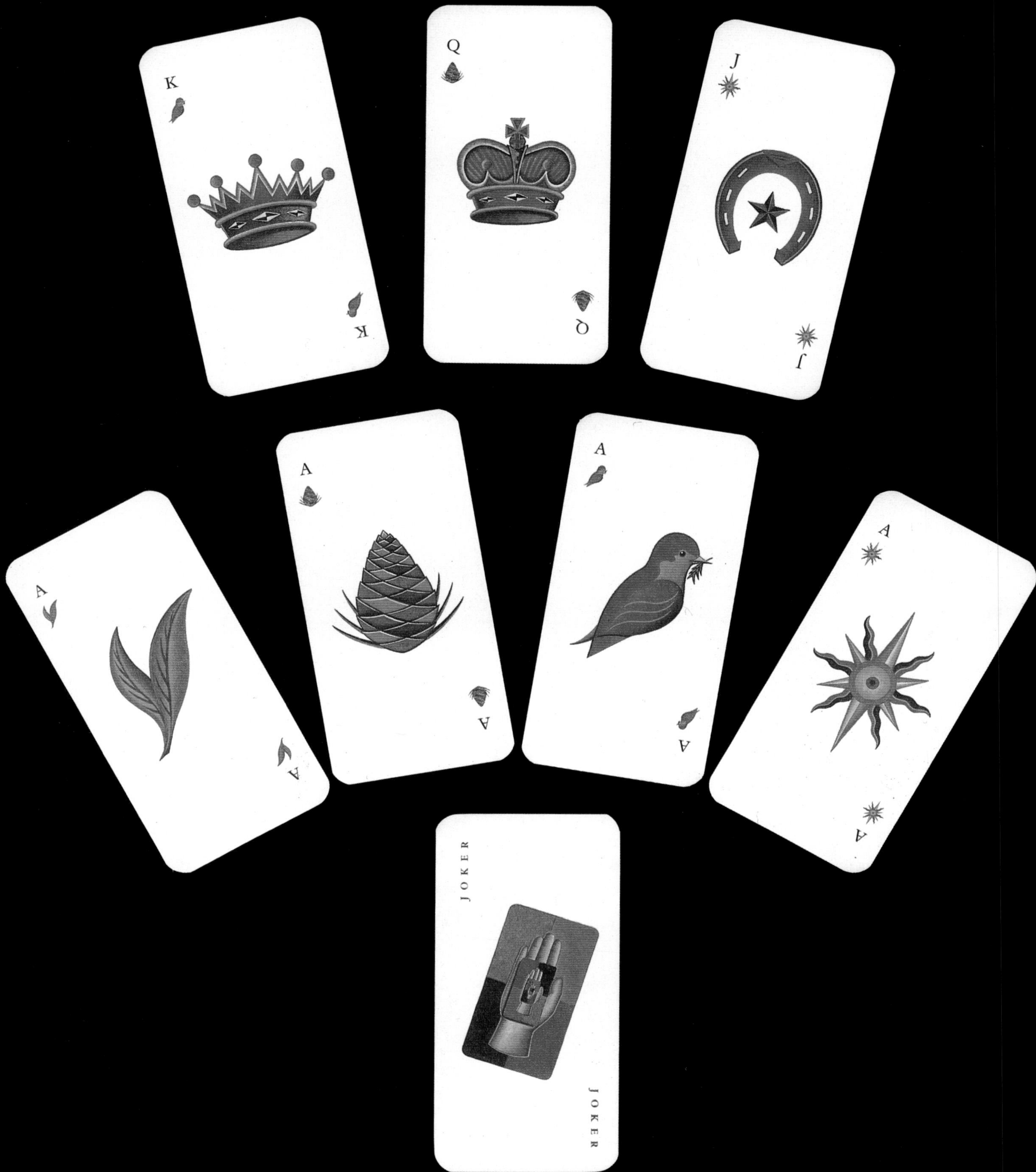
K
Q
J
A
A
A
A
JOKER

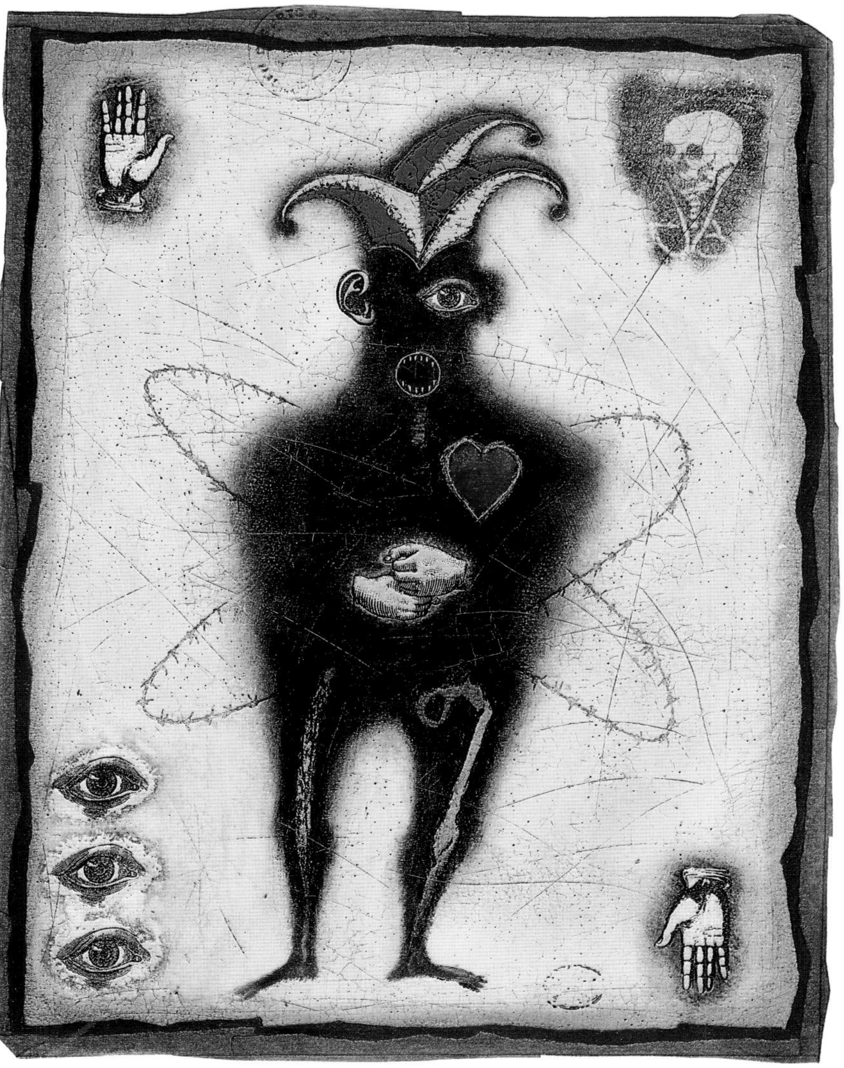

Pol Turgeon

Art Director) Lori Siebert Design Firm) Siebert Design Associates, Inc. Client) Beckett Paper
Agency) Northlick, Stolley, La Warre Writer) Bob Gard Date) Winter 1992 Medium) Photocopy, oil, ink, gouache, tape and varnish
This illustration, part of a promotional series exploring different emotions, represents the emotion hate (above).

∞

Art Director) Sunil Bhandari Design Firm) Harris-Bhandari Writer) Helen Battersby Medium) Acrylic
With each suit representing a different season, these playing cards were sent out as Christmas greetings (left).

Sandra Dionisi

Bill **Mayer**

Art Director) Jerry Sullivan **Client) Graphic Ads** Medium) Gouache and dyes
This ad, entitled "Graphic Ads is **Having an Identity Crisis**," ran originally in Ego Magazine (below).

∞

Art Director) Kim Champagne Client) Warner Brothers **Records Date) August** 11, 1992 Medium) Multi-media three dimensional art
This illustration was created for **the Elmore James "King of** the Slide Guitar" CD package (right).

Josh **Gosfield**

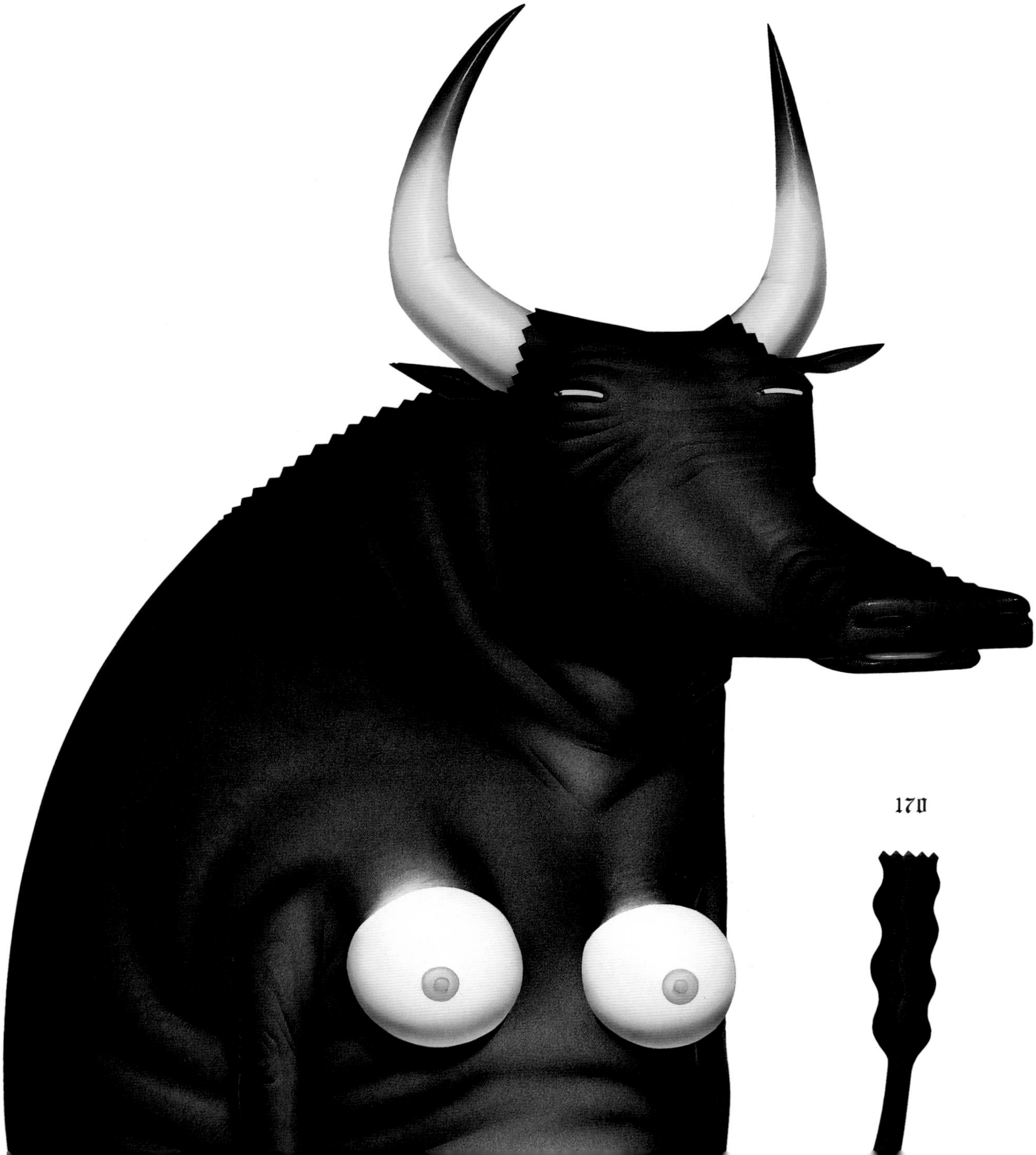

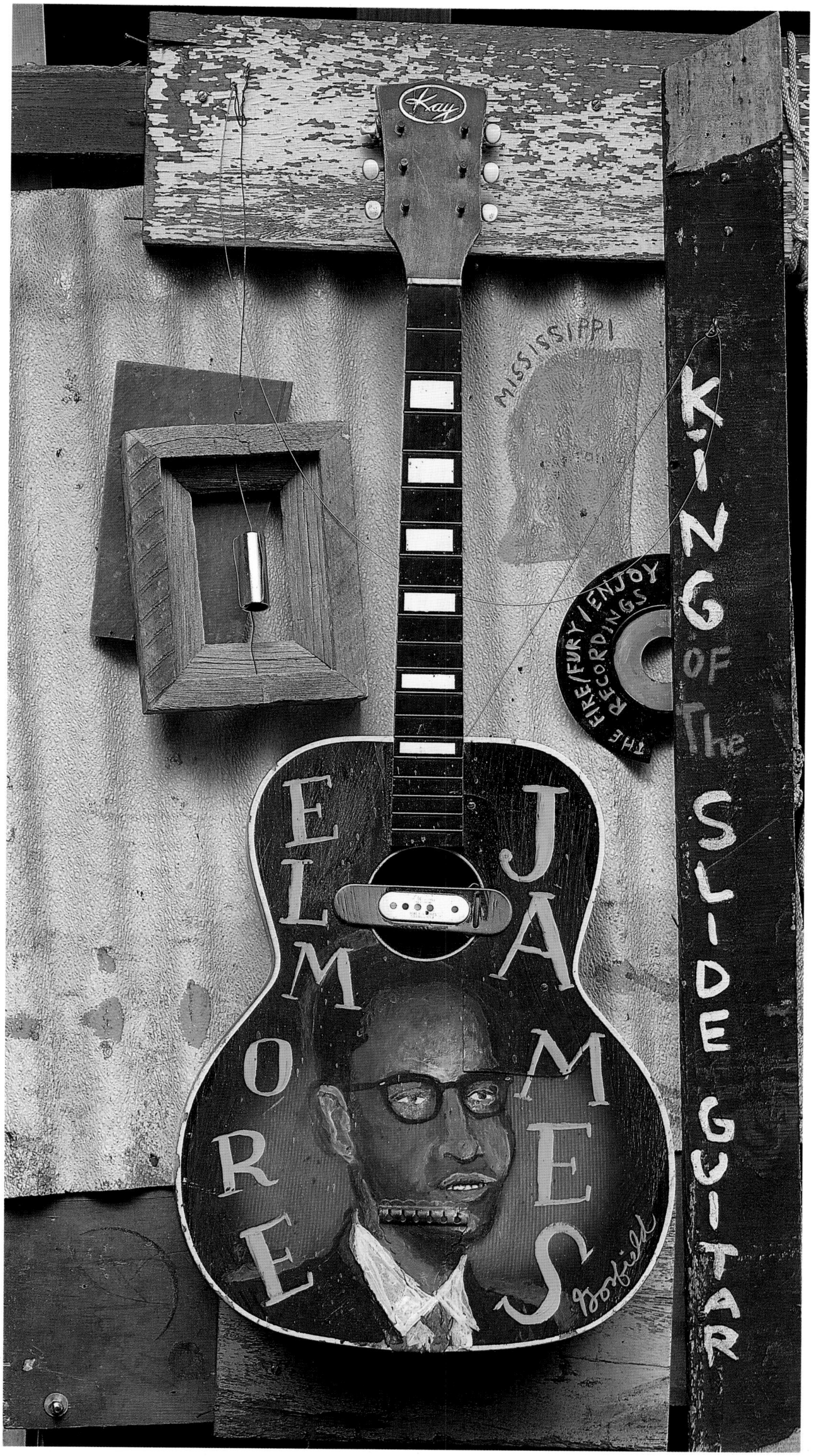
Kay
MISSISSIPPI
THE FIRE/FURY/ENJOY RECORDINGS
ELMORE JAMES
KING OF THE SLIDE GUITAR

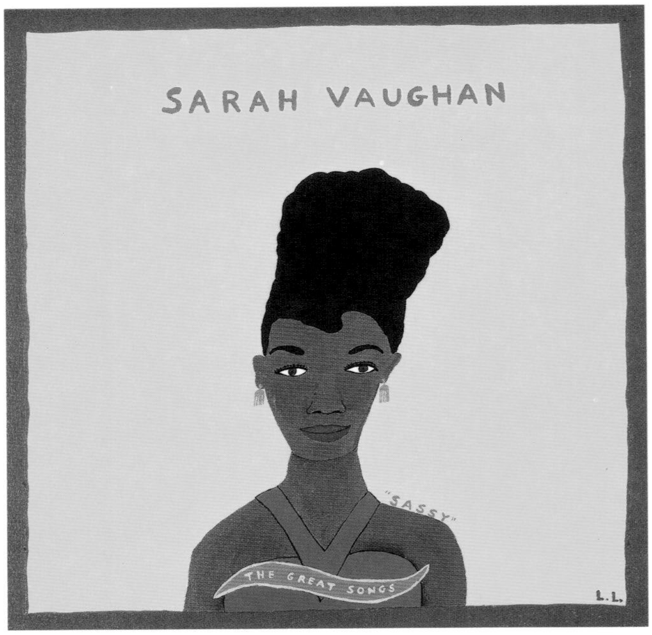

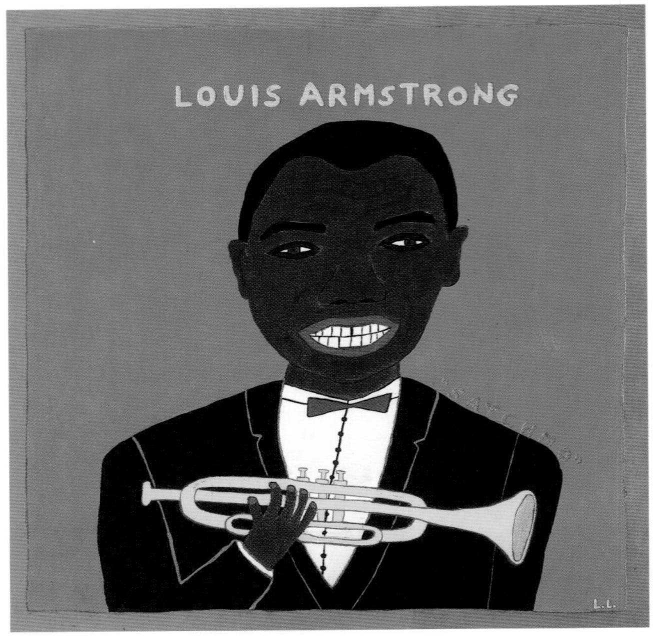

Laura Levine

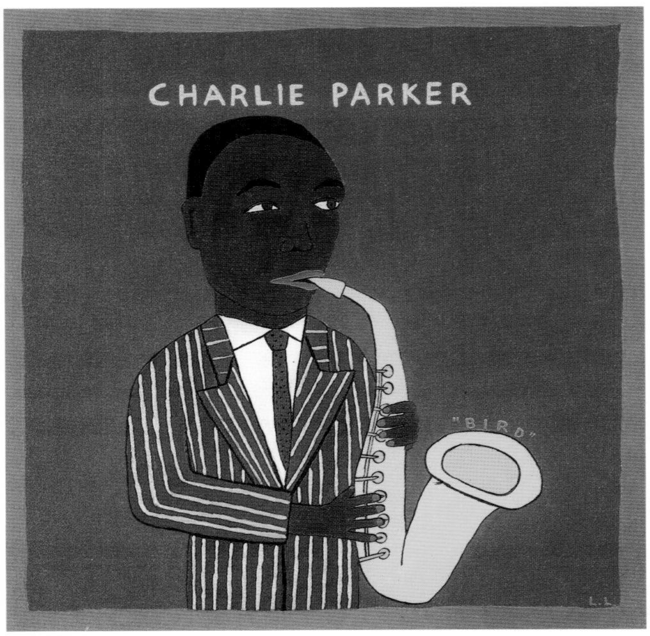

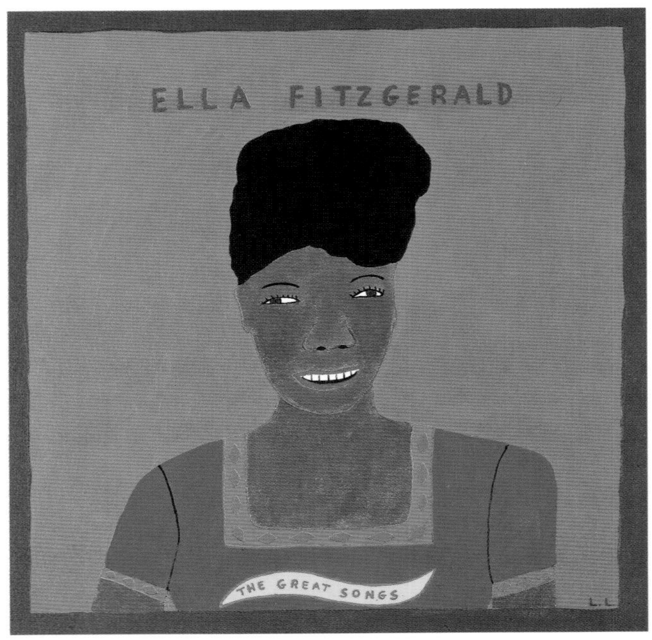

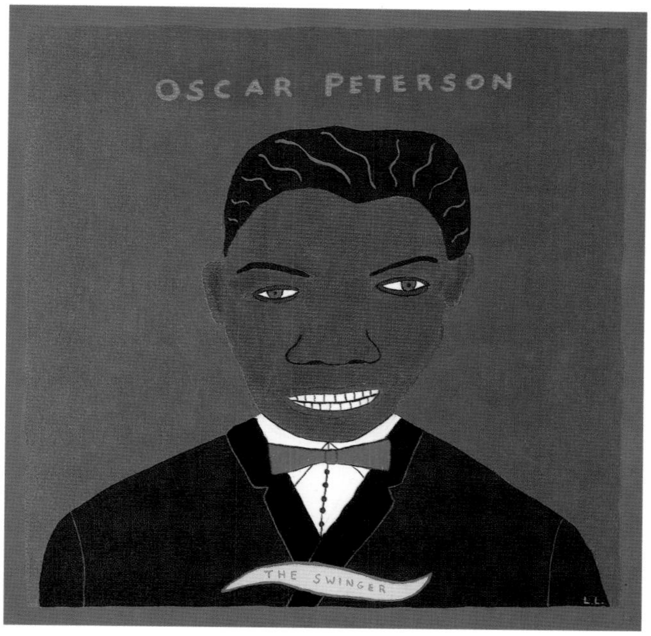

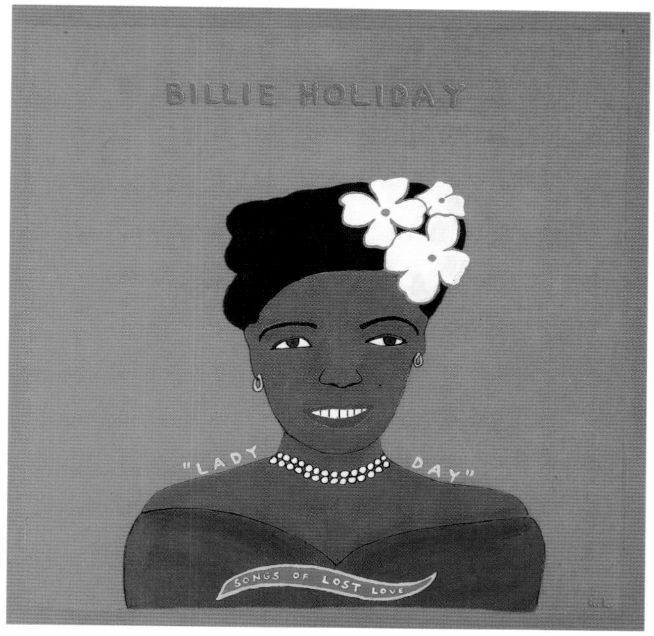

Art Director) Alli Truch Client) **Verve/Polygram Records** Medium) Acrylic on masonite
These portraits appeared on the CD covers of the "Essential Series."

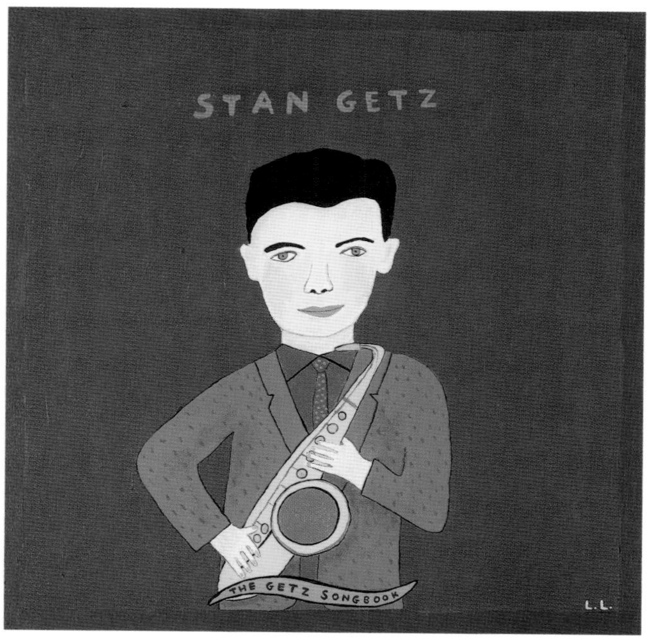

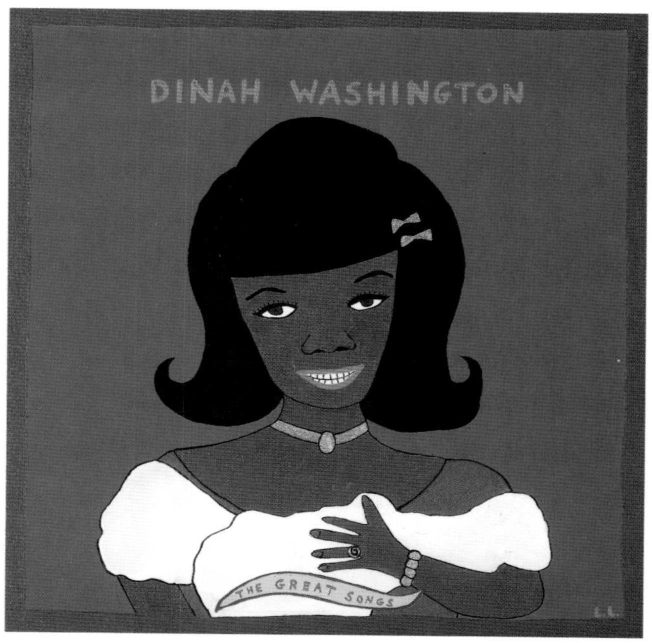

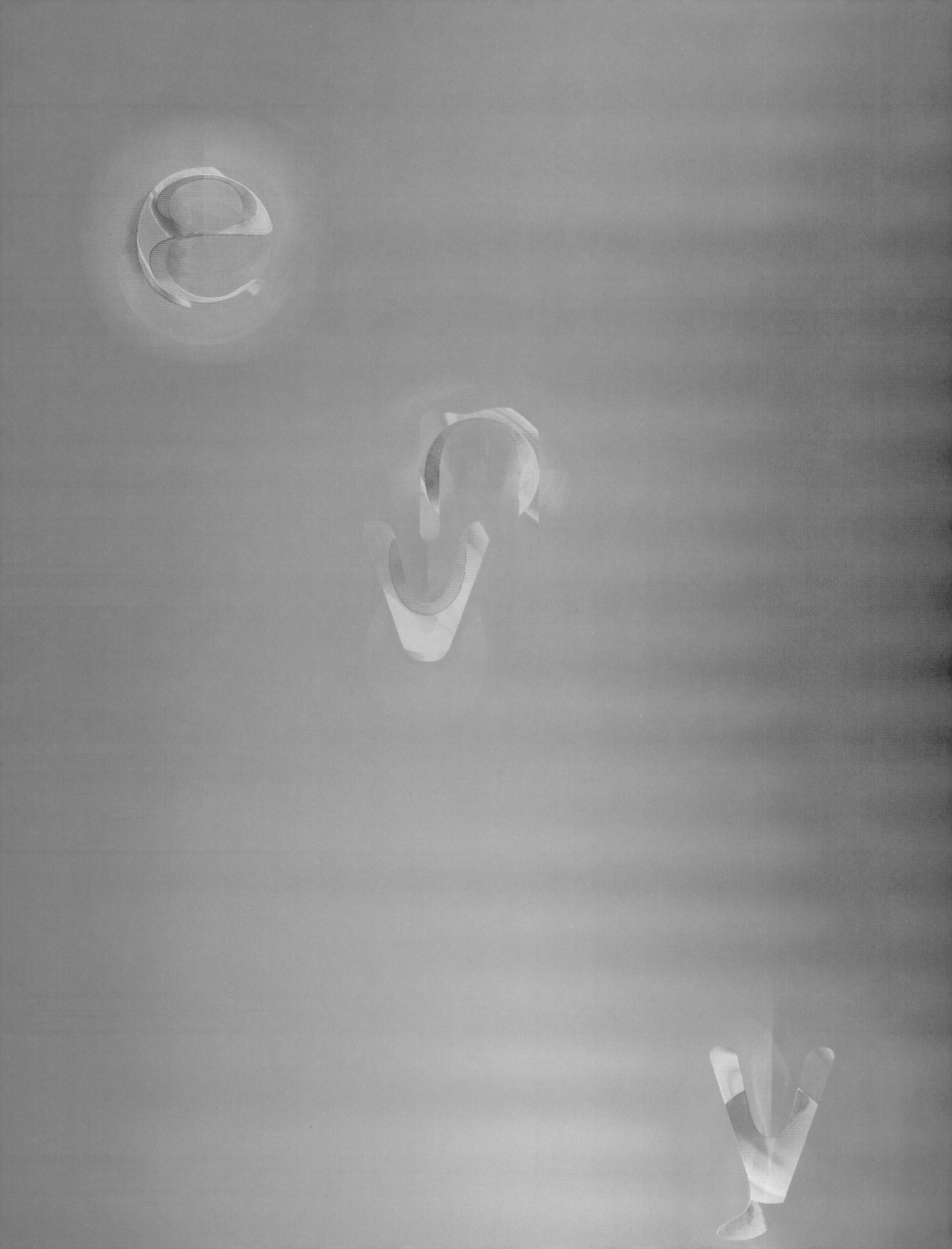

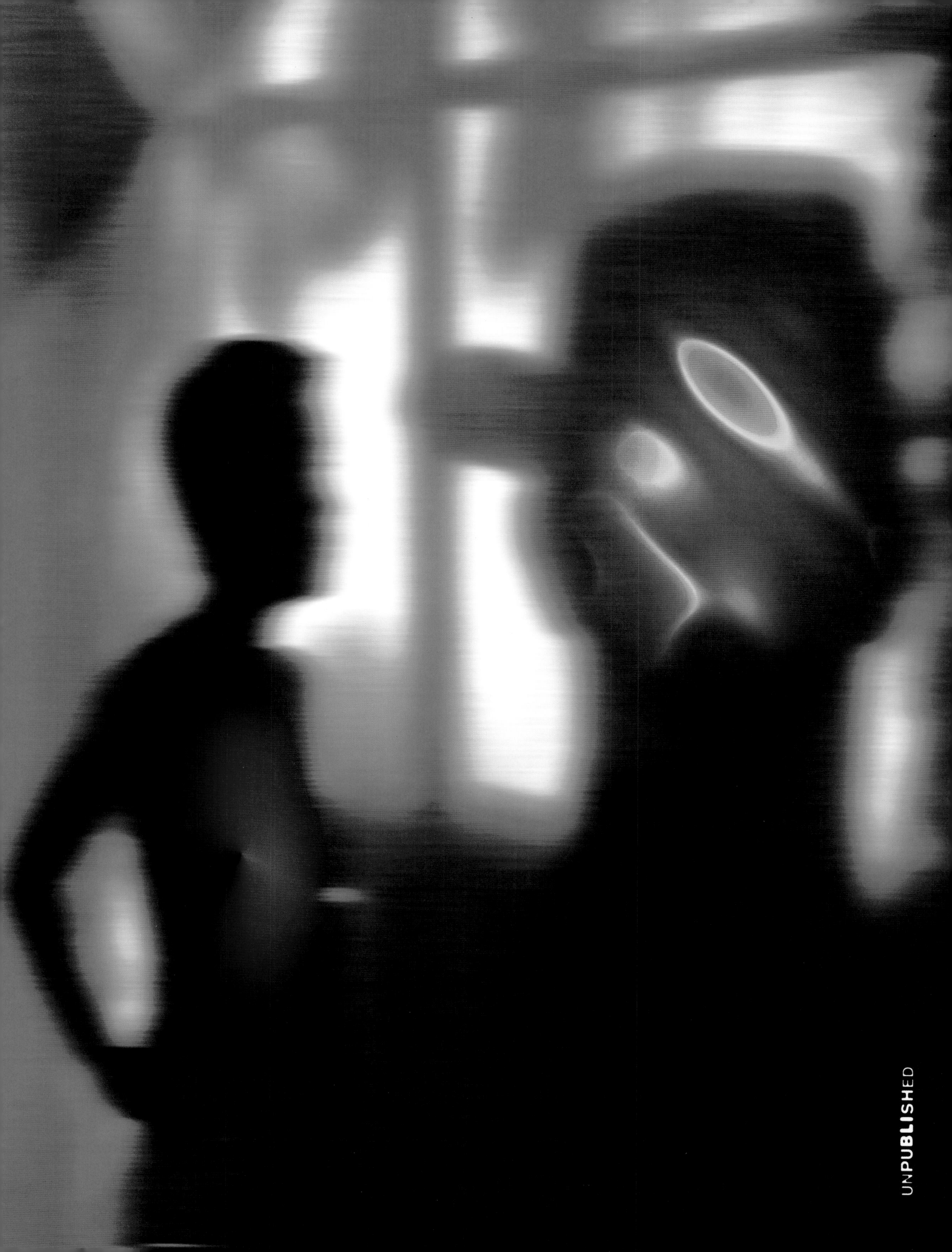

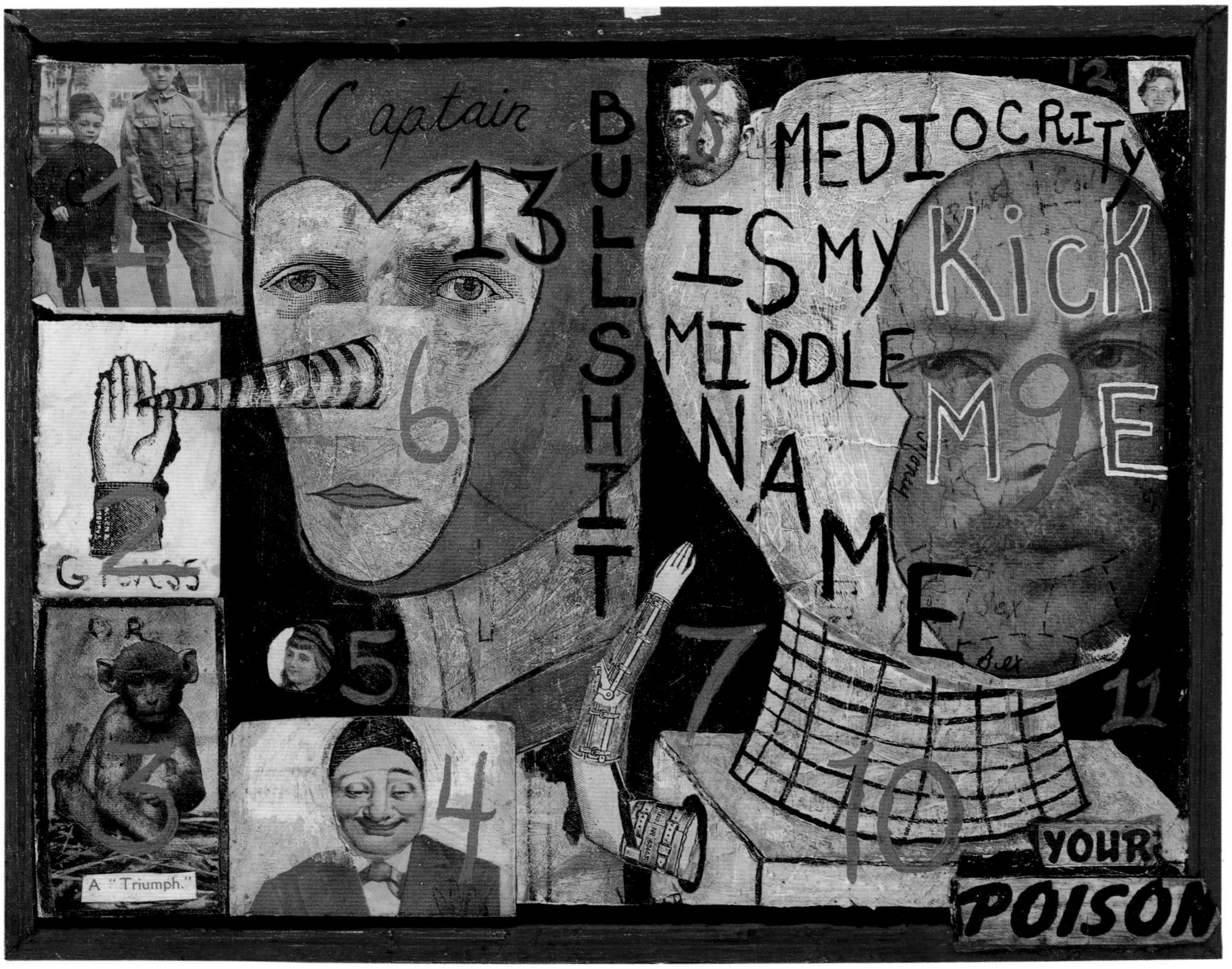

Christian Northeast

Medium) Mixed media The following three images were created for the illustrator's portfolio.

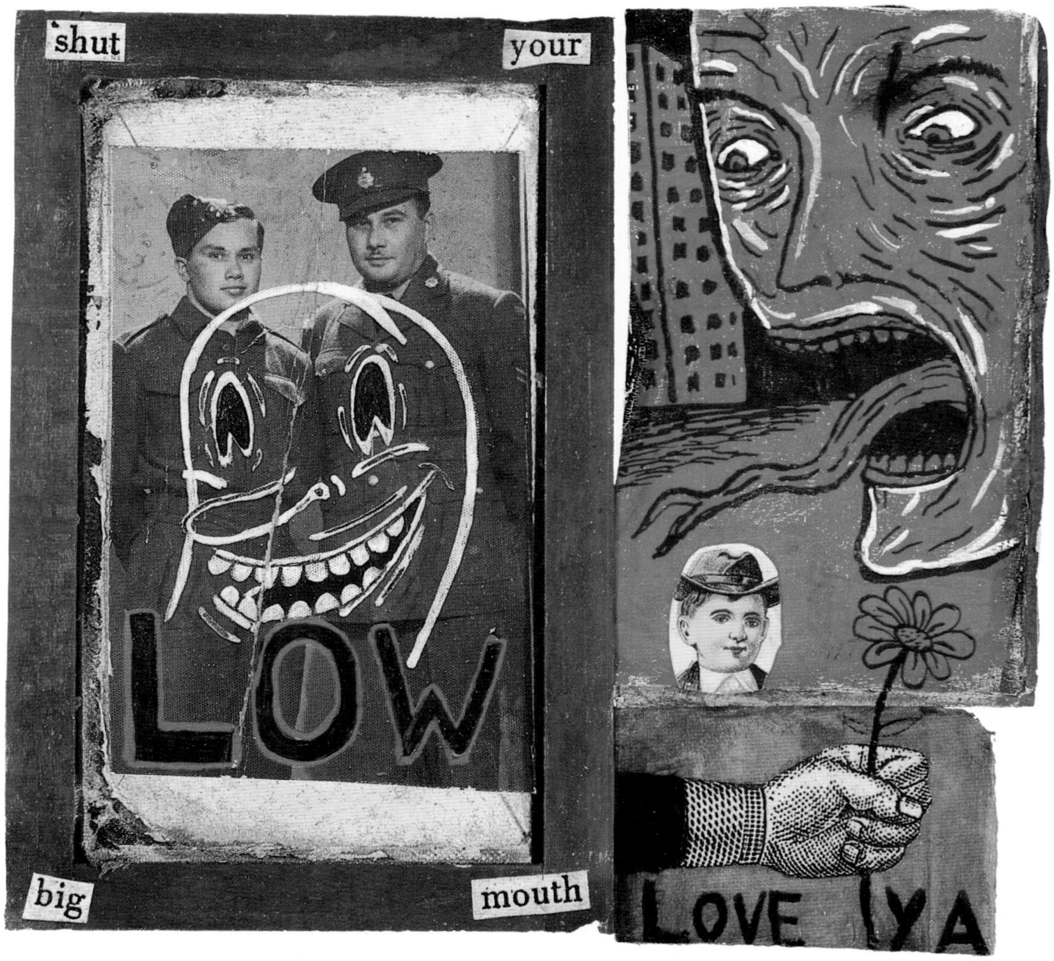
shut
your
LOW
big
mouth
LOVE YA

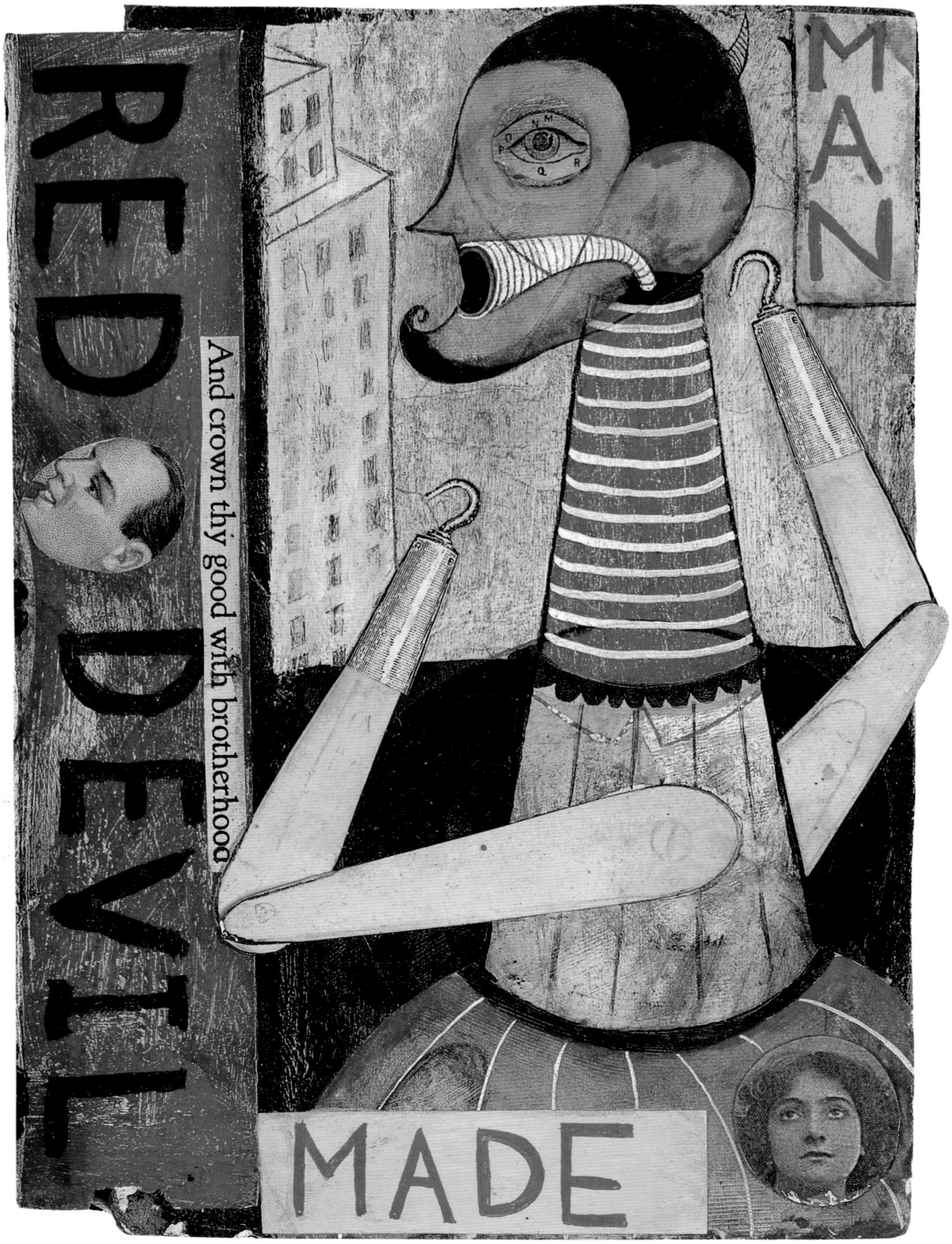
RED DEVIL
And crown thy good with brotherhood
MAN
MADE

Medium) Acrylics, spray paint and cardboard A personal work entitled "Firewater."

Gerald Bustamante

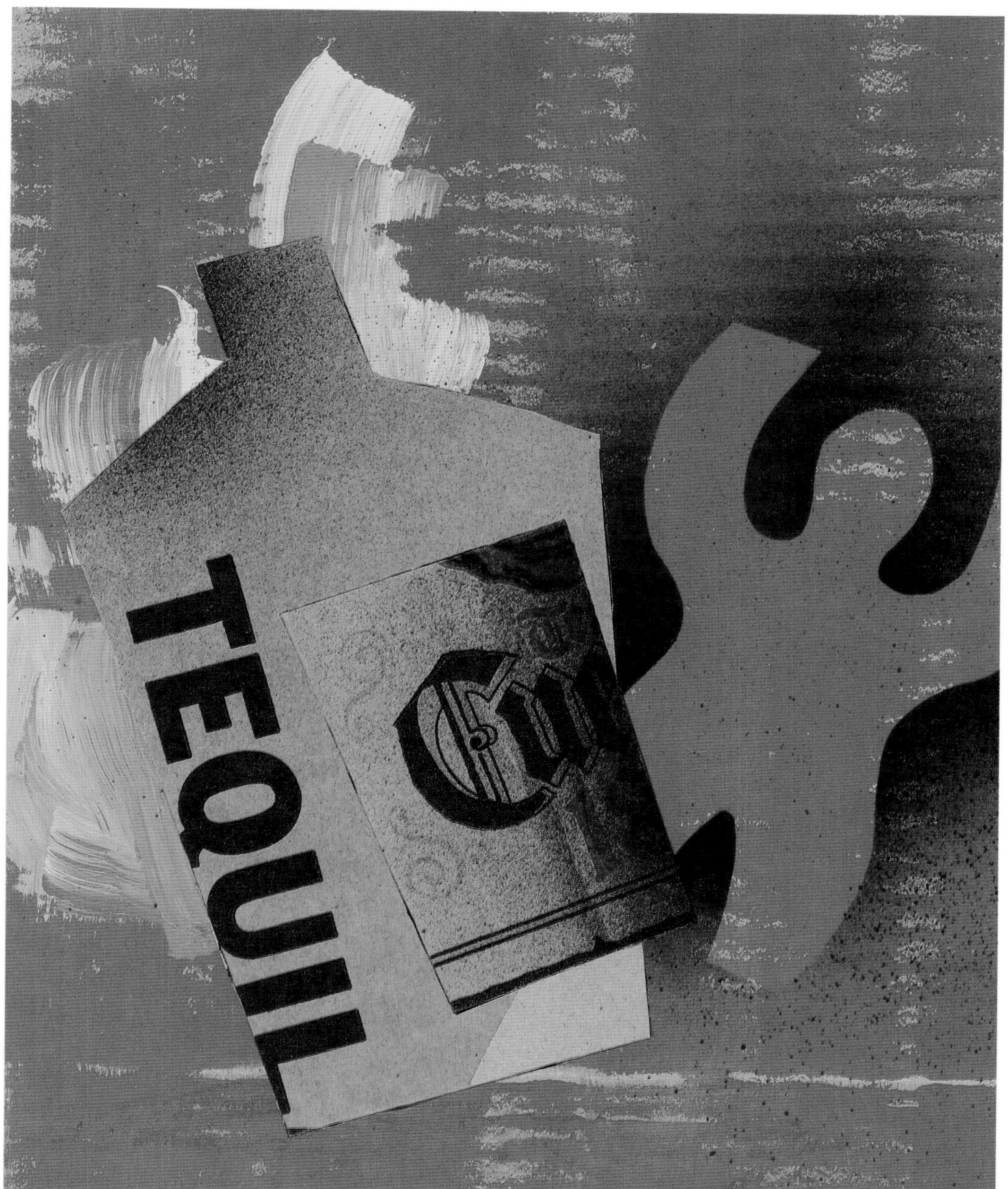

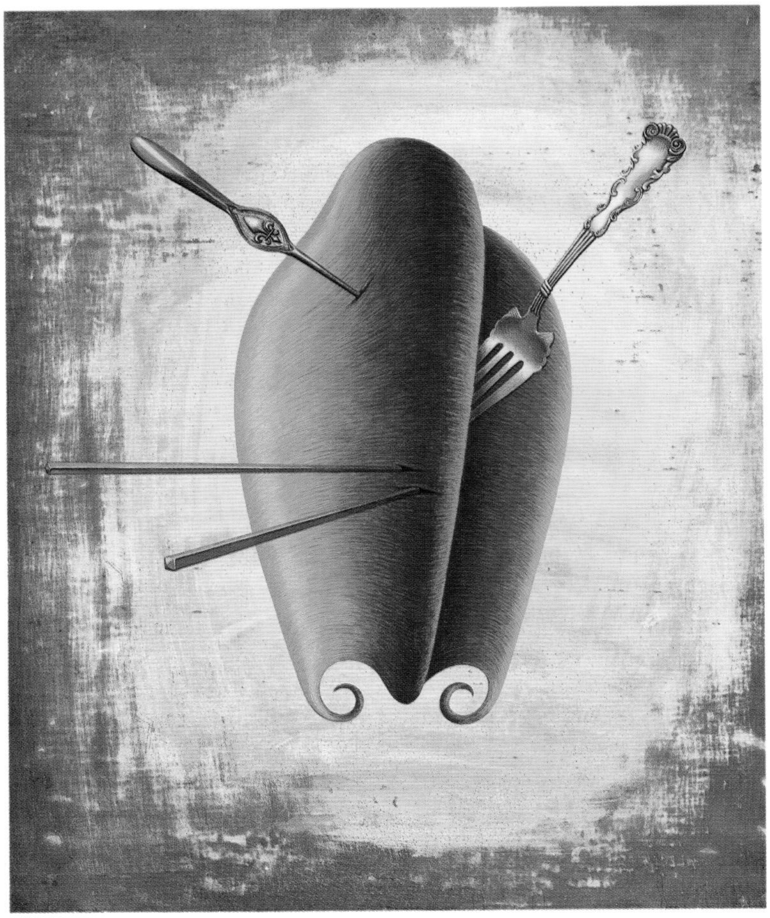

Ruth Marten

Medium) Egg tempera on wood "Havana Red" (above).

∞

Medium) Egg tempera on wood "Portrait of Saul" (right).

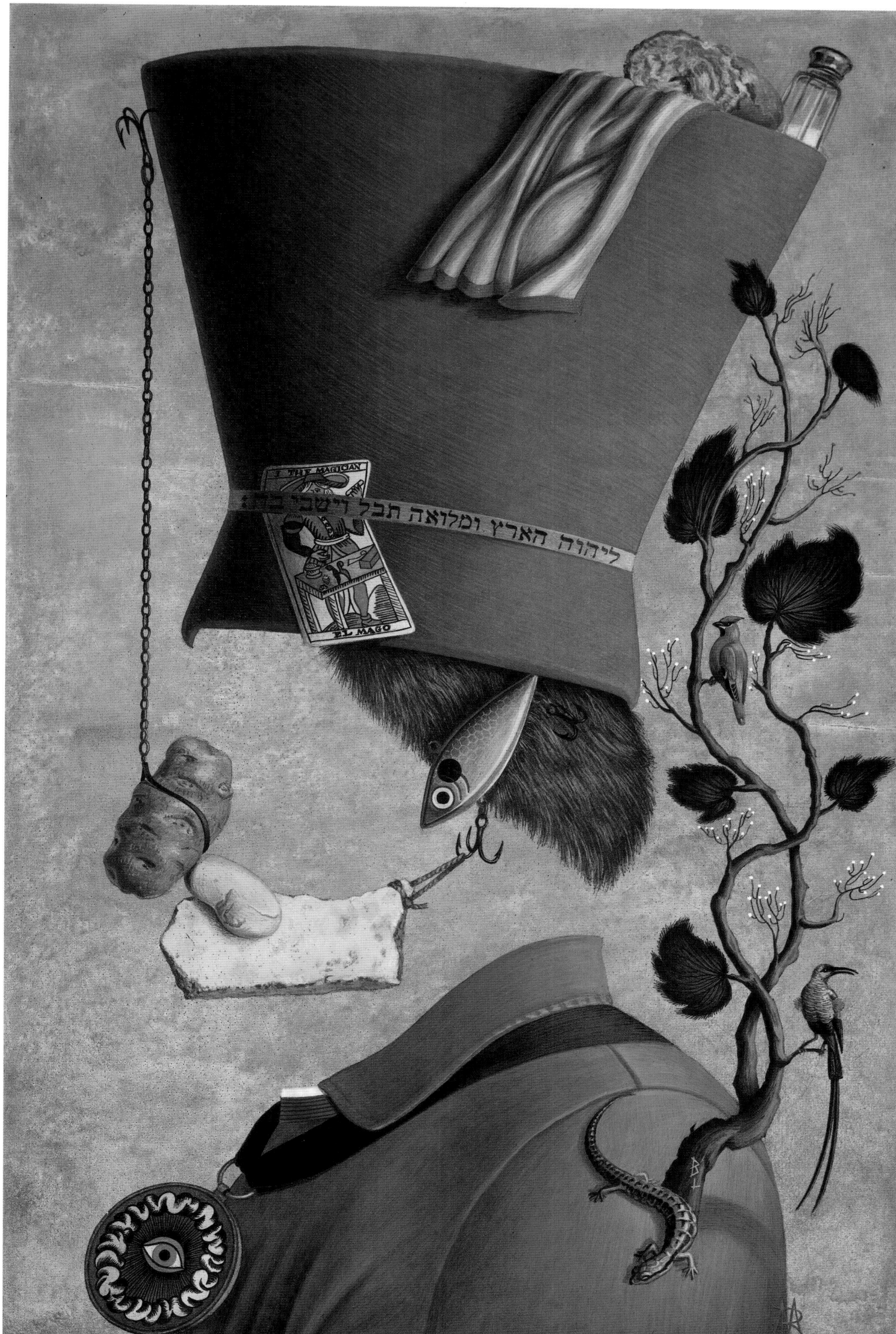
THE MAGICIAN
ליהוה הארץ ומלואה תבל וישבי
EL MAGO

Medium) Acrylic A personal piece entitled "Being Fat in the USA."

Lisa Manning

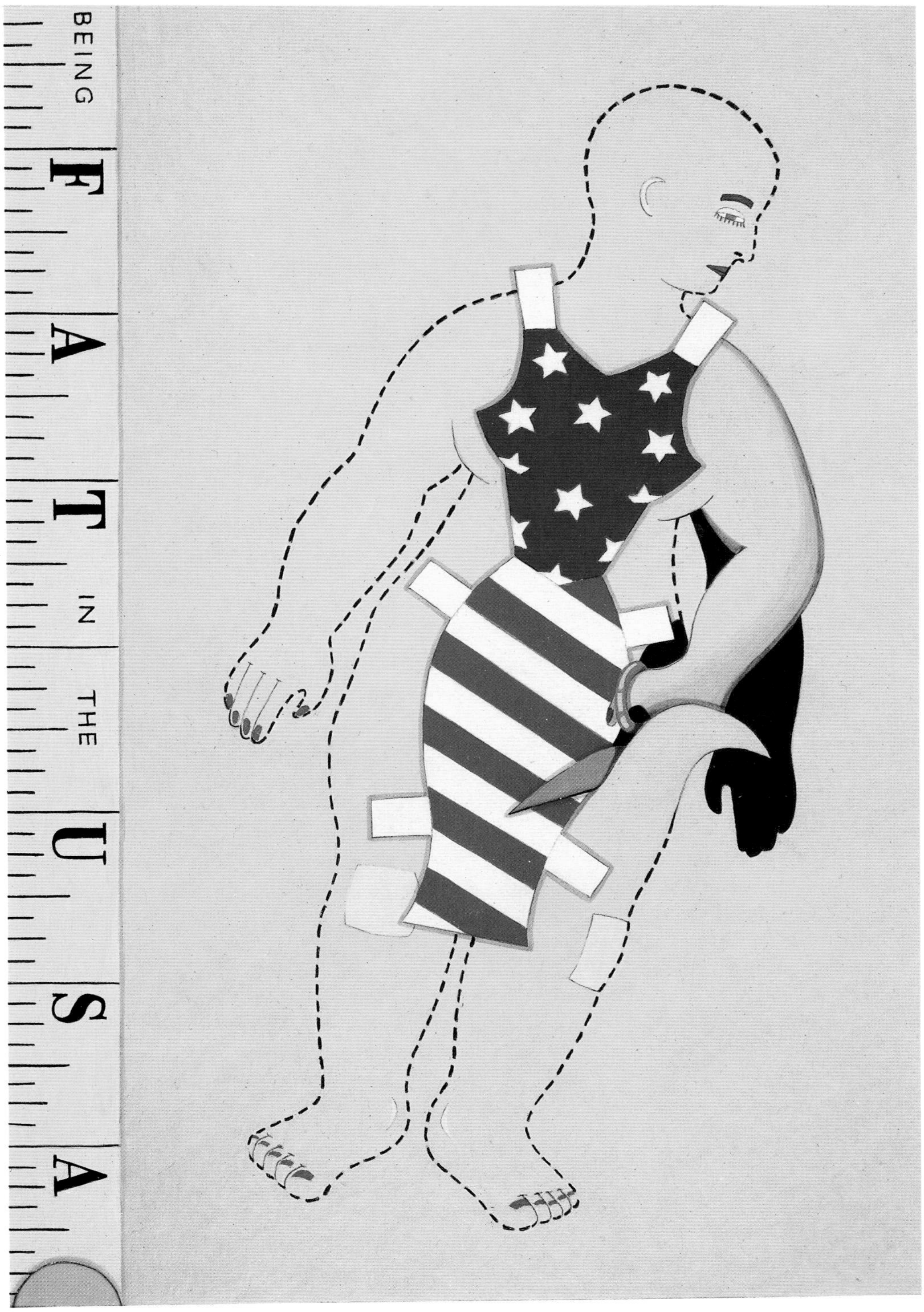

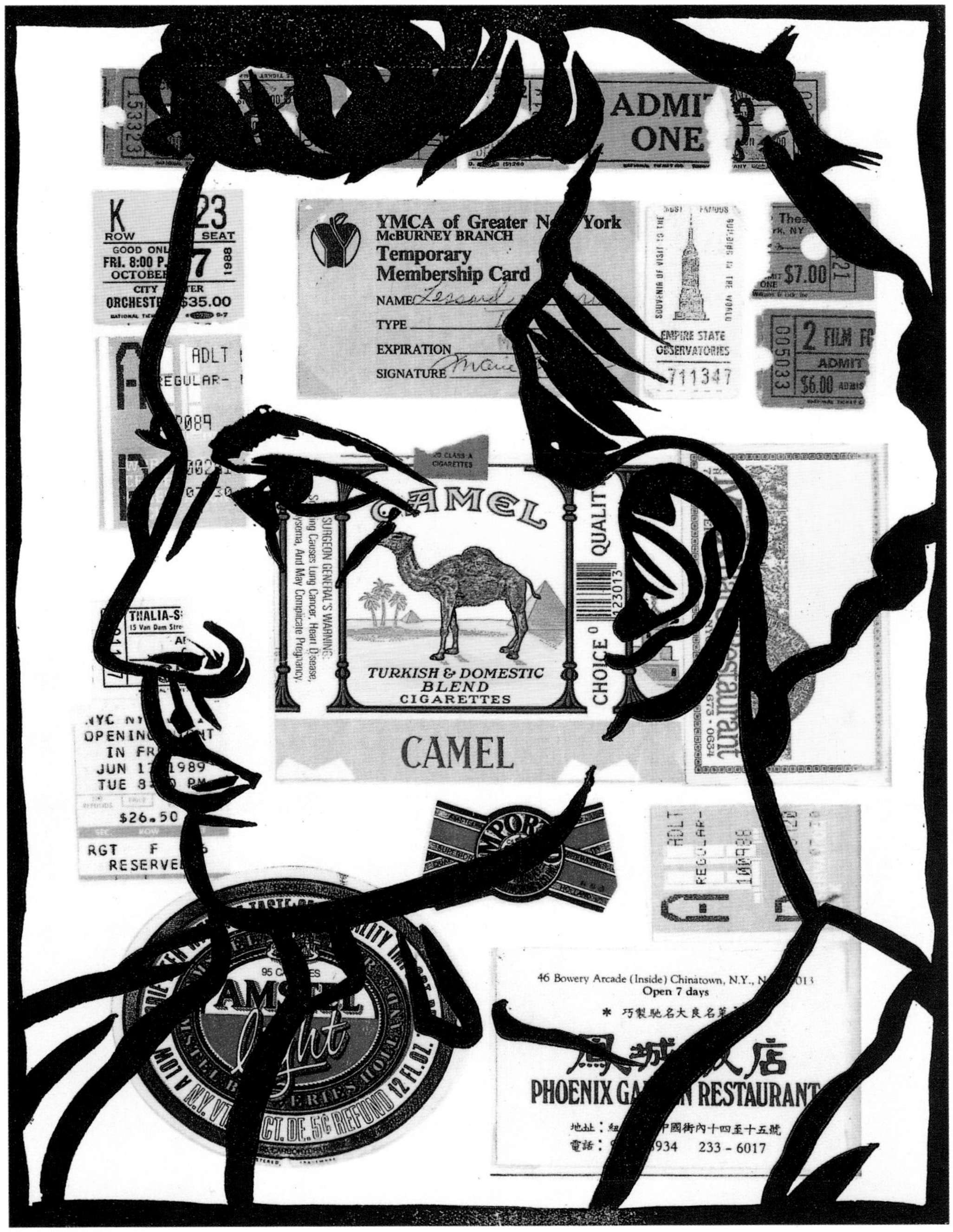

Marie Lessard

Medium) Linocut and transfer on paper An untitled personal work.

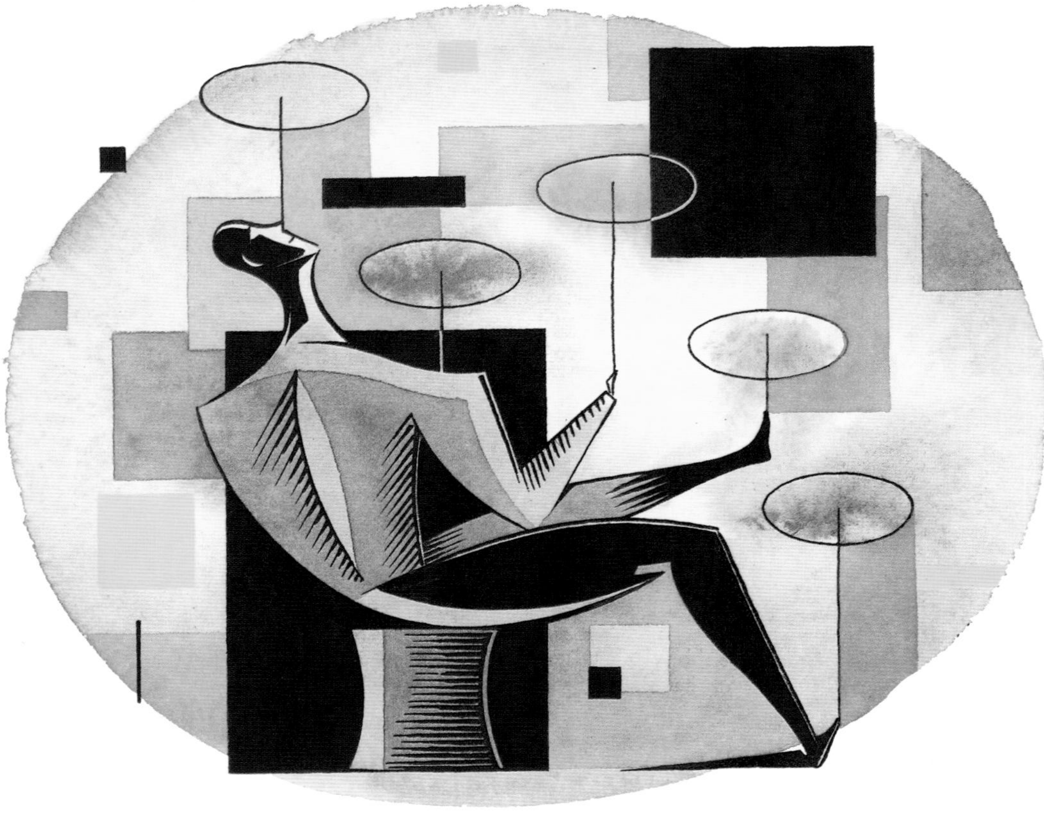

Tim Lewis

Medium) Water color over Xeroxed copy of drawing A personal piece entitled "Plate Spinner" (above).

Medium) Water color over Xeroxed copy of drawing
Entitled "Profile Puzzle," the figures are holding shapes that form another profile (right).

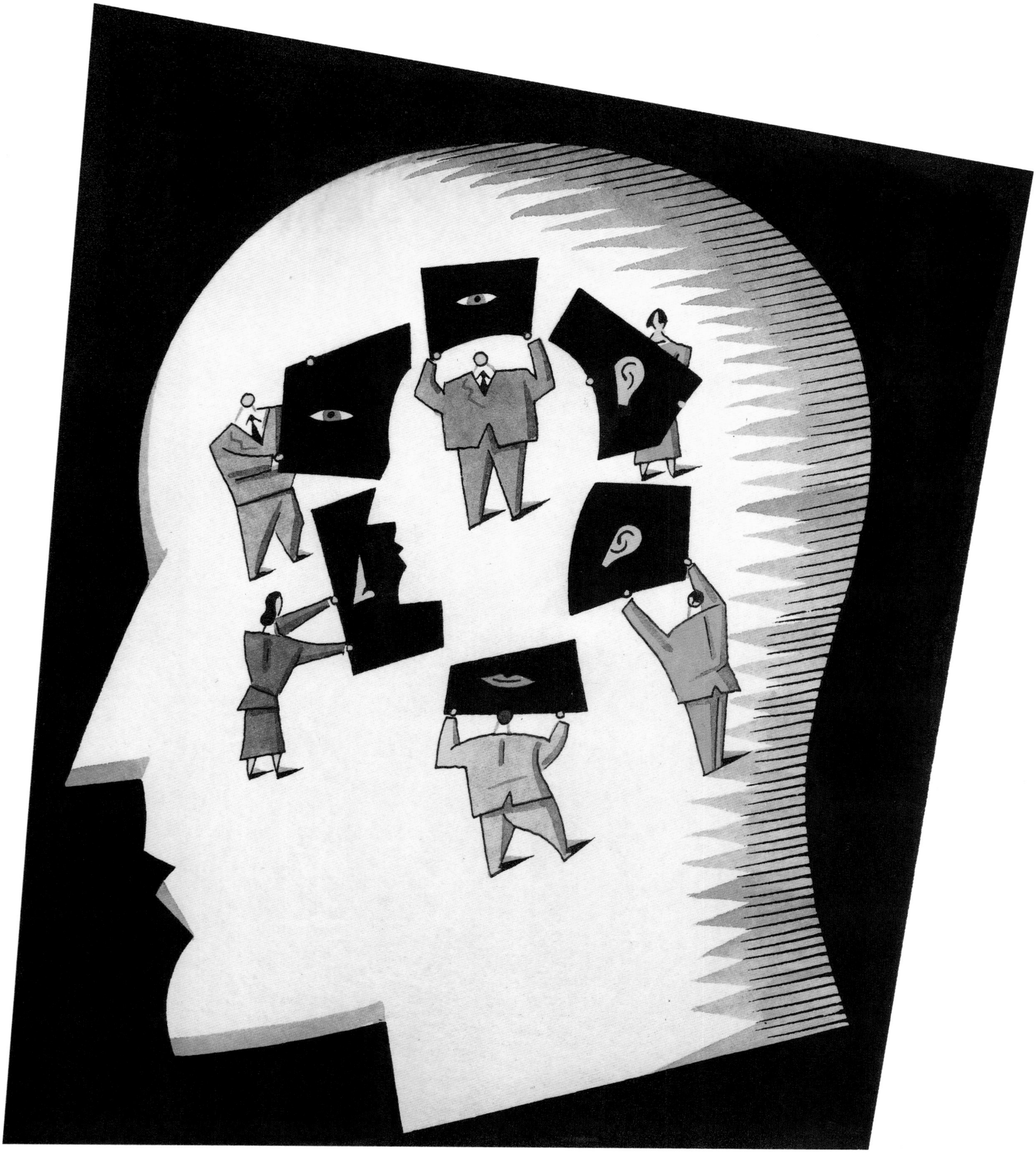

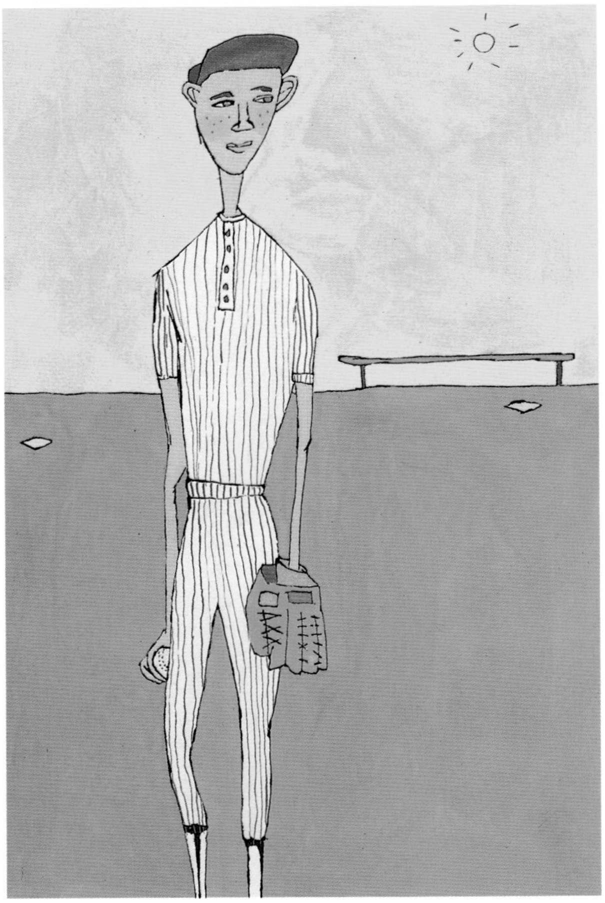

Beth O'Grady

Medium) Pen and ink, gouache A self-promotional piece completed in June 1992.

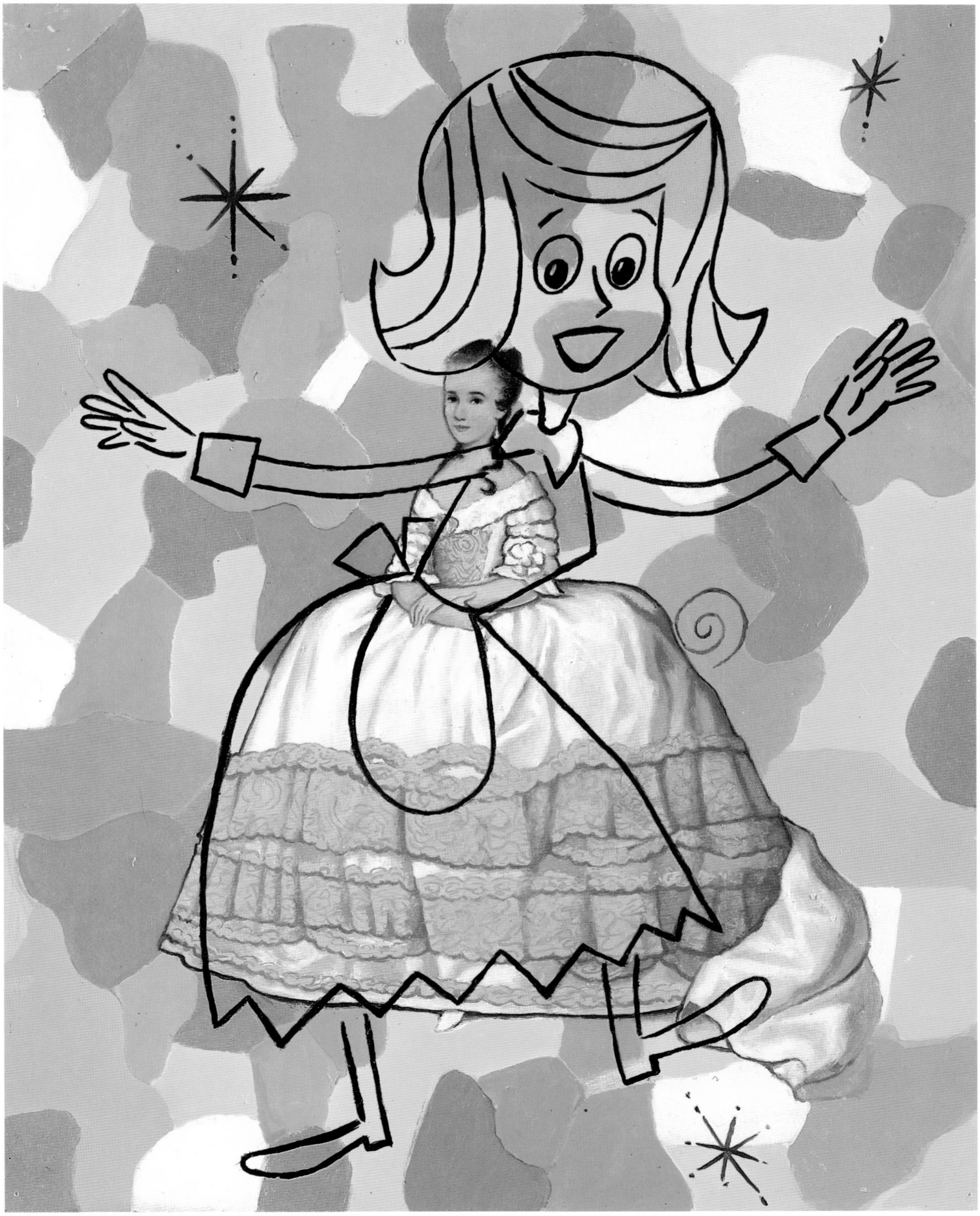

Irene Rofheart Pigott

Medium) Oil on paper This illustration was created for self-promotional purposes, entitled "Portrait of a Woman."

Art Director) Jim Christie **Client)** Bloomingdale's **Medium)** Acrylic paints on paper
For the new store campaign, "Only at Bloomingdale's," this shopping bag was commissioned, but never used.

Jessie Hartland

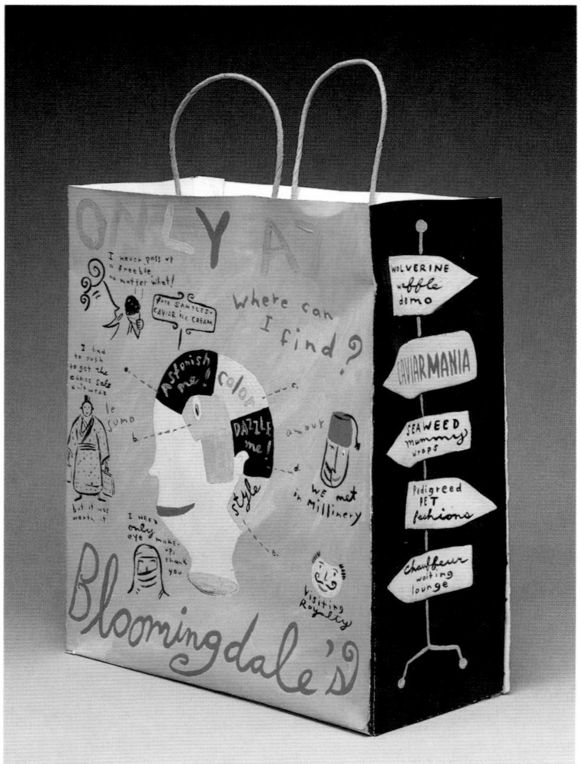

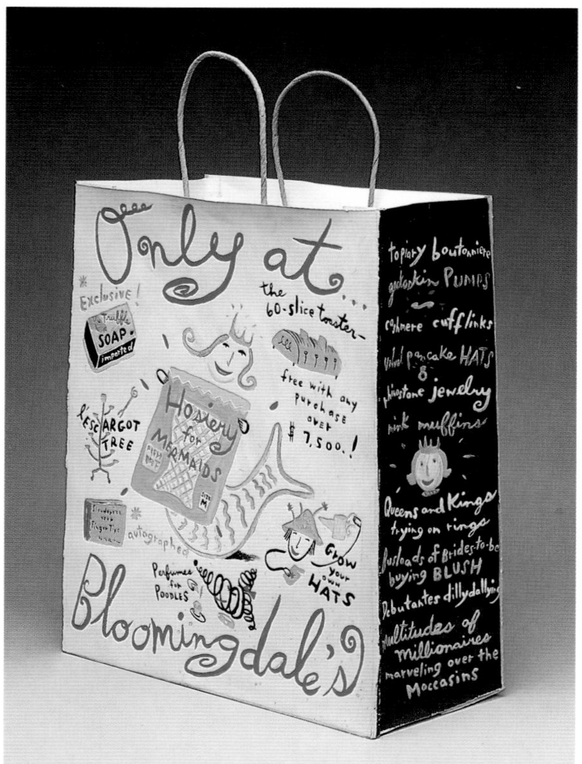

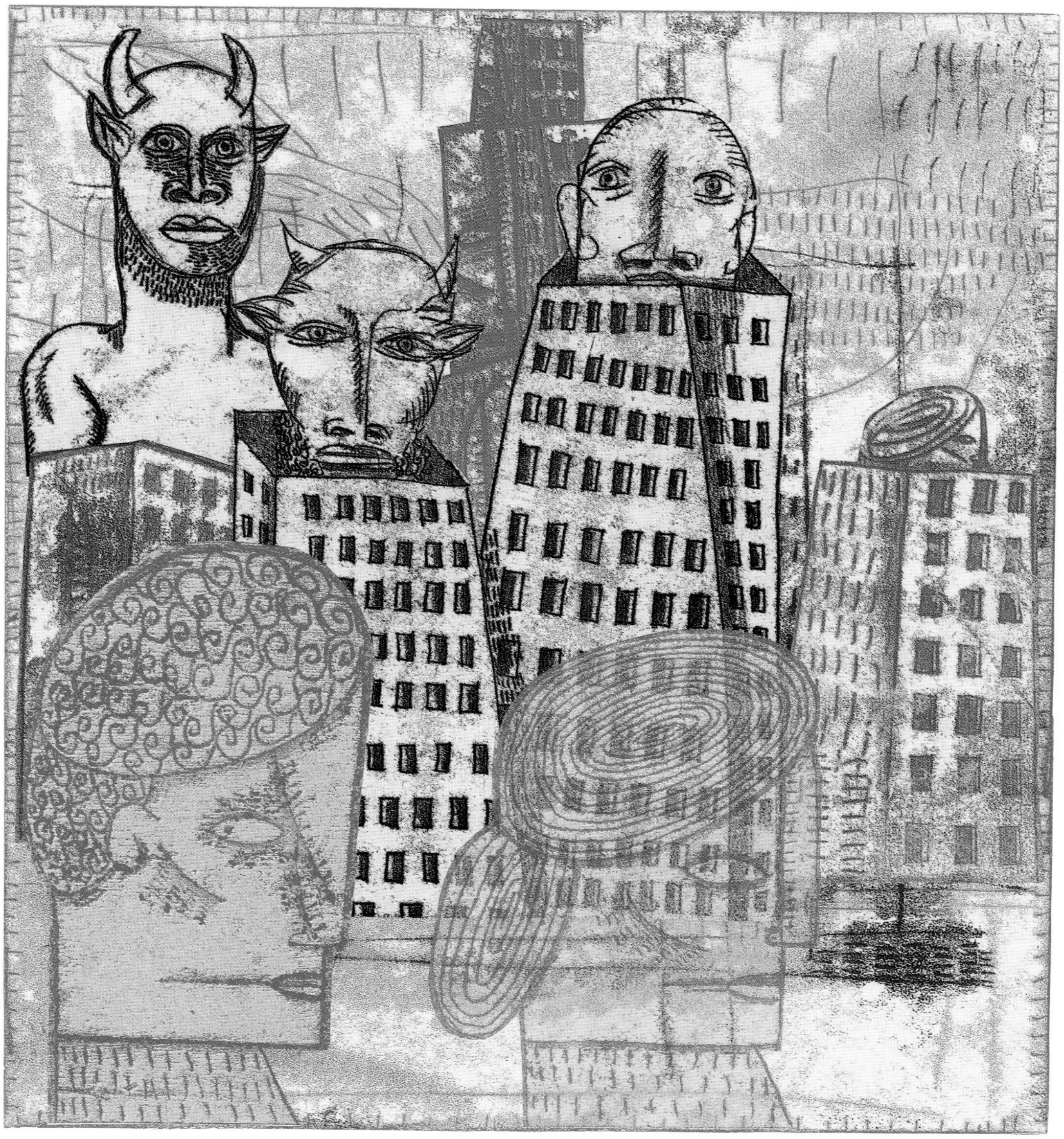

Richard Downs

Medium) Mixed media This is the **artist's Interpretation** of "Life and Love in the Big City."

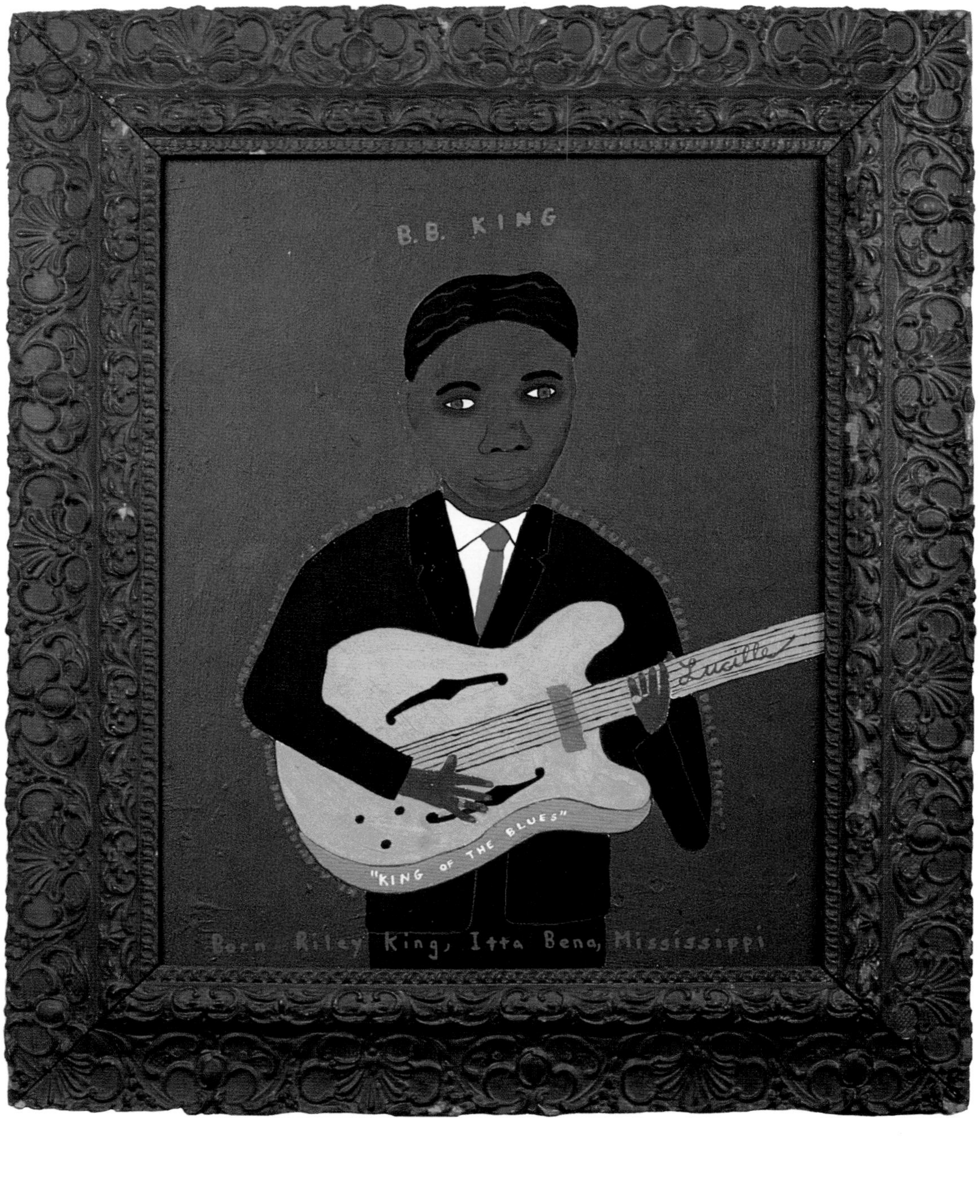

Laura Levine

Medium) Acrylic on masonite with antique frame
This portrait of B.B. King is one in a series of musicians for a show at the Julie Rico Gallery.

191

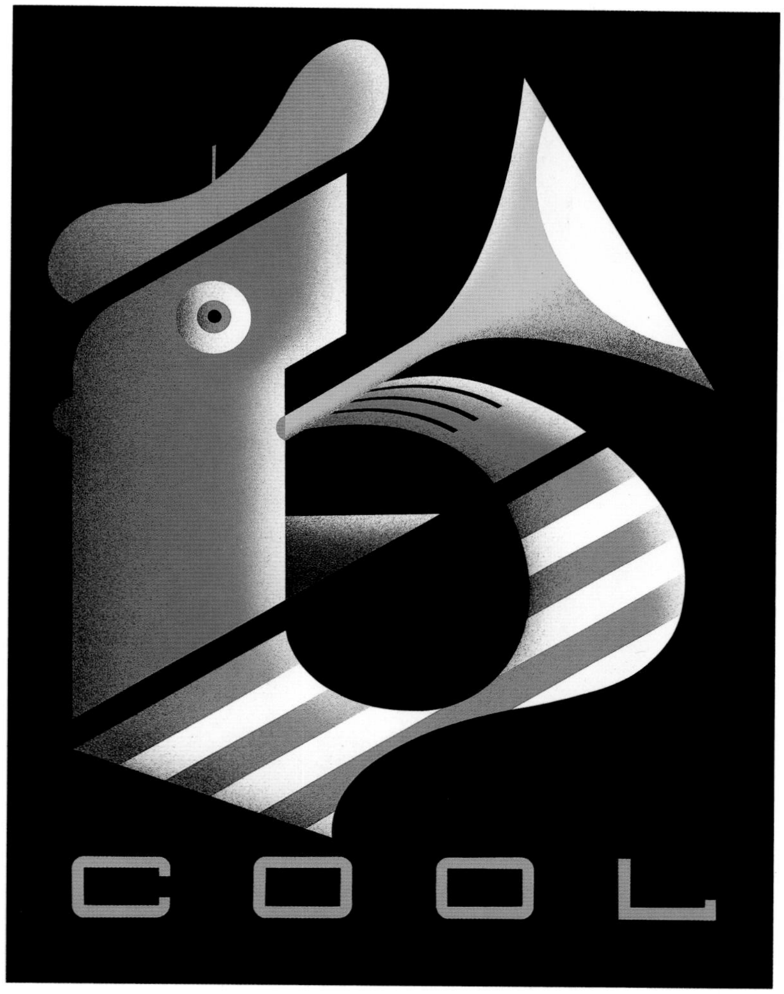

Terry Allen

Medium) Gouache **A personal piece entitled** "Cool," May 1992.

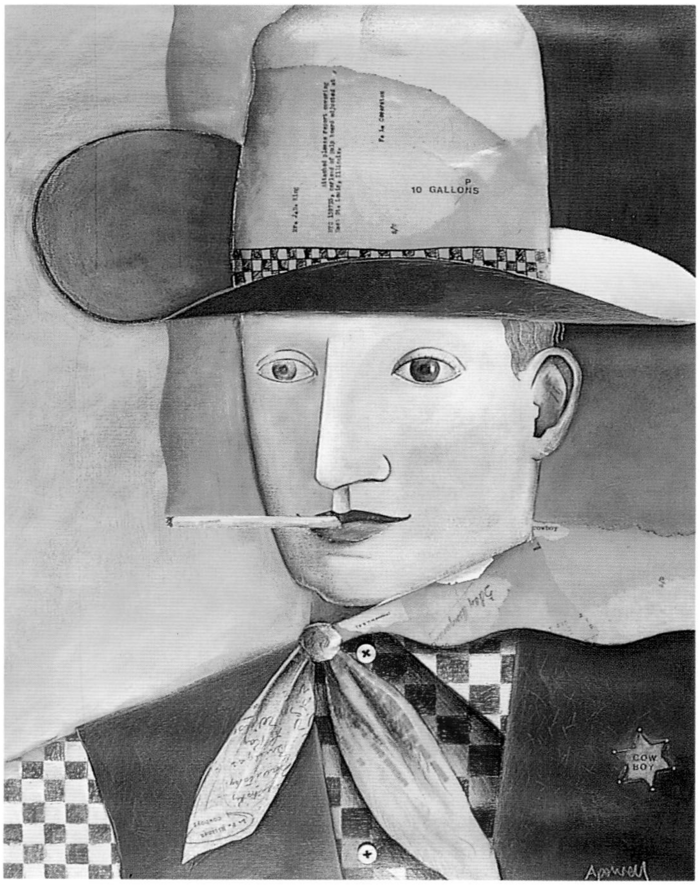

Andrew Powell

Medium) Acrylic, collage and pastel **This illustration explores** the image of the long-lost cowboy.

Medium) Oil and **acrylic** **A personal work** about smoking.

Calef Brown

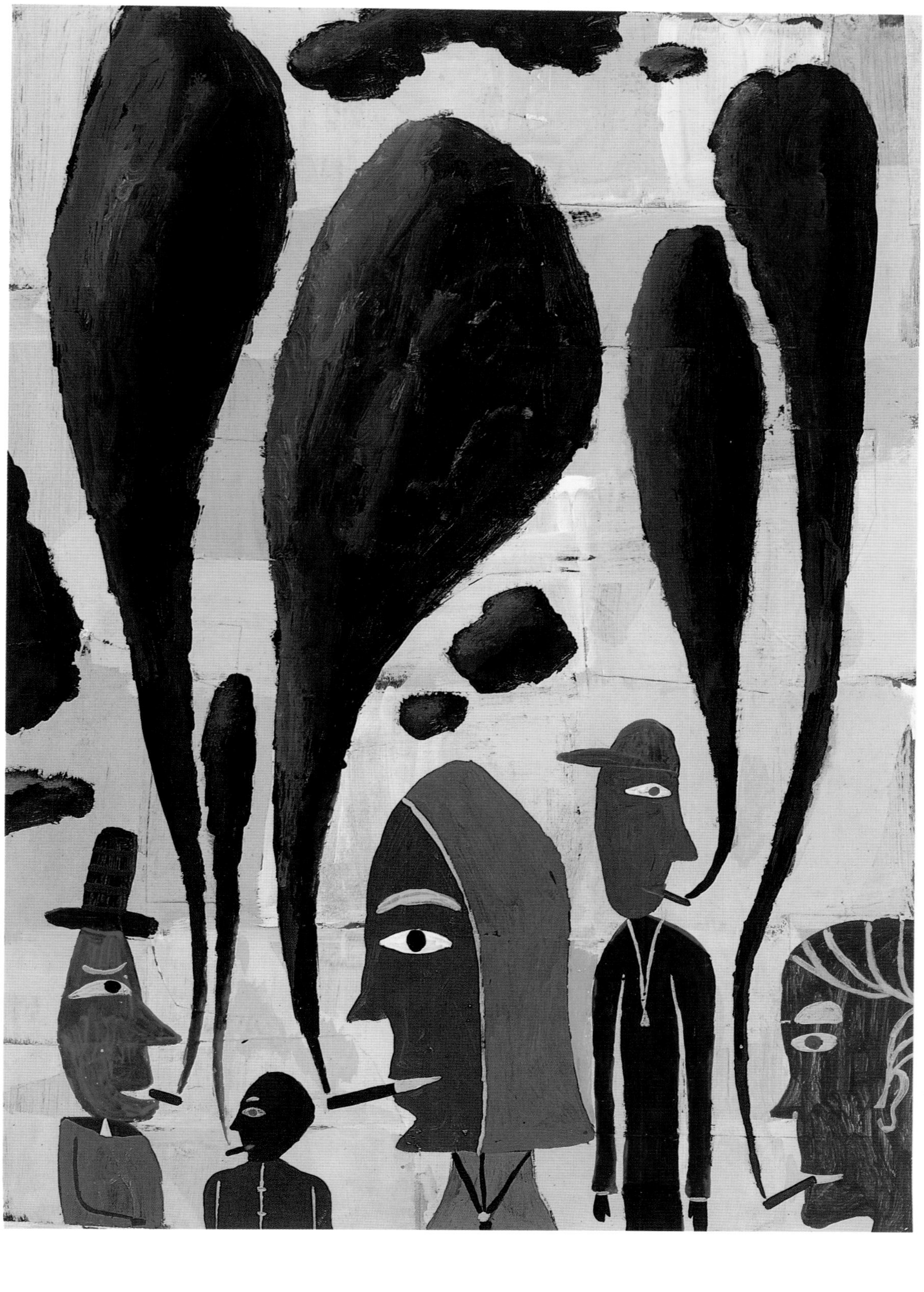

Medium) Oil and acrylic This illustration was created for a proposed children's book about death.

Calef Brown

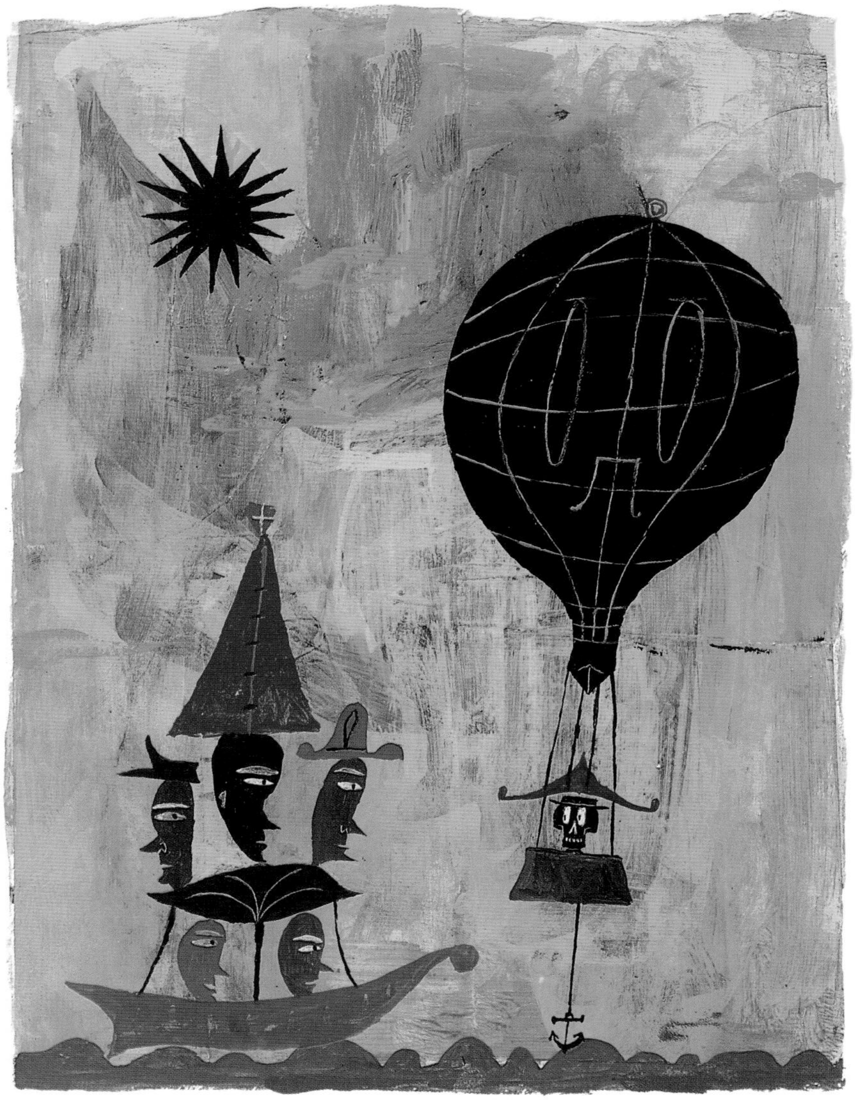

195

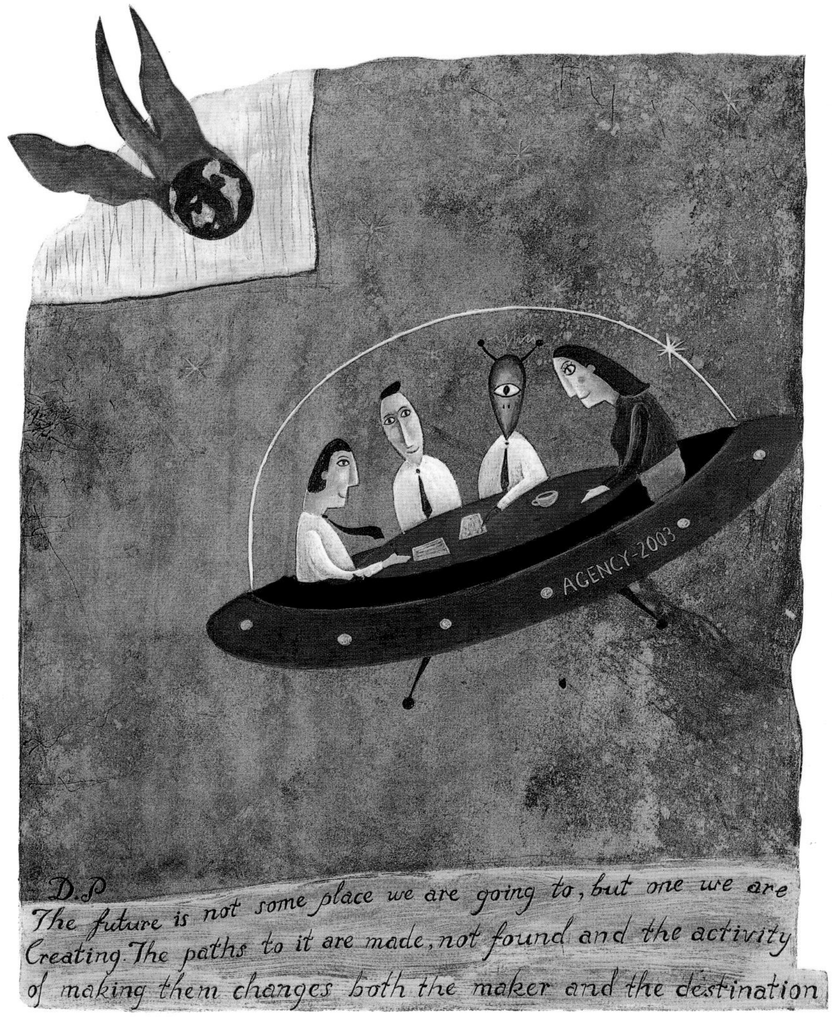

Darren Pryce

This personal piece, entitled "Agency 2003," depicts the world after its complete ozone depletion.

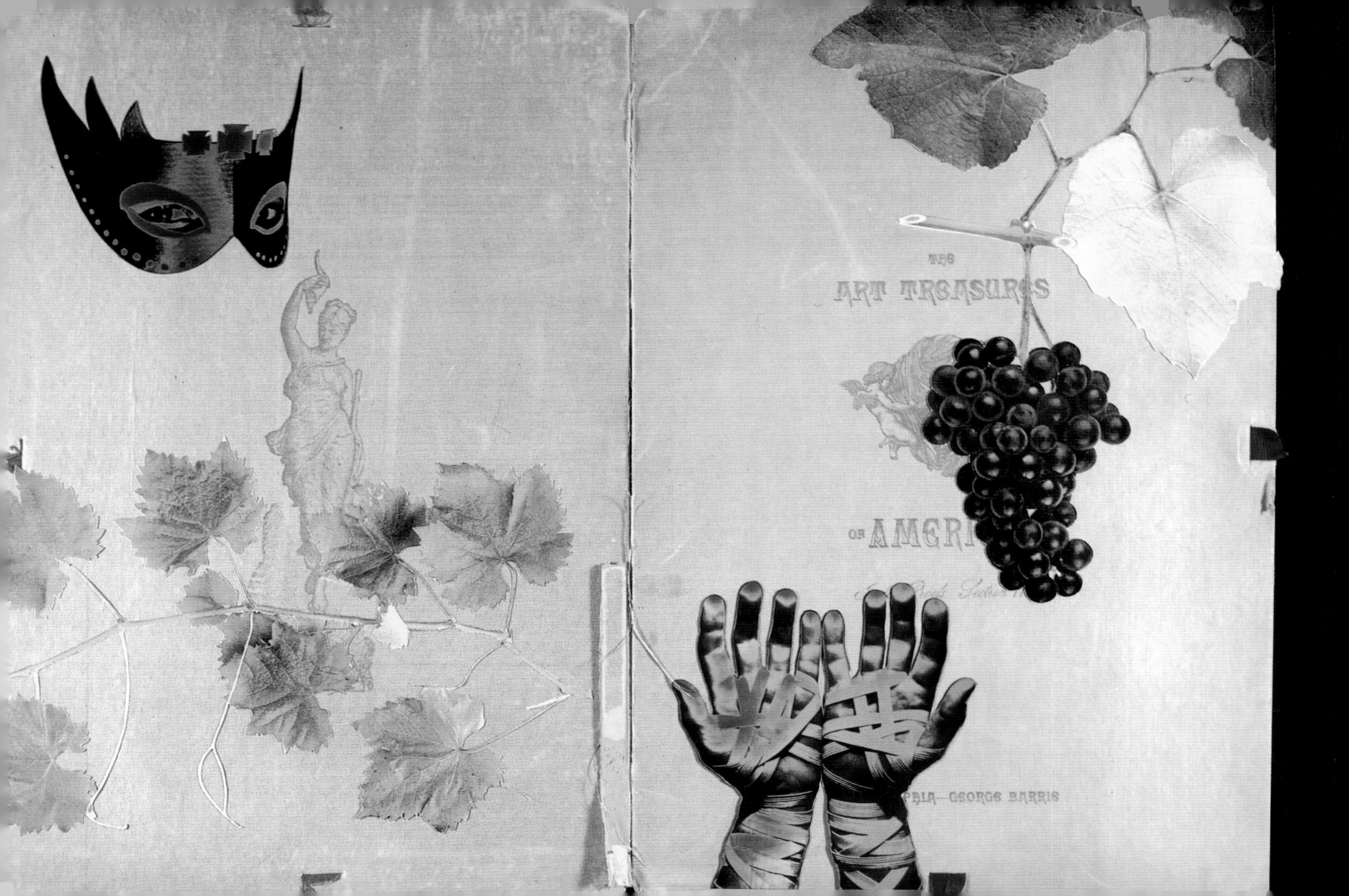
THE
ART TREASURES
OF AMERI
PHIA—GEORGE BARRIE

Medium) Alkyd on paper A personal piece entitled "Spaz the Cat."

Greg Clarke

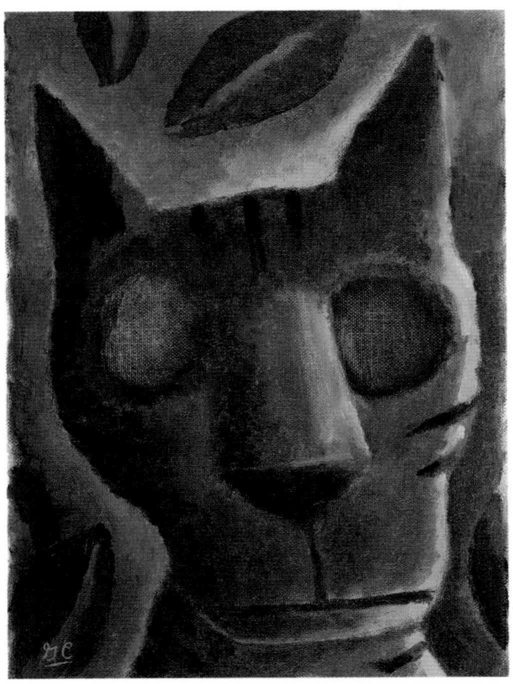

Art Director) Michael Walsh Medium) Ink and watercolor This commissioned but unpublished book jacket is in part a self-portrait. The illustrator wore a rubber gorilla nose during the execution.

Alan E. Cober

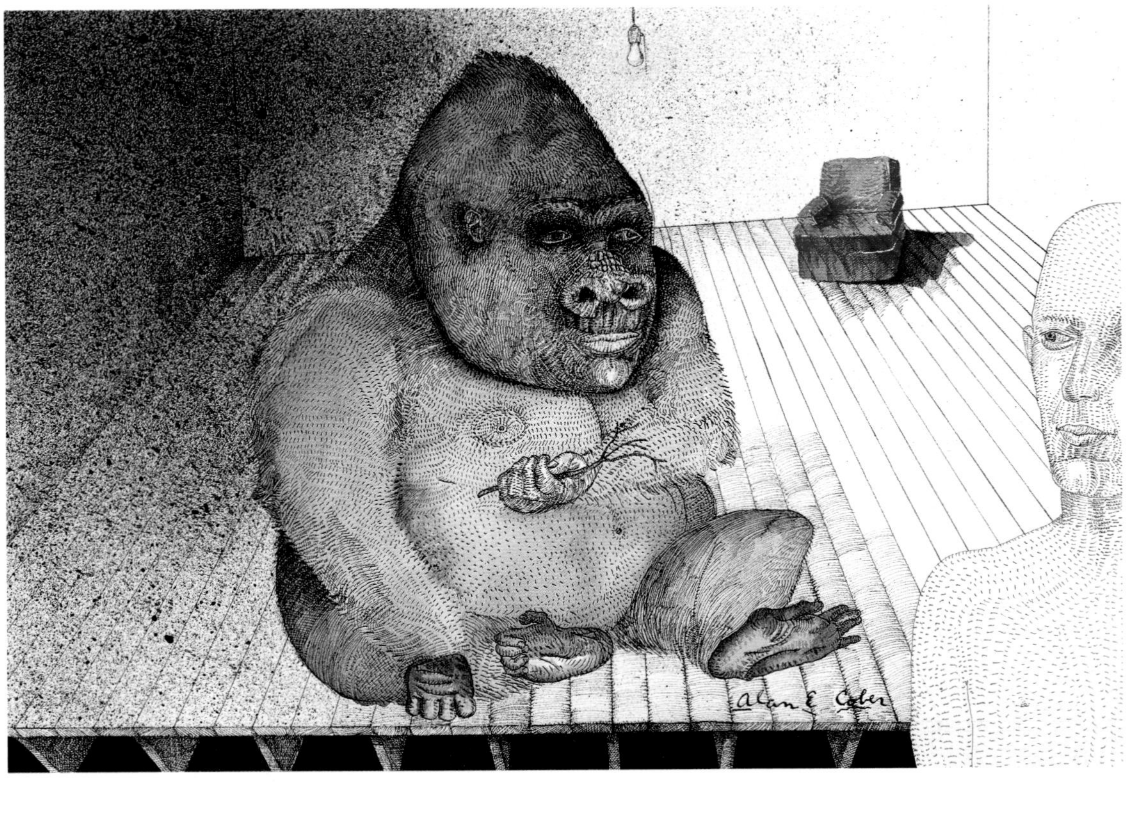

199

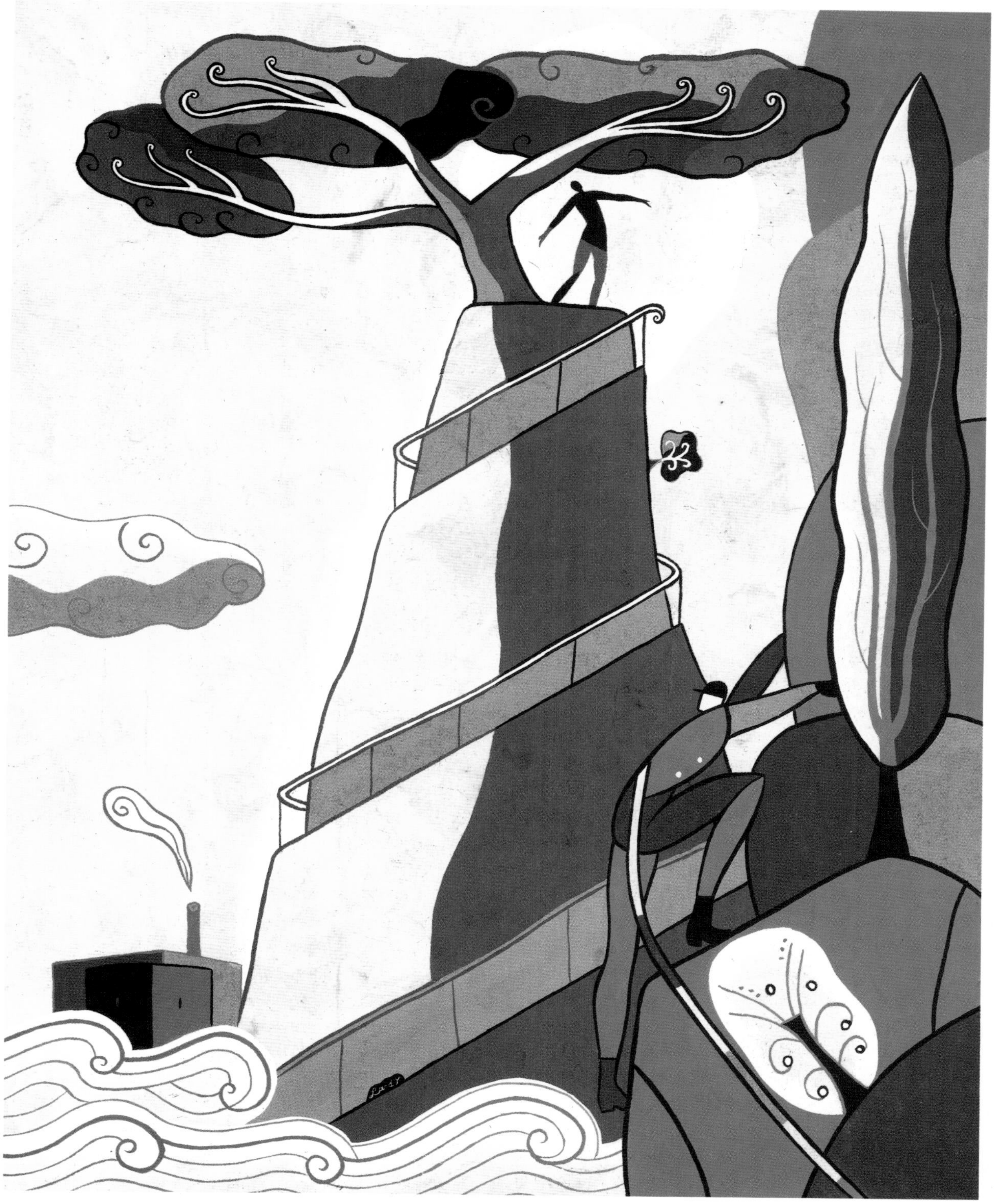

Philippe Lardy

Art Director) Alison Grevstad Client) Nordstrom Publication) Employee Benefits/Program Cover Medium) Gouache
A different version of this illustration will appear in an upcoming brochure describing Nordstrom's employee benefits.

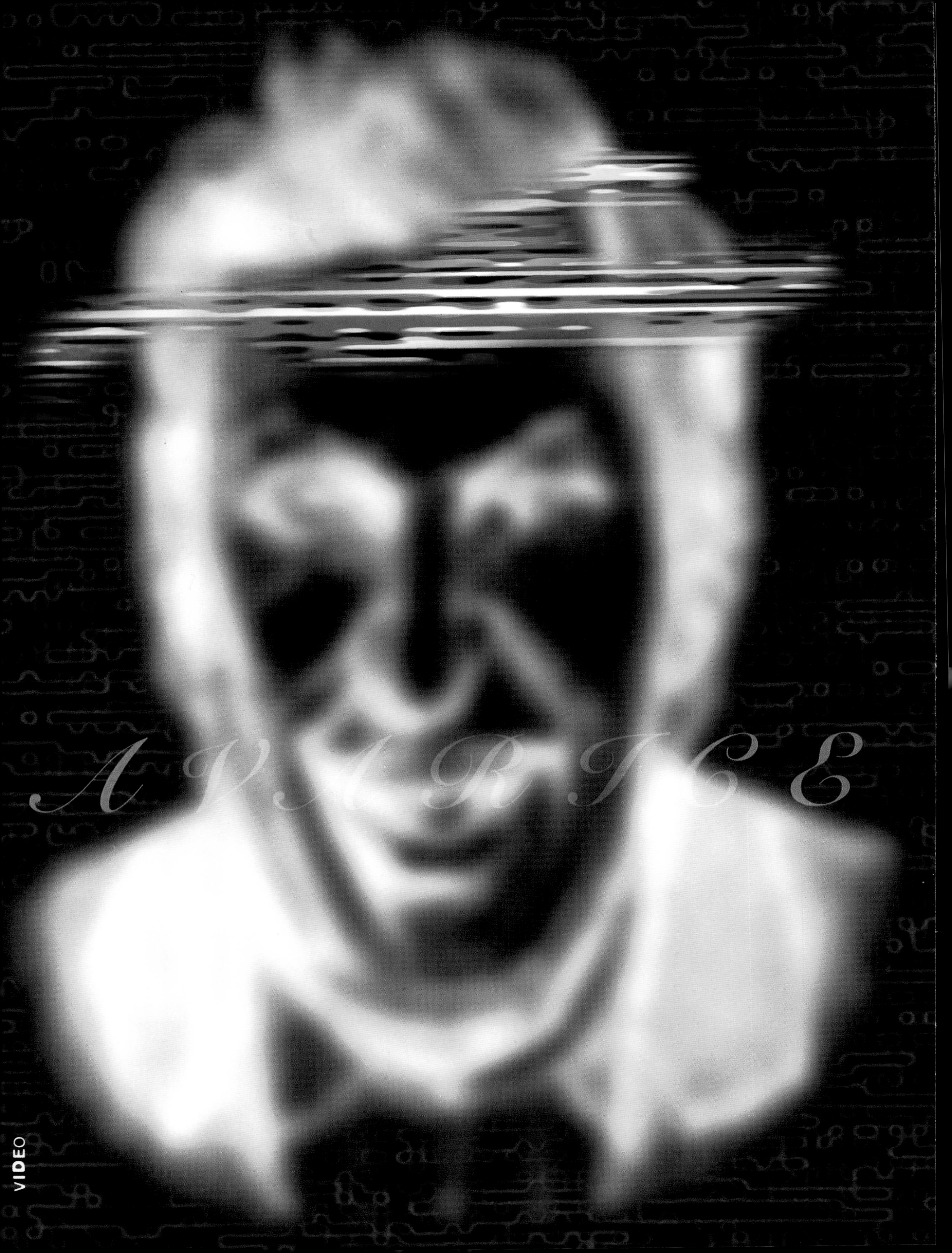
AVARICE

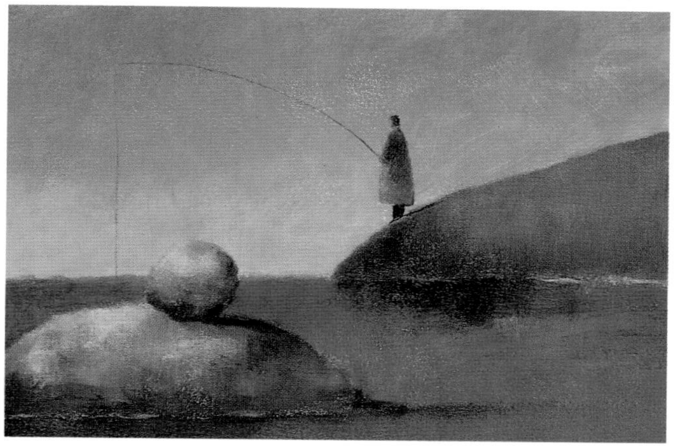

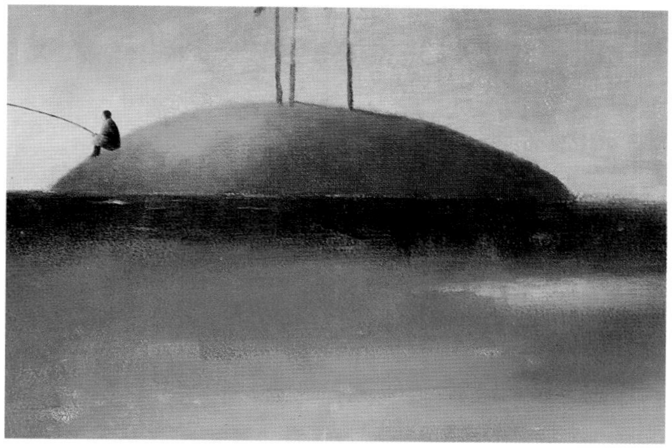

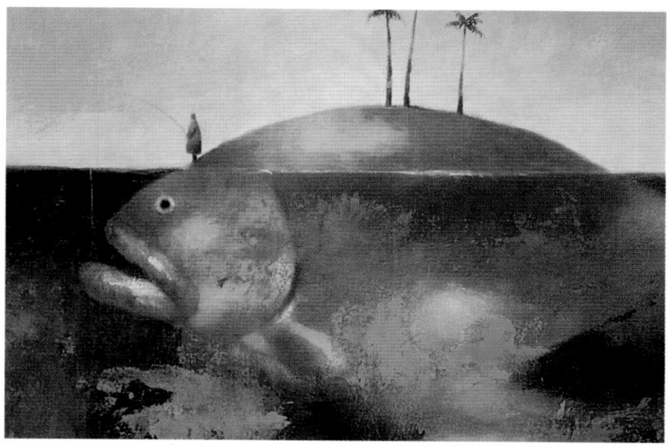

Brad **Holl**and

Creative Director) **Parry Merkley** **Art Director) Guy Marino** **Copywriter)** Bill Stone **Agency) Merkley** Newman Harty
Client) Bankers Trust Company **This video for Bankers Trust Company entitled** "Fish/Island" **began running in** October 1992 on CNN.

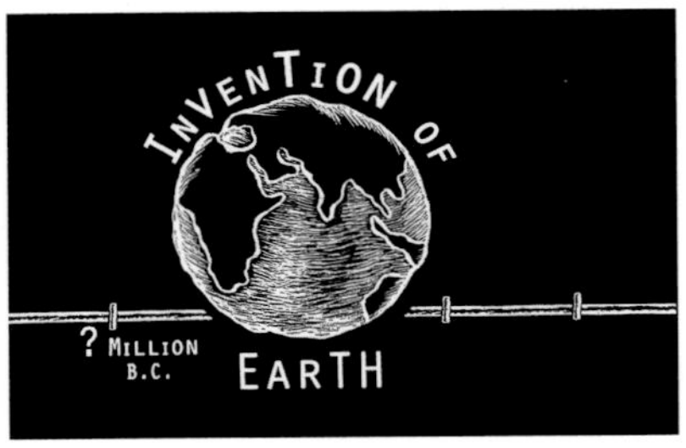

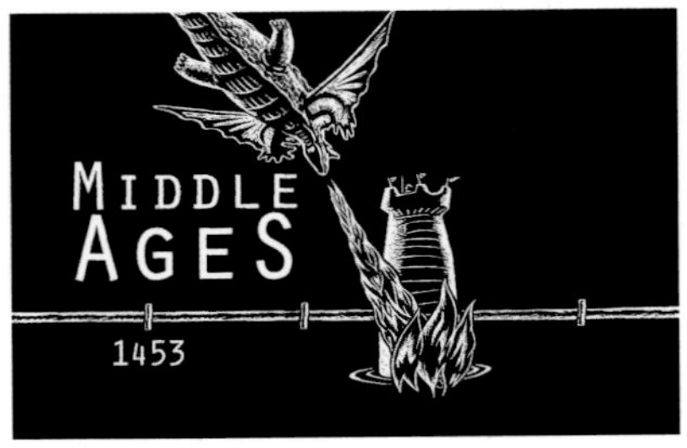

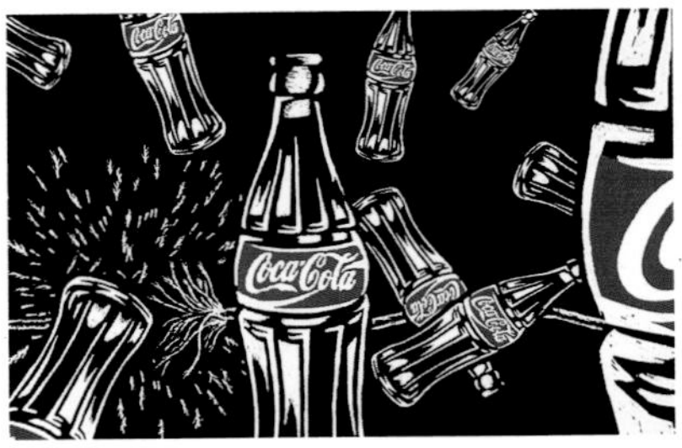

Geoffrey Grahn

Animators) Rob Palmer, Kate Flather and Geoffrey Grahn Art Director) Kate Flather Writer) Mark Fenske Agency) Creative Artists Agency Production Company) The Bomb Factory Client) Coca-Cola Sound) Warren Dewey Medium) Scratchboard, Macintosh computer with Adobe Photoshop and Macromind Director "Coca-Cola Time Line," a thirty-second animated televison commercial, began airing nationally in February 1993 and internationally in March 1993.

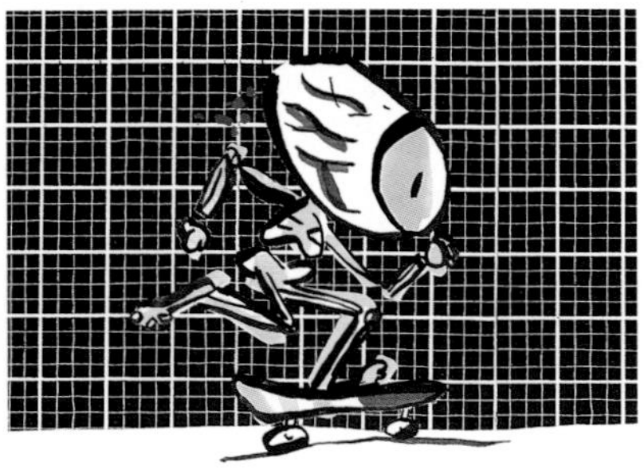
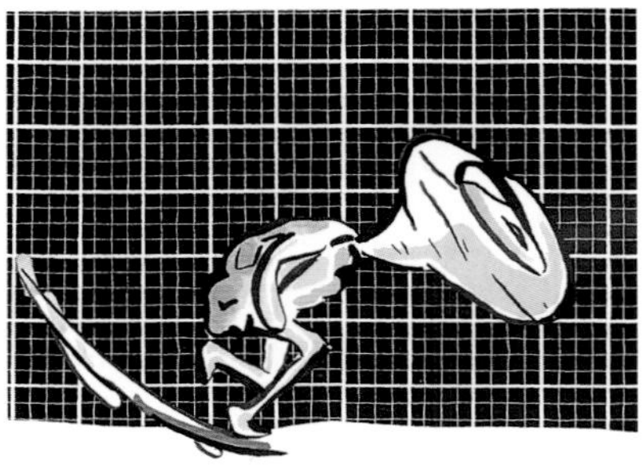
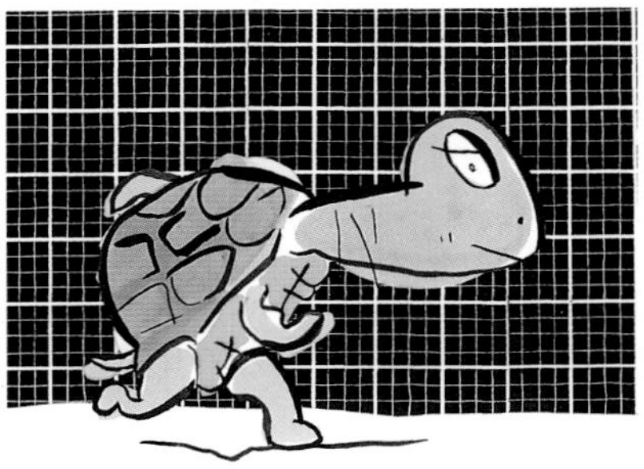

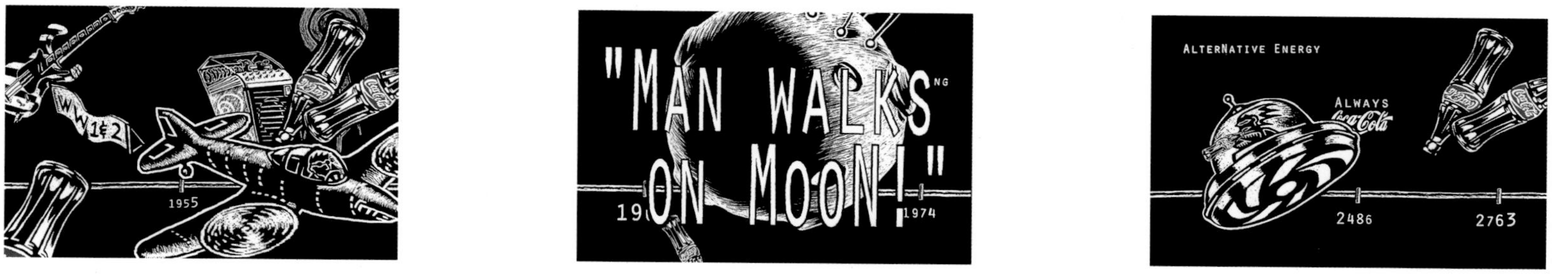

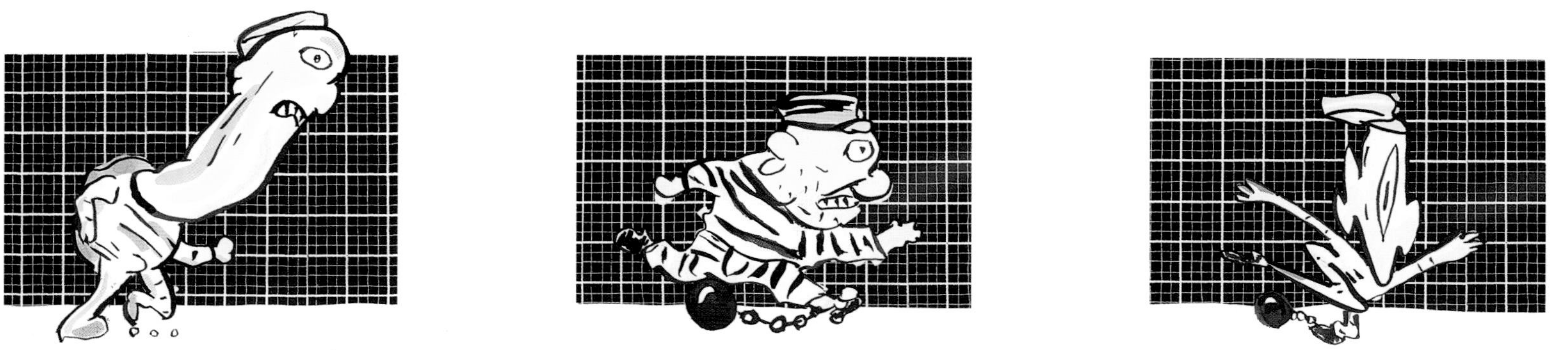

Mark Marek

Animator) Mike DeSeve Art Director) R.O. Blechman Production Company) The Ink Tank
This sequence, from a promotional thirty-five second reel opener, was created in-house for the Ink Tank.

Index

Philippe Lardy
478 West Broadway #5A
New York, NY 10012
101/199

Marie Lessard
4641 Hutchison
Montreal, Quebec
Canada H2V 4A2
183

Laura Levine
444 Broome Street
New York, NY 10013
172-173/190

Tim Lewis
184 St. Johns Place
Brooklyn, NY 11217-3402
184/185

Warren Linn
4915 Broadway #2A
New York, NY 10034
28/96

Matt Mahurin
666 Greenwich Street #16
New York, NY 10014
79

Lisa Manning
12 Ledge Lane
Gloucester, MA 01930
182

Mark Marek
199 Owatonna Street
Haworth, NJ 07641
202-203

Ruth Marten
8 West 13th Street #7RW
New York, NY 10011
149/180-181

Bill Mayer
240 Forkner Drive
Decatur, GA 30030
170

Richard McGuire
45 Carmine Street #3B
New York, NY 10014
126-129

Chesley McLaren
228 West 82nd Street
New York, NY 10024
150

Scott Menchin
640 Broadway
New York, NY 10012
109/110/151

Christian Northeast
48 Abell Street #245
Toronto, Ontario
Canada M6J 3H2
54-56/176-178

José Ortega
524 East 82nd Street
New York, NY 10028
81/100

Beth O'Grady
161 Fourth Street #3E
Hoboken, NJ 07030
186

C.F. Payne
758 Springfield Pike
Cincinnati, OH 45215
94/95

Hanoch Piven
310 West 22nd Street #4A
New York, NY 10011
62-65

David Plunkert
3647 Falls Road
Baltimore, MD 21211
49-52/72/74

Andrew Powell
420 North 5th Street #706
Minneapolis, MN 55401
192

Darren Pryce
90 Clyde Street St. Kilda
Victoria 3182 Australia
195

Robert Risko
155 West 15th Street #4B
New York, NY 10011
39

Irene Rofheart Pigott
75 Prospect Park West #1A
Brooklyn, NY 11215-3054
187

Lilla Rogers
6 Parker Road
Arlington, MA 02178
136-140/162-163

Jonathon Rosen
408 Second Street #3
Brooklyn, NY 11215
90-91/104-105

Mark Ryden
221 West Maple
Monrovia, CA 91016
131

Wiktor Sadowski
c/o Marlena Torzecka
211 East 89th Street, Suite A-1
New York, NY 10128
45

Rick Sealock
112 C 17th Avenue N.W.
Calgary, Alberta
Canada T2M 0M6
88

J. Otto Seibold
38 West 21st Street 11th Floor
New York, NY 10010
122-125

Lane Smith
12 West 18th Street #6W
New York, NY 10011
118-121

Owen Smith
4370 Faulkner Drive
Fremont, CA 94536
30

Edward Sorel
156 Franklin Street
New York, NY 10013
22

Ralph Steadman
c/o Andrea Harding
146 East 19th Street
New York, NY 10003
42

Gary Tanhauser
3018 Orange Avenue
Santa Ana, CA 92707
70-71

Malcolm Tarlofsky
P.O. Box 786
Glen Ellen, CA 95442
77

Pol Turgeon
5187 Jeanne-Mance #3
Montreal, Quebec
Canada H2V 4K2
169

Maurice Vellekoop
c/o Reactor Art & Design
51 Camden Street
Toronto, Ontario
Canada M5V 1V2
21

Stefano Vitale
478 Bergen Street #4
Brooklyn, NY 11217
99

Alexandra Weems
58 East 80th Street #2B
New York, NY 10021
17/18

Philippe Weisbecker
c/o Riley Illustration
155 West 15th Street #4C
New York, NY 10011
103

Mick Wiggins
1103 Amador Avenue
Berkeley, CA 94707
60

Thomas Woodruff
29 Cornelia Street #17
New York, NY 10014
143

Janet Woolley
c/o Alan Lynch
11 Kings Ridge Road
Long Valley, NJ 07853
25/93

Art/Creative Directors and Designers

Animators

Editors

Writers

Publications

Publishing Companies

Advertising Agencies

Clients

Design Firms

Production/Studios

Sound